Jeremiah's First Confessions
A Pentecostal Hearing

Jeremiah's First Confessions

A Pentecostal Hearing

Jared S. Runck

CPT

CPT Press
Cleveland, Tennessee

Jeremiah's First Confessions
A Pentecostal Hearing

Published by CPT Press
900 Walker ST NE
Cleveland, TN 37311
USA
email: cptpress@pentecostaltheology.org
website: www.cptpress.com

Library of Congress Control Number: 2021942393

ISBN-13: 9781953358196

To my wife Tiffany
And to my daughters Shaelyn and Abagael

CONTENTS

ACKNOWLEDGMENTS

It is still difficult for me to accept that I have finally completed the work that lies before you, in part because it does not seem all that long ago that I despaired this day would ever arrive and also in part because now that the work is completed, I am beginning to feel a sense of loss, as if I am missing a dear friend. It is, then, a prime opportunity to reminisce over the past few years and take a moment to thank those who played vital roles in the completion of this project.

First of all, I would like to give thanks to my family. My wife, Tiffany, was constant in her patient encouragement; my older daughter Shaelyn was my ever-faithful 'study buddy', spending countless summer break hours with me in the library; and my younger daughter Abagael could always be counted on to provide a much needed 'study break' with her cheerful silliness.

I was privileged to complete this project while serving as full-time faculty and now Academic Dean at Urshan College as well as part-time Associate Pastor for the Pentecostal Church of our Lord Jesus Christ. The faculty, students, and congregation that I serve were so supportive and understanding, but I owe a very special thanks to my Executive Vice President, Jennie Russell, and my pastor, Ernest Dumarseq, not only for allowing me time away from other duties but also for being always available with wise counsel, encouragement, and constant prayer when the stress of competing obligations seemed too great to bear.

I would be remiss not to thank the many wonderful colleagues who inspired, challenged, and encouraged me during this process. Robin Johnston and David Norris, who together ignited my interest in the distinctiveness of Pentecostal hermeneutics; Jeffrey Brickle, whose work on aurality in the Johannine letters has helped me learn how to listen carefully to Scripture; and John W. Bracke, who guided me so ably into the wondrous world of Jeremiah studies and always challenged me to use my scholarship in service of the church. These teachers, perhaps more than any others, have shaped my identity as a Oneness Pentecostal OT scholar, and I am forever grateful.

I would also like to thank John Christopher Thomas for extending an invitation to join the CPT doctoral seminar; those bi-annual meetings will remain among my most-cherished memories of this time. Gathered around that front-room table, I was always challenged, encouraged, affirmed, and spiritually uplifted. Truly, the members of the CPT seminar have been my own 'family of Shaphan', particularly through my unexpected trials of misunderstanding and false accusation. I must also extend a special thank you to my very dear friend, Rick Wadholm, Jr, who has truly become a brother to me; I pray God allows us many more years of fellowship, friendship, and scholarly collaboration.

I must thank both my doctoral supervisor, Willie Wessels, and my co-supervisor, Lee Roy Martin, for their kind and careful guidance throughout the process of research and writing. It has been a true joy to be able to complete a study that brings together my two greatest passions – the book of Jeremiah and Pentecostal hermeneutics – with such tremendous scholar-teachers as my guides. They have been unfailingly quick to answer questions, address concerns, and give helpful critiques at every crucial point in this process.

Finally, I must give thanks to God for bringing me to an 'expected end'. Immediately after beginning my doctoral work, I was faced with the worst trial of my life to date, a trial caused by colleagues' false accusations and misrepresentations. In fact, I learned of their betrayal when I returned from my very first CPT seminar. As crushed as I was by the actions of those whom I had thought were my friends, I do recall being overwhelmed by a strong presence of the Lord when the thought suddenly came, 'I am sure this is exactly how Jeremiah felt when he was betrayed by his friends'. In that terrible moment, the realization that I was experiencing Jeremiah-like rejection was, I believe, a word of the Lord to me. That terrible trial served as my confirmation that I was truly in God's will. I can testify today that God has reversed all that was against me and has silenced the voices of my enemies. Therefore, I present this monograph as both an act of worship and as a testimony to the power of God to save and deliver in any circumstance. God's Word will forever endure as will those who live in accordance with it.

PREFACE

The present book is a rhetorical-theological study of the Jeremiah's first two confessions (Jer. 11.18-23; 12.1-13) utilizing an affective perspective rooted in a Pentecostal hermeneutic. Combining insights gleaned from rhetorical, narrative, and reader-response interpretive methods, this study seeks to demonstrate how the initial confessions work as a kind of affective 'listening guide', working to tune the audience's ear to the emotive key of the Confessions and, more broadly, the entire book of Jeremiah. The work asserts the Confessions are integral to the overall theological message of the book, creating a space where the audience is invited to identify with and be transformed by the shared *pathos* of YHWH and prophet.

ABBREVIATIONS

AB	Anchor Bible
AcBib	Academia Biblica
ABD	Freedman, David Noel (ed.), *Anchor Bible Dictionary* (New York: Doubleday, 1992).
AJBI	*Annual of the Japanese Bible Institute*
AOAT	Alter Orient und Altes Testament
AOTC	Abingdon Old Testament Commentaries
BA	*Biblical Archaeologist*
BASOR	*Bulletin of the American Schools of Oriental Research*
BDB	Brown, Francis, S. Driver, and C. Briggs, *The New Brown-Driver-Briggs-Gesenius Hebrew and English Lexicon* (Peabody, MA: Hendrickson, 1996).
BFT	Biblical Foundations in Theology
BHS	*Biblia Hebraica Stuttgartensia*
BHT	Beiträge zur historischen Theologie
BibSem	The Biblical Seminar
BST	Basel Studies of Theology
BZAW	Beihefte zur Zeitschrift für die alttestamentliche Wissenschaft
CBC	Cambridge Bible Commentary
CBQ	*Catholic Biblical Quarterly*
CDCH	Clines, David J.A. (ed.), *The Concise Dictionary of Classical Hebrew* (Sheffield: Sheffield Phoenix Press, 2009).
CHALOT	Holladay, William (ed.), *A Concise Hebrew and Aramaic Lexicon of the Old Testament* (Grand Rapids: Eerdmans, 1971).
CTM	Calwer Theologie Monographien
Enc	*Encounter*
EuroJTh	*European Journal of Theology*
EvQ	*Evangelical Quarterly*
Exp Tim	*Expository Times*
FB	*Forschung zur Bibel*
GBS	Guides to Biblical Scholarship
HALOT	Köhler, Ludwig, *The Hebrew and Aramaic Lexicon of the Old Testament* (Leiden: Brill, 1994–2000).
HTR	*Harvard Theological Review*
HUCA	*Hebrew Union College Annual*

IB	*Interpreter's Bible*
IBC	Interpretation: A Bible Commentary for Preaching and Teaching
ICC	International Critical Commentary
Int	*Interpretation*
ISBE	*International Standard Bible Encyclopedia,* rev. edn.
JBL	*Journal of Biblical Literature*
JETS	*Journal of the Evangelical Theological Society*
JJS	*Journal of Jewish Studies*
JNES	*Journal of Near Eastern Studies*
JPT	*Journal of Pentecostal Theology*
JPTSup	Journal of Pentecostal Theology Supplement Series
JSOT	*Journal for the Study of the Old Testament*
JSOTSup	Journal for the Study of the Old Testament Supplement Series
JTS	*Journal of Theological Studies*
KAT	Kommentar zum Alten Testament
KEH	Kurzgefasstes exegetisches Handbuch zum Alten Testament
LHB/OTS	Library of Hebrew Bible/Old Testament Studies
LXX	Septuagint
MT	Masoretic Text
NET	New English Translation
NIB	*New Interpreter's Bible*
NIDOTTE	Van Gemeren, Willem A. (ed.), *New International Dictionary of Old Testament Theology and Exegesis* (5 vols; Grand Rapids: Zondervan, 1997).
NICOT	New International Commentary on the Old Testament
NIV	New International Version
NJPS	*Tanakh: The Holy Scriptures, The New JPS Translation according to the Traditional Hebrew Text*
NKJV	New King James Version
NLT	New Living Translation
NRSV	New Revised Standard Version
OBT	Overtures to Biblical Theology
OTE	*Old Testament Essays*
OTL	Old Testament Library
OtSt	*Oudtestamentische Studiën*
Pneuma	*Pneuma: Journal of the Society for Pentecostal Studies*
PEQ	*Palestine Exploration Quarterly*
PTMS	Princeton Theological Monograph Series
RevExp	*Review & Expositor*
S	Syriac

SBLDS	Society of Biblical Literature Dissertation Series
SBLMS	Society of Biblical Literature Monograph Series
SBLSP	Society of Biblical Literature Seminar Papers
SBT	Studies in Biblical Theology
SemeiaSup	Semeia Supplements
SHBC	Smyth & Helwys Bible Commentary
SJOT	*Scandinavian Journal of Old Testament*
SOTI	Studies in Old Testament Interpretation
STI	Studies in Theological Interpretation
T	Targum
TCT	Textual Criticism & the Translator Series
TDOT	Botterweck, G. Johannes, Helmer Ringgren, and Heinz-Josef Fabry (eds.), *Theological Dictionary of the Old Testament* (Grand Rapids: Eerdmans, 1974-2006).
TLOT	Jenni, Ernst, and Claus Westermann (eds.), *Theological Lexicon of the Old Testament* (3 vols; trans. Mark E. Biddle; Peabody, MA: Hendrickson Publishers, 1997).
TOTC	Tyndale Old Testament Commentaries
TWOT	Harris, R. Laird, Gleason L. Archer, Jr., and Bruce K. Waltke (eds.), *Theological Wordbook of the Old Testament* (2 volumes; Chicago, IL: Moody Press, 1980).
TynBul	*Tyndale Bulletin*
USQR	*Union Seminary Quarterly Review*
V	Vulgate
VT	*Vetus Testamentum*
WBC	Word Biblical Commentary
WMANT	Wissenschaftliche Monographien zum Alten und Neuen Testament
WTJ	*Westminster Theological Journal*
WW	*Word & World*
ZAW	*Zeitschrift für die alttestamentliche Wissenschaft*

1

INTRODUCTION

1.1 Introduction

'His Word was in my heart like a burning fire shut up in my bones.'[1] I cannot count how many times I heard this verse quoted in sermons as a young boy growing up in a Pentecostal church. I have no memory of this verse *ever* being read in a normal tone of voice; rather, in my boyhood recollections, the preacher's voice always echoes with that same 'burning fire' mentioned in the text.

It was, therefore, with some shock that I learned in a class on the prophets in my first year at a Pentecostal Bible college that these words are an expression of grief and anguish and not an expression of zealous desire to proclaim God's Word. Though I did not understand it fully at the time, this was perhaps my very first experience of an academic reading of the biblical text conflicting with my prior Pentecostal understanding. In that jarring moment, I discovered the apparent unnerving distance between academic research and Pentecostal experience.

In further academic studies, I learned that the so-called Confessions in the book of Jeremiah, which conclude with Jer. 20.7-18,[2] reflect a unique genre of prophetic literature virtually unseen in any other prophetic book in the OT. Namely, while most prophetic literature presents the prophet's addresses to the people, the Confessions

---

[1] Jeremiah 20.9b, NKJV.
[2] The other texts considered as part of this group are Jer. 11.18-12.6; 15.10-21; 17.14-18; 18.18-23.

disclose the prophet's private words to God. Given their uniqueness, they have generated much scholarly discussion but little, if any, agreement as to their origin, purpose, and function within the life of the historical prophet Jeremiah and the book which bears his name.

I was equally shocked to find fundamental rifts within the current academic discussion of the Confessions that were no less jarring than the clash between my Pentecostal experience and my academic understanding of Jer. 20.9. Thus, the larger goal of this book is to bring together the divided scholarly discussion of the Confessions with the emerging formulations of a Pentecostal hermeneutic to observe how these are mutually enlightening and beneficial. In this sense, the study proves necessary both to the development of a distinctive Pentecostal approach to the OT and to a more fruitful understanding of the Confessions.

1.2 Research Question

The present study concerns itself with the classic texts identified above as Jeremiah's Confessions. The history of interpretation, briefly sketched below, offers essentially two interpretive strands. The first strand, assuming the majority of the material is authentic to the prophet or his disciple Baruch, sees in the laments 'personal expressions of Jeremiah in the face of great opposition to his prophetic ministry'.[3] A second, and perhaps more dominant strand, assumes that the book is largely the product of an intensive Deuteronomistic redaction presenting 'Jeremiah as standing in the line of the prophets like Moses'.[4] The text, then, presents to us not an actual historical figure but an idealized one.

There is present in this scholarly history an oddly inverted relationship between the opinion of the *biographical/historical* status of the Confessions and their *theological* import within the book. In most other areas, scholars of the book of Jeremiah see the historical authenticity of a passage as directly increasing its theological import – the more authentic the passage, the more valuable its theology. In the case of the Confessions, however, most scholars who are convinced that the Confessions reveal to us the inner emotions of the historical

---

[3] Mark S. Smith, *The Laments of Jeremiah and Their Contexts: A Literary and Redactional Study of Jeremiah 11-20* (SBLMS 42; Atlanta: Scholars Press, 1990), p. xvii.

[4] Smith, *The Laments of Jeremiah and Their Contexts*, p. xvii.

prophet Jeremiah are often quite skeptical of their value to the overall theological message of the book, while scholars who argue that the Confessions represent editorial additions unconnected to the historical prophet are often much more sensitive to their literary and theological function within the larger framework of the book!

I intend to show that, by moving beyond the historically focused interpretations in favor of more literary and canonically focused approaches, a Pentecostal hermeneutic focuses on the agonized cries of the literary figure of the prophet Jeremiah, the one in whom God's Word dwells as fire. Thus, the Pentecostal hearer is compelled to ask, what *kind* of literary figure does hearing the Confessions reveal Jeremiah the prophet to be and how is that figuration instructive for those who hear the Word of YHWH *from* the book of Jeremiah as Jeremiah the prophet hears that Word *within* it?

1.2.1 Aims and Objectives

Given the centrality of these texts to the book of Jeremiah,[5] such a question births other inquiries. How do Pentecostal hermeneutical commitments illuminate the Confessions within their present literary context? How do they inform and illuminate the theology of the Word presented in the book of Jeremiah? Finally, how does such a theology impact the Pentecostal understanding of the Word of God and the human relationship to that Word?

The present study aims to demonstrate that several glaring inadequacies in the current academic discussion of the Confessions can be helpfully addressed by revisiting the texts with the distinctive ear of a Pentecostal hermeneutic. It also aims to demonstrate that the Confessions are integral to the message of the book and form an essential part of its interpretive framework. The ultimate aim is to attempt to discern a profile of an ideal hearer of the text in the literary figure of the prophet presented in the Confessions and chart that profile's implications for contemporary hearers of the book.

1.2.2 Rationale and Relevance

The reason for the present book is that current scholarly discussion has largely missed a key feature of the Confessions, namely that they are not simply recorded *reactions* to the Word but are the book of

---

[5] They essentially span the heart of the first half of the book, Jeremiah 1-25.

Jeremiah's models for ideal *reception* of the Word. Within the imaginative world of the book, these texts offer us deeply emotional responses to the reception of the Word of God. Therefore, one does not simply hear the Word of God in Jeremiah; one also *over*hears the prophet's own hearing of that Word! It is precisely in this *over*hearing that one learns *how* to hear the Word and is transformed by that Word, the book of Jeremiah. The literary figure of Jeremiah presented to us in the Confessions is *first* an ideal hearer *even before* he is an ideal prophet.[6] Given the fundamentally affective nature of these texts, any hearing of these texts should properly account for their affective impact within the hearer of the book.

The present study is relevant to the scholarly discussion of the Confessions precisely because its explicit commitment to a Pentecostal hearing serves to highlight this affective dimension and emphasis of the text in ways that previous interpretive strategies have either undervalued or entirely missed. This study is not solely interested in describing the contributions that critical scholarship can make to the Pentecostal understanding of the book of Jeremiah; it is also interested in demonstrating how Pentecostal experiences – e.g. the bearing of prophetic burdens and the resistance Pentecostals have experienced from the larger mainline Protestant world – aid Pentecostal audiences in comprehending the message of the book, giving Pentecostal interpretation an important way to contribute to and develop the larger academic discussion.[7] The study is also relevant to the further development and description of a Pentecostal interpretive strategy for the OT because it applies those developing insights to a textual unit whose content is neither explicitly pneumatological nor prophetic, in typical Pentecostal definitions of those terms.

1.2.3 Scope

The present study will concern itself with two texts that have been classically identified as the first of Jeremiah's Confessions: Jer. 11.18-23 and 12.1-13. The texts will be considered individually, together, and then briefly within the broader context of the entire Confessions corpus. The analysis will both demonstrate the texts' unique features

---

[6] Perhaps it might even be said that Jeremiah is an 'ideal prophet' *because* he is an 'ideal hearer'.

[7] In brief, not only does Pentecostalism need the scriptural insights provided by 'the academy' but also 'the academy' can gain better insight into the text by listening to the voices of Pentecostal exegetes.

and their careful theologically motivated integration into the present book of Jeremiah.

1.3 A Brief History of Interpretation

The scholarly literature on Jeremiah's Confessions is nothing if not immense; however, given the numerous interpretive difficulties that the Confessions present, the depth of literature is not all that surprising. In many ways, the history of interpretation of the Confessions simply serves as another illustration of Childs' observation that there are 'literary and historical elements both of strong discontinuity and of continuity … present within the Jeremianic tradition'.[8] Perhaps a more obvious reason that the study of the Confessions occupies such a central place in modern scholarship on the book of Jeremiah is that the book gives its readers 'a deeper insight into the life of the prophet than is found with any other Old Testament prophet'.[9]

Despite the amount of scholarly attention devoted to these texts, O'Connor only finds two virtually uncontested points. First, that the Confessions first circulated as an independent collection before being incorporated into the book of Jeremiah and, second, that the Confessions employ in some measure the form of the psalm of lament.[10] Otherwise, the scholarly discussion has been marked by deep divisions.

The present review has two main purposes: first, to trace briefly the major historical movements in the study of the Confessions; second, to offer an extended analysis of the key works that are most relevant to the current study. Given the immensity of the secondary literature, a literature review of everything ever written on the Confessions is neither possible nor helpful. For our purposes, this literature review will focus primarily on scholarly books and monographs explicitly devoted to the Confessions; the copious material from the

---

[8] Brevard S. Childs, *An Introduction to the Old Testament as Scripture* (Philadelphia: Fortress Press, 1979), p. 344.

[9] Childs, *Introduction to the Old Testament*, p. 348. 'It needs no demonstration that the figure of Jeremiah plays a more prominent role in the prophecy that bears his name than any other prophet does in his'. J.G. McConville, *Judgment and Promise: An Interpretation of the book of Jeremiah* (Winona Lake, IN: Eisenbrauns, 1992), p. 61.

[10] Kathleen M. O'Connor, *The Confessions of Jeremiah: Their Interpretation and Role in Chapters 1-25* (SBLDS 94; Atlanta: Scholars Press, 1988), p. 81.

commentaries will be discussed as needed in the actual exegesis of the Confession texts.

1.3.1 An Analytical Rubric

The goal here is to offer an interpretive rubric for understanding the development of the scholarly discussion, providing the reader with a way to categorize the various interpretations and to situate the present work within that larger scholarly landscape. It would be expected that the discussion of the Confessions would track with larger discussions of the book of Jeremiah since Sigmund Mowinckel first proposed that three different literary strata could be discerned in the book of Jeremiah.[11] He then argued that the earliest stratum, source A, represented the authentic words of the historical prophet and should thus be considered the most original theological material in the book. Though many scholars have since challenged Mowinckel's analysis, they have retained his key operative assumption that theological value is directly related to historical authenticity.[12] As Polk notes: 'Theological interests invariably become entwined with questions of literary and religious history'.[13]

It is precisely here that the study of the Confessions moves in a surprising direction,[14] going against the grain of the other dominant discussions in Jeremianic scholarship[15] by inverting the typical relationship between historicity and theological value: a greater emphasis on the Confessions' authenticity typically leads to a devaluing of their

---

[11] Mowinckel, building on the work of Bernhard Duhm, proposed that the earliest layer of the book consisted of 'the prophetic oracles of Jeremiah which are poetic and mostly found in the early part of the book'. The second layer comprised 'a significant amount of biographical material and narrate[d] incidents from the life of Jeremiah'. The final layer consisted of 'prose discourses of a highly rhetorical nature closely resembling the language and style of the Deuteronomists'. Robert P. Carroll, *From Chaos to Covenant: Uses of Prophecy in the Book of Jeremiah* (London: SCM Press, 1981), p. 18. Mowinckel perhaps unimaginatively labeled these as sources A, B, and C. See Bernhard Duhm, *Das Buch Jeremia* (Tübingen: J.C.B. Mohr, 1901) and Sigmund Mowinckel, *Zur Komposition des Buches Jeremia* (Oslo: Kristiania, in Kommission bei J. Dybwald, 1914).

[12] For example, a key aspect of William Holladay's work on Jeremiah has been the reclamation of much of the material marked by Duhm and Mowinckel as 'secondary' or 'redactional' as the authentic words of Jeremiah.

[13] Timothy Polk, *The Prophetic Persona: Jeremiah and the Language of Self* (JSOTSup 32; Sheffield: JSOT Press, 1987), p. 8.

[14] As noted above in the statement of the research question.

[15] For a helpful summary, see J. Andrew Dearman, 'Jeremiah: History of Interpretation', in Mark J. Boda and J. Gordon McConville (eds.), *Dictionary of the Old Testament Prophets* (Downers Grove, IL: InterVarsity Press, 2012), pp. 441-49.

theological import, while a greater emphasis on their theological value typically is found with a bias against their authenticity.

Scholarship on the Confessions, therefore, could be categorized on both biographical and theological axes,[16] defining a continuum of opinion categories. It could be (and has been) argued that the Confessions are purely biographical with no theological connection to the message of the book, are purely theological and integral to the message of the book but with no real biographical value, are primarily biographical but retain theological value, or are primarily theological and central to the book while retaining some biographical value. In the main, the history of the interpretation of the Confessions has moved from the first to the last option. This survey will follow a similar pattern, pointing to several scholars who would fall within three major categories.

1.3.1.1 The Confessions as a Psycho-Biographical Profile of the Historical Prophet[17]

In the first phase of critical scholarship, the Confessions 'with few exceptions … [were] taken as primary sources of psychological and biographical data for the construction of a "life of the prophet"'.[18] They were considered the 'private prayers and musings of Jeremiah in which are recorded his inner spiritual struggles occasioned by the hardships of his prophetic office'.[19] Such an approach seemed to coincide with the book's own focus on the figure of the prophet; thus, the Confessions 'were the very nerve-center of the book'.[20]

The scholarly investigation of the Confessions centered on the Confessions' quite obvious formal relationship to the individual

---

[16] With the caveat that there are near infinite distinctions of degree on each axis.

[17] David K. Jobling's term. See 'The Quest for the Historical Jeremiah: Hermeneutical Implications of Recent Literature', *USQR* 34 (1978), pp. 3-12 (3).

[18] A.R. Diamond, *The Confessions of Jeremiah in Context: Scenes of Prophetic Drama* (JSOTSup 45; Sheffield: JSOT Press, 1987), p. 11.

[19] Diamond, *Confessions*, pp. 11-12.

[20] Jobling, 'Quest', p. 3.

psalms of lament in the book of Psalms.[21] In fact, Walter Baumgartner's scholarly study of the Confessions[22] presented a formidable
form-critical analysis of that relationship that has yet to be effectively
challenged.[23] He argued quite convincingly that 'the confessions were
personal laments modeled after the personal laments of the Psalms
… [that] reflected the inner struggle of Jeremiah'.[24]

However, this position fails to 'address the theological relevance
of his data' or to explain 'how the Confessions fit into the book as a
whole'.[25] To prove the words authentic to the prophet but to refuse
the next necessary step of addressing their theological import for Jeremiah's message seems mistaken. When it came to the actual meaning of these authentic texts, the arguments often ran toward explicat-
ing the inner psychology of the historical prophet Jeremiah.[26] Such
descriptions often ended up being little more than in-depth character
sketches. However, such narratives were 'rooted no more in the text
than in an idealist metaphysics and a *religionsgeschichtliche* thesis'.[27] Furthermore, though scholars were adamant that these Confessions reflected the words of the historical prophet, they seemed not so sure
that they were worthwhile words. In many of the lives of Jeremiah
from this era, the prophet comes across as extremely weak and

---

[21] 'Form-critically the relevant body of material is of course the individual laments among the Psalms.' William L. Holladay, *Jeremiah 1* (Hermeneia; Minneapolis,
MN: Fortress Press, 1986), p. 358.

[22] Cited here in its English translation. Walter Baumgartner, *Jeremiah's Poems of
Lament* (trans. D.E. Orton; Sheffield: Almond Press, 1987).

[23] Baumgartner's study of the Confessions is still considered a classic in the
field of both Jeremiah and form-critical scholarship; not coincidentally, Walter
Baumgartner was a student of Sigmund Mowinckel. Following Baumgartner's
works, all scholars are forced to address two related problems, 'the problem of
explaining [the Confessions'] relationship to the Psalms and at the same time,
properly discerning their relationship to the prophetic mission'. Diamond, *Confessions,* p. 11.

[24] 'He consequently gave Jeremiah a large role in the creation of the confessions.' Peter C. Craigie, Page H. Kelley, and Joel F. Drinkard, Jr., *Jeremiah 1-25* (WBC
26; Dallas: Word Books, 1991), p. 173.

[25] Polk, *Prophetic Persona,* p. 127.

[26] Skinner is quite clear that the Confessions' interest is 'the struggle in Jeremiah's mind between fidelity to his prophetic commission and the natural feelings
and impulses of his heart'. Skinner, *Prophecy and Religion* (Cambridge: The University
Press), p. 210.

[27] Polk, *Prophetic Persona,* p. 11, speaking especially of Skinner's *Prophecy and Religion.*

almost unworthy of the title 'prophet' when compared, say, to an earlier prophet such as Isaiah or Amos.[28]

1.3.1.2 The Confessions as Redactional Constructs
Unconnected with the Historical Prophet

The second phase of scholarship on the Confessions was inaugurated
nearly fifty years after Baumgartner published the first form-critical
study of those texts. This new perspective was driven by the realization that form criticism had proven nearly every biblical text used
some type of conventional speech-form that reflected the social and
cultic institutions that produced the form; the historical event to
which the text referred was of secondary importance.[29] The very
method that had been instrumental in launching the retrieval of the
historical person of the prophet in the Confessions was now understood as pointing to the ahistorical nature of those very same texts!
Such a drastic realization had the effect of creating a new wave of
studies, these particularly concerned with the final compilation of the
book and largely utilizing redaction-critical methods of inquiry.[30]

This seismic shift in interpretive strategy was spearheaded by H.G.
Reventlow[31] who 'concluded that the confessions did not represent
Jeremiah's inner struggle at all'. Rather, the Confessions were to be
read as communal laments. 'The prophet identified with the community in his role as cultic intercessor and the prophetic "I" is the
prophet's personalization of the community's concerns.'[32] In these

---

[28] I.e. Skinner's speculation that the severity of the persecution 'almost un-
manned' the prophet Jeremiah. Skinner, *Prophecy and Religion*, p. 210. See above.

[29] Erhard Gerstenberger, 'Jeremiah's Complaints: Observations on Jeremiah
15.10-21', *JBL* 82.4 (1963), pp. 393-408 (393-94).

[30] Some good examples of this perspective are Dong-Hyung Bak, *Klagender Gott
– Klagende Menschen: Studien zur Klage in Jeremiabuch* (BZAW 192; Berlin: Walter de
Gruyter, 1990); Hannes Bezzel, *Die Konfessionen Jeremias: Eine redaktiongeschichtliche
Studie* (BZAW 379; Berlin: Walter de Gruyter, 2007); Carroll, *From Chaos to Covenant*;
Karl-Friedrich Pohlmann, *Die Ferne Gottes – Studien zum Jeremiabuch. Beiträge zu den
'Konfessionen' im Jeremiabuch und ein Versuch zur Frage nach den Anfängen der Jeremiatradi-
tion* (BZAW 179; Berlin: Walter de Gruyter, 1989); Smith, *The Laments of Jeremiah
and Their Contexts*.

[31] Henning Graf Reventlow, *Liturgie und prophetisches Ich bei Jeremia* (Gütersloh:
Gütersloher Verlagshaus G. Mohn, 1963).

[32] Craigie, Kelley, and Drinkard, Jr., *Jeremiah 1-25*, p. 173.

Confessions, Jeremiah is executing the prophetic office as a mediator 'as he addresses God on behalf of the people'.[33]

It should be clear that this new argument effectively meant that the Confessions were theologically central to the message of the book of Jeremiah; but they were also more reflective of the perspective of the compilers/redactors of the Jeremiah tradition than they were of the historical prophet. By shifting from form-critical to redaction-critical methods of inquiry, scholars began operating with the basic assumption that these texts were intentionally placed within the book and conveyed key aspects of its overall message. In one of the more apparent oddities, scholars working within this framework often ended up simultaneously denying the text's connection to the historical prophet Jeremiah[34] and highlighting the unique presentation of the prophet within the text.[35] In a sense, the search for additional meaning in the redaction of the Confession texts has led to a troubling subtraction of the historical connection to the prophet.

1.3.1.3 The Confessions as Psycho-Biographical Profiles with Theological Connection to the Book

The third phase of Confessions scholarship opened the still-continuing quest to discover some middle ground between the interpretive poles established in the first two phases of critical study. While Baumgartner and others had forcefully argued that the Confessions preserved authentic words of the prophets, they often failed to give an adequate explanation of why such words were ultimately included in the book. This is, by far, the broadest of the three categories. In many ways, the initial scholars within this new category still operated within the parameters of a form-critical approach and with a primary dedication to proving the authenticity of the Confessions, but also pushed toward an integrative theological understanding of the confessions.[36] Newer scholarship within this category retains the

---

[33] 'By its very nature, his office was a two-sided one; it was his task to bring the divine word to the people and, equally to present their plaints and prayers before God as their official intercessor.' John Bright, 'Jeremiah's Complaints: Liturgy or Expressions of Personal Distress?' in J.I. Durham and J.R. Porter (eds.), *Proclamation and Presence: Old Testament Essays in Honour of G.H. Davies* (London: SCM Press, 1966), pp. 189-214 (191).

[34] To avoid the over-psychologizing of earlier approaches.

[35] For example, see Gerstenberger, 'Jeremiah's Complaints', pp. 393-408.

[36] See Sheldon H. Blank, *Jeremiah, Man and Prophet* (Cincinnati, OH: Hebrew Union College Press, 1961). Though they did not produce book-length studies of

historicity of the Confessions more as a safeguard of their status as expressions of real emotions. However, these scholars show a greater interest in the arrangement and function of the Confessions within the book.[37]

Perhaps it would be best to characterize this phase as a continuation of Baumgartner's work steeped in a deep appreciation for Reventlow's critique, achieving various balances between a historical understanding of the Confessions and a theological interpretation of them. Here, scholars were committed to treating the Confessions as the words of the historical prophet Jeremiah and as theologically integral to the message of the book bearing the prophet's name.[38]

Scholars in this category are convinced of the uniqueness of the Confessions as a literary form. They are undoubtedly prayers related to the lament as seen in the Psalms, but they are more than that. Since they were the prayers of a prophet, YHWH's responses to those prayers were received as YHWH's Word for the people as well as for the prophet.[39] Thus, they were also important to the message of the book. In the book of Jeremiah, the historical prophet functions not just as the spokesman to the people but as an exemplar for the

---

the Confessions, it would be remiss not to mention the seminal articles of Gerhard von Rad and John Bright as well; John Bright, 'A Prophet's Lament and Its Answer: Jeremiah 15.10-21', *Int* 28 (1974), pp. 59-74; and Gerhard von Rad, 'The Confessions of Jeremiah', in Leo G. Perdue and Brian W. Kovacs (eds.), *A Prophet to the Nations: Essays in Jeremiah Studies* (trans. Anne Winston and Gary Lance Johnson; Winona Lake, IN: Eisenbrauns, 1984), pp. 339-47.

[37] See Ferdinand Ahuis, *Der klagende Gerichtsprophet: Studien zur Klage in der überlieferung von den alttestamentalichen Gerichtspropheten* (CTM 12; Stuggart: Calwer Verlag, 1982); A.R. Diamond, *Confessions in Context*; Franz D. Hubmann, *Untersuchungen zu den Konfessionen Jer 11, 18-12, 2, und Jer 15, 10-21* (FB 30; Zürich: Echter Verlag, 1978); Norbert Ittmann, *Die Konfession Jeremias Ihre BeDeutung für die Verkundigung des Propheten* (WMANT 54; Neukirchen-Vluyn: Newkirchener, 1981); Ulrich Mauser, *Gottesbild und Menschwerdung: eine Undersuchung zur Einheit des Alten und Neuen Testaments* (BHT 4; Tübingen: Mohr, 1971); Kathleen M. O'Connor, *The Confessions of Jeremiah*.

[38] According to von Rad, 'a theological examination of these sections … must begin with the assumption that they stem directly from the mouth of the prophet … that his soul, indeed his unique subjective life and experiences occupy the center'. Rad, 'Confessions', p. 340.

[39] These responses 'lent his confessions … more than personal significance' and 'prompted Jeremiah to share with his people his … prayer experience. God's word to him was a word for them.' Sheldon H. Blank, 'The Prophet as Paradigm', in James L. Crenshaw and John T. Willis (eds.), *Essays in Old Testament Ethics* (New York: KTAV, 1974), pp. 111-30 (122).

people; the prophet now not only 'serves God with the harsh proclamation of his mouth' but also 'with his person; his life becomes unexpectedly involved in the cause of God on earth'.[40] He became their model for surviving the experience of the Exile.

Perhaps the single greatest weakness of the early scholarship within this category was its lack of attention to the Confessions' placement within the book of Jeremiah. For example, Sheldon Blank argued that there is 'no apparent logic in the distribution of these pieces' nor 'any meaningful order in their arrangement'.[41] However, more recent scholarship has revisited and effectively disproven Blank's claim.

1.3.2 Scholarly Background of the Present Work

This brief analysis of the past scholarship on the Confessions demonstrates something of an impasse. Over time, advancements in the critical study of the Confessions have been reduced to ever-greater specification of diverse forms or redactional layers and have issued noticeably diminished returns on investment from each successive scholarly engagement.

However, embedded within the scholarly tradition are the beginnings of a new way forward that displaces useless dichotomies and endless debates. Scholars today cannot fall prey to a false choice between the authenticity of the Confessions as words of the historical prophet Jeremiah or their theological value to the book as redactional pieces created whole cloth from the mind of some nameless editor. Walter Brueggemann pointed this out when he wisely described the portrayal of Jeremiah in the book that bears his name as a portrait rather than a photograph. He expounds:

> It is clear that we do not have in any simple way a descriptive, biographical report. Indeed this portrait, like every portrait, is passed through the perceptions of the artist. The person of Jeremiah offered us in some sense (as in every such piece of literature) [is] a construction of literary imagination. But it is also probable that the person, memory, and impact of Jeremiah were so

---

[40] Rad, 'Confessions', p. 346.
[41] Blank, 'Prophet as Paradigm', p. 126.

powerful and enduring that that personal reality presided over and shaped the imaginative reconstruction.[42]

This study is concerned with presenting just such a portrait. However, as with all such artistic endeavors, it stands within the stream of prior scholarship. This section will revisit in some detail key pieces of critical scholarship that should be considered foundational to the endeavor of the present work.

1.3.2.1 Walter Baumgartner, *Jeremiah's Poems of Lament* (1917)

Baumgartner's study of the Confessions is still rightly considered a classic of both Jeremiah and form-critical scholarship. Here, Baumgartner argued quite convincingly that 'the confessions were personal laments modeled after the personal laments of the Psalms … [that] reflected the inner struggle of Jeremiah'.[43]

a) Summary

Baumgartner's discussion begins with an analysis of the form of the individual lament. He helpfully identifies their main components.

> As an introduction there is the 'invocation' of the deity. The main part, the 'corpus', contains the 'lament' and the 'petition', which is often accompanied by special motifs. The 'assurance of being heard', the 'vow', and often the hymnic 'thanksgiving' form the conclusion.[44]

He also sees the individual psalms of lament as identified by several recurring motifs. There is an honor motif where 'the petitioner likes to complain to Yahweh that he is having to suffer so much for his sake'. The petitioner, therefore, appeals to the divine *honor*, hoping also to convince YHWH that the petitioner's 'own reputation is at stake'.[45] The trust motif is present when 'the psalmist clings to God in the firm confidence that he will not let him down'. Such trust

---

[42] Walter Brueggemann, 'Jeremiah: Portrait of the Prophet', in Patrick D. Miller (ed.), *Like Fire in the Bones: Listening for the Prophetic Word in Jeremiah* (Minneapolis: Fortress Press, 2006), pp. 3-17 (4).

[43] 'He consequently gave Jeremiah a large role in the creation of the confessions'. Craigie, Kelley, and Drinkard, Jr., *Jeremiah 1-25*, p. 173.

[44] He does admit there is 'some degree of freedom in the sequence of the components' though he also thinks that 'all songs of lament contain essentially the same subject-matter'. Baumgartner, *Jeremiah's Poems of Lament*, p. 20.

[45] Baumgartner, *Jeremiah's Poems of Lament*, p. 31.

'forms the basis on which the [petition] rests. Without this trust he would not even dare to cherish a hope and make a petition.'[46]

The repentance motif acknowledges that, according to the theology of retribution, the reality that all suffering is rooted somehow in guilt. Thus, the petitioner 'is moved to soul-searching and contemplation'.[47] Confession is designed to relieve the burdened conscience and appease the wrath of YHWH. However, almost as frequently, we discover an innocence motif where the petitioner claims to be completely righteous, even declaring that YHWH would find the petitioner to be faultless.[48]

Baumgartner's analysis of the individual lament form leads him to several important observations. First, he notes that 'the lament and the petition should be regarded as the indispensable constituents of the song of lament'. In fact, the psalmists are 'especially partial to alternating between lament and petition two or three times'.[49]

This alternating structure 'necessarily creates an impression of great disorder. Instead of a strict progression of ideas there is a restless to-ing and fro-ing.' However, 'it would be quite wrong to try to introduce some order by always placing similar ideas together. The apparent disorder corresponds to the psalmist's excited state of mind.'[50]

Baumgartner also argues that the 'purely spiritual' songs of lament preserved in the book of Psalms must have been preceded by '*cultic* psalms of lament'.[51] This is significant because 'cultic language is less free and is always inclined to the formation of established forms …

---

[46] Baumgartner, *Jeremiah's Poems of Lament*, pp. 31-32.

[47] Baumgartner, *Jeremiah's Poems of Lament*, p. 33.

[48] The petitioner 'appeals to the fact that he has always avoided the company of evil men and has been mindful of Yahweh … fulfilled his cultic duties … [and] acted quite differently towards those who are now behaving so shabbily towards him'. See, for example, Ps. 35.12-14. Baumgartner, *Jeremiah's Poems of Lament*, pp. 33-34.

[49] 'It is an attempt, albeit a schematized one, to express the ups and downs of [the Psalmist's] own mood … wavering between dark hopelessness and firm confidence'. Baumgartner, *Jeremiah's Poems of Lament*, p. 38.

[50] Baumgartner, *Jeremiah's Poems of Lament*, p. 38.

[51] The key evidence Baumgartner cites is the presence of metaphors such as 'washing of hands in innocence' (see Pss. 26.6; 73.13) and the request to be 'purged with hyssop' (Ps. 51.9 [7]), which, in his eyes, are most certainly derived from actual cultic customs (cf. Deut. 21.6; Lev. 14.4, 51). Baumgartner, *Jeremiah's Poems of Lament*, p. 38, italics original.

with the constant repetition of the same forms a firm style was bound to develop'.[52]

Having established the components of the individual lament, Baumgartner embarks on a detailed study of each Confession, demonstrating how those formal elements are noticeably present. However, Baumgartner is not only intent on demonstrating the Confessions' formal relationships to the individual psalms of lament but is also set to defend their authenticity as words of the historical prophet Jeremiah. Baumgartner argues that such a possibility should not be discounted if three key criteria can be met; Baumgartner sets out to demonstrate that (1) 'the psalms of the book of Jeremiah differ from those of the Psalter in characteristic ways'; (2) 'that these characteristics are associated with the prophetic matter'; and (3) '[that] similar lyrical sections are to be found in the genuine parts of the book of Jeremiah'.[53]

Baumgartner first analyzes the deviations between the psalms of lament in the Psalter and the Confessions of Jeremiah. The place of the 'assurance of being heard' is often 'taken by a divine speech', something that is a 'very rare occurrence in the psalms of lament'.[54] But more significant are the inclusions of elements that demonstrate 'prophetic substance'. For example, the author of the Confessions 'receives special knowledge from Yahweh[55] … Yahweh's name is called over him[56] … and it is in Yahweh's name that he speaks'.[57] Essentially, in the Confessions, we see a 'prophet who clothes his most personal experiences in psalmic form'.[58]

---

[52] To Baumgartner, the 'fixed' quality of the form's language was a 'consequence of the originally magical significance of their wording'. Baumgartner, *Jeremiah's Poems of Lament*, p. 39.

[53] 'Then we should have positive proof of their authenticity'. Baumgartner, *Jeremiah's Poems of Lament*, p. 80.

[54] Baumgartner, *Jeremiah's Poems of Lament*, p. 80.

[55] Jeremiah 11.18.

[56] Jeremiah 15.16.

[57] Jeremiah 20.9. Baumgartner, *Jeremiah's Poems of Lament*, 80. 'Baumgartner shows that in Jeremiah's laments there is stress on the prophetical office, unparalleled in the book of Psalms.' Michael Avioz, 'The Call for Revenge in Jeremiah's Complaints (Jer 11-20)', *VT* 55.4 (2005), pp. 429-38 (433).

[58] 'What we see [in Jeremiah's laments] is the man and his struggle to come to terms with his prophetic role … we see the prophet … from the inside.' Baumgartner, *Jeremiah's Poems of Lament*, pp. 82-83.

As important as it is to find points of prophetic distinction from the psalms of lament, it is equally important to find points of prophetic coherence with the prophetic material universally recognized as authentic to Jeremiah.[59] If it is 'incontestable that Jeremiah occasionally adopts a lyrical tone, the possibility must also be admitted that he makes use of thoroughly lyrical types in other places too'.[60]

The greatest assurance of the Confessions' authenticity to the historical prophet Jeremiah is the shared presentation of the 'position he adopts toward his God and the prophetic ministry'. Contrary to the presentation of such prophets as Amos, Hosea, Isaiah, and Micah, who 'give themselves unreservedly to their prophetic "profession" and are devoted to it', Jeremiah 'obeys the prophetic impulse under protest and only out of necessity'.[61] In fact, Baumgartner goes so far as to claim that a 'deep crack ... runs through Jeremiah's personality ... at least for periods of time, the human being and the prophet in him part company'.[62]

Finally, Baumgartner reaches the apex of his argument. the claim that Jeremiah's Confessions derive, at least formally, from the psalms of lament in the Psalter. He notes that the biography of Jeremiah given us in the book that bears his name indicates deep, abiding suffering:

> He suffered ... from the fact that his life was now a great, ceaseless struggle, that in his work for Yahweh his reward was nothing but scorn and mockery, even severe persecution, that his clairvoyance, which showed him the horrors of the future as if in the present, stopped him enjoying life's harmless pleasures, and that he had to stand so completely alone and without joy in life.[63]

---

[59] These sections include Jer. 4.19-21; 8.18-23; 10.19-22; 13.17; 14.17-18; 23.9. Baumgartner, *Jeremiah's Poems of Lament*, pp. 83-85.

[60] Baumgartner, *Jeremiah's Poems of Lament*, pp. 86-87.

[61] 'A good indication ... lies in the difference between his call and that of Isaiah. While Isaiah responds to Yahweh's query as to whom he should send by immediately offering himself (6.8), Jeremiah shrinks back at the immensity and difficulty of the task imposed upon him; he tries to withdraw from it.' Baumgartner, *Jeremiah's Poems of Lament*, p. 87.

[62] Baumgartner, *Jeremiah's Poems of Lament*, p. 87.

[63] Baumgartner, *Jeremiah's Poems of Lament*, p. 95.

The typical prophetic style Jeremiah had inherited 'did not really offer him an appropriate medium for expression. So he took hold of that type of song which came closest to his experiences and feelings'.[64]

b) Appraisal

Baumgartner's impact on the study of the Confessions cannot be overstated. His form-critical analysis of the Confessions has made their connection to the psalms of lament one of the two points of 'universal agreement' to which Kathleen O'Connor can point.[65] Baumgartner effectively laid to rest the argument that the Confessions were inauthentic[66] based on perceived inconsistencies with idyllic images of the prophet.[67] For Baumgartner, the Confessions' multiple connections to the psalms of lament indicated their role as accurate representations of the inner emotional state of the prophet Jeremiah vis-à-vis his prophetic ministry.

This is not to say that Baumgartner's argument is flawless. His restricted sense of the use of psalms of lament in the Psalter[68] leads him to argue that Jeremiah's use of the lament to express his pain 'could be no more than an incomplete success'. Thus, the 'song of lament style lies like a thick veil over what is actually intended to be said'.[69] It seems curious to claim that Jeremiah, who is certainly among the more eloquent of the OT prophets, chose for the expression of his inmost feelings a literary form that actually *distorts* or *disguises* his true feelings.

However, that should not distract us from the fact that, from the very beginning of scholarly study of the Confessions, there was an implicit recognition of the affective power of their rhetoric and form. For Baumgartner, the essential lament pattern adopted in the Confessions was the alternation of lament and petition which gave an impression of structural disorder. However, that disorder in lament

---

[64] Baumgartner, *Jeremiah's Poems of Lament*, p. 96.

[65] O'Connor, *The Confessions of Jeremiah*, p. 81. See above.

[66] See, for example, Gustav Hölscher, *Die Profeten: Untersuchungen zur Religionsgeschichte Israels* (Leipzig: J.C. Heirhices'sche Buchhandlung, 1914).

[67] See Rad, 'Confessions', p. 339, note 1.

[68] In the history of the cultic form of the individual lament, they had been 'intended for external suffering', particularly for use in times of physical sickness. Baumgartner, *Jeremiah's Poems of Lament*, pp. 22-24, 96.

[69] Baumgartner, *Jeremiah's Poems of Lament*, p. 96.

psalms was evidence of the 'psalmist's excited state of mind',[70] that is, the psalmist's emotions! To Baumgartner's way of thinking, it was the emotive nature of the form of lament that made it so attractive to the struggling Jeremiah.

1.3.2.2 A.R. Diamond, *The Confessions of Jeremiah in Context* (1987)

Beginning with the work of Franz Hubmann and Ferdinand Ahuis, scholars began to see through the false dichotomy between the historical and theological value of the Confessions; the Confessions could be *both* personal expressions of the historical Jeremiah's distress and pain *and* key parts of the theological message of the book of Jeremiah.[71] The question then became *how* these texts functioned simultaneously in those dual capacities.

a) Summary

After a helpful and incisive review of the history of interpretation of the Confessions, Diamond chooses to begin his work with a careful exegesis of each Confession text that paid close attention to 'their literary sequence and immediate literary context'.[72] This close reading of the texts revealed 'two progressive cycles … connected by a transitional passage'.[73] The first cycle centered on 'the presentation of a dispute between the prophet and Yahweh over the nature of the prophetic mission'. The second cycle shifted to the dispute 'between prophet and nation over the fate of his prophetic message … which was challenged and rejected by the nation'.[74] The crises of both cycles are resolved by 'the very nature of the prophet's mission and message'.[75]

Diamond calls the effect of this dual axis a 'prophetic drama', explaining: 'For as a play … which relies primarily upon dialogue in order to create a sense of narrative development, so the literary complex 11-20 narrates or portrays the course of Jeremiah's prophetic

---

[70] Baumgartner, *Jeremiah's Poems of Lament*, p. 28.

[71] Though, in this phase, much more attention is paid to the theological weight of the Confessions' position within the book of Jeremiah than to their relationship to the historical prophet. Hence the distinction from the work of scholars such as Bright and von Rad.

[72] Diamond, *Confessions in Context*, p. 177.

[73] The two main cycles are Jer. 11.18-15.21; 18.18-20.18; the transitional passage is Jer. 17.14-18. Diamond, *Confessions in Context*, p. 177.

[74] Diamond, *Confessions in Context*, pp. 177-78.

[75] Diamond, *Confessions in Context*, p. 178.

mission as a dialogue in which prophet, Yahweh, and nation are participants'.[76]

Each side of this double axis presents 'a justification for the destruction of Israel', by pointing 'to the incorrigible faithlessness and alienation of the nation in its relationship to Yahweh'. The 'hopelessness of this situation is crystallized by the nation's response … to Jeremiah's mission'.[77] Thus, Diamond sees the *primary* purpose of the Confessions as presenting a theodicy of the nation's downfall.

If Diamond's view of the role of the Confessions is correct, he recognizes that 'much that is characteristic in the normal approach to reading the confessions needs modification':[78]

> It is not the personal experience of the prophet in the context of his mission per se and its value for the depiction of Jeremiah as an exemplary spiritual figure which lie at the heart of the editorial interest. Instead, the portrayal of the prophetic mission represents an element in the promotion of the theodicy theme and is subordinate to it.[79]

Even the paradigmatic readings of the Confession promoted by scholars like Blank and Bright are inadequate for Diamond. They retain the view that the Confessions are 'a type of spiritual biography with a theological and hortatory focus', even when 'their contextual utilization has assigned them a more apologetic role rather than the purely biographical'.[80]

While Diamond is willing to consider a polyvalent reading of the Confessions, he feels that if it 'is going to succeed, then it must do so with proper regard to the regulatory and excluding role offered in the presence of the double-axis pattern'. Any 'discovery of additional levels of meaning will have to result from the accumulative presence of features within the integrated literary complex … that impel one to speak of sub-themes subordinated to the primacy of the theodicy theme and unexhausted by it'.[81]

---

[76] Diamond, *Confessions in Context*, p. 181.
[77] Diamond, *Confessions in Context*, p. 182.
[78] Diamond, *Confessions in Context*, p. 182.
[79] Diamond, *Confessions in Context*, p. 183.
[80] Diamond, *Confessions in Context*, p. 183.
[81] Diamond, *Confessions in Context*, pp. 184-85.

b) Appraisal

Diamond's approach to the Confessions provides a very clear reason
why the texts were included in the book; they are integral to its theological explanation of the nation's downfall. Though Diamond does
not categorically deny that the Confessions refer to the historical
prophet, he certainly downplays that aspect of their understanding in
favor of their function as a theodicy.

It is precisely here that Diamond's work runs aground. J.G.
McConville finds Diamond's 'relegation of the prophet's 'suffering
servant' role to the status of a subtheme ... unsatisfying'. He thinks
that this view does not fairly handle the 'burst of perplexity which
emanates from Jeremiah in chapter 20'[82] and 'seriously underesti-
mates his representative capacity'.[83]

1.3.2.3 Timothy Polk, *The Prophetic Persona* (1987)

a) Summary

Polk sets as his task to 'trace the picture drawn of the prophet by the
first-person poetic, so-called autobiographical, passages and to describe the function this picture performs'.[84] He is clear that to distinguish his methodology as synchronic meaning that 'we propose to
view the Bible as a *literary* work [which] constructs its own world'.[85]
Like a language, the Bible is so constructed that 'the meaning of any
of its parts depends on that part's relation to the whole'.[86]

Viewing the text holistically brings two forms of textual temporality to the fore. 'The first is the temporal scheme delineated by the
text itself, that which belongs to the world the text constructs ... the
second is the temporality of the [sequential] reading process'.[87] Thus,
Polk does not attempt to fix the chronology of the book nor does he
avoid 'reading juxtaposed materials sequentially even though they

---

[82] Where, according to Diamond, the tension has already been resolved.
[83] McConville, *Judgment and Promise*, p. 72.
[84] Polk, *Prophetic Persona*, p. 8.
[85] Polk, *Prophetic Persona*, p. 15.
[86] More than the part's relationship to (1) 'some datum of intention that is supposed to have existed in the author's mind at the time of composition'; (2) 'a reconstructed historical reference to something outside the world of the text'; or (3)
'the part's function and meaning at a stage prior to the work's final shape'. All these
are simply different ways of 'etymologizing the text'. Polk, *Prophetic Persona*, p. 15.
[87] Polk, *Prophetic Persona*, p. 15.

may be generically and genetically different'.[88] In broad terms, the synchronic approach shifts the focus from the writing process of the text to its reading process.[89]

According to Polk, the problem with the prevalent historical-critical approaches to the book is 'not so much that we have two Jeremiahs but … that only one, the historical figure, has received adequate attention'. The 'biblically depicted Jeremiah has been virtually forgotten'.[90] Polk's focus is the literary *persona* of the prophet Jeremiah rather than his historical person. That literary *persona* 'is always depicted in terms of his vocation, which is fully corporate in orientation, and the public vocation always involves him at a level most personal'.[91] Polk's exegetical move puts us beyond the endless historical debate over whether Jeremiah's Confessions were public or private prayers.

Polk sees this move as involving strategic shifts in the understanding of the book's genre, its conception of the self, and its use of the pronoun 'I'. First, it must be understood that the ancient conception of biography would undoubtedly be different than the modern conception, given the fact of very different understandings of personal identity. 'Private life and the development of personal identity would have been of less importance than one's public life and the performance of a social role'.[92] Thus, the ancient biography would emphasize 'however unwittingly, a subject's typicality … at the expense of … particularity'.[93] However, this does not somehow mean that such texts are *un*biographical.

It seems that modern biography has forgotten that 'the concept of "self" entails a world which is constituted, at the very least, by a network of relations rooted in the self. The self can thus not be described apart from its world'.[94] Thus, Western individual identity is 'not just one "I" but many, or rather an "I" with a *variety* of uses,

---

[88] 'It bears remembering that the meaning that tends to accrue from, say two expressions which are ten verses apart can be quite different from that which accrues by thinking of them as being ten decades apart'. Polk, *Prophetic Persona,* p. 15.

[89] Polk, *Prophetic Persona,* p. 16.

[90] Polk, *Prophetic Persona,* p. 9.

[91] Polk, *Prophetic Persona,* p. 9.

[92] Polk, *Prophetic Persona,* p. 20.

[93] Polk, *Prophetic Persona,* p. 20.

[94] Polk, *Prophetic Persona,* pp. 21-22.

some of which have a primitive ... logic and remain quite untouched by *any* philosophy or movement'.[95] Thus, from this synchronic standpoint, it is perfectly logical to argue for a polyvalent 'I' in the book of Jeremiah. Polk argues, though, that 'principal among the uses of "I" in Jeremiah ... is the expression of emotion'.[96]

Polk sees Jeremiah as both 'exemplar' and 'metaphor' within the book of Jeremiah. This idea fits well with the 'prophet-as-paradigm' model earlier proposed by Sheldon Blank.[97] To conceive of the prophetic 'I' as an exemplar includes the notion of imitation. In Jeremiah, 'the prophetic persona's piety ... is to be imitated by the reader'. In other words, 'since Jeremiah's person is inextricably bound up with his proclamation, the piety is really part of the kerygma, not something extrinsic to it'.[98]

Polk recognizes what could be labeled a kind of psychological interpretation; however, it differs from a typical profile because it does not focus on 'reconstructing the Jeremiah of history in order to identify there a watershed in the history of human consciousness and religious spirituality'. Rather, the purpose is to 'limn the features of the persona rendered by the text as a model of obediential suffering'.[99]

b) Appraisal

Polk's approach to the Confessions is very near in purpose to the present work. Polk does not attempt to 'take sides in the debate over the occasion of the Confessions ... [rather] the point is to question the relevance of the debate itself. However the text achieved its present shape, it is that shape that confronts the reader and is the primary determinant of meaning.'[100]

Probably the only weakness of Polk's study is that he chooses to deal more broadly with the autobiographical passages in the book and chooses to address only two of the Confessions. Though this choice

---

[95] Polk, *Prophetic Persona*, p. 23.

[96] 'Jeremiah's emotion-language will also be seen to attest a notable degree of interiority and particularity ... which should counteract any too-hasty or overdrawn generalizations about the corporate nature of personality in ancient Israel'. Polk, *Prophetic Persona*, p. 24.

[97] Polk, *Prophetic Persona*, p. 128.

[98] Polk, *Prophetic Persona*, p. 129.

[99] 'This in our opinion is the locus of the theological value and interest of the text, when understood as scripture'. Polk, *Prophetic Persona*, p. 129.

[100] Polk, *Prophetic Persona*, pp. 129-30.

to focus on other texts besides the Confessions is no doubt intentional, it does seem to leave an unexpected gap in his argument.

1.3.2.4 Kathleen M. O'Connor, *The Confessions of Jeremiah* (1988)

a) Summary

In many ways, O'Connor's work is eerily similar to Diamond's. She likewise attempts a contextual and multivalent reading of the Confessions. She acknowledges that 'these poetic pieces create the impression that Jeremiah was a man of small vision and narrow self-centeredness' and that their 'abrupt vacillations in mood give the appearance not only of psychological disorder within the prophet but also of textual displacement within the poems'.[101] However, she 'challenges these prevailing interpretations of the prophet, the confessions, and the Book', contending that 'Jeremiah's use of the personal voice … does not provide evidence of a petulant and disturbed personality' but rather 'is a weapon in his battle for acceptance as a true prophet of Yahweh'.[102]

O'Connor agrees the Confessions had both public and private roles during the historical prophet's lifetime but differs from other scholars on 'the nature and importance of their public function'.[103] Her careful exegesis of each Confession demonstrated that 'the primary purpose of each confession was to establish the authenticity of Jeremiah's claim to be the true prophet of YHWH'.[104]

In her analysis, these arguments for Jeremiah's legitimacy fall into three categories. The first category presents 'Jeremiah as a prophet faithful to his task',[105] innocent of wrong and faithful to his mediatorial role,[106] all the while maintaining a unique relationship with YHWH.[107] It is precisely these two elements that distinguish Jeremiah from the false prophets he indicts in Jer. 23.18-22.[108]

---

[101] O'Connor, *Confessions*, p. 2.

[102] Thus, 'the confessions served a public prophetic function in the original life setting of the prophet'. O'Connor, *Confessions*, p. 3.

[103] O'Connor, *Confessions*, pp. 84-85.

[104] O'Connor, *Confessions*, p. 85.

[105] O'Connor, *Confessions*, p. 84.

[106] Jeremiah 11.19; 12.3; 15.10cd, 16; 18.20. O'Connor, *Confessions*, p. 86.

[107] Jeremiah 11.18; 12.3; 15.16; 17.17; 20.11. O'Connor, *Confessions*, p. 86.

[108] 'The false prophets … are evil and they refuse to turn from their evil ways (v. 22). Nor do they have any relationship with Yahweh.' O'Connor, *Confessions*, p. 86.

The second category or argument 'presents Yahweh as the controlling power and originator of the prophet's work'.[109] Jeremiah depicts YHWH as an overpowering, compelling force; Jeremiah's message 'was not his own but Yahweh's'.[110] The final category comprises YHWH's replies to the prophet which reveal the expectations of a true prophet. The true prophet must 'anticipate suffering and mounting persecution … [and] must meet certain conditions or behavioral expectations'.[111]

Finally, the entire collection is bounded by Jeremiah's petition to YHWH (Jer. 11.20; 20.12).[112] This stock legal language 'is a tool used to give shape and texture to the argument of legitimation'.[113] It also helps to explain the presence of Jeremiah's accusations against YHWH.

O'Connor makes three key points about the Confessions. First, 'the framing of the confessions by the doublet sets all the poems within the boundaries of a subtle assertion that Yahweh is the Just Judge who will hear and act on behalf of the prophet'. Second, it 'sets Jeremiah against the enemies who refuse to hear the word (11.20; 15.10; 20.12)' and 'provides Jeremiah with the language to blame Yahweh for his predicament (12.1-3)'. Finally, the use of the term יָדַע 'allows Jeremiah to strengthen his claim that he exists in a special relationship with Yahweh who will ultimately vindicate him'.[114]

b) Appraisal

O'Connor is much more persuasive than her contemporary Diamond in her claim to support the authenticity of these texts to the historical prophet. 'The "I" of these poems must be understood as the personal voice of Jeremiah.' It 'can in no way be interpreted to represent the voice of the community' because 'the speaker in the confessions stands over against the community'.[115] However, she does agree that the Confessions are preserved for more than

---

[109] O'Connor, *Confessions*, p. 85.

[110] Jeremiah 15.16ab, 17; 17.16. This leads to the prophet's accusations against YHWH. 'It is the word of God which caused all the prophet's sufferings (20.8).' O'Connor, *Confessions*, p. 86.

[111] O'Connor, *Confessions*, p. 87.

[112] O'Connor, *Confessions*, p. 88.

[113] O'Connor, *Confessions*, p. 88.

[114] O'Connor, *Confessions*, p. 91.

[115] O'Connor, *Confessions*, p. 92.

biographical interest in the historical prophet; they were preserved 'because they claimed that Jeremiah's prophecy was true and they appealed to God's authority for that truth'.[116]

As with the work of Baumgartner, von Rad, and Blank, O'Connor finds a way to preserve history and theology in her reading of the text. However, I find it very intriguing that her form-critical analysis of the shape of the Confessions corpus reveals a 'movement toward praise and confidence in Yahweh'. That the confessions are classified form-critically as psalms of lament means to her that their purpose 'is to praise God with confidence and assurance in the midst of suffering'.[117] It is not clear that O'Connor would agree that their purpose was the expression of true human emotion to God. It seems that her rejection of 20.14-18 as part of the collection on form-critical grounds[118] is perhaps more based on her discomfort with a truly human affective dimension to the texts.

1.3.2.5 J.G. McConville, *Judgment and Promise* (1992)

a) Summary

McConville's short but incisive work on Jeremiah operates with similar assumptions as Polk's work and is, in part, based upon it. When discussing the Confessions, McConville sets out to answer the following question: 'To what extent [does] the portrayal of Jeremiah [cohere] with … the message of the book?' For McConville, the portrayal of the prophet relates to the core theological question of the book: 'What is a true prophet, and which of those "prophets" who were prominent in the life of the people in the days before the exile, truly had the authority to speak for YHWH?'[119]

McConville agrees with Polk that Jeremiah's 'message is bound up with his own suffering, which has been a part of his announcement of the suffering which the people too must endure'. Jeremiah's

---

[116] O'Connor, *Confessions*, p. 92.

[117] O'Connor, *Confessions*, p. 94.

[118] 'In this study, 20.14-18 has been disqualified both as an element of the fifth confession and as a separate confession in itself. The pericope does not conform to the form-critical features of the Psalm of individual lament as do all the other confessions, but, with Job 3, includes appropriate elements to classify it as a cursing poem, placed after the confessions for redactional purposes.' O'Connor, *Confessions*, pp. 88-89.

[119] McConville, *Judgment and Promise*, p. 61.

identification with his people 'forces an interpretation of his experience, which cannot be detached from his message'.[120] Jeremiah equally identifies with 'the will of YHWH, which condemns the people's sin'.[121] This creates a tension within the prophet which is described in the Confessions.[122] The Confessions, then, *do* have a function in the proclamation of the divine word in Jeremiah. In effect, 'life and word mesh in his ministry. Both in his speech and in himself he sets YHWH forth.'[123]

It is also important to McConville to see these Confessions in the context of chapters 11-20. The overall thrust of this section is 'that the hope for Judah is deliberately closed down'.[124] However, McConville is convinced that 'the relationship of Jeremiah to Judah is not exhausted by his addressing to them words of judgment'.[125] For instance, McConville notes that in Jeremiah 14-15,

> Jeremiah looks to YHWH for deliverance (14.22) and receives in the end an assurance of it (15.19). If that assurance relates in the first instance to a deliverance of Jeremiah from his enemies within the people, it has overtones too of a deliverance of the nation from its enemies by virtue of the representative role of the prophet.[126]

McConville also agrees with Polk on the complexity of the presentation of the prophet in the Confessions; Jeremiah represents the people and YHWH both and yet remains an individual. Thus, all the sections where Jeremiah speaks as a representative would naturally be complicated. For example, Jeremiah's words in 14.19-22 simultaneously are 'a kind of criticism of the nation, sealing their fate', and, 'by virtue of [Jeremiah's] representative role ... the prayer becomes, after all, a genuine prayer of the people'.[127] Yet, even in his role as representative, Jeremiah 'can still be distinguished from the

---

[120] McConville, *Judgment and Promise*, p. 62.

[121] 'If the prophet feels keenly the horror of the "alarm of war" (4.19), he feels equally keenly the stupidity and evil of the people (4.22).' McConville, *Judgment and Promise*, p. 62.

[122] McConville, *Judgment and Promise*, p. 62.

[123] McConville, *Judgment and Promise*, p. 62.

[124] McConville, *Judgment and Promise*, p. 69.

[125] McConville, *Judgment and Promise*, p. 69.

[126] McConville, *Judgment and Promise*, p. 69.

[127] McConville, *Judgment and Promise*, p. 73.

people, as in his expressed feelings of isolation and anger with them'.[128]

b) Appraisal

McConville's understanding of the figure of Jeremiah within the Confessions is one of the most nuanced explanations currently on offer: 'The figure of Jeremiah is neither merely an example of an individual's great personal piety, nor a detached cultic functionary. Rather there is an incarnational aspect to his role, by which he embodies both the experience of the people and that of YHWH, yet without ever ceasing to be an individual personality.'[129]

However, one point of critique may be offered. McConville observes that, in the context of Jeremiah 11-20, 'YHWH suffers an inner tension because of his need to punish the people that [YHWH] has chosen and loves'.[130] It seems that McConville has simply extended the psychologizing tendency of interpretations into the heart and mind of YHWH. If Baumgartner's claim of a disjuncture within Jeremiah's psyche is problematic, much more would be a claim of such a fissure within YHWH.

1.3.2.6 Amy Kalmanofsky, *Terror All Around* (2008)

a) Summary

Amy Kalmanofsky's published dissertation presents us with a unique study of the book of Jeremiah, fitting in with the broad tradition of rhetorical criticism of the book inaugurated by James Muilenburg. Recognizing that prophetic texts use 'many strategies of persuasive speech', she focuses her attention on the overlooked 'rhetoric of horror'. Unlike the contemporary understanding of 'horror' literature and movies as having only shock value, this rhetoric serves important theological purposes.[131] She also recognizes from the outset that the key reason for this rhetoric's impact is the *emotion* that it provokes,

---

[128] Jeremiah 15.10-12; 20.7-12. McConville, *Judgment and Promise*, p. 73.

[129] McConville, *Judgment and Promise*, p. 76.

[130] McConville, *Judgment and Promise*, p. 76.

[131] 'Threats of impending disease and graphic images of rotting corpses work to scare audiences straight.' Amy Kalmanofsky, *Terror All Around: The Rhetoric of Horror in the Book of Jeremiah* (LHB/OTS 390; New York: Bloomsbury, 2008), p. 1.

and that that emotive impact is still felt by the contemporary reader.[132]

In fact, horror as a literary genre is identified by the emotional response it evokes in its readers. Horror 'provides a literary mirror that enables critics to gauge audience reaction and consequently identify the genre'.[133] The character's reaction when encountering a horrifying entity is meant to guide and shape the reader/viewer's own response.[134]

Using this as her criterion, Kalmanofsky identifies key passages that fit the 'horror corpus' of the book of Jeremiah.[135] She makes clear that not all texts that frighten or threaten are horror texts, using Jer. 16.16-21 as an example: 'God threatens to hunt and fish sinful Israel and to fill the land with corpses (a terrifying prospect)', but 'the text does not include the reactions of those hunted or fished'.[136] Within these texts, Kalmanofsky identifies two key Hebrew roots that characterize the horror genre within the book. The key Hebrew roots are חָתַת ('be dismayed/terrified')[137] and שָׁמַם ('be desolate/appalled').[138] These root terms point to two subcategories of horror passages in Jeremiah that Kalmanofsky labels 'direct' and 'indirect' horror. In simplest terms, some horror passages in the book deal directly with 'the emotional reaction to the destroyer', while other passages deal more indirectly with 'the emotional reaction to the destruction'.[139] To put it another way, direct horror deals with the emotional reaction of those who are destroyed while indirect horror deals with the emotional reactions of those who witness that destruction.

Before dealing directly with the rhetoric of horror in the book of Jeremiah, Kalmanofsky provides a detailed analysis of the complex

---

[132] 'This study ... provides a powerful glimpse into the emotional life of the Bible's audience – which may include its current readers – by examining what moves and terrifies them ... Perhaps no other genre of literature is as geared to audience response.' Kalmanofsky, *Terror All Around*, p. 2.

[133] Here, Kalmanofsky follows closely critic Noël Carroll's theory of the 'mirroring effect' of horror literature. Kalmanofsky, *Terror All Around*, p. 3. See Noël Carroll, *The Philosophy of Horror* (New York. Routledge, 1990), p. 18.

[134] Character reactions 'counsel the audience how to react'. Kalmanofsky, *Terror All Around*, p. 3.

[135] Jeremiah 4.5-6.30; 8.1-23; 13.15-27; 14.1-15.9; 18.13-17; 19.1-20.6; 23.9-22; 24.1-10; 30.5-9; 34.8-22; 46.1-51.64.

[136] Kalmanofsky, *Terror All Around*, p. 4.

[137] 'Be dismayed, terrified'. Cf. Jer. 1.17; 8.9. *CDCH*, s.v. 'חתת I'.

[138] Jeremiah 2.12; 12.11. *CDCH*, s.v. 'שמם'.

[139] Kalmanofsky, *Terror All Around*, p. 31.

biblical emotion described as horror. For her, the experience of horror is rooted in the fear of shame.[140] She notes that the Hebrew term for shame, בּוֹשׁ is paired with חָתַת in key 'horror' texts.[141] In the OT, shame refers specifically to an emotive awareness of failure to live up to personal or social standards. She describes it as 'essentially a feeling of personal failure'[142] that leads to a fear of rejection. Similarly, חָתַת expresses a 'self-conscious emotion perhaps best understood as the awareness of one's own weakness and vulnerability'.[143] Furthermore, such awareness is usually only ever achieved in an instant of threat and is usually an overwhelming emotion; thus חָתַת expresses a paralyzing fear rooted in the sudden shame of awareness of vulnerability.[144]

Building on this posited relationship of terror to shame in the Hebraic affective paradigm, Kalmanofsky further notes that shame is often expressed in disgusting images such as rotting figs (Jer. 24.8) or festering wounds (Jer. 6.7-8). Thus, fear and disgust become 'the essential components of the emotional response of horror'.[145] However, the point of this rhetoric in the book of Jeremiah is not simply to evoke this strong emotional reaction. Horrific images demand response; the rhetoric of horror seeks 'to scare, shame, and ultimately reform the prophet's audiences'.[146]

b) Appraisal

Kalmanofsky's study provides an important precursor to the present work, even though it is not directly focused on the Confession texts. Rather, it provides an important example of a rhetorical-critical

---

[140] Kalmanofsky references two other scholars who have done seminal work in the OT conception of shame. See Johanna Siebert, *The Construction of Shame in the Hebrew Bible: The Prophetic Contribution* (JSOTSup 436; Sheffield: Sheffield Academic Press, 2002) and Lyn M. Bechtel, 'The Perception of Shame within the Divine-Human Relationship', in Lewis M. Hopfe (ed.), *Uncovering Ancient Stones: Essays in Memory of H. Neil Richardson* (Winona Lake, IN: Eisenbrauns, 1994), pp. 79-92.

[141] E.g. Jer. 8.9; 48.1; 50.2.

[142] Thus, the differentiation between 'shame' and 'guilt' is this: shame is related to 'who I am', while guilt is related to 'what I did'. Kalmanofsky, *Terror All Around*, p. 12.

[143] Kalmanofsky, *Terror All Around*, p. 19.

[144] חָתַת expresses 'the terror of impotence and certain disaster'. Kalmanofsky, *Terror All Around*, p. 20.

[145] Kalmanofsky, *Terror All Around*, p. 9.

[146] Kalmanofsky, *Terror All Around*, p. 5. She later explains. 'Shame discourse provides the goals-horror, the method.' Kalmanofsky, *Terror All Around*, p. 14.

methodology that takes seriously the emotive dimensions of the text. Furthermore, she understands the emotional reaction of the audience as part of the intended purpose of the book.

However, this study does have several limitations. First of all, it only deals with one particular emotion, horror. Clearly, there are multiple emotions at work (at war?) within the book; focusing on a single emotive strand in some ways flattens the richness of the affective dimension of the book of Jeremiah. Another aspect that Kalmanofsky chose not to address is the issue of whether the identified horror passages serve any sort of structuring function within the book. I found it particularly intriguing that she identified the entire cycle of oracles against the nations that ends the book of Jeremiah MT as a horror text but made no real comment on what it might mean in terms of the reader's overall reaction or the book's overall shape that the book's ending is an overload of horror. While I recognize the wisdom and pragmatism of narrowing the concluding exegetical focus to Jeremiah 6, such a choice leaves some important questions related to the current investigation unanswered, especially when identified horror texts provide the most immediate contexts for the two longest Confession texts.[147]

1.3.2.7 Kathleen M. O'Connor, *Jeremiah: Pain and Promise* (2011)

a) Summary

O'Connor introduces her latest work on the book of Jeremiah with a fascinating story. She reminds the reader that her first introduction to the book of Jeremiah was the Confession texts[148] which, as she says, 'touched something very deep within me'.[149] However, as she launched her teaching career, she confesses that she found the book of Jeremiah 'harder and harder to teach'. In particular she recalls one class:

> I met strong resistance to Jeremiah even before we had studied five or six chapters of the book. These students found the prophet's angry, punishing God nearly unbearable. They said that Jeremiah's theology blamed the victims, was deeply sexist, and was

---

[147] E.g. Jer. 14.1-15.9, 19.1-20.6.

[148] The subject of her published dissertation; see analysis above.

[149] Kathleen M. O'Connor, *Jeremiah: Pain and Promise* (Louisville, KY: Westminster/John Knox Press, 2011), p. 1.

not useful for churches today. When their lives met the biblical text, the results of the encounter were toxic.[150]

O'Connor was so shocked by the negative reaction that she did not teach a course on the book of Jeremiah again for some years. When she finally did work up the courage to offer another course, she was astounded to find her students giving a completely different response: 'This time, the book of Jeremiah called forth stories of their lives, stories of deep suffering only partially visible to them, of pain still alive in them'.[151] She credits the day-and-night difference in student response to an intervening modification in her approach to the book utilizing research from the emerging field of trauma and disaster studies.[152] O'Connor testifies that these studies 'help me to refocus my attention from questions of the book's creation[153] … to the matter of why these words were kept alive at all'.[154]

The field of trauma and disaster studies really opened up with the analysis of the 'long lasting effects upon victims and their offspring of the Holocaust, or Shoah … but the list of modern disasters is broad and sweeping'.[155] Trauma and disaster studies is an important interdisciplinary field that draws from other disciplines such as 'cognitive psychology, counseling, sociology, anthropology, and literary criticism'.[156]

---

[150] O'Connor, *Jeremiah: Pain and Promise*, p. 1.

[151] O'Connor, *Jeremiah: Pain and Promise*, p. 1.

[152] She notes one particular effect of applying trauma/disaster studies to her work on the book. 'Not only was Jeremiah more accessible and acceptable to the students, it also elicited from them their own stories of violence and trauma'. O'Connor, *Jeremiah: Pain and Promise*, p. 4.

[153] 'Such as which words belonged to Jeremiah, which were words of later writers and editors'. O'Connor, *Jeremiah: Pain and Promise*, p. 2.

[154] O'Connor, *Jeremiah: Pain and Promise*, 2. See also Kathleen M. O'Connor, 'The Book of Jeremiah: Reconstructing Community after Disaster', in M. Daniel Carroll R. and Jacqueline E. Lapsley (eds.), *Character Ethics and the Old Testament: Moral Dimensions of Scripture* (Louisville: Westminster/John Knox Press, 2007), pp. 81-92.

[155] E.g. the Armenian genocide (1915-1917), the nuclear bombing of Hiroshima and Nagasaki (1945), and the Rwandan genocide (1994). O'Connor, *Jeremiah: Pain and Promise*, p. 2. She follows closely the important work of Cathy Caruth. See Cathy Caruth, 'Introduction II, Recapturing the Past', in *Trauma: Explorations of Memory* (Baltimore: Johns Hopkins University, 1995), pp. 151-57, and *Unclaimed Experience: Trauma, Narrative, and History* (Baltimore: Johns Hopkins University, 1996).

[156] O'Connor, *Jeremiah: Pain and Promise*, p. 2.

In medical parlance, the term 'trauma' refers specifically to 'the violence that inflicts injury, not to the injury itself'.[157] The effect of this definition is that the victim is always understood as the passive recipient of trauma.[158] 'Disaster' then is magnified or multiplied trauma. As O'Connor explains it, trauma *becomes* disaster when 'violence reigns down upon a whole society ... When suffering and loss heaped upon one person is no more than a miniscule moment in the massive destruction of a society and its habitat, violence magnifies its effects in uncountable ways'.[159]

Disaster, then, has a *different* effect than trauma. Most importantly, disaster 'creates a kind of mental vacuum. It so overwhelms the capacities of victims to take it in, that the violence cannot be absorbed as it is happening'. This violence 'comes as a shocking blow, a terrifying disruption of normal mental processes, distorting reality, even as it becomes the only reality'.[160]

Disaster literally causes people to 'shut down'. O'Connor provides a comprehensive list of the elements that are overwhelmed in 'disaster' conditions: human capacities and resources,[161] human senses and normal responses, sense of safety, daily life routines, social resources and stability,[162] ability to communicate,[163] and all 'systems of meaning'. O'Connor concludes this summary by noting the lack of distinction between 'disaster' and the 'effects' of disaster. In fact, 'the effects are the disaster'.[164]

Even this list of disaster's effects is a bit overwhelming, but what makes these times of crisis even more difficult are the long-term 'hidden effects'. O'Connor carefully delineates four. First, disaster fragments memory. Victims of violence and disaster often have trouble recalling the precise events or their proper sequence. In effect, 'trauma survivors can experience violence as a kind of stunning non-

---

[157] Thus, not all injuries are necessarily traumatic. O'Connor, *Jeremiah: Pain and Promise*, p. 2.

[158] 'Victims are acted upon rather than actors who chose what happens to them.' O'Connor, *Jeremiah: Pain and Promise*, p. 2.

[159] O'Connor, *Jeremiah: Pain and Promise*, p. 3.

[160] O'Connor, *Jeremiah: Pain and Promise*, p. 3.

[161] Physical, emotional, and environmental injury.

[162] Many disasters create conditions of hunger, fear, and greed that prompt such violent responses as robbing and/or looting.

[163] Both a psychological (inability to articulate emotions) and a logistical (normal physical modes interrupted) problem.

[164] O'Connor, *Jeremiah: Pain and Promise*, p. 21.

event, or more aptly, as such an overwhelming experience that they cannot receive it or assimilate it into consciousness'.[165] Memory of the disaster event is little more than 'glimpses of horror' that distort reality.[166] Second, disaster leads to the 'loss' of language; that is, victims of disaster are unable to articulate their experiences. In fact, 'pain does not merely resist being put into language; it destroys both language and the power to think symbolically'.[167] This is really a direct outgrowth of the fragmentation of memory.

Third, the experience of disaster leads to what O'Connor labels 'numbness'. That is, people lose the ability to feel *any* emotion. True 'grief and anger become unreachable' and the grieving process is prematurely foreclosed.[168] Disaster victims exist 'in a shut-down, half-alive state … no longer fully alive in the world'.[169] Fourth, disaster leads to a loss of faith.[170] O'Connor explains: 'Like a solar eclipse blotting out the sun, calamity blots out God because death and destruction obscure any sense of God's protective and faithful presence'.[171]

Having established this framework understanding of the nature and effects of disaster, O'Connor then turns her attention to how this interpretive framework illuminates the book. In the preface, she states clearly this work is 'not a commentary on the biblical book of Jeremiah'. Rather, it is 'an interpretation of aspects of Jeremiah'.[172] Given the framework provided, it would perhaps seem most natural to expect an interpretation somewhat along the lines of a 'reader-response' methodology, so it is a bit surprising that O'Connor begins her discussion with the historical background of the book. She explains: 'I attempt to set the prophet's work into its historical context,

---

[165] O'Connor, *Jeremiah: Pain and Promise*, p. 22.

[166] Such broken memories also may 'disappear briefly and pounce again later, triggered by the smallest sight, sound, smell, or encounter'. O'Connor, *Jeremiah: Pain and Promise*, p. 22.

[167] It is a 'kind of "unmaking" of speech' that reduces sufferers to 'groans and screams disconnected from traditional, culturally accepted meanings'. O'Connor, *Jeremiah: Pain and Promise*, p. 23.

[168] People who cannot truly 'feel' anything are inhibited from fully 'recovering' from traumatic experiences.

[169] O'Connor, *Jeremiah: Pain and Promise*, p. 25.

[170] Or, better, a 'disintegration of belief'. O'Connor, *Jeremiah: Pain and Promise*, p. 26.

[171] O'Connor, *Jeremiah: Pain and Promise*, p. 26.

[172] O'Connor, *Jeremiah: Pain and Promise*, p. ix.

not to show how the book was composed but to imagine the destroyed world in which the book intervenes like a survival manual for
people wavering between life and death'.[173] She finds that the book
of Jeremiah is both more and less than a 'historical record' of the
events of the fall of Jerusalem. Rather, it is testimony, which is
'speech from the inside of events; it does not seek to prove something but to portray and interpret the experience from the inside'.[174]

Seeing the book as 'testimony' offers O'Connor a different perspective on perhaps the most vexing issue in Jeremiah studies – the
unstructured appearance of the book. When looked at through the
lens of disaster studies, especially its insights into the way disasters
fragment memory and end language, the 'jumbled' nature of the
book appears to be purposeful. The book's 'chaotic over-abundance,
its 'too-muchness', its very disorder itself turns the book into a helpful text for survivors of disaster'.[175] Forcing readers to 'make sense'
of the book subtly forces them to begin the process of 'making
sense' of the disaster they have just experienced in Jerusalem's fall.
Thus, the disorder of the book is 'a moral act, a literary work that
turns disaster victims into people who must make sense of the literature'.[176] In reading Jeremiah, survivors of Jerusalem's fall (and survivors of modern-day disasters) are forced to be no longer passive
recipients but active shapers of the text and the world that it presents.
Thus, 'the book's lack of order itself works as a mode of recovery'.[177]
The prophet Jeremiah provides the key point of coherence in this
text. However, he is a 'complex figure who stands both against this
people as God's spokesperson and with them as a symbolic figure
whose prayers and captivities gather up their sufferings'.[178]

In her chapter on the Confession texts, O'Connor's analysis
moves in a somewhat surprising direction. O'Connor recognizes that
Jeremiah speaks to God in his 'own' voice[179] but also in *more* than his

---

[173] O'Connor, *Jeremiah: Pain and Promise*, p. 6.

[174] Such testimony cannot be impartial and unbiased, but that fact adds to its
overall impact rather than detracting from it. O'Connor, *Jeremiah: Pain and Promise*,
p. 16.

[175] O'Connor, *Jeremiah: Pain and Promise*, p. 31.

[176] O'Connor, *Jeremiah: Pain and Promise*, p. 31.

[177] O'Connor, *Jeremiah: Pain and Promise*, p. 31.

[178] O'Connor, *Jeremiah: Pain and Promise*, p. 34.

[179] 'As an "I" besieged by doubt and desperate in the face of all he is suffering.'
In fact, O'Connor goes so far as to say the Confessions essentially record a 'voca-
tional meltdown'. O'Connor, *Jeremiah: Pain and Promise*, pp. 81-82.

own voice – his words give voice to the sorrows of the people. Jeremiah's words 'enact in the life of one person Judah's shattered faith. They dramatize the shutting down of trust among disaster victims and put it into the public sphere.'[180] For the survivors of the disaster, Jeremiah becomes here 'a kindred soul who mirrors their suspicion, skepticism, and outrage'.[181]

In terms of 'helping' survivors work through their experience of the disaster, though, O'Connor concludes that the Confessions have something of a *destabilizing* effect. Whereas the rest of the book squarely places the blame for the fall of Jerusalem on the *people's* failure, these Confessions unrelentingly point the finger of blame at YHWH.[182] The presence of the Confession texts means for O'Connor that the 'rhetoric of [human] responsibility' is 'not a definitive interpretation of the disaster but one among many'.[183] In effect, as a 'counterview'[184] of the disaster, the Confessions 'generate questions about causes and complicate interpretation of disaster'.[185]

b) Appraisal

O'Connor is the only scholar to appear twice within this history of interpretation. This affords a unique opportunity to see both the broadening and deepening of her work. Her initial work on the Confessions treated them as texts that work for the legitimation of the prophet and his message. She clearly has not moved on her assertion that there is an authentic 'I' of the historical prophet discernible in these words. In fact, in some ways, her 'traumatic' reading of the text perhaps makes the historicity of the prophet's experiences even *more* crucial. She has also retained the conviction that the Confessions 'push toward' a resolution of praise and confidence in God.[186] Clearly, her core convictions born out of her study of the Confessions have

---

[180] O'Connor, *Jeremiah: Pain and Promise*, p. 84.

[181] O'Connor, *Jeremiah: Pain and Promise*, p. 88.

[182] 'God has failed, betrayed, turned away, left the prophet to suffer'. O'Connor, *Jeremiah: Pain and Promise*, p. 83.

[183] O'Connor, *Jeremiah: Pain and Promise*, p. 85.

[184] It seems here that O'Connor is clearly picking up on Brueggemann's tension between 'testimony' and 'counter-testimony'. See Walter Brueggemann, *Theology of the Old Testament: Testimony, Dispute, Advocacy* (Minneapolis: Fortress Press, 1997).

[185] O'Connor, *Jeremiah: Pain and Promise*, p. 91.

[186] 'Following the form of lament, his accusations against God are, for the moment, absorbed in praise, and relationship with God again seems sure.' O'Connor, *Jeremiah: Pain and Promise*, p. 89, cf. O'Connor, *Confessions of Jeremiah*, p. 92.

fruitfully carried her forward into other parts and puzzles of the book of Jeremiah. A key additional strength of her newer work is how she delves into the effects of the book on the reader, both ancient and modern. For her, the insights of disaster studies resolve the intractable problem of the book's formation and the endless theories it has generated. 'Rather than overlooking the book's confusions, they point them out and try to make sense of them.'[187]

There are still some difficulties. First of all, for all her 'swearing off' of key historical-critical concerns, she does seem to still be governed by the questions of the book's formation. For example, her reading of the prose sermons in the text as a 'narrowing and simplifying interpretation of the disaster' is based on her assumption of their later provenance.[188]

Perhaps the other key difficulty is her view of the Confessions as a 'counterview'. While placing these within the 'world' of the book of Jeremiah, they remain virtually unconnected to the rest of the text. Unlike the prose sermons, they do not represent a clear stage of progression in the grieving process; they are almost regressive. While it is certainly true the book of Jeremiah does not offer a simplistic explanation for the fall of Jerusalem but, in reality, lingers in the complexity, to conclude that 'biblical language about human sin and divine punishment is, after all, as culturally-conditioned as ancient biblical practices of slavery and the subjugation of women … Like all speech about God, biblical words … are provisional, partial, and incomplete',[189] seems to undercut the conclusions of what appeared at first to be a search for some overarching principle of coherence within the book.

1.4. Methodology & Structure

1.4.1 Research Methodology

As the above brief review has demonstrated, the scholarly discussion of the Confessions has slowly moved from early opinions which effectively polarized historical and theological interpretations to much

---

[187] O'Connor, *Jeremiah: Pain and Promise*, p. 126.

[188] In terms of disaster recovery, they *must* be later. 'One sign of recovery is that explanations become more uniform.' O'Connor, *Jeremiah: Pain and Promise*, p. 34.

[189] O'Connor, *Jeremiah: Pain and Promise*, p. 85.

more nuanced recent work attempting to resolve the dichotomy. Part of this has been accomplished by a shift from historical-critical methodologies to literary-theological approaches. Though still much in the minority, these latter approaches seem to offer the most fruitful way forward and the way most amenable to a Pentecostal hermeneutic. Given their minority status within scholarship on the Confessions and the still-developmental stages of a recognizable Pentecostal OT hermeneutic, it will be necessary to devote a separate chapter to development and justification of the research methodology.

This book will utilize a rhetorical-theological method that pays close attention to the affective dimensions of the Confession texts. It will be operationalized in a three-stage analysis of the selected Confession texts. The analysis will begin with an attempt to hear each chosen confession, paying close attention to the Confessions' position within the flow of the book of Jeremiah, their rhetorical internal structure and interrelationship, and the significance of their affective language and its role in constructing the literary figure of the prophet Jeremiah as an ideal hearer to be emulated by implied and actual hearers of the book.

After considering the introductory Confessions texts, the final stage will be hearing these texts within the larger Confessions corpus (Jeremiah 11-20), investigating how rhetorically significant affective language and figures echo throughout. However, the overarching concern of both phases of this exegetical investigation will be to hear the Word *with* Jeremiah not just *from* Jeremiah, listening for ways the prophetic figure's affective profile impacts the theology of the Word in the book of Jeremiah and the listener's reception of that Word.

1.4.2 Structure

This study will be separated into six chapters. The present first chapter has covered the establishment of the research question, including its rationale and relevance, aims and objectives, and basic scope. It then offered a brief history of interpretation with the dual purpose of demonstrating the need for a fresh approach to the Confessions that moves beyond historical-critical reading strategies and situating the present work within that broader scholarship. Some of the noted turns in recent studies of the Confessions toward a more literary-theological focus indicate an opportune moment to bring these texts into conversation with the emerging conversations about unique

Pentecostal strategies for reading the OT. Thus, the tasks of the second chapter will be carefully defining the special nature of Pentecostal strategies of interpreting the OT and their unique application to the study of Jeremiah's Confessions.

After establishing this important methodological framework, the third chapter will test the proposed hearing strategy on Jeremiah 1-10, exploring the ways in which the affective movements in the first major section prepare us to hear the Confessions. The fourth and fifth chapters move to an analysis of the first two Confessions (Jer. 11.18 -23; 12.1-13), paying particular attention to their use of affective language. The sixth chapter will conclude by demonstrating that the introductory Confessions establish affective patterns that are replicated throughout the rest of those of texts and even, it will be suggested, throughout the rest of the book. As the affective tones of these texts are heard within these expanding contexts, they accrue ever-greater theological value.[190] The chapter will then summarize the main conclusions and the major implications for further study both in the book of Jeremiah and in the developing field of Pentecostal hermeneutics.

---

[190] Thus, no level of meaning is 'lost' at any higher level; rather, prior levels provide the foundation for new understandings.

2

HEARING CONFESSIONS – A PENTECOSTAL STRATEGY

2.1 Introduction

The Confessions of Jeremiah are a unique genre of prophetic literature not seen in any other prophetic book in the OT. Given their uniqueness – especially their combination of the lament and prophetic genres – it should come as no surprise that such literature would benefit from a specialized hermeneutical approach. The specific emphases of a Pentecostal hearing strategy are well suited to helpfully illuminate Jeremiah's Confessions.

Defining such a strategy presents its own challenges. Though much work has been done on the distinctive Pentecostal approach to interpreting Scripture,[1] it is still easier to speak of a 'Pentecostal culture of Bible reading'[2] than to speak of a particular methodological approach. Pentecostal hermeneutics is still more defined by a series

---

[1] See particularly the work of Kenneth Archer, which is probably the most thorough study of the topic published to date. Kenneth J. Archer, *A Pentecostal Hermeneutic: Spirit, Scripture, and Community* (Cleveland, TN: CPT Press, 2009). See also Jacqueline Grey, *Three's a Crowd: Pentecostalism, Hermeneutics, and the Old Testament* (Eugene, OR: Pickwick, 2011), Bradley Truman Noel, *Pentecostalism and Postmodern Hermeneutics: Comparisons and Contemporary Impact* (Eugene, OR: Wipf and Stock, 2010), and Chris E.W. Green, *Sanctifying Interpretation: Vocation, Holiness, and Scripture* (Cleveland, TN: CPT Press, 2015). A thorough bibliography of Pentecostal biblical hermeneutics is provided by Lee Roy Martin (ed.), *Pentecostal Heremeneutics: A Reader* (Leiden: Brill, 2013), pp. 285-90.

[2] Andrew Davies, 'What Does It Mean to Read the Bible as a Pentecostal?' *JPT* 18.2 (2009), pp. 216-29 (223).

of theological commitments than a singular interpretive strategy.[3] This is not to give the false impression that proposing a Pentecostal reading strategy is simply license to invent an interpretive method; Pentecostal interpretations should rather be envisioned as a 'remixing' of hermeneutical concerns common to what could be defined as pre- and post-critical hermeneutics.[4]

The interpretive strategy will, therefore, require some definition. We will briefly survey some important examples of Pentecostal OT scholarship and then utilize the insights garnered there to provide a coherent statement of the strategy of the present work.

2.2 The Development of a Pentecostal Hermeneutic of the Old Testament

In defining a Pentecostal approach to the OT, the work of scholars Rickie Moore (on Deuteronomy), Larry McQueen (on Joel), and Lee Roy Martin (on Judges) is exemplary. Their work not only demonstrates the variety of ways in which a Pentecostal hermeneutic can be constructed but also provides a solid foundation on which to construct new interpretive strategies. We will examine these scholars' own explanations of their interpretive strategies and the uniquely Pentecostal contributions of their interpretive work.

2.2.1 Rickie D. Moore

An abiding interest of Rickie Moore's work has been the book of Deuteronomy. It seems safe to say that his article 'Canon and Charisma in the Book of Deuteronomy' is one of the very first Pentecostal explorations of an OT text.[5] His later 'Deuteronomy and the Fire

---

[3] 'While no consensus has emerged as of yet, it appears that many scholars working within the Pentecostal tradition are less content to adopt a system of interpretation that is heavily slanted toward rationalism and has little room for the role of the Holy Spirit'. John Christopher Thomas, 'Women, Pentecostals, and the Bible: An Experiment in Pentecostal Hermeneutics', *JPT* 5 (1994), pp. 41-56 (41).

[4] 'The pathway [of Pentecostal hermeneutics] is newly constructed only in some of its parts, while other parts of the path are actually ancient ways rediscovered, uncovered, and restored.' Lee Roy Martin, *The Unheard Voice of God: A Pentecostal Hearing of the Book of Judges* (JPTSup 32; Blandford Forum: Deo Publishing, 2008), p. 54.

[5] See Rickie Moore, 'Canon and Charisma in the Book of Deuteronomy' in *The Spirit of the Old Testament* (JPTSup 35; Blandford Forum: Deo Publishing, 2011), pp. 19-34 (originally published in *JPT* 1 (1992), pp. 75-92).

of God'[6] presents a continuation and development of his previous essay. Together, both essays present a well-rounded description of a distinctively Pentecostal OT hermeneutic.

Moore's first essay is a conscious attempt 'to integrate [his] Pentecostal vocation and perspective with critical OT scholarship'. Moore admits: 'Such an integration is not easy for me, for I spent many years learning to keep these things mostly separate from one another'.[7] His key argument is that a careful reading of Deuteronomy reveals that a dialectical interrelationship of 'inscripturated word' and 'prophetic utterance',[8] found especially in Deuteronomy 4 and 5, forms a central theme of the book.[9]

As far as the features of his interpretive methodology, Moore first states that his Pentecostal perceptions 'surface elements in the text that have been hidden and suppressed by other perspectives of long standing'.[10] Modern critical scholarship has failed to notice the 'dialectical possibilities' because any 'tension' or 'shift of emphasis' within the text is automatically credited to 'different literary sources or redactional layers'.[11] Both critical and Evangelical scholarship fail due to inflexibility – methodologically on the one side and theologically on the other.

Moore points out that the Word of God delivered through the prophet and the Word of God delivered through the Torah are both related to the 'themes of heeding God's word and fearing him',[12]

---

[6] Moore, 'Canon and Charisma', pp. 35-55.

[7] Moore, 'Canon and Charisma', p. 20.

[8] Or 'canonical word' and 'charismatic revelation'. Moore, 'Canon and Charisma', p. 20.

[9] Moore, 'Canon and Charisma', p. 20.

[10] Moore, 'Canon and Charisma', p. 20.

[11] Modern Evangelical scholarship has fared no better in discerning this central feature of Deuteronomy 'insofar as they have been committed to a larger theological scheme that sees a radical and dispensational break between charismatic utterance and completed canon'. Moore, 'Canon and Charisma', pp. 20-21.

[12] The 'equivalence of canon and prophecy' is found 'in their stated goals of engendering fear of and obedience to God'. Moore, 'Canon and Charisma', p. 23. See Deut. 31.11-13; 17.19; 18.19.

themes most closely linked in Deut. 4.5-8,[13] which highlights the twin concerns that encapsulate the thrust of the entire book.[14]

In the subsequent 'Deuteronomy and the Fire of God', Moore returns to his 'dialectical' interpretation of the Deuteronomy based on a strategy with a 'self-conscious commitment to read the biblical text through the lens of Pentecostal experience and confession'.[15] It is Moore's Pentecostal heritage that ultimately leads him to see that 'the book of Deuteronomy is itself an act of interpretation that is ... both charismatic and critical'.[16] Thus, though Moore's interpretation represents what he feels is a distinctive Pentecostal perspective, it better aligns with the inherent theological viewpoint of the book of Deuteronomy.

The uniqueness of Moore's method is revealed in his choice to begin with a personal testimony 'that tells not only how I have come to interpret Deuteronomy but also how Deuteronomy has come to interpret me'.[17] In a very real way, though, Moore's recitation of his journey of integrating academic scholarship with his Pentecostal roots, using Deuteronomy as his example, mirrors the way that

---

[13] Verse 8 'most emphatically points to the vital and incomparable character of Israel's *canon*', while 'v. 7, with parallel wording, points to the equally vital and incomparable endowment of having a "god so near"', a phrase Moore says is used to designate the gift of prophecy. In this key passage, 'the written word and the charismatic word ... were seen to be held together from this foundational moment of Israel's covenant'. Moore, 'Canon and Charisma', pp. 26-27.

[14] Moore observes that the Hebrew term *dabar* 'would accord with the argument above for seeing divine revelation as bringing closely together the notions of written word, spoken word, even manifested or embodied word'. Moore, 'Canon and Charisma', p. 32, italics original.

[15] Moore recognizes that his work represents a 'fresh approach toward something scarcely seen in biblical scholarship until recently – a literary theological reading of the entire book of Deuteronomy'. Rickie D. Moore, 'Deuteronomy and the Fire of God: A Critical Charismatic Interpretation', in *The Spirit of the Old Testament* (JPTSup 35, Blandford Forum: Deo Publishing, 2011), p. 35.

Moore consciously contrasts his reading of Deuteronomy with the work of Dennis Olson, who argues that the 'death of Moses' forms the theological center of the book. See Dennis T. Olson, *Deuteronomy and the Death of Moses: A Theological Reading* (OBT; Minneapolis: Fortress Press, 1994). Moore points out that though they use the same method (a literary-theological reading), their theological commitments lead to radically different interpretations.

[16] Moore, 'Canon and Charisma', p. 35. Moore shares Grey's concern that any Pentecostal hermeneutical strategy be consistent with the ethos of the movement yet acknowledge and respect the critical distance between the ancient text and the contemporary audience. Grey, *Three's a Crowd*, pp. 143-46, 154.

[17] Moore, 'Deuteronomy and the Fire of God', p. 36.

Deuteronomy opens with Moses' recitation of Israel's journey.[18] Moore's Pentecostal approach allows him to approach the book of Deuteronomy on its own terms, rather than through the imposition of some external critical frame.

Moore acknowledges that his first experience of 'critical' engagement with the biblical text was 'a far cry from the ethos and impulses of my Pentecostal confession'. He felt that he was being unwillingly yet 'relentlessly conditioned to experience criticism and confession as mutually exclusive opposites'.[19] However, Moore points to a series of three interrelated 'shifts' that began to break down the wall between critical and confessional approaches to biblical exegesis, opening the door for a distinctively Pentecostal approach.

The first of these important 'shifts' was postmodernism's abandonment of the scholarly quest for absolute objectivity. Such objectivity is both unattainable and even unwanted; this shift 'eliminated any credible basis for keeping marginal perspectives [e.g. Pentecostalism] … from being given a hearing in the academic arena'.[20] The second of these important shifts occurred within Pentecostal scholarship, where Moore witnessed a move away from dominant historiographical concerns toward more narratological viewpoints.[21] Finally, the third key shift occurred as Moore completed his doctoral work at Vanderbilt University and joined an explicitly Pentecostal scholarly community. As Moore testifies:

> This conscious move to begin bringing my own faith confession into interaction with my technical work on the text … was actually encountered as the most *critical* step I had ever taken in studying biblical texts. It is precisely what enabled me and forced me to realize that many of my earlier research choices and conclusions, which had passed for *critical* scholarship, had actually been the

---

[18] Moore, 'Deuteronomy and the Fire of God', p. 36.
[19] Moore, 'Deuteronomy and the Fire of God', p. 37.
[20] Moore, 'Deuteronomy and the Fire of God', p. 38.
[21] This meant a revival of 'interest in the narrative orientation of Pentecostalism's own theological heritage', especially in the role that testimony played in early Pentecostal theological formulation and understanding. Moore, 'Deuteronomy and the Fire of God', p. 38. There is no doubt that this shift is also reflective of the broader shift from modernism to postmodernism.

product of largely *uncritical* impulses, such as social conformity and intellectual intimidation.[22]

Moore insists that he 'did not see some great new hermeneutical formula' for interpreting Deuteronomy, but rather more points 'where Pentecostalism's narrative orientation and instincts seemed capable of freshly informing and benefiting from a literary-theological approach to the book'.[23]

2.2.2 Larry R. McQueen

We now turn to the work of Larry McQueen on the book of Joel. Whereas Moore's work on Deuteronomy has been restricted to two published journal articles, McQueen's work presents a book-length engagement; not only does he offer a reading of Joel, but he also explores how the book of Joel was appropriated in the NT and in early Pentecostal literature. Consequently, McQueen offers the first book-length treatment of a biblical book from a Pentecostal reading strategy.

McQueen names three key implications of a Pentecostal hermeneutic for the interpretation of Joel. First, a Pentecostal hermeneutic will illuminate aspects of the text overlooked or unseen by other interpreters as the text of Joel illuminates various aspects of Pentecostal theology and practice in new ways. Second, such a strategy will consider Joel 'in terms of its historical and literary significance' and in 'its character as a 'living' word of God'.[24] Finally, McQueen's reading of Joel should be seen as only 'one member's voice among the other members of the Christian community'.[25] McQueen does not claim that his reading is *the* authoritative interpretation of Joel; rather, it is simply one faithful interpretation appropriate to its time. This implies that other times and places will require fresh work to yield faithful interpretations; it is this way that the Word of God in Pentecostal theology maintains its status as a prophetic Word.

McQueen begins with a brief literature survey demonstrating the lack of scholarly consensus regarding the unity of the book. The

---

[22] Moore, 'Deuteronomy and the Fire of God', p. 39.

[23] Moore, 'Deuteronomy and the Fire of God', p. 39.

[24] 'The question is not only "how do we interpret the book of Joel?" but also "how does the book of Joel interpret us?"' Larry R. McQueen, *Joel and the Spirit: The Cry of a Prophetic Hermeneutic* (Cleveland, TN: CPT Press, 2009), p. 5. (originally published as JPTSup 5; 1995).

[25] McQueen, *Joel and the Spirit*, p. 6.

problem with the typical historical-critical approach to the book, other than the fact that it shifts focus 'away from the final form of the text toward its assumed redactional history',[26] is that the 'original' text – free from the passages identified as later interpolations – takes priority in the theological understanding of the text. While McQueen does not *abandon* historical-critical interpretive concerns,[27] he thinks it is important to focus readerly attention on the canonical form of the text.

McQueen's literary approach to the book of Joel is built on paying close attention to 'the shifts in subject matter as well as in who is speaking and who is being addressed'.[28] The book demonstrates a broad 'movement' from lamentation (1.1-2.17) to salvation (2.18-32) to judgment (3.1-21).[29] Over the course of the book, the speech of YHWH 'builds both in quantity and in intensity,'[30] matching an increase in the daring of the prophet's speech to God. The 'moments of human-divine interaction in the text serve as transition points' for the text.[31]

The final phase of McQueen's exploration is the appropriation of Joel's language in early Pentecostalism; here he again finds striking parallels to the lament/salvation/judgment structure of the book of Joel. In the literature of early Pentecostalism, McQueen discerns the language of lament is preserved in the practice of 'praying through,' also commonly referred to as 'tarrying'.[32] McQueen shares a very personal prayer experience that occurred during his time of study in the book of Joel in which the Lord gave him a vision of his life as a broken cup glued together which God would have to shatter to make

---

[26] McQueen, *Joel and the Spirit*, p. 9.

[27] McQueen notes that several historical-critical scholars *have* affirmed the unity of the text, an affirmation with which he agrees: 'It is … my assumption that the literary unity of the book points to single authorship by the historical prophet Joel'. McQueen, *Joel and the Spirit*, p. 9.

[28] The key shift being a movement from speech *from* YHWH to speech *to* YHWH. McQueen, *Joel and the Spirit*, p. 12.

[29] However, McQueen admits 'none of these themes is restricted to the section in which it predominates'. The lamentation section contains 'anticipations of judgment' in 1.15; 2.1-11 and 'hopeful hints of salvation' in 2.13b-14. McQueen, *Joel and the Spirit*, p. 13.

[30] McQueen, *Joel and the Spirit*, p. 14.

[31] McQueen, *Joel and the Spirit*, p. 16.

[32] Both terms were used almost interchangeably to express 'the existence of deep pathos in the practice of prayer'. McQueen, *Joel and the Spirit*, p. 72.

him anew. This visionary experience led McQueen into an emotional time of prayer (i.e., 'praying through') which resulted in a liberating and refreshing move of the Spirit.

McQueen notes that this personal experience shaped his reading of Joel in several significant ways. First, McQueen's understanding of the literary and theological 'unity' of the book of Joel is more than a literary-critical or canonical-critical decision; it was born out of his own spiritual encounters with God and the book of Joel.[33] Also, McQueen's experience caused him to resist the temptation to subsume the theme of judgment under the theme of salvation.[34] Finally, the 'transitions' in Joel, marked by a movement from human cry to divine response, helpfully corresponded to 'the testimony of the Pentecostal community that God responds to prayer, sometimes in dramatic ways'.[35]

2.2.3 Lee Roy Martin

By far, the most extensive Pentecostal exploration of an OT passage to date is Lee Roy Martin's *The Unheard Voice of God: A Pentecostal Hearing of the Book of Judges*, in which he devotes an entire chapter to explaining his methodology. Martin proposes 'an approach to Scripture that is theologically motivated, canonically based, and narratively oriented'.[36] Like Moore, Martin does not identify a Pentecostal hermeneutic with one particular methodology but 'claims the freedom to wrestle with difficult texts … utilizing an integration of multiple interpretive approaches'.[37]

Martin observes that traditional methods of interpretation have been concerned with three 'worlds': the world 'behind' the text (the purview of historical criticism); the world 'in' the text (the purview of literary criticism) and the world 'in front of' the text (the purview of reader-response criticism). He wants to add a fourth world for

---

[33] 'The theological and orthopathic interrelationships of lament, salvation, and judgment in my own and my community's encounter with God elucidated their corresponding literary interrelationships in the book of Joel.' McQueen, *Joel and the Spirit*, p. 107.

[34] 'The early Pentecostals perhaps had a better communal sense of the dreadful presence of God' that has been lost in contemporary Pentecostalism's 'individualism and consumerism'. McQueen, *Joel and the Spirit*, p. 108.

[35] McQueen argues that this prior understanding of the function of prayer within the Pentecostal community helped to highlight the 'crucial' nature of these transitions within the book of Joel. McQueen, *Joel and the Spirit*, p. 108.

[36] Martin, *The Unheard Voice of God*, p. 52.

[37] Martin, *The Unheard Voice of God*, p. 52.

consideration: 'the world of the living, dynamic, charismatic word of God' where the text 'is no longer the object of my critical critique, but I become the object of critique to the voice of God'.[38]

Given the rise of postmodern interpretive concerns and methodologies,[39] Pentecostals no longer face a false choice between participation in the academy and honoring their spiritual heritage. Today, Pentecostal scholars 'can adopt integrative models of biblical studies that engage the academy, the Church, and the postmodern world'.[40]

Martin's reading of Judges takes seriously its place in the Hebrew canon as part of the Former Prophets. This indicates that the book 'does not function as historiography to be examined or as ideology to be evaluated; rather it functions as a prophetic voice to be heard'.[41] That Judges is a 'prophetic word' means that it is a divine word confronting the human community and is thus an authoritative word for the believing community that will transform its hearers. Such 'prophetic' texts require 'prophetic interpretation' which is essentially 'a reenactment of earlier events, making them present for a new generation'.[42]

Given these concerns, Martin describes his interpretive strategy as a 'hearing' of the text rather than a 'reading'.[43] There are several reasons for this decision. First, 'hearing' is a more biblical term; it is the 'most frequent method of encounter with the word of God ... to hear is to act upon what which is heard'.[44] Furthermore, 'hearing' respects the orality of biblical and Pentecostal contexts.[45] 'Hearing'

---

[38] Martin, *The Unheard Voice of God*, p. 52.

[39] Which accommodates well the 'Pentecostal ethos [that] regards Scripture as the dynamic and living "Spirit-Word"'. Martin, *The Unheard Voice of God*, p. 56.

[40] Martin, *The Unheard Voice of God*, p. 68.

[41] As 'prophetic history', Judges' goal is not 'to offer an explanation of the past, but to function as scripture for the new generation of Israel who are instructed from the past for the sake of the future'. Martin, *The Unheard Voice of God*, p. 61.

[42] Similar to the function of the book of Deuteronomy. Martin, *The Unheard Voice of God*, p. 63.

[43] A truly Pentecostal hermeneutic prefers obedience over correctness, openness over exactness, humility over certitude, and faithfulness over objectivity. Martin, *The Unheard Voice of God*, p. 57.

[44] Martin, *The Unheard Voice of God*, p. 58.

[45] That Pentecostals represented a largely 'oral culture' within a larger educated 'literate' culture means that Pentecostals are uniquely equipped to understand 'Scripture as oral discourse, particularly when it comes to narrative, non-propositional texts'. Martin, *The Unheard Voice of God*, p. 67.

highlights the 'relational' nature of Truth because it places emphasis on the one speaking truth; while the hearing is individual, it usually occurs 'takes place within the community of faith'.[46]

Once again, a Pentecostal approach to the text serves to highlight aspects of the text long ignored in scholarly circles. In this case, Martin sees that the 'underlying cause of Israel's problems in Judges is their lack of attention to the voice of God'.[47] Modern critical scholarship has virtually ignored the role and speech of God in Judges.[48] Martin finds the key to the structure and message of the book of Judges in the three recorded speeches of YHWH.[49]

2.3 Important Features

Having surveyed these important pieces of Pentecostal OT scholarship, it is now necessary to attempt to define the methodological characteristics that have emerged and their relevance to the present project. Broadly stated, a Pentecostal hermeneutic is distinguished by its understanding of the role of the Spirit, personal and communal experience, and Scripture.

2.3.1 Role of the Holy Spirit
While it probably goes without saying that Pentecostal hermeneutics is differentiated by its focus on the role of the Spirit, this renewed emphasis is 'an important contribution as the Western church seeks to reclaim its sense of mysticism and the immanence of the transcendent'.[50] Clark Pinnock credits the current neglect of the Spirit's work in biblical interpretation to the strong influence of rationalism

---

[46] Martin, *The Unheard Voice of God*, p. 71.

[47] Judges 2.2, 17a, 20; 6.10. Martin, *The Unheard Voice of God*, p. 75.

[48] There are probably several reasons for this. The greater part of the book is taken up with the stories of the so-called 'Major Judges'. Further, critical studies have focused either on the historicity of the book or the ideological importance of the violence (especially against women) in the book rather than on the theological message of the text. 'Like the Israelites, modern biblical scholarship has failed to hear the voice of Yahweh in the book of Judges.' Martin, *The Unheard Voice of God*, pp. 76-79.

[49] Judges 2.1-5; 6.7-10; 10.10-16.

[50] Timothy B. Cargal, 'Beyond the Fundamentalist-Modernist Controversy: Pentecostals and Hermeneutics in a Postmodern Age', *Pneuma* 15.2 (1993), pp. 163-87 (186).

in Western societies.[51] For much of Western theology, defining a role for the Spirit of God in interpretation is tantamount to dragging 'mysticism into hermeneutics'.[52]

Pentecostalism's dependence on the working of the Spirit in the process of interpretation 'clearly goes far beyond the rather tame claims regarding 'illumination' which many … have often made regarding the Spirit's role in interpretation'.[53] Rather, in Pentecostal theology, the emphasis is not placed on distinguishing 'inspiration' from 'illumination' but rather on considering both as works of the Spirit. Not only did the Spirit play a role in the Scripture's formation; it now 'guides the community as it walks with God in the light of its Scriptures toward the fulfillment of its mission':[54]

> God did not speak in the Scriptures and then become silent. God did not stop breathing and illuminating the community after he had inspired the Bible. There is not a gap of thousands of years between us and the biblical witness for the simple reason that the Spirit is putting us in touch with the same subject matter even today, helping us to understand what the ancients said, making God's saving truth present to us now.[55]

In all three of the examples mentioned above, attention to the pneumatic dimensions of the text served to open up fresh avenues of interpretation that were effectively closed to traditional methods of exegetical inquiry. The focus lies on the Word *as speaking* rather than simply on the Word *as spoken*.

2.3.2 Role of Experience
Another important feature of the works surveyed above is the important role played by personal and communal experience in the interpretive process. Moore's essay 'Deuteronomy and the Fire of God' is equal parts personal memoir and biblical exegesis, and McQueen

---

[51] Clark H. Pinnock, 'The Work of the Holy Spirit in Hermeneutics', *JPT* 2 (1993), pp. 3-23 (8). See also 'The Work of the Spirit in the Interpretation of Holy Scripture from the Perspective of a Charismatic Biblical Theologian', *JPT* 18.2 (2009), pp. 157-71.
[52] Pinnock, 'The Work of the Holy Spirit in Hermeneutics', p. 8.
[53] Thomas, 'Women, Pentecostals, and the Bible', p. 49.
[54] Pinnock, 'The Work of the Holy Spirit in Hermeneutics', p. 3.
[55] Pinnock, 'The Work of the Holy Spirit in Hermeneutics', pp. 6-7.

informs us that the linchpin of his interpretation of Joel was dramatically reinforced in a personal experience of 'praying through'.

That personal experience plays a role in interpretation is past doubt. Arden C. Autry writes, 'Whenever understanding takes place, experience will have its effect in how that understanding occurs and even to what extent it can be expected to occur adequately'.[56] However, while the experience is personal; the context is always communal. Later in the same article, Autry observes: 'The subjectivity inherent in personal religious experience is best kept on track not simply through comparison with objective data in the text (important as that is) but also through the sharing of experiences in a community of believers'.[57] A key function of the Spirit-filled community is to 'give and receive testimony as well as assess the reports of God's activity in the lives of those who are part of the community'.[58]

This is actually one of those parts of the path of Pentecostal hermeneutics that is *not* 'newly constructed' but is rather an ancient way 'rediscovered, uncovered, and restored'.[59] For the early Church, 'the interpretation of Scripture is itself subject to the hermeneutic of the Spirit: prophetic truth is never just a matter of individual interpretation'.[60] In fact, Scripture cannot be properly understood apart 'from the space they have inhabited, and continue to inhabit, as the canonical Scripture of the Christian Church'.[61]

One final point must be made about the role of experience and community within Pentecostal hermeneutics. The pneumatic community is narratologically constructed; Pentecostals see themselves as

---

[56] Arden C. Autry, 'Dimensions of Hermeneutics in Pentecostal Focus', *JPT* 3 (1993), pp. 29-50 (39). He continues: 'Any effective preacher will know that if the meaning is not perceived to be significant for personal or corporate needs or aspirations, the response will be indifference'. Two things about this statement are compelling:
1) That Autry refers to the practice of preaching, which is one of the main hermeneutical arenas within Pentecostalism.
2) That the measure of 'effectiveness' is applicability. This highlights the fact that, for Pentecostal interpretive strategies, 'meaning' and 'application' cannot be separated.
[57] Autry, 'Dimensions of Hermeneutics', p. 45.
[58] Thomas, 'Women, Pentecostals, and the Bible', p. 49.
[59] Martin, *The Unheard Voice of God,* p. 54.
[60] Markus Bockmuehl, 'Reason, Wisdom, and the Implied Disciple of Scripture', in David F. Ford and Grahahm Stanton (eds.), *Reading Texts, Seeking Wisdom: Scripture and Theology* (Grand Rapids: Eerdmans, 2004), p. 63.
[61] Bockmuehl, 'Reason, Wisdom, and the Implied Disciple', p. 54.

the 'eschatological people of God … caught up in the final drama of God's redemptive activity'.[62] Archer speaks of a set of 'central narrative convictions'[63] that serve as a coherent story and 'primary filter used to sift the Scriptures for meaning'.[64] This central narrative is used to connect the experiences of the early and contemporary Church; it is this pneumatic connection across time and space – this claim that we share the same experience as the apostolic Church – that gives meaning to Pentecostal experience today.[65]

2.3.3 Role of Scripture

Finally, within this pneumatic-experiential framework, Scripture takes on a unique but no less authoritative role within the community. In his essay 'Women, Pentecostals, and the Bible,' John Christopher Thomas looks carefully at the role of Scripture in the deliberations of the Jerusalem Council recorded in Acts 15. He draws out several significant implications of the text.

First, the exegetical method demonstrated in Acts 15 is 'far removed from the historical-critical or historical-grammatical approach where one moves from text to context'. The interpretive direction seen in Acts 15 is rather 'from context to text'.[66] Second, there were multiple texts in the OT that could have either supported or denied Gentile inclusion in the Church; the choosing of the Amos text was far from an 'obvious' choice: 'It appears that the experience of the Spirit in the community helped the church make its way through this hermeneutical maze'.[67] Finally, Scripture was also used to create a series of temporary stipulations for table fellowship, indicating 'the biblical text was assigned and functioned with a great deal of authority in this hermeneutical approach [however] … the text's authority is

---

[62] Archer, *A Pentecostal Hermeneutic*, p. 134.

[63] 'The primary story used to explain why the Pentecostal community existed, who they were as a community, [and] how they fit into the larger scheme of Christian history.' Archer, *A Pentecostal Hermeneutic*, p. 156.

[64] Archer, *A Pentecostal Hermeneutic*, p. 157.

[65] Autry says, 'I need … to see myself and my story as part of the greater, continuing story of God's people'. Autry, 'Dimensions of Hermeneutics', p. 40. Cf. Grey, *Three's a Crowd*, pp. 167-69.

[66] Thomas, 'Women, Pentecostals, and the Bible', p. 50.

[67] Thomas, 'Women, Pentecostals, and the Bible', p. 50.

not unrelated to its relevance to the community' or 'its own diversity of teaching on a given topic'.[68]

2.4 A New Interpretive Strategy for Hearing the Confessions

The prior section concerned itself primarily with surveying past works by Pentecostal scholars on the OT to discern, if possible, a broad outline of the characteristics of Pentecostal interpretive work on the OT. Obviously, these scholars working within the framework of a Pentecostal hermeneutic have quite brilliantly brought the insights afforded by their Pentecostal roots to bear on very diverse interpretive questions and problematic texts. The factors that connected these efforts seem to have been their insistence on the ongoing role of the Spirit in the work of biblical interpretation, the importance of personal and communal experience as both a source and a judge of various interpretive options, and a view of biblical authority that allowed for multiple 'meanings' as Scripture was brought to bear on new contexts and issues.

The next task is to distill these insights into a working interpretive method appropriate to Jeremiah's Confessions. The primary goal is to allow, as far as possible, the text to control the method rather than to force the text to fit into an already-selected hermeneutical method. This ensures that the text remains in focus throughout the interpretive process.

2.4.1 A 'Transformative-Formative' Hermeneutical Paradigm

2.4.1.1 The Narrative of Jeremiah's Call as a Hermeneutical Key

While a detailed exegesis of Jeremiah's call is neither possible nor necessary at this juncture, there are several reasons why it must be briefly considered. First and foremost for the task before us, almost all scholars are agreed that Jeremiah's 'Confessions' serve in some way as a reflection upon his call.[69] In fact, Holladay argues that the

---

[68] Thomas, 'Women, Pentecostals, and the Bible', p. 50.

[69] 'Before proceeding in [the Confessions'] analysis, it is necessary to examine the account of Jeremiah's call to the prophetic service, because in it we are given the first glimpse into the working of Jeremiah's mind.' Joseph L. Mihelic, 'Dialogue with God: A Study of Some of Jeremiah's Confessions', *Int* 14 (1960), pp. 43-50 (43).

only way one can understand Jeremiah's claim that, 'Your words were found … and I ate them',[70] is by recognizing that the 'thought link' is found in the narrative of Jeremiah's call, when YHWH says to him: 'Now, I have put my words in your mouth'.[71] Thus, if our ultimate goal is to discern interpretive direction for reading the book of Jeremiah in the Confessions, it seems not too great a stretch to begin discerning such direction within the call narrative.[72]

The calling is also important because it defines the nature of the Word Jeremiah is called to proclaim. Two things are obvious about the nature of that Word. First, this Word is addressed to *the nations*, not just Judah. Second, this Word is predominantly *destructive* in nature – it will 'uproot and tear down', 'destroy and overthrow' – but is also significantly *constructive*; the same Word will 'build and plant' (see Jer. 1.10).

In his seminal study of the call narrative, Wilhelm Vischer argues the key interpretive question is: 'How does Jeremiah perform an international ministry? … Jeremiah only left his homeland at the end of his life when the last Jews of Palestine forced him to go Egypt'.[73] Vischer insists that Jeremiah did not exercise 'two' ministries, one ministry to 'the nations' and another to Judah. Rather, 'the word that the Lord speaks to Jerusalem and Judah determines by itself the destiny of the nations'.[74] Vischer sees Jeremiah's destructive word of judgment on Judah as preparing the way for the constructive word of salvation to the nations:

> The nations are to be instructed because the Israelites dispersed among them are the witnesses of the Good Shepherd who one day will gather them all into one flock. Ezekiel … through his prophetic ministry among the Babylonian exiles confirms Jeremiah's message that the dispersed tribes are the witnesses among the nations … and that it is through them that God is preparing the way for the vocation of the Gentiles. Where the sin of the

---

[70] Jeremiah 15.16.

[71] Jeremiah 1.9. William L. Holladay, 'Jeremiah and Moses: Further Observations', *JBL* 85.1 (1966), pp. 17-27 (25).

[72] Not least because the call narrative appears as the introduction to the book.

[73] Wilhelm Vischer, 'The Vocation of the Prophet to the Nations: An Exegesis of Jer 1.4-10', *Int* 9.3 (1955), pp. 310-17 (313).

[74] 'The history of Israel is at all times closely related to the history of other peoples and all great empires'. Vischer, 'The Vocation of the Prophet', p. 314.

elect abounds, the mercy of the Lord superabounds on the nations.[75]

The destruction of divine judgment brought on Judah by Jeremiah's words 'makes room' for the coming day of divine salvation for all the nations.[76] The divine Word has a dual purpose; its 'destructive' and 'constructive' functions are necessary to each other.

2.4.1.2 Grant Wacker's 'Primitive-Pragmatic' Paradigm

How then does this 'destructive-constructive' function of the divine Word translate into a working hermeneutical model? Such a tensive understanding of the Word is, it seems, a key part of what makes the book of Jeremiah so difficult for the modern mind to comprehend. However, it is precisely at this point that the distinctive Pentecostal worldview may help in comprehending the book of Jeremiah's seemingly contradictory theology of the Word. That tension within the foundational theology of the Word of God in Jeremiah seems to mirror a fundamental tension in the Pentecostal worldview that Grant Wacker named the 'primitive-pragmatic' paradigm which represents the two 'poles' of Pentecostal experience in North America.[77]

Wacker argues that there was a 'primitivism' at the root of Pentecostal experience of spiritual power. On occasion, 'the longing to touch God bordered on mysticism'. However, it usually 'suggested a yearning simply to know the divine mind and will as directly and as purely as possible, without the distorting refractions of human volition, traditions, or speculation'.[78]

This desire to return to the pure faith experience described in Scripture led the early Pentecostals to a deep suspicion of theological traditions and organizational structures. '[Creeds] all suffered from the same fatal flaw. All represented humanly fabricated-and therefore error-riddled-structures that had to be *torn down* so that true churches

---

[75] Vischer, 'The Vocation of the Prophet', p. 316.

[76] Isaiah 2.1-4; Mic. 4.1-6.

[77] Grant Wacker, *Heaven Below: Early Pentecostals and American Culture* (Cambridge, MA: Harvard University Press, 2001), p. 14, writes,

The Old Testament's portrait of the alien and the resident, or the New Testament's image of the pilgrim and the citizen, offer ... possibilities [for thinking about] the two impulses ... No effort to describe the world of early Pentecostalism can be complete without accounting for both impulses and the way they worked together to secure the movement's survival.

[78] Wacker, *Heaven Below*, p. 11.

of God could be *erected* in their place'.[79] Thus, this 'primitive' impulse in early Pentecostalism defines 'a determination to return to first things, original things, fundamental things'.[80]

This impulse has certainly affected Pentecostalism's view of Scripture. Wacker points out that the earliest Pentecostal educational institutions usually used the Bible as their sole textbook. The motive 'was neither intellectual narrowness nor cultural parochialism'.[81] Instead, 'they simply felt certain that no other resource of significant information existed'.[82] This absolute trust in the Bible was more than rational acceptance of Scripture's veracity. It was a desire 'to enter the apostolic world, to breathe its air, feel its life, see its signs and wonders with their own eyes'.[83] Certainly, such a return to the text would be experienced as a virtual 'uprooting' of our understanding and an 'overturning' of all preconceived notions about the meaning of the text.

Yet, Wacker was surprised to discern in the early Pentecostal literature, alongside this restorative impulse, a very pragmatic set of concerns. He notes that, as he read, 'I heard about adjusting doctrine to the needs of the moment'.[84] This inherent, though sometimes unadmitted, pragmatism meant 'that at the end of the day pentecostals proved remarkably willing to work within the social and cultural expectations of the age'.[85]

While the early Pentecostals understood the Word of God almost as a portal to return to the days of the Apostles, they also deeply believed 'the Bible contained all the information one needed to know in order to navigate life's tough decisions'. Wacker calls this the 'principle of plenary relevance'.[86] While the Bible might be an almost-mystical book, it most certainly was an always-practical book, granting direction in even the most mundane decisions of daily life often

---

[79] Wacker, *Heaven Below*, p. 12, italics mine.

[80] 'With this term I hope to connote not so much an upward reach for transcendence as a downward or even backward quest for the infinitely pure and powerful fount of being itself.' Wacker, *Heaven Below*, p. 12.

[81] 'Though', Wacker notes, 'that may have been the effect'. Wacker, *Heaven Below*, p. 71.

[82] Wacker, *Heaven Below*, p. 71.

[83] Wacker, *Heaven Below*, p. 72.

[84] Wacker, *Heaven Below*, p. 12.

[85] Wacker, *Heaven Below*, p. 13.

[86] Wacker, *Heaven Below*, p. 70.

in surprising ways. Thus, the text gave context-specific direction that allowed one to 'build' a life that was pleasing to God, making sure to keep believers firmly 'planted' in the way of righteousness in the midst of life's shifting circumstances.

Also helpful here is the oft-used model of the hermeneutical circle. Dunn sees this as occurring in three forms in the interpretive process.[87] The first form is found in the relationship of the parts to the whole. The parts only make sense in light of an understanding of the whole; the whole can only be made known through the parts. The second form is the relationship between the 'Word' and the 'words'.[88] The concept of canon includes a rule of faith that serves as an interpretive guide/narrative for the canonical texts. The final form is the relationship of reader and text.

2.4.2 A 'Transformative-Formative' Hermeneutic

A key argument here is that Pentecostalism could add a fourth form of the hermeneutical circle to Dunn's list. the relationship between transformation and formation. A crucial, but oft-ignored, feature of encounters with the biblical text is the way in which they not only *transform* our relationship with God but also *form* our obedience to God. Pentecostals encounter the Bible as a book that both 'roots up' (a kind of primitive experience) and 'builds up' (a pragmatic encounter) faith. Autry is convinced, 'The Pentecostal-charismatic experience of the Holy Spirit enhances our sense of both the unchanging authority[89] of Scripture and its measureless capacity to be relevant and applicable[90] in new situations'.[91] While Scripture is unified in its call to encounter the Holy Spirit, which is universal, it is diversified in its call to obedience, which is always context-specific. 'Texts of Scripture have multiple complex senses rather than one single meaning.'[92]

---

[87] James D.G. Dunn, 'Criteria for a Wise Reading of a Biblical Text', in David F. Ford and Graham Stanton (eds.), *Reading Texts, Seeking Wisdom: Scripture and Theology* (Grand Rapids. Eerdmans, 2003), pp. 38-52.

[88] 'One thinks, for example, of the gospel ... serving as the critical scalpel for Luther, or the universal ideals of Jesus indicating for nineteenth-century liberalism an "essence" from which the merely particular could be stripped.' Dunn, 'Criteria for a Wise Reading', p. 50.

[89] Read 'Transformative power'.

[90] Read 'Formative power'.

[91] Autry, 'Dimensions of Hermeneutics', p. 31.

[92] In many ways, this 'complexity' of Scriptural meaning was already understood in the premodern Church's 'fourfold' approach to interpretation. See L.

2.4.2.1 Hearing for Transformation

It seems helpful to understand a transformative hearing of Scripture as any interpretive strategy that backgrounds exegesis and fore-grounds encounter.[93] Hearing Jeremiah's Confessions for transformation requires much more than a one-dimensional interpretation of the text. The Pentecostal hearer seeking encounter must seek entrance into the world of the text presented in the book of Jeremiah,[94] discern the character[95] of the prophet Jeremiah as portrayed in that world, and then faithfully submit to the transforming power of the Word heard there.

The primitivist drive[96] of transformational hearing manifests itself in a deliberate focus on the canonical form and literary-rhetorical dimensions of the text. The diversity within the canon is a beauty to be appreciated rather than a puzzle to be solved. In fact, a good part of the creativity of Pentecostal hermeneutics derives from its inter-textual reading of the canon. Pentecostal immersion within the canonical story means that 'a casual reference to "Babel" should call up an entire network of story and teaching'.[97]

Once immersed in the textual world, the reader's task is to discern 'those predispositions … necessary for a literary work to exercise its "effect"'.[98] It is obvious that 'each reader's presuppositions, questions,

---

Gregory Jones, 'Formed and Transformed by Scripture: Character, Community, and Authority in Biblical Interpretation', in William P. Brown (ed.), *Character and Scripture: Moral Formation, Community, and Biblical Interpretation* (Grand Rapids. Eerdmans, 2002), pp. 18-32 (29).

[93] It must be noted that just because exegesis is moved to the 'background' does not mean that it is taken out of the picture altogether! In all the examples of scholarship given above, there was no avoidance of the work of rigorous scholarly exegesis; rather, that work became a 'staging ground' on which to build a fresh spiritual encounter.

[94] 'Texts do not just sit passively by while readers plunder their meanings. They project a world into which we may enter, a world which may impact upon us.' Pinnock, 'Work of the Holy Spirit in Hermeneutics', p. 13.

[95] Particularly the affective profile.

[96] A drive to 'get back' to the text not to the historical event.

[97] Robert W. Jenson, 'The Religious Power of Scripture', *SJT* 52.1 (1999), pp. 89-105 (92).

[98] For Wolfgang Iser, 'implied reader' was a short-hand term for this. Robert O. Baker, 'Pentecostal Bible Reading: Toward a Model of Reading for the Formation of Christian Affections', *JPT* 7 (1995), pp. 34-48 (42). See Wolfgang Iser, *The Act of Reading: A Theory of Aesthetic Response* (trans. D.H. Wilson; Baltimore: Johns Hopkins University Press, 1978), pp. 34-38.

and circumstances ... will always differ somewhat and may differ profoundly from those of the author';[99] however, though the text may be filled with 'gaps' and 'indeterminacies', a good book instructs the reader 'on how those gaps should be correctly filled'.[100]

Once the character of the ideal hearer is discerned, the task of the faithful reader of Scripture is submission to the transformation of their own character by the power of the Spirit. The 'implied hearer' of Scripture is always a disciple; therefore, 'the object of biblical interpretation ... is the interpreter as much as it is the text, and it is *performative* as much as it is hermeneutical'.[101]

It is here that the oft-ignored affective dimension of the text comes into crucial focus. More so than any other Christian tradition, Pentecostalism is uniquely suited to 'deconstruct the Enlightenment myth and ideal of critical and passionless objectivity'.[102] Pentecostals expect Scripture to transform their feelings as much, if not more so, than their beliefs and actions. In fact, Pentecostals would probably agree that 'to seek to understand the ideational/rational content of a text without also seeking to experience and reflect upon its emotive effect is to skew the text's message'.[103]

In a text like the book of Jeremiah, the focus on the affective domain is undeniable. In fact, Baumgartner notes:

> Like none of his predecessors, the man with the gentle, sensitive disposition suffered ... from the fact that his life was now a great, ceaseless struggle, that in his work for Yahweh his reward was nothing but scorn and mockery, even severe persecution, that his clairvoyance, which showed him the horrors of the future as if in the present, stopped him enjoying life's harmless pleasures, and that he had to stand so completely alone and without joy in life.[104]

It is in the Confessions that we see this rawness of Jeremiah's reaction to the Word, and for the attentive hearer, such revelations serve to transform their own reading of God's Word to Jeremiah.

---

[99] Autry, 'Dimensions of Hermeneutics', p. 35.
[100] Baker, 'Pentecostal Bible Reading', p. 41.
[101] Bockmuehl, 'Reason, Wisdom, and the Implied Disciple', p. 64. On the transforming effect of Scripture, see also Grey, *Three's a Crowd*, p. 155.
[102] Baker, 'Pentecostal Bible Reading', p. 35.
[103] Baker, 'Pentecostal Bible Reading', p. 34.
[104] Baumgartner, *Jeremiah's Poems of Lament*, p. 95.

To allow oneself to be engulfed by the emotions in the book of Jeremiah – to be affectively transformed by Jeremiah's outcries – requires a great deal of faith and trust. One must be convinced that 'when a text is actually read, it is not merely text but … living address'.[105] Andrew Davies would agree: 'Pentecostals read the Bible not to learn of the history of Israel, the development of the earliest Christian theology or even of the life of Christ, but to meet God in the text, and to provide an opportunity for the Holy Spirit to speak to our spirits'.[106]

Reading for transformative encounter in addition to exegetical insight adds new dimension and depth to the text.[107] As Jones observes: 'Readers who attempt to remain detached and neutral in their interpretation of the Bible will typically understand it less deeply than those who discipline their lives by studying Scripture as the vehicle of God's Word'.[108]

But a question hangs over the discussion: what exactly does the Bible transform in this hermeneutical model? The transformative power of Scripture changes the faithful hearer at the level of the religious affections. An affection is not simply a mood or an emotion; it has greater stability and is 'more akin to the language used in the New Testament'.[109] The development of religious affections requires the cooperation of mind and will and has its ultimate 'origin in the person of Christ … actualized by the activity of the Holy Spirit'.[110] The affections thus integrate orthodoxy and orthopraxy.[111]

2.4.2.2 Hearing for Formation

Furthermore, a Pentecostal hearing of Scripture must be 'more than antiquarian'; it must be a hearing 'which opens up to the present

---

[105] Jenson, 'Religious Power', p. 89.

[106] Davies, 'What Does It Mean', p. 219.

[107] McQueen noted that his experience of 'praying through' radically concretized his understanding of the literary unity of Joel. 'The theological and orthopathic interrelationships of lament, salvation, and judgment in my own and my community's encounter with God elucidated their corresponding literary interrelationships in the book of Joel.' McQueen, *Joel and the Spirit*, p. 107.

[108] Jones, 'Formed and Transformed', p. 31.

[109] Daniel Castelo, 'Tarrying on the Lord: Affections, Virtues, and Theological Ethics in Pentecostal Perspective', *JPT* 13.1 (2004), pp. 31-56 (40).

[110] Castelo, 'Tarrying on the Lord', p. 37.

[111] Steven Jack Land, *Pentecostal Spirituality. A Passion for the Kingdom* (Cleveland, TN: CPT Press, 2010), p. 33.

situation'.[112] Timothy Cargal cautions, 'If Pentecostals in particular ... do not find ways of interpreting the Bible which are meaningful to people living in this postmodern age, their interpretation of the Bible will increasingly be perceived as irrelevant'.[113] Transformation is only the originating point on the hermeneutical circle. It is not enough merely to enter the textual world; the text must also enter the *hearer's* world and provoke the audience to be a 'doer of the Word and not a hearer only' (Jas 1.22).

As in the process of transformation outlined above, this next process we have designated 'formation' includes the backgrounding explanation in favor of foregrounding embodiment. Formation submerges the typical distinction between interpretation (what the text meant) and application (what the text means), recognizing that a text is not fully interpreted until it is properly applied – this is hermeneutics' 'total task'.[114] Hearing Jeremiah's Confessions then would mean the affectively-transformed hearer must re-enter their world, discern the proper ways in which to embody the theology of the Word found in the Confessions within the contemporary context,[115] and then live in faithful obedience.

Re-entering the world of the reader is just as much a work of the Spirit as any other aspect of the interpretive process here described. Early Pentecostals 'effectively sacramentalized the divine power by locating it within their own bodies, within time and space'.[116] Pinnock says:

> The truth of the Bible into which the Spirit would lead us does not consist only of matters of fact and bits of information. It includes truth for thought, for life, for feeling. The Spirit is concerned as much with the truth of our walk as the truth of our talk.

---

[112] Pinnock, 'Work of the Holy Spirit in Hermeneutics', p. 23.

[113] Cargal, 'Beyond the Fundamentalist-Modernist Controversy', p. 165.

[114] Autry, 'Dimensions of Pentecostal Hermeneutics', p. 32.

[115] 'Pentecostals generally have a vacuum when acknowledging ways of embodying their faith commitments, for the traditional means of sustaining an identity apart from and in witness to the world has been discounted.' Castelo, 'Tarrying on the Lord', p. 34.

[116] Castelo, 'Tarrying on the Lord', p. 50, quoting Grant Wacker.

His interests encompass all these things and to this end he makes full use of the Scriptures' ability to be opened up.[117]

If, as was argued above, personal experience plays a key role in initiating the interpretive process, it would make sense for the interpretive process to come full circle and impact behavior. 'If meaning starts with me, then it is only correct that the responsibility for implementing that meaning as practical application should also end there.'[118]

The crucial process here is the final embodiment of the text. The goal is not merely 'belief in objectively true propositions taught by the text' nor 'the adoption … of an authentic self-understanding evoked by the text's symbols' but ultimately 'the formation of a community whose forms of life correspond to the symbolic universe rendered or signaled by the text'.[119] In other words, texts only acquire meaning when 'they function intelligibly within specific cultures or subcultures'. This would seem to imply that 'the hermeneutical circle is not completed until the text finds a fitting social embodiment'.[120] Stephen Fowl and Gregory Jones see the embodiment of Scripture as Christians' primary vocation. However, they admit that 'discerning *how* to go about embodying Scripture … is a complex matter'.[121] This is due to the cultural distance between the world of the Bible of the world of contemporary readers. 'What the [text] meant – the work it did – belonged to a specific cultural-linguistic complex, which no effort of translation however fine and no act of will however faithful can call again into existence in our so different world'.[122]

Once ways of embodiment are discerned, we again come to a point requiring faith and courage, the point of obedience. Jones shrewdly notes: 'We find it easier, and morally convenient, to evade

---

[117] Pinnock, 'Work of the Holy Spirit in Hermeneutics', p. 14. See A.K.M. Adam *et al.*, *Reading Scripture with the Church: Toward a Hermeneutic for Theological Interpretation* (Grand Rapids: Baker Academic, 2006).

[118] Davies, 'What Does It Mean', p. 229.

[119] This is George Lindbeck's 'cultural-linguistic' model of theological language. Wayne Meeks, 'A Hermeneutics of Social Embodiment', *HTR* 73.1-3 (1986), pp. 176-86 (184-85).

[120] Meeks, 'A Hermeneutics of Social Embodiment', pp. 183-84.

[121] Stephen Fowl and L. Gregory Jones, *Reading in Communion: Scripture and Ethics in Christian Life* (BFT, Eugene, OR: Wipf and Stock, 1998), p. 1.

[122] Meeks, 'A Hermeneutics of Social Embodiment', p. 181.

the actual claims of Scripture through debates about Scripture.'[123] Here again, the early Pentecostals' approach to Scripture actually addressed this very issue because 'their concern was to live the Gospel faithfully before God'.[124]

Again, a question arises in this discussion: what precisely is to be embodied? The Scripture's formative power is felt at the level of the hearer's virtue. Castelo notes that the categories of affections and virtues have similar, even complementary, aspects. In fact, they could easily be two sides of the same coin, if you will. Religious affections 'emphasize the necessity of an inner transformation that can be wrought only by the presence of the Holy Spirit'; virtues, however, 'demonstrate the necessity of habitually sustaining those capacities that exist in us … in order that these may increase in the approximation of their proper ends'.[125]

In many ways, affections and virtues, then, are the inner and outer manifestations of the work of the Spirit in the interpretive process, and each works to support the other.[126] As Autry says, 'The 'successful' exegete has made Scripture's aim (and God's aim) his or her own … knowing God and helping others to know God and live as God's people'.[127]

2.5 Primary Hermeneutical Tools

The only remaining element is to identify specific hermeneutical tools that will serve to achieve those transformative and formative ends that, as described above, are the core of a uniquely Pentecostal approach to the Confessions. This discussion is guided by two key understandings. First, contemporary exegesis can never, in good conscience, simply advocate an abandonment of critical methods of textual engagement in favor of pre-critical approaches. Secondly, contemporary exegesis must move away from the myopic tendency to engage texts with a single interpretive methodology.

---

[123] Jones, 'Formed and Transformed', p. 31.
[124] Archer, *A Pentecostal Hermeneutic*, p. 87.
[125] Castelo, 'Tarrying on the Lord', p. 45.
[126] For a fascinating discussion of readerly 'virtues' applied to OT interpretation, see Richard S. Briggs, *The Virtuous Reader: Old Testament Narrative and Interpretive Virtue* (STI; Grand Rapids: Baker Academic, 2010).
[127] Autry, 'Dimensions of Hermeneutics', p. 48.

Wesley Kort's observations about the complexity of narrative seem equally applicable to the nature of Scripture. He sees the 'pluralism of critical methodology' as directly related to the 'complexity of the narrative form'.[128] This is so because each methodology is primarily oriented to some outside interest and is designed to focus on one particular feature.[129] Kort is aware that 'the critic of biblical narrative may not want to affirm all the theoretical assumptions behind any one method'; however, he also observes, 'the methods can be used together because they also have, by virtue of the narrative form itself, a certain coherence'.[130] It is precisely this understanding of the inherent complexities of the biblical text that lies behind Martin's 'integration of multiple interpretive approaches'.[131]

The interpretive strategy promoted here is based on such methodological multiplicity governed by the uniqueness of the text/s under investigation. Thus, the present work will use the tools of rhetorical, narrative, and reader-response criticisms to ground its hearing of Jeremiah's Confessions. It is not necessary here to define each of these well-known methodologies,[132] yet it is incumbent that some defense and explanation of their unique combination here be offered.

2.5.1 Rhetorical Criticism

The monumental influence of James Muilenburg's 1968 SBL presidential address, 'Form Criticism and Beyond'[133] is widely recognized and cannot be gainsaid. Rhetorical criticism's status within the repertoire of critical methodologies need not be defended. However, one significant point must be noted. The very first published dissertation that utilized the Muilenburg program of rhetorical criticism focused on the rhetorical features of the book of Jeremiah.[134] Thus, by

---

[128] Wesley A. Kort, *Story, Text, Scripture: Literary Interests in Biblical Narrative* (University Park, PA: The Pennsylvania State University Press, 1998), p. 15.

[129] 'The diversity of critical method is determined by the complexity of the narrative form as well as by the theoretical commitments by which each method is shaped before it begins to address particular narratives.' Kort, *Story, Text, Scripture*, p. 50.

[130] Kort, *Story, Text, Scripture*, p. 51.

[131] See above.

[132] For definitions, see Eryl W. Davies, *Biblical Criticism* (Guides for the Perplexed; London: T & T Clark, 2013).

[133] James Muilenburg, 'Form Criticism and Beyond', *JBL* 88.1 (1969), pp. 1-18.

[134] Jack. R Lundbom, *Jeremiah: A Study in Ancient Hebrew Rhetoric* (Winona Lake, IN: Eisenbrauns, 2nd edn, 1997); for a brief summation of the features of

beginning with rhetorical analysis, the present work stands within a long-established tradition of scholarly interest and investigation in Jeremiah studies.

2.5.1.1 From Form Criticism to Rhetorical Criticism

The difficulty is that the term 'rhetorical criticism', especially as described by Muilenburg, is more than a little vague. Part of this ambiguity is no real fault of Muilenburg's but simply a feature of ancient Semitic languages. 'The conventions appropriate to discourse and literature seem not to have been as sharply discriminated in the ancient world as in the modern. The interconnections among oratory, dialectic, drama, and epistolography are genuine, albeit hazy.'[135] It is also important to remember that Muilenburg's keynote defined rhetorical criticism over against the already-established method of form-criticism. Muilenburg saw the fault in classical form criticism this way: 'There has been a proclivity among scholars in recent years to lay such stress upon the typical and representative that the individual, personal, and unique features of the particular pericope are all but lost to view'.[136] Or, in the words of Muilenburg's student Phyllis Trible, form criticism 'neglects the individual' and focuses sole attention on 'the general'.[137] It is this deficiency that he sought to correct and to give each individual text its due hearing.[138]

Jeremiah's rhetoric, see Jack R. Lundbom, 'Jeremiah' in *ABD* III, pp. 690-97. The present work differs from Lundbom in its use of the results of rhetorical analysis and in its inclusion of the critical concerns of reader-response theory. Lundbom is more interested in discerning textual *structure* (e.g. the rhetorically-matched pieces that establish textual boundaries), whereas the present study is more interested in discerning textual *flow* (e.g. the dynamic movement that occurs between rhetorical boundary points).

[135] He notes the legitimacy of inquiring whether or not 'Graeco-Roman standards are as congenial to Old Testament rhetoric as to the New'. C. Clifton Black, 'Rhetorical Criticism and Biblical Interpretation', *Exp Tim* 100.7 (1989), pp. 252-58 (257).

[136] Muilenburg, 'Form Criticism and Beyond', p. 5. See also Roy F. Melugin, 'Muilenburg, Form Criticism and Theological Exegesis', in Martin J. Buss (ed.), *Encounter With the Text: Form and History in the Hebrew Bible* (SemeiaSup; Philadelphia. Fortress Press, 1979), pp. 91-100.

[137] Phyllis A. Trible, *Rhetorical Criticism: Context, Method, and the Book of Jonah* (GBS; Minneapolis: Fortress Press, 1994), p. 26.

[138] Muilenburg, 'Form Criticism and Beyond', p. 5, writes,

Form and content are inextricably related. They form an integral whole ... Exclusive attention to the *Gattung* may actually obscure the thought and intention of the writer or speaker. The passage must be heard and read precisely as it is

2.5.1.2 The Main Ingredient of Rhetorical Criticism

The key focus of all rhetorical criticism[139] is on methods and modes of persuasion. In fact, Martin Kessler finds Aristotle's definition of rhetoric as 'the best possible means of persuasion' still worthy of note: 'An obvious advantage of this definition is that it brings together the formal and functional aspects'.[140] In respect to the larger academic discussion, Patricia Tull notes that many 'have come to view rhetoric and persuasion as inherent in all forms of communication', which has led 'to a recognition of speech as inevitably value-laden'. This shift within the larger academic community has led many biblical scholars 'to direct attention to the hortatory nature of much of the Bible – that is, its effort to persuade audiences not merely to appreciate the aesthetic power of its language but, even more importantly, to act and think according to its norms'.[141] To acknowledge, identify, and interpret the rhetorical features of a biblical text is to admit to its persuasive intentions.

In his commentary on Jeremiah, Walter Brueggemann, also a student of James Muilenburg, explains that his method keys off the persuasive nature of human language. He describes his interpretive program for book this way:

> In this method, one pays attention to the power of language to propose an imaginative world that is an alternative to the one that

---

spoken. It is the creative synthesis of the particular formulation of the pericope with the content that makes it the distinctive composition that it is.

[139] Classical, biblical, and modern.

[140] Martin Kessler, 'A Methodological Setting for Rhetorical Criticism', in David J.A. Clines, David M. Gunn, and Alan J. Hauser (eds.), *Art and Meaning: Rhetoric in Biblical Literature* (JSOTSup 19; Sheffield: Sheffield Academic Press, 1982), pp. 1-19 (2).

[141] Patricia K. Tull, 'Rhetorical Criticism and Intertextuality', in Steven L. McKenzie and Stephen R. Haynes (eds.), *To Each Its Own Meaning: An Introduction to Biblical Criticisms and Their Application* (Louisville: Westminster/John Knox Press, rev. edn, 1999), pp. 156-80 (157-58, 160). David J.A. Clines agrees:

> Even the 'authority' of the Bible as Scripture is experienced in no different way from that in which the 'authority' of any great literary work is felt ... the way in which they impose themselves upon their readers, impel them to reexamine their values, and win for themselves lodgement in those recesses of the mind where behavior is determined, is one and the same.

See 'Story and Poem: The Old Testament as Literature and Scripture', *Int* 34.2 (1980), pp. 115-27 (117).

seems to be at hand – alternative to the one in which the reader or listener thinks herself or himself enmeshed. Literature then is not regarded as descriptive of what is, but as evocative and constructive of another life world ... This approach permits literature to be enormously daring and bold, and often abrasive and subversive in the race of the presumed world of the listener. It places the listener in crisis, but also presents the listener with a new zone for fresh hope, changed conduct, and fresh historical possibility.[142]

To see rhetorical strategies as simultaneously 'world-destroying' and 'world-building' shows the affinity such studies have with both the literary features and theological message of the book of Jeremiah.

2.5.1.3 The Missing Ingredient in Rhetorical Criticism

However, contemporary rhetorical criticism is often *missing* the key ingredient of serious consideration of the role of emotive appeal in persuasive speech. Thomas Olbricht says: 'Biblical scholars have long recognized appeal to emotions in biblical documents. But they have not given specific attention to ways in which these may be reflected upon systematically.'[143]

Stanley Fish is certainly not overstating the case when he writes, 'In any linguistic experience we are internalizing attitudes and emotions, even if the attitude is the pretension of no attitude and the emotion is a passionate coldness'.[144] Then why has the emotive dimension of persuasion been virtually ignored? Probably the most central reason is that most 'post-Enlightenment discussions of emotion commonly regarded anything having to do with affective response ... as nonrational, if not irrational, and primarily physiological reactions'.[145] What sense would it make to analyze rationally such a process?

---

[142] Walter Brueggemann, *A Commentary on Jeremiah. Exile and Homecoming* (Grand Rapids: Eerdmans, 1998), p. 15.

[143] Thomas H. Olbricht, '*Pathos* as Proof in Greco-Roman Rhetoric', in Thomas H. Olbricht and Jerry L. Sumney (eds.), *Paul and Pathos* (SBL Symposium Series 16; Atlanta: Society of Biblical Literature, 2001), pp. 7-22 (7).

[144] Stanley K. Fish, 'Literature in the Reader: Affective Stylistics', *New Literary History* 2.1 (1970), pp. 123-62 (149).

[145] Karl Allen Kuhn, *The Heart of Biblical Narrative: Rediscovering the Biblical Appeal to the Emotions* (Minneapolis: Fortress Press, 1999), p. 16.

However, newer studies of human emotion recognize such processes as containing cognitive elements.[146] It would be false to say the emotive process can be articulated easily or completely, but 'the knowledge we know as human feeling is not irrational'.[147] What follows are two important examples of recent biblical scholarship that attempt to give an account of the affective nature of rhetoric and construct a program for its analysis.

The Work of Karl Allen Kuhn
Already cited above, the focus of Kuhn's work is the role of emotional appeal in biblical narrative. 'Not only is affect crucial to the construction and experience of narrative, it is also essential to the *rhetorical* function and force of narrative.'[148] He credits the 'emergence of narrative critical methods' and the 'resurgence of theological interpretation' with dramatic improvements in understanding how texts 'tell the story'; yet, when it comes to analyzing the message of the text, 'commentators often leave its affective dimensions unearthed and fail to consider how pathos may be employed by the biblical author in the shaping of the narrative'.[149]

Scholars today still agree with Aristotle that a narrative's plotting and characterization drive the affective dimension. This is important because, 'By pointing out … the emotional freight of plotting and characterization, psychologists and literary critics have shown that the affective dimension of narrative is integral to the function of narrative itself'. However, these same studies give no real 'specification of what *particular* techniques of plotting or characterization may be especially well suited to stimulating reader emotion'.[150]

The goals that Kuhn sets for his work will also shape the present investigation. The first goal is the obvious starting point: to acknowledge the presence of a significant affective dimension to biblical narrative. 'My sense is that we have a lot to learn about this dimension of biblical narrative, and our understanding of pathos as a

---

[146] Although, Kuhn notes, there is 'widespread disagreement, however, on the nature of that cognition, and therefore the actual character of emotion'. Kuhn, *The Heart of Biblical Narrative*, p. 17.

[147] Ronald J. Allen, 'Feeling and Form in Biblical Interpretation', *Enc* 43.1 (1982), pp. 99-107 (100).

[148] Kuhn, *The Heart of Biblical Narrative*, pp. 2-3.

[149] Kuhn, *The Heart of Biblical Narrative*, p. 28.

[150] Kuhn, *The Heart of Biblical Narrative*, pp. 30-31.

rhetorical device will be enhanced as we keep an eye out for it.'[151] There are two basic ways to accomplish this goal. One would be to analyze the affective impact of the various rhetorical devices the authors used; the other would be to assess our own responses to the biblical text as we read it.[152]

The second goal is discerning how the affective appeal is meant to impact the response to the passage. Kuhn again perceptively comments: 'The tone we give to a passage when reading it aloud is a major interpretive decision, for it will greatly affect the way in which a passage is heard'.[153] The emotional tone attributed to the passage directly influences how one interprets its function in its present context, fills in narrative gaps, and discerns between plausible readings.[154]

The third goal is discerning the implied author's own rhetorical agenda. Very often, such agendas are carefully hidden or, better, the implied hearer is led on a carefully paced journey toward the revelation of that agenda. When discerning these intentions, it is quite common to look 'to the prominence of certain themes' and 'structuring features', but the 'affective appeals' of the work must also be considered for 'emotively charged narration will lead us to the worldview the author is urging readers to embrace'.[155]

The Work of Lee Roy Martin

While Kuhn's insights into affective analysis are extremely helpful and vital to this interpretive task, it is important to keep in mind that Kuhn's remarks relate specifically to biblical *narrative*. It seems fair to ask after the distinctions, if any, of an affective analysis of prophetic texts which are largely poetic or non-narrative prose.

Once again, Lee Roy Martin's recent work is contributing to this very inquiry. After some initial exegetical work in the Psalms,[156]

---

[151] Kuhn, *The Heart of Biblical Narrative*, p. 57.

[152] This latter approach is effectively 'intuiting the affective function of the text', an approach Kuhn admits 'will not sit well with many in our field'. Kuhn, *The Heart of Biblical Narrative*, p. 57.

[153] Kuhn, *The Heart of Biblical Narrative*, p. 58.

[154] 'When different readings for a passage are proposed, affective analysis can be employed to determine which reading is more consistent with the affective tendencies and rhetorical interests of the author.' Kuhn, *The Heart of Biblical Narrative*, pp. 58-59.

[155] Kuhn, *Heart of Biblical Narrative*, p. 58.

[156] Lee Roy Martin, 'Delighting in the Torah: The Affective Dimension of Ps 1', *OTE* 23.3 (2010), pp. 708-27. See also Lee Roy Martin, 'Longing for God: Ps 63 and Pentecostal Spirituality', *JPT* 22.1 (2013), pp. 54-76.

Martin has published a piece that seems to serve as a programmatic summary of his understanding of affective interpretation.[157] Much of what he proposes there concurs with Kuhn's ideas, but with a broader application to the various genres of biblical literature.

With Kuhn, Martin avers that 'one area of rhetoric continues to be undervalued and generally avoided … the affective argument of the text'.[158] While that is plainly seen, it is also abundantly self-obvious that 'biblical writers adopted a rhetorical approach that took advantage of what they knew to be true about human dependence upon *pathos* as a constituent of the decision making process'.[159] Thus, the emotional aspect of a text's appeal should be taken as seriously as its rational and behavioral aspects.

Martin then delineates what he sees as the two basic steps of such an analysis. First, 'the interpreter must acknowledge and identify the affective dimensions of the text'. It seems clear that Kuhn would agree with Martin that such a step is neither 'automatic' nor 'common', and must be undertaken with some care. Though 'every text includes an affective dimension', it is also true that 'the level of affective content varies from one text to another, depending on the genre'.[160]

The next step is identifying explicitly affective words and phrases and the affective impact of the text's overall structure. Martin admits that the latter aspect of this task is more difficult than the former but is no less important.[161] The larger goal here is to ascertain a sense of

---

[157] Lee Roy Martin, 'Rhetorical Criticism and the Affective Dimension of the Biblical Text', *Journal for Semitics* 23.2 (2014), pp. 339-53.

[158] Martin, 'Rhetorical Criticism', p. 340.

[159] 'This is not an affirmation of non-critical approaches, nor … a move to create a new interpretational method, but only to suggest that no matter what methods are used, an examination of the affective component of the text must be included.' Martin, 'Rhetorical Criticism', p. 341.

[160] Martin, 'Rhetorical Criticism', p. 346.

[161] Martin, 'Rhetorical Criticism', p. 348, points to the interwoven narratives of Saul, Samuel, and David:

> Samuel is presented in such a way that the reader develops confidence in Samuel's integrity and authority … Furthermore, Saul is presented in ways that make the reader distrustful of him. Finally, David enters the story as a humble, faithful, and brave youth who is the ideal leader. The reader comes to love David so much that even when David commits adultery and murder and even when David fails to protect his daughter Tamar, the reader is willing to forgive him.

the tone of the text which 'may contribute to the reader's perceptions of the text'.[162]

It is important throughout this analysis that the affective language be treated with the 'same care … afforded to propositional or rational content'.[163] The objective here is not to give affective rhetoric *special* treatment but *equal* treatment. As Martin cogently observes: 'Ideas are propelled not only by reasoned argument but also by emotive packaging. To ignore … either the reasoned argument or the [e]motive package, I would argue, is to be incomplete in one's interpretation.'[164]

2.5.2 Narrative Criticism

Besides the abundance of affective rhetoric, only one other feature predominates in the Confessions of the book of Jeremiah: the literary figure of the prophet. The emotional outbursts given voice in these peculiar texts are, for all intents and purposes, a character sketch.[165] Thus, a holistic approach to the Confessions cannot ignore the role of these texts in the characterization of the prophet nor that characterization's central role in the theological message of the book. Though the book of Jeremiah is clearly not a narrative in any traditional sense of the term,[166] the central role of the figure of the prophet justifies the utilization of narrative criticism's insights into character development to comprehend that figure's role in the Confessions.

Of all the literary elements, character is probably the most familiar to modern readers given its dominance in the modern novel.[167] It is through characters that hearers learn how to relate to the story; in a very real sense, it is the characters that bring the text to life.

---

[162] This may be done by exploring the role of the 'implied reader' or the reactions of 'readers from any specific reading community or context'. Martin, 'Rhetorical Criticism', p. 349.

[163] Martin, 'Rhetorical Criticism', p. 346.

[164] Martin, 'Rhetorical Criticism', p. 346.

[165] Alter describes the basic mode of character portrayal in biblical narrative as a strategy of 'studied reticences', which 'generate an interplay of significantly patterned ambiguities'. We are presented with an art of characterization that 'leads us through varying darknesses which are lit up by intense but narrow beams, phantasmal glimmerings, [and] sudden strobic flashes'. Robert Alter, *The Art of Biblical Narrative* (New York. Basic Books, 1981), p. 126.

[166] Like, for example, the book of Jonah; however, it should be noted that the book of Jeremiah does contain several extended narrative sections, especially found in Jeremiah 26-45.

[167] The period 'has been preoccupied with individual existence, personal resourcefulness, or development, and the tensions between the person and society'. Kort, *Story, Text, and Scripture*, p. 16.

Commenting on the book of Judges – a text with some of the most colorful characters in the OT – Kort notes 'an interplay between constancy and variety. That is, the positioning and career of the judge have a certain fixed pattern, but within this uniformity there is great variation.'[168]

Thus, in Judges, 'character depiction and variance from pattern are closely interrelated'.[169] Theologically, 'the religious meaning ... arises from the effect of contrasting a consistent function of deliverer with a wide diversity of characters. While the characters are human, at times all too human, deliverance is divine'.[170] This kind of contrast is a unique feature of biblical characterization. 'The depiction of character in biblical narrative is often derived from an interplay, then, between a stable and standard role and the individuality of the character ... the constancy and the diversity, are interdependent'.[171] The application of these observations to the Confessions should be clear: one element that makes these texts so intriguing is that we see a prophet *not* behaving like a/n (ideal) prophet! There is, it seems, a dramatic contrast in these texts between the person of Jeremiah and the office of the prophet which he holds.[172]

For a moment, let us return to the Kuhn's work on narrative; as mentioned above, Kuhn sees characterization as one of two primary carriers of a text's affective content/agenda. Good stories introduce us to characters we deeply understand and, usually, grow to love. Thus, characterization, Kuhn says, plays three key affective roles.

First, good characterization invites sympathy and empathy[173] with key characters. The amount of empathy or sympathy seems to be

---

[168] Announced in 2.18-20 and embodied in 3.7-12. Kort, *Story, Text, and Scripture*, p. 29.

[169] Kort, *Story, Text, and Scripture*, p. 30.

[170] Kort, *Story, Text, and Scripture*, p. 34.

[171] Kort, *Story, Text, and Scripture*, p. 70. See also David McCracken's articulation of 'threshold characters' in 'Character in the Boundary: Bakhtin's Interdividuality in Biblical Narratives', *Semeia* 63 (1993), pp. 29-42.

[172] To the extent that the prophet Jeremiah attempts to 'resign' his prophetic office (see Jer. 20.9)!

[173] Sympathy and empathy are not contrary emotions. According to Kuhn, *Heart of Biblical Narrative*, p. 50, sympathy is 'typically defined as a reader's wishes for a character to achieve a beneficial state or to be delivered from some sort of threat or suffering'. Empathy, on the other hand, 'occurs when a reader becomes so intimately engaged with a character that the reader actually experiences the same or similar emotions as the character'.

directly related to the time spent in developing a character's complexity. The greater the character's complexity, the more empathy and/or sympathy readers experience. Secondly, good characterization invites identification. This has to do simply with 'the extent to which a reader considers him- or herself similar to a character in the narrative'.[174] More often than not, readers 'identify' with characters they admire and develop a 'sense of solidarity' with them; however, this is not always the case, and, identification with a character one does *not* admire often leads to golden opportunities for critical self-reflection. [175] Ultimately, good characterization invites us to admire certain characters while disdaining others, and a well-composed text will utilize this feature to promote its own worldview and agenda.[176] Thus, as this investigation progresses, we must continually revisit the question of when and how we are to sympathize, empathize, and/or identify with the literary figure of the prophet and whether or not that figure is set up for our admiration and/or disdain.[177]

2.5.3 Reader-Response Criticism

If we are right about the centrality of the affective rhetoric and the literary figure of the prophet to the Confession texts, then the claim that these texts are meant to shape those who hear them is nearly self-evident. Identifying textual emotions cannot help but elicit

---

[174] Kuhn, *Heart of Biblical Narrative*, p. 50. See also Seymour Chatman's 'paradigmatic' theory of character where character is not so much revealed by the narrative as it is constructed by the reader from clues and evidences provided in the narrative; thus, good character portrayal almost automatically invites readerly speculation about the interior life of the literary figure. Seymour Chatman, *Story and Discourse: Narrative Structure in Fiction and Film* (Ithaca, NY: Cornell University Press, 1978), pp. 96-145.

[175] Kuhn, *Heart of Biblical Narrative*, p. 50.

[176] 'An author may lead us to admire certain characters and then use these characters to promote ideas the author wishes us to adopt. Conversely, the author may identify those we disdain with a competing worldview he or she would have us reject.' Kuhn, *Heart of Biblical Narrative*, p. 51.

[177] This is not always clear. Kuhn remarks: 'At ... times, the author may seek to elicit mixed feelings for certain characters', primarily by depicting otherwise admirable characters doing wrong things [e.g. think David's rape of Bathsheba and murder of Uriah] 'in order to lead readers to "affective dissonance"'. Such affective crises are deeply transformational. Kuhn, *Heart of Biblical Narrative*, p. 51. Ilona Rashkow points out: 'The more "realistic" a biblical character [is] in the sense of responding fully and believably to his or her world ... the more difficult it may be to assign a complex of motives'. Ilona N. Rashkow, 'In Our Image We Created Him, Male and Female We Create Them: The E/Affect of Biblical Characterization', *Semeia* 63 (1993), pp. 105-13 (106).

personal emotions; that is not under contention. What is being contended is the claim the Confessions are *designed* to elicit certain patterns of emotions and to thereby transform and form competent hearers of the Word in Jeremiah.[178]

What is in view here is much more than a simple recording of personal feelings as these texts are heard. First, such an approach would probably say more about the vicissitudes of the interpreter's life than it would about the text; second, such a record would be virtually meaningless to other hearers whose experiences and emotional responses did not correspond. While it is clear that many hearers are open to such emotional transformations, it is equally true 'they are difficult (if not impossible) to accomplish within a written document. They are experiences that may be validated by testimony and description … but the transformative experience itself is outside the bounds of written discourse'.[179]

What *is* possible within the framework of this investigation is to follow carefully the development of the rhetoric and characterization in the Confessions and note the possible affective responses at crucial points. In a sense, this goal can be accomplished by following the lead of Stanley Fish and, instead of asking, 'What does this text *mean?*', inquiring, 'What does this text *do?*'[180]

With that one change of the basic structure of inquiry, the text 'is no longer an object … but an *event,* something that *happens* to, and with the participation of, the reader'.[181] The question of what a text 'does' is not a question asked once at the conclusion; rather, it is a question that is asked continually throughout the process. Perhaps it would be more appropriate to rephrase the question, 'And what is the text doing *now?*'[182]

Fish is certainly correct that such a method is 'simple in concept' but 'complex … in execution'. The question itself is quite simple, but its execution requires *'an analysis of the developing responses of the reader*

---

[178] Christopher R. Seitz, 'The Place of the Reader in Jeremiah', in Martin Kessler (ed.), *Reading the Book of Jeremiah: A Search for Coherence* (Winona Lake, IN. Eisenbrauns, 2004), pp. 67-75.
[179] Martin, 'Longing for God', p. 60.
[180] Fish, 'Literature in the Reader', p. 125.
[181] Fish, 'Literature in the Reader', p. 125, emphasis original.
[182] As opposed to what it did 'then' and what it will do 'later'.

in relation to the words as they succeed one another in time'.[183] It turns the attention from the static meaning to the temporal flow of the text.[184]

It is important to note that Fish does not restrict response to merely emotional reactions. For Fish, response includes 'any and all activities provoked by a string of words: the projection of syntactical and/or lexical probabilities; their subsequent occurrence or non-occurrence; attitudes toward persons, or things, or ideas referred to; the reversal or questioning of those attitudes'.[185] This again highlights the inseparability of cognitive and emotive processing. For Fish,

> Essentially what the method does is *slow down* the reading experience so that 'events' one does not notice in normal time, but which do occur, are brought before our analytical attentions. It is as if a slow motion camera with an automatic stop action effect were recording our linguistic experiences and presenting them to us for viewing.[186]

Most fascinating about this careful analysis of the development of response is that the described response structure may be only tangentially or even contrastively related to the apparent formal structure![187] However, when it comes to the transformational and formational impact of the Confessions, the *way* they mean is maybe even more important than *what* they mean.

Fish notes several key advantages to this approach. First, 'attention is shifted away from the message to its reception, and therefore from the object to the reader'. The advantage here is that it both eliminates the need for a 'fixed and artificial inventory of stylistic devices' while opening itself up to discover a text's full rhetorical power.[188]

---

[183] Fish, 'Literature in the Reader', pp. 126-27, italics original.

[184] Fish, 'Literature in the Reader', p. 127.

[185] Fish, 'Literature in the Reader', p. 127.

[186] 'Of course, the value of such a procedure is predicated on the idea of *meaning as an event*, something that is happening between the words and in the reader's mind, something not visible to the naked eye, but which can be made visible (or at least palpable) by the regular introduction of a "searching" question ...' Fish, 'Literature in the Reader', p. 128.

[187] Fish, 'Literature in the Reader', p. 139.

[188] 'In terms of contextual norms anything can be a stylistic device.' Fish, 'Literature in the Reader', p. 139. While this may seem to militate against the important role claimed for rhetorical criticism above, this observation strikes me as a tacit recognition of the rhetorical power and intent of *all* language, not just a specific set ('bag o' tricks') of recognized rhetorical devices.

A second advantage is that 'its operation is long-term and never ending'.[189] Though it is an interpretive strategy that, at first, is very difficult,[190] over time a hearer has the hope of 'becoming good at the method'. This happens as the hearer inquires about what the text is doing 'with more and more awareness of the probable (and hidden) complexity of the answer … with a mind more sensitized to the workings of language'.[191] Fish continues: 'In a peculiar and unsettling (to theorists) way, it is a method which processes its own user, who is also its only instrument. It is self-sharpening and what it sharpens is *you*. In short it does not organize materials, *but transforms minds*.'[192]

In an article that, intriguingly, also addresses both rhetorical analysis and characterization, Jonathan Magonet concludes with a comment on the nature of biblical text:

> This modern awareness of the 'multidimensionality' of the text is a rediscovery of the old Rabbinic dictum … that there are 'seventy faces to Torah' … This is an uncomfortable view but a liberating one. The responsibility is firmly placed back on the reader to make of the text what he or she can. There is no one view but rather a variety of perspectives that have to be taken into account. The best one can hope for is … the possibility of being surprised again and again into rediscovering the text afresh.[193]

Magonet's concluding line could do a couple things. It could present the hearer with a fixed interpretive situation that disallows, with a despairing sigh, a hoped-for hermeneutical resolution, or it could, as I think it does, present us, with a merry twinkle of the eye, a uniquely living Word that, across countless centuries, retains its ability to speak in ways we all can hear.

---

[189] Fish, 'Literature in the Reader', p. 160.

[190] 'You can't hand it over to someone and expect them at once to be able to use it.' Fish, 'Literature in the Reader', p. 160.

[191] Fish, 'Literature in the Reader', p. 160.

[192] Fish, 'Literature in the Reader', p. 160, italics mine.

[193] Jonathan Magonet, 'Character/Author/Reader: The Problem of Perspective in Biblical Narrative', in L.J. de Regt, J. de Waard, and J.P. Fokkleman (eds.), *Literary Structure and Rhetorical Strategies in the Hebrew Bible* (Winona Lake, IN: Eisenbrauns, 1996), pp. 3-13 (13).

2.6 Conclusion

By way of concluding this lengthy discussion, it seems best to attempt to re-outline the interpretive steps to be taken. As was mentioned above, a transformational-formational hearing brings to the foreground the affective dimension of interpretation, described above as encounter and embodiment. That such strategies background exegesis and explanation[194] should not be understood as a denigration of their importance; in a very real sense, it means that these important activities are *foundational* to a Pentecostal interpretive strategy. Scholarly, careful exegesis of the text will always serve as the initiation point in the Pentecostal interpretive process.

Thus, the initial stage of this analysis of Jeremiah's Confessions will still require an attentive hearing of the text itself. Specifically, this hearing will work to hear each confession as it is written,[195] pay close attention to the rhetorical significance of the Confessions' affective language and structures, and analyze their role in 'characterizing' the prophet Jeremiah and, by extension, the ideal hearer. It will also be vital to consider the Confessions of Jeremiah as a unit within the book of Jeremiah, listening for both their echoes of each other and their reverberations throughout the book.

Thus, a Pentecostal hearing of Jeremiah's Confessions, specially attuned to the affective dimensions of the texts, promises to yield intriguing interpretive and theological results. In a unique way, the emotive language of the Confessions serves to express the inexpressible; that is, by the very act of giving voice to Jeremiah's almost inarticulate and primitive emotions, the text offers a pragmatic structure for their expression. Stated in literary terms, the promised result seems to be that the affective profile of Jeremiah provided in the Confessions connects directly to the profile of the implied hearer. We are invited to hear *with* Jeremiah even more than we are asked to read *about* Jeremiah. In more explicitly theological terms, it seems that the Confessions of Jeremiah invite the reader literally to become the prophet, experiencing the dread of coming judgment and disappointment of betrayal brought by the unyielding, almighty Spirit-Word of God as an integral part of the process of receiving words of hope.

---

[194] Understood here as exploring what the text 'meant' and what it 'means'.

[195] Rather than as we wish it were written … or rearranged … or reconstructed. The focus will be on the canonical form of the passages.

The ultimate goal of Pentecostal hermeneutics is to be obedient to Scripture, which necessitates first hearing the text in both its cognitive and affective dimensions. This full-orbed experience of the text is ultimately enabled through the working of the Spirit in the life of the hearer. A successful Pentecostal hearing of Scripture will lead to an experience of the glorious overpowering presence of God in such a way that when we return to our daily lives, we will be forced to confess like Jeremiah, 'Your Word was in me …'

3

HEARING THE PROPHECIES IN JEREMIAH 1-10

3.1 Introduction

The conclusion of the previous chapter outlined a series of three important interpretive steps to be taken in this exploration of the Confessions: 1) listen closely to the Confessions' affective language; 2) analyze the rhetoric's impact on the literary characterization of the prophet,[1] then 3) discern the affective profile of the prophetic figure who serves as the text's ideal/first hearer. In brief, we first hear the Confessions through the book of Jeremiah (especially their context of Jeremiah 1-20) in order that we may be enabled to hear the book through the Confessions.

Immediately, we encounter a challenge. If we are to follow the kind of sequential affective reading process that Fish has described[2] to understand the Confession texts, we must first say something about Jeremiah 1-10 as an affective groundwork for our hearing of Jer. 11-20. The affective aspects of texts are, ultimately, elements of *response*. In a sense, if these Confession texts were the very first words heard in the book of Jeremiah, they could not be so understood, and an affective hearing would be extremely difficult if not impossible. To be understood as the figural prophet's 'response' to the word of

---

[1] 'Rhetorical critics have generally been content to look at how Jeremiah might have affected his audience without asking also how the prophet and his message were affected.' Ellen Davis Lewin, 'Arguing for Authority: A Rhetorical Study of Jeremiah 1.4-19 and 20.7-18', *JSOT* 10.32 (1985), pp. 105-19 (106).

[2] See above ch. 2, section 2.5.3.

YHWH, the Confessions must necessarily be preceded by actual word/s of YHWH. Otherwise, these texts become context-less and virtually un-hearable.

Therefore, though in an appropriately abbreviated fashion, the present chapter will concern itself first with a review of the rhetorical structure of Jeremiah 1-10, highlighting the presence of affective tensions that empathetically 'tune the ear' to receive the prophetic words of complaint, distress, and even anger. The next chapter will then turn attention to a careful and extended hearing of the Confession texts in Jeremiah 11-12, demonstrating the affective cohesion of message and messenger in the book of Jeremiah and preparing the way for a careful 're-hearing' of the Confessions.[3]

3.2 Jeremiah 1-10

3.2.1 Overview

It is important to note from the outset that an affective hearing of the Confessions decenters many of the ongoing debates. Vast amounts of interpretive energy have been expended on determining who (and who is not) speaking while relatively little attention has been paid to the tone of what is said.[4] Furthermore, interpretive interests in particular sections of the book of Jeremiah, especially the Confessions, have almost inadvertently biased approaches to other sections of the book. Biddle, whose analysis can be at points unnecessarily stringent, is assuredly right that this interweaving of prose narrative, prophetic prayer, and divine response is already present

---

[3] The first section of ch. 5.

[4] One of the best examples of this debate is found in Mark Biddle's strenuous critique of Timothy Polk's work on the 'prophetic persona'. At several key points in his second chapter, Biddle critically engages Polk's thesis which 'seems to be that, since the tradition identifies the prophet Jeremiah as the human agent of all speech contained in the book, every first person specimen involves, to some degree or on some level, the prophetic persona. Can the integrity of distinct voices survive such an interpretive program?' Mark E. Biddle, *Polyphony and Symphony in Prophetic Literature: Reading Jeremiah 7-20* (SOTI 2; Macon, GA: Mercer University Press, 1996), p. 21, n. 11.

Later in his analysis of Jer. 13.5-7, Biddle openly admits that Polk's reading of the text as both prophetic and divine speech *is* faithful to the text, though he remains insistent that Polk misconstrues it because the text is not explicitly attributed to Jeremiah. Biddle, *Polyphony and Symphony*, p. 37.

before Jeremiah 11, creating a complicated dialogical pattern. [5] What we are searching for in the following analysis is a '"red thread" running through the book with its central theological thoughts'. [6]

Below is offered a multi-layered summary of the rhetorical structure and unity of chs. 1-10 with a focus on how this section establishes a rhetorical-theological foundation for the Confession texts in chs. 11-20. The use of an affective model of hearing texts enables the consideration of the harmonious possibilities of what, on the surface, appear to be radically diverse interpretive strategies.

Mark Biddle's explorations of the presence of polyphony in Jeremiah 7-20 provide some very helpful initial insights into our understanding of this section's literary and rhetorical structure. Biddle begins his work with an important preliminary caution. Hearers of a prophetic text must be aware that the implied author of *any* text may actually use different voices. Careful hearers must avoid, on the synchronic side of their analysis, the pitfall of confusing persona and implied author,[7] and, on the diachronic side, the automatic equation of multiple voices with multiple historical authors and/or redactors.[8]

Biddle argues that the final form of the book of Jeremiah is best described as an open forum. In it 'one hears various Jeremiahs … the indignant prophet, the plaintive sufferer, the hopeful visionary'. One also hears 'various YHWHs, various incarnations of the people, various personifications of Jerusalem, and various incarnations of the postexilic worshiping community'.[9] Thus, Biddle perceives the book as an extended dialogue, which he seeks to construe in a way that enlightens structural, compositional, and theological questions

---

[5] 'Jeremiah 7-10 shares several features with the collections constitutive of 11-20, including a body of "lament" materials which function analogously to the confessions of 11-20.' Biddle, *Polyphony and Symphony*, pp. 4-5.

[6] Such an approach should not be taken as a claim that the book is a 'seamless unity. It [clearly] offers a great variety of thoughts, styles, and genres.' Joep Dubbink, 'Getting Closer to Jeremiah: The Word of YHWH and the Literary-Theological Person of the Prophet', in Martin Kessler (ed.), *Reading the Book of Jeremiah: The Search for Coherence* (Winona Lake, IN: Eisenbrauns, 2004), pp. 25-32 (25).

[7] An implied author could potentially use multiple literary personae. Biddle comments: 'Both classical historical-critical and new literary-critical approaches exhibit a methodological tendency to homogenize voices, to treat poetry somewhat one-dimensionally, and to overlook nuances of voice and characterization'. Biddle, *Polyphony and Symphony*, p. 5.

[8] Biddle, *Polyphony and Symphony*, p. 6.

[9] Biddle, *Polyphony and Symphony*, p. 7.

related to this text.[10] In this understanding of the book, a dialogical 'voice' is more than a grammatical category[11] or a metaphor or simile. A voice is a *speaking subject* who participates in dialogue with other voices.[12]

The major difficulty with Biddle's proposal is his refusal to allow for the possibility of multiple personas being used simultaneously, especially since there is nothing inherent to Biddle's polyphonic analysis that warrants this prohibition.[13] While the very nature of Jeremiah's response to the prophetic call (Jer. 1.6) puts the reader on notice regarding the basic dialogical pattern of the prophetic word in Jeremiah, it seems very arbitrary and a little bit illogical to assume, for example, that a prophetic voice that speaks on behalf of the people cannot also simultaneously speak as one of the people[14] or that prophetic words of divine anger and hurt could not resonate with similar feelings that appear quite natural to the literary presentation of the prophetic figure.

Louis Stulman seems to have come closest to articulating concisely a coherent literary-theological structure for the present MT book of Jeremiah; he makes his case based on four key points that are vital to our present exploration. First, Stulman assumes the intentional presence of an identifiable literary structure and an overarching theological message; he picturesquely describes this macrostructure as 'a symbolic tapestry of meanings with narrative seams'. Second, this literary and theological intentionality makes it natural to

---

[10] Biddle, *Polyphony and Symphony*, p. 11.

[11] I.e. a shift from 3rd person plural to 2nd person singular.

[12] In some places in the book of Jeremiah (e.g. Jer. 4.14-21), Jerusalem has been given 'literary independence. She is no longer simply the object of discussion but a subjective participant in dialogue with other participants.' Biddle, *Polyphony and Symphony*, p. 11.

[13] Biddle's insistence on this point is undergirded by a largely extra-textual commitment to the importance of acknowledgement that 'some voices in Jeremiah are so distinct that they must reflect distinct social and historical settings'. Biddle thinks that, because the 'author's or redactor's dilemma, ideology, politics, or theology' leaves such an indelible mark on the text, it is 'entirely valid for exegesis to employ historical-critical tools capable of analyzing this aspect of characterization and voicing'. Biddle, *Polyphony and Symphony*, pp. 6-7. I would only say that proving an exegetical process' *validity* is not the same thing as proving its *necessity* or its *benefit*.

[14] At the end of the day, it is simply incontrovertible that a key to the literary presentation of the figure of Jeremiah is his presumed existence as a citizen of Jerusalem, facing the threat of invasion and destruction.

assume the presence of large macro-units that give the book its architecture. Third, Stulman insightfully identifies the so-called 'prose sermons' as an important set of these structural pillars. They serve the important function of introducing 'equilibrium and symmetry into a wild world of poetry that is laden with incongruence and dissymmetry'.[15] With these interpretive principles in place, Stulman then identifies the book of Jeremiah as a 'two-part drama that maps out the death and dismantling of a national-cultic symbol system and piety in preparation for stunning new theological and social structures arising from the ruins of exile'.[16]

Within this structure, Stulman notes four principal configurations that give the book its unity: (1) reimagination of a community who finds its entire 'symbolic world' reduced to ruin; (2) renewed confession of God's sovereignty, demonstrated in the defeat of evil and the inauguration of a just reign; (3) rejuvenated adherence to a book around with the community is gathered/formed; and (4) two alternative theodicies.[17]

Finally, Stulman points out that the prophetic *persona* is irreducibly connected to the key motif of dismantling and rebuilding. The text of the book works hard to delineate this interconnection between Jeremiah's life and the fortunes of the nation of Judah;[18] within the symbolic world of the book, Jeremiah is 'an archetypal figure who stands between two worlds'.[19]

Stulman, then, would suggest the following macrostructure for Jeremiah 1-10:

Jeremiah 1 (prose): Introduction and call of the prophet Jeremiah[20]

---

[15] One wonders if Stulman could have substituted instead the terms 'feeling' and 'emotion' here.

[16] 'The present shape of the text ... bears witness to a God who "shatters and overthrows" *only* to "[re]build and plant"'. Louis J. Stulman, *Order Amid Chaos: Jeremiah as Symbolic Tapestry* (BibSem 57; Sheffield: Sheffield Academic Press, 1998), pp. 17-20, italics original.

[17] One is 'coherent and retributive'; the other 'is counter-coherent and replete with ambiguity'. Stulman, *Order Amid Chaos*, pp. 19-20.

[18] 'Both prophet and nation descend into utter hopelessness and desolation ... and emerge as wounded survivors.' Stulman, *Order Amid Chaos*, p. 21.

[19] Stulman, *Order Amid Chaos*, p. 21. See also Louis J. Stulman, 'Jeremiah the Prophet: Astride Two Worlds', in Martin Kessler (ed.), *Reading the Book of Jeremiah: A Search for Coherence* (Winona Lake, IN: Eisenbrauns, 2004), pp. 41-66.

[20] The actual call narrative (vv. 4-10) is poetic.

Jeremiah 2-6 (poetry): Indictment of Judah/Defense of YHWH[21]

Jeremiah 7 (prose sermon): Symbolic destruction of the Jerusalem Temple as a symbol of divine favor and national security[22]

Jeremiah 8-10 (poetry): Enactment of judgment on Judah for her sins[23]

Within this framework, especially Jer. 7.1-15 serves as both a response to Jeremiah 2-6[24] and as an anticipation of Jeremiah 8-10. The Temple Sermon then pulls together and, in a way, epitomizes the surrounding poetry's depiction of Judah as a wayward, rebellious people engaged in wrong worship and destined only for death.[25]

Another important and refreshing perspective on these chapters is offered by Joe Henderson, who questions the predominance of what he calls the 'archaeological approach' to interpreting the Jeremianic poetry.[26] For Henderson, the archaeological approach is based on faulty discernment of the true nature of prophetic texts, treating them as collections of historical documents and therefore not giving them their due as true literary creations.[27] This approach is undergirded by three virtually-unquestioned assumptions: 1) the

---

[21] Stulman notes that 'as the indictments develop ... they become more scathing and passionate'. Stulman, *Order Amid Chaos*, p. 39.

[22] 'The picture emerging from this prose "commentary" is that of Judah using the temple *as a sanctuary from the devastating indictment pronounced in chs. 2-6*'. Stulman, *Order Amid Chaos*, p. 40, italics original.

[23] There is, Stulman notes, a 'panic-stricken topos for Jeremiah 8-10 ... [as] death draws closer, the poetry becomes more jumbled and the voices more blurred. With Yahweh and Jeremiah, Judah is not a grief-stricken participant in the dialog (see, e.g. Jer. 8.14-17) ... the voices of fear, pain, and profound sadness converge with force at the certain prospect of Judah's downfall'. Stulman, *Order Amid Chaos*, p. 42.

[24] 'In the sermon we discover that the confidence and smugness exuded by Judah ... derives in part from its temple ideology.' Stulman, *Order Amid Chaos*, p. 40.

[25] Stulman, *Order Amid Chaos*, p. 42.

[26] In such an 'archaeological' approach, the poetic sections of Jeremiah 1-10 are 'combed through for reliable evidence from the time of the prophet'. Such a reconstruction is considered 'an indispensable framework for interpretation because interpreting the poetry means explaining each piece of poetry in relation to its origin in the historical ministry and message of the prophet'. Joe Henderson, 'Jeremiah 2-10 as a Unified Literary Composition: Evidence of Dramatic Portrayal and Narrative Progression', in John Goldingay (ed.), *Uprooting and Planting: Essays on Jeremiah for Leslie Allen* (LHB/OTS 459; New York: T and T Clark, 2007), pp. 116-52 (116).

[27] Henderson, 'Jeremiah 2-10', p. 117.

authenticity of the poetic form to the historical prophet, 2) the messenger format as the format of all the poetic speeches,[28] and 3) that chs. 2-10 are simply the collection of those speeches in no particular and/or meaningful order.[29] The supposed 'unity' of the prophetic collections is 'about the same degree and kind of unity as marbles collected in a bag because most of them are the same color'.[30]

For Henderson, each of these assumptions is highly problematic. The assumption that poetic speech is the only authentic prophetic speech means that the poetic sections of the book of Jeremiah are valued for 'what it happens to *be*tray about its origins' rather than for what it 'was created to *por*tray for its readers'.[31] The second assumption causes exegetes to ignore the fact that many of the poetic speeches in Jeremiah are highly dramatic *dialogues* between the prophet and YHWH, where both partners have independent voices.[32] Henderson therefore disagrees with the assumption that the collection of poetry in chs. 2-10 shows no order, cogently arguing instead for an understanding of these chapters as a 'cohesive literary composition unified by a temporal progression'.[33]

This renewed focus on the dramatic nature of the poetry means for Henderson that the reader should consider these speeches as a representative of what *would* have been said in those circumstances; the book clearly trusts the competent reader to infer situation and speaker from the text.[34] Such a perspective should not be taken to mean that Henderson finds it impossible that the historical Jeremiah actually *performed* these speeches for real people, but it does most certainly mean that the operative setting of the poetry is not the life of the historical Jeremiah but 'a dramatic situation in the life of Yahweh and his bride'.[35]

---

[28] E.g. the poetry represents YHWH's words in the mouth of Jeremiah.
[29] Thus, the literary structure of Jeremiah 2-10 is 'of little interpretive value'. Henderson, 'Jeremiah 2-10', p. 117.
[30] Henderson, 'Jeremiah 2-10', p. 138.
[31] Henderson, 'Jeremiah 2-10', p. 117, italics original.
[32] E.g. the 'dialogical' nature of the poetry that Biddle analyzes.
[33] Henderson, 'Jeremiah 2-10', p. 117.
[34] Henderson, 'Jeremiah 2-10', p. 124.
[35] Henderson, 'Jeremiah 2-10', p. 128.

The typical approach to discerning unity and structure in the poetic material followed by, for example, Holladay and Lundbom[36] is to discover the intricate network of *inclusios,* chiasms, and other rhetorical devices that stitch these once disparate texts together. Henderson argues the very intricacy of the proposed structural devices 'raises doubts about whether readers or hearers could have been expected to perceive or appreciate them'.[37]

For example, Henderson points out that the Hebrew roots הלך and אכל are found in crucial positions in 2.1-3 and 10.23-25, an *inclusio* that is ignored by Holladay and Lundbom.[38] However, the claim that this *inclusio* serves a structural purpose is supported by a much stronger argument for connecting the passages in terms of their temporal settings. The images at the beginning of ch. 2 related to the Israelite exodus while the speeches at the end of ch. 10 are clearly spoken from the exilic time period. Thus, Jer. 2.2-3 and 10.23-25 'depict two contrasting moments in Israel's history,'[39] and the observation of the verbal *inclusio* in chs. 2 and 10 is only meaningful if 'the whole [intervening] nine chapters are unified by a temporal progression'.[40]

Working, then, from the idea that chs. 2 and 10 are 'the opening and closing scenes of a story',[41] Henderson proposes a tripartite 'story of Israel' being retold in Jeremiah 2-10:

Jeremiah 2-3: Israel's history of idolatrous infidelity from entering the land until the exile of Samaria

Jeremiah 4-9: Judah's refusal to repent after Samaria's destruction, resulting in Jerusalem's own fall

---

[36] E.g. William L. Holladay, *The Architecture of Jeremiah 1-20* (Lewisburg, NJ: Bucknell University Press, 1976), and Jack R. Lundbom, *Jeremiah: A Study in Ancient Hebrew Rhetoric.*

[37] In effect, these approaches 'do not go much beyond defining units and noting parallel units … It may be a solid observation that unit A' in ch. 6 has verbal and formal similarities with unit A in ch. 4, but it is not clear how this observation adds to the reader's understanding or experience of these passages.' Henderson, 'Jeremiah 2-10', p. 137.

[38] 'Neither Holladay nor Lundbom make much of this *inclusio.*' Henderson, 'Jeremiah 2-10', p. 138.

[39] There is also an implicit comparsion. 'In the time of the exile as in the time of the exodus, Israel finds itself without land, king, or temple, wholly dependent upon Yahweh for protection and guidance.' Henderson, 'Jeremiah 2-10', p. 139.

[40] Henderson, 'Jeremiah 2-10', p. 139.

[41] Henderson, 'Jeremiah 2-10', p. 139.

Jeremiah 10: Israel's renewed reliance upon YHWH after the Exile

Following these suggestions by Stulman and Henderson, my approach to the rhetorical analysis of Jeremiah 1-10 will assume both its dialogical and its narratological nature. To put it more simply: Jeremiah 1-10 is a dialogue between prophet, people, and YHWH about the people's own history with YHWH. In some sense, this model subsumes the predicting of Jerusalem's destruction within a larger category of 'retelling' Israel's story in a way that legitimates that coming destruction. With that understanding of the structure in mind, we are better sensitized to the affective parameters within which such a text is bound to operate. We have before us a text meant to simultaneously evoke both a sense of impending doom and a sense of inescapable guilt/responsibility.

3.2.2 Rhetorical Structure and Affective Movement

That the text under consideration here is largely poetic demands that we acknowledge such speech is 'intentionally crafted';[42] poetic form, diction, and techniques are used for the achievement of specific effects.[43] Poetry is thus *reader*-oriented rather than *author*-oriented, 'more concerned with imitation or representation in the imagination of the audience'.[44] Those concerns, like the poetic form, are predominant here. Since the following analysis is meant only as a preparation for a close hearing of the Confessions, remarks and analysis will be necessarily brief. It seems best to focus on a series of short texts that serve as crucial waypoints in this poetic re-imagination of Israel and Judah's idolatrous history and coming judgment. For purposes of

---

[42] I.e. it is 'artificial rather than naturally occurring'. Henderson, 'Jeremiah 2-10', p. 118.

[43] Henderson, 'Jeremiah 2-10', p. 118.

[44] Henderson points out that the fact poetry has 'been artfully contrived to move an audience or to create an impression' would render it 'inadmissible' as evidence in a modern court of law. By those evidentiary standards, a poetic rendition of an event would be an 'unreliable witness to the mind of the author or the historical event that lies behind it'. However, when poetry *does* deal with a historical event or personal experience, it makes it so that the events/experiences 'no longer lie behind the work to be uncovered by researchers; instead they are projected in front of the work to be experienced by the audience'. Henderson, 'Jeremiah 2-10', p. 119.

brevity, I have chosen to comment first on the following passages: Jer. 1.4-10; 2.2-9; 7.1-7; 10.17-25.

3.2.2.1 Jeremiah 1.4-10: Jeremiah as Called Yet Reluctant

Clearly, the key element of a prophetic call narrative is the prophet's 'setting apart'.[45] By far, the most detailed example of the pattern is the call of the prophet in Ezekiel 1-3,[46] but Jeremiah's call stands out from the typical pattern in three ways. First, Jeremiah is the only Israelite prophet called as a prophet to 'the nations' (נּוֹיִם) [see Jer. 1.5]. Avioz believes that Jeremiah's title served as a reminder that YHWH is not simply the God of Israel but the God of *all* nations.[47] The moniker could also be taken as a not-so-subtle commentary on Judah's spiritual condition and the coming judgment; Judah's love of idols made her just another of the pagan 'nations' and left her subject to YHWH's wrath and judgment.

The second unique matter of Jeremiah's calling is that he is the only prophet chosen before birth, a way of emphasizing the uniqueness of YHWH's choice of Jeremiah. Again, Avioz points out that such language was familiar in the ANE, used as a means of legitimation and authority, especially for rulers.[48] However, here, this chosen language rather serves to highlight Jeremiah's *displeasure* at being so 'chosen'.

Finally, Avioz notes that Jeremiah's call is replete with verbs of mission (vv. 5, 7): 'I knew you' (יְדַעְתִּיךָ), 'I sanctified you' (הִקְדַּשְׁתִּיךָ), 'I appointed you' (נְתַתִּיךָ), 'I am sending you' (אֶשְׁלָחֶךָ). While Avioz is

---

[45] E.g. their 'appointment to the role of prophet and imposing the divine mission upon him or her'. For the prophet, it is a 'constitutive experience'. Michael Avioz, *'I Sat Alone': Jeremiah Among the Prophets* (Piscataway, NJ: Gorgias Press, 2009), p. 15.

[46] Avioz delineates the basic literary pattern.
– God's sudden personal revelation
– God's initiation of a conversation (usually with a description of distress)
– God's appointment to a mission (usually indicated by the word 'send')
– The prophet's refusal of or anxiety about the mission. Importantly, 'God allows the prophets to express words of reservation'.
– God's assurance of continued presence and help
– A miraculous sign is given to the appointed prophet 'in order to remove all doubt from his or her mind'
Avioz, *'I Sat Alone'*, p. 16. See also Norman Habel, 'The Form and Significance of the Call Narratives', *ZAW* 77.3 (1965), pp. 297-323.

[47] Avioz, *'I Sat Alone'*, p. 19.

[48] Avioz, *'I Sat Alone'*, p. 19.

certainly correct that this plethora of authorization terms would serve to counter-act the claims of the very active false prophets,[49] it should also be seen as serving in some way as a breaking down of the prophet's own resistance to God's call. As Lewin says:

> In the clash (vv. 6-7) and reconciliation (v. 8) of the prophet's 'I' with God's, it becomes clear that Jeremiah is more than a passive vehicle for a one-way transmittal from heaven to earth; his own questioning, challenging ego is part of his qualification for the mediatorial office.[50]

In a book that will be so heavily focused on the destructive-creative force of YHWH's words, it is vital that we keep in mind that the first words from the prophet's mouth are *emotional* words of objection and protest: 'Ah, Lord God, I cannot speak for I am a youth!' (Jer. 1.6). In fact, these words serve to *interrupt* the divine commissioning. This serves several important purposes in preparing to understand the type of interpretive work that lies ahead. First, the Word of YHWH will be heard in dialogue. Second, the literary figure of the prophet is placed 'front and center';[51] Jeremiah is a prophet who speaks *to* God as much as *for* God. Third, the hearer is put into a position of judging the prophet's speaking ability;[52] in effect, the prophet's disclaimer nudges the hearer toward a careful evaluation of the power of the prophetic rhetoric. At some level, the prophet's *reluctance* to prophesy seems to be key to the authenticity of the prophetic calling.[53]

The tension apparent between the prophet and YHWH is also seen within the prophetic word itself. Again, we have an intense series

---

[49] William McKane points out: 'The call narrative is retrospective rather than proleptic … it is an estimate of him after he has run his course. It affirms that nothwithstanding the opposition which he aroused, the hostility which he awakened, and the rejection which he suffered, he was indeed a prophet called by Yahweh.' William McKane, *A Critical and Exegetical Commentary on Jeremiah: Jeremiah I-XXV* (ICC; Edinburgh: T and T Clark, 1986), p. 14.

[50] Lewin, 'Arguing for Authority', p. 107.

[51] I disagree with Brueggemann's claim that 'interpretive interest is immediately shifted away from the person of the prophet toward the prophetic text'. Brueggemann, *Commentary on Jeremiah*, p. 25.

[52] Jeremiah protests his 'lack of fitness' based on 'inexperience and lack of rhetorical expertise … He is young and without a commanding presence and authority, and he has had no practice in the skills of public speaking.' McKane, *Jeremiah*, p. 7.

[53] Carroll, *Jeremiah*, p. 98.

of verbs describing the functional power of the word: 'pluck up' (לִנְתוֹשׁ), 'pull down' (לִנְתוֹץ), 'destroy' (וּלְהַאֲבִיד), 'throw down' (לַהֲרוֹס), 'build' (לִבְנוֹת), and 'plant' (לִנְטוֹעַ). While the first four verbs in the sequence describe negative actions, the final two are positive. This statement thus simultaneously asserts that 'no historical structure, political policy, or defense scheme can secure a community against Yahweh' and that 'God can work newness [and] create historical possibilities *ex nihilo*'.[54] Carroll points out that this is the *only* time in the entire book where the human prophet is the subject; in every other occurrence, it is *YHWH* who destroys or builds; thus, in effect, the prophet is hereby elevated to act *as YHWH* in international affairs.[55] The important relationship of these tensions is clear when one remembers that YHWH has placed this word 'in Jeremiah's mouth' (Jer. 1.9).

If we are to take the call narrative seriously as a hermeneutical key to the book, then we must acknowledge not just the presence of affective language but the structuring role of that language within this crucial text. Furthermore, we have demonstrated that the affective language is contradictory or, better yet, tensive. The prophet both resists and is conquered by the divine call; the prophetic word both destroys and rebuilds.[56] It would seem that many of the accusations related to the jumbled nature of the book, its lack of coherence, and the resultant difficulties in achieving an articulate interpretation are simply reflections of a lack of proper attention to this fundamental tension. The divine word presents a 'balance which [the prophet] will have to maintain, a tug of war which he will have to endure'.[57] The book of Jeremiah is not disorganized as much as it is organized for affective impact more than for rational argument.

---

[54] Brueggemann, *Commentary on Jeremiah*, p. 25.

[55] Carroll, *Jeremiah*, pp. 95-96.

[56] In the vision cycle at the end of ch. 1, we also learn that the prophet will face enormous opposition but will be as impervious as a 'bronze wall' (Jer. 1.18-19). McKane comments: 'If the verse is to be regarded as proleptic in relation to a prophetic activity which is about to commence … what is indicated [so Weiser] is less a temporal order of operations than a perception that the true prophet will never secure release from a tension between warning and promise'. McKane, *Jeremiah*, p. 11.

[57] McKane, *Jeremiah*, p. 11.

3.2.2.2 Jeremiah 2.2-9: YHWH as Saddened yet Angered

We now turn to the opening oracles of the book of Jeremiah. Holladay has described Jer. 2.2-3 as the 'seed oracle' of Jeremiah 1-20.[58] Verses 2-3a function as a summative review of Israelite history, providing the basis for the coming oracles.[59] It is a generalized denouncement of the nation for rejecting YHWH to serve false idols. Since this is an appropriate depiction of 'any period of Israelite history',[60] it is an ideal introduction not only to Jeremiah 1-10 but to the entire book.

The terminology here is covenantal/marital language. 'devotion' (חֶסֶד), 'love' (אַהֲבָה),[61] 'following' (לֶכְתֵּךְ). Thus, the opening images of this oracle are a *positive,* even warm, image. Leslie Allen remarks: 'In another context Yahweh's recollection could have the flavor of a proclamation of salvation'.[62] However, here 'it refers to a nostalgic appreciation of a past memory'.[63] The imagery is that of a young bride (Israel), loyally following her husband (YHWH). The pursuant descriptions of false worship and turning away from YHWH then, derive their rhetorical power from the contrast here established 'between the idyllic origins of the community and its recent experience. The honeymoon was wonderful but the marriage – a complete failure!'[64]

In the second half of this oracle (v. 3), we are given sacrificial imagery. In fact, the word קֹדֶשׁ is placed first for emphasis. The shift in metaphor follows the narrative shift from life in the wilderness to

---

[58] 'The words of 2.2 are matched systematically, in a kind of chiastic fashion, with what turn out to be the two halves of the harlotry cycle ... so as to map out the outlines of each half'. Holladay, *Architecture,* p. 32.

[59] Brueggemann, *Commentary on Jeremiah,* p. 32.

[60] Carroll, *Jeremiah,* p. 117.

[61] אַהֲבָה and חֶסֶד are 'virtual synonyms'. Connecting it with a marriage metaphor 'shows indebtedness ... to Hosea, with the one qualification that Hosea speaks only about Yahweh's love for Israel, not Israel's love for Yahweh'. Lundbom, *Jeremiah 1-20,* p. 252.

[62] 'With the sense "I remember and will act accordingly by blessing or saving you" (cf. Ps. 105.42; 132.1).' Leslie C. Allen, *Jeremiah* (OTL; Louisville, KY: Westminster/John Knox Press, 2008), p. 34. Lundbom uses the term 'romanticizing'. Lundbom, *Jeremiah 1-20,* p. 252.

[63] Allen, *Jeremiah,* p. 34.

[64] Carroll, *Jeremiah,* p. 119. McKane concurs that we are presented the contrast 'of a perfect beginning and a failure to maintain that relationship characterized by simplicity and wholeness'. McKane, *Jeremiah,* p. 28.

settlement in the Promised Land.[65] Israel's holiness derives from her set-apartness, her belonging to YHWH. This was primarily established in the Exodus (Exod. 19.4-6; Deut. 7.6, 14.2, 21b; 26.19), but its roots lie even earlier in YHWH's choosing of Abraham, Isaac, and Jacob.[66] In a general sense, the picture of Israel as the firstfruits of a harvest indicates Israel's status as the best of YHWH's produce.[67] However, just as the firstfruits offering was only to be consumed by the priests,[68] so the people of Israel are presented here as being untouchable (i.e., secure in YHWH's protection) during those early days of the occupation. Clearly, that protected status has now been revoked. These remarks also, very subtly, draw parallels between the nation and the prophet Jeremiah, who is likewise young and yet set apart and protected.[69] These similarities of initial status provide the stage on which the promised conflict between the nation and the prophet will develop. Jeremiah's continued faithfulness to YHWH versus the nation's pandemic unfaithfulness.

This glowing recollection of past faithfulness disappears in the opening lines of the second oracle (vv. 5-9).[70] The banal historical recital becomes a condemnation as the 'audience is drawn into an objective, relatively nonthreatening discussion, only to be trapped into finding themselves condemned'.[71] The oracle is clearly structured as a chiasm with references to past and present generations in vv. 5 and 9 and new and old rhetorical questions in vv. 6-8.[72] Verse 7 then becomes central with its description of entry into the Promised Land the people's subsequent defilement of it.

Two things are important to notice about this accusation. First, the accusation of Israel's infidelity is framed as a question rather than a declaration. The language is from a formal divorce proceeding.[73]

---

[65] Lundbom, *Jeremiah 1-20*, p. 253.

[66] Lundbom, *Jeremiah 1-20*, p. 253.

[67] Deuteronomy 33.21; Amos 6.6. Carroll, *Jeremiah*, p. 120.

[68] Numbers 18.12-13.

[69] Carroll, *Jeremiah*, p. 121.

[70] 'Like the prior oracle in 2.2b-3, these verses are framed by two messenger formulas.' Lundbom, *Jeremiah 1-20*, p. 257.

[71] This is reminiscent of rhetorical effect of Nathan's parable to David in 2 Sam. 12.1-7. Allen, *Jeremiah*, p. 40.

[72] See Carroll, *Jeremiah*, pp. 122-23.

[73] Deuteronomy 24.1. Brueggemann, *Commentary on Jeremiah*, p. 34; Fretheim, *Jeremiah* (SHBC; Macon, GA: Smyth and Helwys, 2002), p. 64.

The assertion is that there is no fault with YHWH; therefore, the entire blame must be placed on Israel.[74] Fretheim comments: 'Given God's exemplary participation as a spouse, it is a mystery even to God why Israel would run after other gods'.[75] In other words, Israel's idolatry is presented here to us in terms of a family quarrel and the 'breakdown of relationship',[76] with all the attendant feelings of anger, betrayal, and wounded love.[77] In that sense, the language is not simply stereotyped legal language but should be treated as a 'real' question. Given Israel's later accusation of YHWH,[78] this may very well be God's invitation to the wayward people to enter into dialogue.[79]

It is important to take a moment, however, to consider the affective impact of this statement. Though it is a legal accusation, the presentation serves to highlight YHWH's position as the jilted husband, one who is both deeply committed to Israel and deeply pained by rejection.[80] In this context, it is important to notice that the term הָלַךְ ('to go after') forms something of a catchword connecting the two oracles together. However, the term's usage in 2.5b (worship of false gods) effectively *inverts* its meaning in 2.2 (full devotion/obedience to YHWH). A term used to describe Israel's *devotion* to YHWH is now used to describe the nation's *rebellion*. Becoming 'worthless', (וַיֶּהְבָּלוּ), then, is not so much an imposed penalty but a place or state of suffering in which the rebellious nation now finds herself.[81]

The rest of the oracle serves to give definition to the people's apostasy in terms of what they had *not* done. Israel's sin was that they had chosen to ignore their 'shaping memory'.[82] Verses 6-7 serve as a

---

[74] Brueggemann, *Commentary on Jeremiah,* p. 34.

[75] Fretheim, *Jeremiah,* p. 64. הֶהְבֵּל is used here as a 'dismissive pun' on the name Ba'al; he is literally called 'the Nothing'. See Allen, *Jeremiah,* p. 40.

[76] Carroll, *Jeremiah,* 123. Furthermore, this is an *ongoing* 'family quarrel'. 'The prophet appears to address all generations of Israel and not just his own generation. There is an indivisibility of responsibility and the hearers have to answer not only "Why did you remove yourselves from me?", but also, "Why did your fathers remove themselves from me?"' McKane, *Jeremiah,* p. 31.

[77] Or 'concern and pained bewilderment'. So McKane, *Jeremiah,* p. 32.

[78] Jeremiah 2.35; 3.5.

[79] Fretheim, *Jeremiah,* p. 64.

[80] Brueggemann has noted: 'The tone of the initial question is like the hurt of a wounded lover'. Brueggemann, *Commentary on Jeremiah,* p. 34.

[81] See McKane, *Jeremiah,* p. 31, following Volz and Rudolph.

[82] Brueggemann, *Commentary on Jeremiah,* p. 35.

recitation of the forgotten creed.[83] The dominant word in this recitation is 'land' (אֶרֶץ), contrasting the threatening territories of Egypt and wilderness with the secure and blessed territory of the Promised Land. A key rhetorical feature is the subtle contemporizing of the 'you' in the passage;[84] the rhetorical effect is to collapse the temporal distance between ancient ancestors and contemporary audience, indicating the present hearers were just as faithless as their forbears and could not escape the coming judgment just by casting blame.[85]

Along with this generational transition, we have a transition in the land's status from the idea of the land as a gift to the land as defiled. The language of defilement and abomination is used to symbolize the people's change of religious allegiance, while the continued use of the expressions 'my country' (אַרְצִי) and 'my property' (נַחֲלָתִי)[86] serve to emphasize YHWH's unbreakable claims as the rightful landowner.[87] It is also curious to note that this recitation of Israel's early days seems to completely ignore the fact the land 'would have been profaned already by the idolatrous practices of the pre-Israelite occupants!'[88] In some sense, this accusatory discourse, then, is a significant 'glossing' of historical reality, a revisionist telling of much more complicated story. Carroll sees this as proof that the 'gravamen' of this accusation is rooted more in its emotional appeal rather than its logical argument.[89]

The second repetition of the phrase 'did not say' points to the consequences of Israel's 'forgetting'.[90] We should note that this is a repetition of the earlier 'unasked question' but here applied to the current generation.[91] This spiritual amnesia has impacted all levels of

---

[83] As in Exod. 34.6-7, which is another story of national apostasy, the 'people's confession' is placed 'in the mouth of God', i.e. presented as God's word to the people rather than the people's (much needed) words to God. Fretheim, *Jeremiah*, 67. It is interesting as well that the question, 'Where is YHWH?' is also a 'response to suffering (cf. Pss. 42, 3, 10; 79.10) but here it is intended to indicate a failure of correct procedure'. Carroll, *Jeremiah*, p. 124.

[84] Matches 2.2, except that now the pronouns are plural.

[85] Fretheim, *Jeremiah*, p. 65.

[86] A term that also reverberates with the concept of family inheritance.

[87] See Lev. 25.23. Allen, *Jeremiah*, p. 41.

[88] Carroll, *Jeremiah*, p. 124.

[89] Carroll, *Jeremiah*, p. 124.

[90] 'This passage suggests that where the story of the land is lost, the loss of the land itself will soon follow'. Brueggemann, *Commentary on Jeremiah*, p. 35.

[91] Following the shift in the usage of 'you' in v. 7. Allen, *Jeremiah*, p. 41.

Israelite society, including the leadership.[92] In fact, the spiritual life of the nation has fallen to such a low tide that the worship of YHWH is indistinguishable from the worship of Ba'al.[93]

The final verse of this oracle makes it a plain accusation. Israel has abandoned Yahweh by going after[94] other gods. In fact, the unfaithfulness is so ingrained that judgment is perceived as lasting for several generations.[95] As Allen picturesquely says, 'Not only their forbears were guilty before God ... they had caught the old bug'.[96]

This brief analysis highlights several key affective shifts. We were prepared by the call narrative to expect the presence of conflicting emotions and are not disappointed to find such shifts occurring here. The note of nostalgia in v. 3 slowly gives way to anger in vv. 5-9, following the concomitant shift from YHWH's 'remembering' to Israel's 'forgetting'.[97] The rhetoric of the text is designed to cause us to both experience and comprehend YHWH's pain and anger. We are made to understand that YHWH has a legal claim, but that claim is expressed in deeply relational terms. This is a bitter divorce, if you will. Also, in the truest sense of the term, there is present here an emotionally logical progression from the beauty and sincerity of initial love the depths of anger at being spurned and rejected.

3.2.2.3 Jeremiah 7.1-7: The People of Judah as Deceitfully Pious

We now move ahead to another key text within Jeremiah 1-10, a passage long-known as the 'Temple Sermon'.[98] Brueggemann calls it 'the clearest and most formidable statement ... of the basic themes of the Jeremiah tradition'. Clearly, the words here could only have been

---

[92] All levels, both civic and religious. See Brueggemann, *Commentary on Jeremiah*, p. 35. Allen points out that the priests 'should have taken the lead in praying a communal lament to Yahweh'; this clear 'failure of leadership to propagate Yahwistic ideals was evidence of an underlying tendency to demote Yahweh in the interests of a rival faith'. Allen, *Jeremiah*, p. 41.

[93] So Rudolph. McKane, *Jeremiah*, p. 33.

[94] This is the third occurrence of הלך and forms an *inclusio* with the same verb in v. 5. Brueggemann, *Commentary on Jeremiah*, p. 35.

[95] Fretheim, *Jeremiah*, p. 41.

[96] Allen, *Jeremiah*, p. 41.

[97] See especially Jer. 2.32.

[98] Though Lundbom considers this name a 'misnomer ... best abandoned'. Lundbom, *Jeremiah 1-20*, p. 457.

considered high treason, given the way they decimated the propagan-distic ideology of the Jerusalem ruling elite.[99]

Lundbom sees this as a collection of three oracles demarcated by inclusios.[100] Carroll discerns four key elements by breaking Lundbom's first oracle into two admonitions: first admonition (vv. 2-4); second admonition (vv. 5-7); invective (vv. 9-11); and threat (vv. 12-14).[101] Perhaps what is most clear is that up through v. 7, the passage is clearly both a warning and a call to repent. The accusations related to current behavior begin in v. 8 and culminate in vv. 13-15 in an announcement of certain punishment for the unhearing Judeans.[102]

As in Jeremiah 2, the opening statement is positive;[103] it presents a hopeful alternative to the coming destruction. Overall, the message of the sermon is that the covenantal lifestyle demanded by YHWH is the condition of continued presence in the land and, by extension, the condition of continued Temple worship (see v. 10).[104] Covenant life is so integral a part of Israel's life that, if it is negated, it is capable of 'nullifying in turn both the temple privilege and the land privilege'.[105]

Verses 3 and 4 articulate the main theme of this proclamation. There are only two options before Judah. Judah may 'amend'[106] their ways or continue to trust in the false security of their errant Temple ideology.[107] The interpretation of this passage really hinges on the

---

[99] Brueggemann, *Commentary on Jeremiah*, p. 77.

[100] 'I will let you dwell in this place …' (vv. 3,7); 'Look/Behold!' (vv. 8, 11); 'My place … in Shiloh/the place … to Shiloh' (vv. 12-14). Lundbom, *Jeremiah 1-20*, p. 458.

[101] Carroll, *Jeremiah*, pp. 207-208.

[102] William L. Holladay, *Jeremiah 1*, p. 238.

[103] Avioz says the phrase 'amend your ways and your doings' is a 'classic call for repentance'. Avioz, *'I Sat Alone'*, p. 22.

[104] Jeremiah 7.3.

[105] Allen, *Jeremiah*, p. 96.

[106] The imperative clause here is 'all-embracing'; Holladay suggests the paraphrase, 'Whatever you do, make it good instead of bad'. Holladay, *Jeremiah 1*, p. 241. Newman and Stine agree based on the fact that 'ways' (דַרְכֵיכֶם) and 'doings' (מַעַלְלֵיכֶם) are equivalent in meaning. Barclay M. Newman and Philip C. Stine, *A Handbook on Jeremiah* (UBS Handbook Series; New York: United Bible Societies, 2003), p. 208. Fretheim calls it an 'instance of merismus' and compares it to Jer. 18.11; 26.13. See Fretheim, *Jeremiah*, p. 133.

[107] Brueggemann, *Commentary on Jeremiah*, p. 78.

vocalization of the occurrences of the verb 'dwell' (שׁכן) and the second plural expressions in vv. 3 and 7.[108] The consonantal text permits both the translation, 'I will cause you to dwell'[109] or 'I will dwell with you'.[110] The key here is the ambiguity of the term מקום to refer to *both* the land *and* the Temple.[111] The text offers two interpretive options: the warning could either be, 'Amend your ways and I, Yahweh, will dwell with you (in the Temple),' or, 'Amend your ways and I, Yahweh, will let/cause you to dwell (in the land)'. Each can be argued textually. If we accept *both* readings as essentially correct, then a 'twofold organic relationship between the temple and land' is revealed. 'Land, temple, and people function as a vital triangle, and the sort of people the Judeans should be is the focus with which the oracle begins.'[112] The purposeful ambiguity here reveals that 'both God's presence in the temple and the people's presence in the land are adversely affected by Israel's infidelity'.[113]

This first admonition concludes with a warning against trusting in 'false'[114] words. These words are false precisely because they lull people into a false sense of security as YHWH's 'Chosen People', right or wrong![115] What is shocking is the term that is here defined as a 'false' or 'lying' word (literally): 'The Temple of the Lord *are these*!' As Brueggemann says:

> In one deft move, the prophet has exposed the dysfunctional character of the Jerusalem temple. The temple and its royal liturgy are exposed as tools of social control, which in a time of crisis will not keep their grand promises. The temple is shown to be not an embodiment of transcendence, but simply an arena of social

---

[108] Holladay, *Jeremiah 1*, p. 236.
[109] So MT.
[110] So Volz, Rudolph, and *BHS*. See Carroll, *Jeremiah*, p. 207.
[111] 'The term "place" ... brings with it a host of associations that invite reflection.' Allen, *Jeremiah*, p. 95.
[112] Allen, *Jeremiah*, p. 95.
[113] Fretheim, *Jeremiah*, p. 133.
[114] 'The key word in Jeremiah's proclamation.' Brueggemann, *Jeremiah*, p. 78. In fact, it could be considered a key theme of the entire book, occurring 37 times. Jer. 3.10, 23; 5.2, 31; 6.13; 7.4, 8, 9; 8.8 (2x), 10; 9.2, 4; 10.14; 13.25; 14.14 (2x); 16.19; 20.6; 23.14, 25, 26, 32 (2x); 27.10, 14, 15, 16; 28.15; 29.9, 21, 23, 31; 37.14; 40.16; 43.2 (a false accusation against Jeremiah!), 51.17. See also Thomas W. Overholt, *The Threat of Falsehood: A Study in the Theology of the Book of Jeremiah* (SBT 2.16; London, SCM Press, 1970).
[115] Fretheim, *Commentary on Jeremiah*, p. 133.

manipulation. The poet [delegitimizes] the temple claims of abso-luteness.[116]

The surprising triple repetition of this phrase has caused quite a bit of speculation about its intention. It could possibly reflect the trisagion of Isaiah 6,[117] a magical incantation,[118] or both.[119] The key belief behind this catchy phrase appears to have been that YHWH had irreversibly chosen the Jerusalem Temple as YHWH's personal earthly dwelling, a belief that quickly elided into conceiving the tem-ple as a mere 'fetish'.[120]

Leslie Allen points out that, very much like YHWH's question in 2.5, the words in a different setting, 'could have been meaningful, as when Jacob exclaimed, "This is none other than the house of God, and this is the gate of heaven" (Gen 28.17)'.[121] However, here the phrase is emptied of all religious feeling, for the people are express-ing their faith in *the Temple* rather than in *YHWH*.[122] Jeremiah presents these words[123] as 'mere slogans'[124] to allow his hearers to discern their basic untruth[125] that lived obedience is not a component of true faith.[126]

The second admonition opens with a string of conditional phrases that is essentially a summary of Torah requirements given in reverse order of the Ten Commandments.[127] Surprisingly, even with all the covenant disobedience, the land remains YHWH's land of

---

[116] Brueggemann, *Commentary on Jeremiah*, p. 78.

[117] Holladay, *Jeremiah 1*, p. 242.

[118] Carroll, *Jeremiah*, p. 208.

[119] Holladay's proposal. Holladay, *Jeremiah 1*, p. 242.

[120] Ernest W. Nicholson, *The Book of the Prophet Jeremiah. Chapters 1-25,* (CBC; Cambridge: Cambridge University Press, 1973), p. 77. McKane agrees: 'These are solemn and powerful words; they have a spell-like character ... and they rivet them-selves in the minds of those who recite them or hear them recited'. McKane, *Jere-miah*, p. 161.

[121] Allen, *Jeremiah*, p. 96.

[122] Allen, *Jeremiah*, p. 96.

[123] Proclamations of the false prophets, presumably.

[124] The *reason* these pious words are 'mere slogans' becomes apparent in the accusations of vv. 8-11. Allen, *Jeremiah*, p. 96. These pious words are *made into* slo-gans by the people's lack of covenant obedience in other contexts.

[125] Avioz, *'I Sat Alone'*, p. 24.

[126] Brueggemann, *Commentary on Jeremiah*, p. 78.

[127] Brueggemann, *Commentary on Jeremiah*, p. 79.

promise; the promise has not yet been taken back.[128] The 'place', here meaning *both* the land of Israel *and* the Temple of YHWH, can remain occupied; the covenant can still be renewed and maintained. However, those who persist in unfaithful behavior will *lose* the promise and will be denied participation in its fulfillment.[129] In the end, possession of the land and divine presence in the Temple are dependent upon the people's obedient response to covenant.

It is important to pause again and consider the affective dimensions of this crucial passage, which serves, as Stulman has noted, both to summarize key themes of preceding oracles and point ahead to coming prophetic words.[130] We have traced already the prophet's own reluctant faithfulness and YHWH's deep sadness and anger; here, we direct our attention to the *people's* affective profile and we see 'falsehood' (שֶׁקֶר).[131] Not only does this cast into doubt the veracity of the words the people will speak in the rest of the book, but the pall of skepticism extends to every word they have already spoken.

The alert hearer should already have been expecting this moment, for we heard in ch. 2 the contrast between the people's apparent accusation of YHWH's absence (v. 8) and the obvious gracious provision evident in their bountiful 'garden land' (v. 7). It serves to solidify the case against Israel and Judah. There is and never was any wrong in YHWH; it is the people's own sinful waywardness that has led them to the brink of destruction.

The hearer then is not surprised by the sudden shift in tone in vv. 8-11. In our reading of vv. 3-7, the prophet held forth the possibility of amendment and rescue from coming judgment. Now, however, in vv. 8-11, 'the prophet announces a conclusion and a verdict that suggest the time for amending is past'.[132] The sudden shift is shocking for the list of offenses in vv. 8-11a reveals the exhortations are only hypothetical possibilities; by the time the Temple Sermon is delivered, those possibilities of amendment and restoration are a distant memory. The only possible future is destruction of the Temple and removal from the land.[133] Effectively, the hope of amendment has

---

[128] Fretheim, *Jeremiah*, p. 135.
[129] Fretheim, *Jeremiah*, p. 135.
[130] See above.
[131] This term appears 37x in the book of Jeremiah.
[132] Brueggemann, *Commentary on Jeremiah*, p. 79.
[133] Allen, *Jeremiah*, p. 95.

become *another* 'false word', falsified not by YHWH's betrayal but by the people's own stubborn refusal to change. Again, the text very carefully leads the hearer to the point of *feeling* the sense of doom and betrayal while still understanding the compelling reasons. Avioz is right to recognize how Jeremiah is 'playing on the emotions here'[134] by deconstructing a prized national symbol and its attendant false theology.

3.2.2.4 Jeremiah 10.17-25: The Voice/s of Lament & Distress

We come now to the final section of Jeremiah chs. 1-10, which contains a variety of material: admonition (vv. 17, 22), oracles of judgment (v. 18), lament (vv. 19-21), confession (vv. 23-24), and even a call for vengeance (v. 25).[135] Given this variety of material and the swift movement from descriptions of public calamity to private lament,[136] the structure of the passage has been a matter of speculation and some debate. Lundbom finds a unifying chiasm in vv. 17-22 that centers on v. 20,[137] while Holladay finds unity in a patterned sequence of speakers.[138] In terms of content, the passage clearly addresses the unavoidable reality of exile. Not only does this provide important closure with the opening of the present unit,[139] but also serves to bring the entire first section of the book of Jeremiah to its inevitable close. In broad outline, then, the passage presents to us a judgment speech (vv. 17-18), followed by a lament (vv. 19-20), another

---

[134] Avioz, *'I Sat Alone'*, p. 25.

[135] Lundbom, *Jeremiah 1-20*, pp. 600-601.

[136] E.g. vv. 17-18 are 'public'; vv. 19-20 are 'private'. Brueggemann, *Commentary on Jeremiah*, p. 107.

[137] 'From the land … Look I … land' (vv. 17-18)/ 'My tent … My cords … My tent … My curtains' (v. 20)/'Look … from a land' (v. 22). Lundbom, *Jeremiah 1-20*, pp. 601, 604.

[138] According to Holladay, the cycle is Jeremiah (vv. 17, 21), YHWH (vv. 18, 22), and then the people (vv. 19-20, 23-25). Holladay admits this structure ignores the form-critical problem of v. 22 as an 'audition report' for 'such reports are normally offered by the prophet'. He concludes that placing such words in YHWH's mouth rather than the prophet's is an 'ironic reuse of the form'. Holladay, *Jeremiah 1*, p. 339.

[139] Jeremiah 9.17-22 [16-21]. Allen, *Jeremiah*, p. 130. The verb אָסַף is, Carroll notes, the last word of 9.22 [21] and the first word of 10.17. Carroll, *Jeremiah*, p. 259.

judgment speech that specifies the reason for judgment (vv. 21-22), concluding with a prayer (vv. 23-25).[140]

Clearly, v. 18 is the prophet's address to the personified city, Lady Jerusalem.[141] Much of the exegetical interest in this passage has focused on the best understanding of the *hapax legomenon* כִּנְעָה. While Lundbom is right, it seems, to suggest the basic translation 'bundle',[142] Holladay sees an important potential wordplay here on כְּנַעַן/כְּנַעֲנִי ('Canaan'/'Canaanite') as a symbol of an 'ethic of profit' antagonistic to the 'ethic of covenant'.[143] In fact, the entire address to Lady Jerusalem is characterized by a kind of sarcastic rhetoric. The city is no longer 'enthroned' but 'surrounded',[144] no longer a 'fortress' but 'under siege'.[145] The sarcasm becomes clear when YHWH promises to 'sling out' – literally to 'hurl' violently![146] – the inhabitants of Jerusalem. Holladay labels the final phrase grammatically 'incomprehensible';[147] the sentence has no object, and most literally reads: 'So they will find out'.[148] The attentive hearer would be led to wonder what precisely it is that self-satisfied Judah will discover when YHWH's judgment arrives.[149]

---

[140] Here following Allen's suggestion (against Lundbom) that these verses are an 'oracle of disaster' with the reason provided *first* and the audition report functioning as the actual announcement, as in Jer. 9.19 [18]. Allen, *Jeremiah*, p. 131.

[141] Jeremiah 7.29.

[142] Following Driver, who noted the close relationship to the Arabic *kana'a*, which means 'to be folded in'. Thus, the term refers to 'modest hand luggage'. Lundbom, *Jeremiah 1-20*, pp. 601-602.

[143] The implication of the passage is then, 'Get rid of your lifestyle of profit'. Holladay, *Jeremiah 1*, p. 341.

[144] The verb יָשַׁב is likewise used contemptuously of Egypt in Jer. 46.19. Holladay, *Jeremiah 1*, p. 341.

[145] Cf. Ps. 60.11 [9] for מָצוֹר as 'fortress'. Targum translates 'you who dwell in a strong place' rather than 'You who dwell under siege'. Both meanings are 'nearly the same'. Lundbom, *Jeremiah 1-20*, p. 602.

[146] 'As one slings a stone in a slingshot [see 1 Sam. 25.29]'. Lundbom, *Jeremiah 1-20*, p. 602.

[147] Holladay, *Jeremiah 1*, p. 341.

[148] It is interesting that the NRSV chooses to translate 'so that they shall *feel* it' (italics mine) and the NLT offers the paraphrastic 'at last you will feel my anger'.

[149] Following Lundbom who sees this as intentional ambiguity. 'What we may have is simply a terse ending, a thought intentionally left unfinished ... [so the] audience can then complete [it]'. Lundbom, *Jeremiah 1-20*, p. 602. Likewise, Lalleman speculates that 'the line was possibly left open to make people think'. Hetty Lalleman, *Jeremiah and Lamentations* (TOTC 21; Downers Grove: InterVarsity Press, 2013), p. 130.

Verses 19-20 are clearly a cry of anguish and lament meant to represent a response to the declaration of immutable disaster.[150] However, the complexity here is in identifying the speaker. All commentators are agreed that the speaker here is *not* YHWH, which leaves us the possibility that the speaker is the prophet Jeremiah or the personified city.

Further complicating the question is the presence of וַאֲנִי אָמַרְתִּי ('and/but I said ...') at the beginning of the second line of v. 19 which seems to introduce a *third* speaker. Many scholars choose to deal with this puzzle through textual emendation specifically to counter this impression of a different voice in v. 19b.[151] Seeing this passage as simply the people's response to the announcement of judgment is certainly simple, logical, and (tolerably) compatible with the Hebrew text.[152] Seeing the passage as the prophet speaking for or on behalf of the people, however, is also *not* implausible.[153] And it is this slight shift which 'takes on profound significance for the prophet's identity',[154] a point to which we will return later.

Jerusalem describes her coming distress as a 'break' (שֶׁבֶר) and an 'incurable wound' (נַחְלָה מַכָּתִי).[155] Kalmanofsky finds this complex image of the 'incurable (or infected) wound' distinctly 'able to communicate Israel's degenerative state, as well as God's anger and power,' while still speaking 'to the potential for Israel's

---

[150] Jeremiah 10.19-20 has much in common with Jer. 4.19-20; 8.18-9.1 [8.23]. Carroll, *Jeremiah*, p. 261.

[151] Polk surveys the possibilities. Baumgartner simply deletes it as a gloss. Duhm moves the phrase to the beginning of v. 19 and reads וְאֶשָּׂאֶנּוּ as a *waw*-consecutive rather than a *waw* plus imperfect, rendering the following: 'But as for me, woe is me ... I have said, Surely this is my pain and I *have borne* it'. Volz, whom most commentators follow, makes a similar move but argues the speaker is the *people* rather than the *prophet*. Polk, *Prophetic Persona*, p. 60.

[152] Polk, *Prophetic Persona*, p. 61.

[153] In fact, this seems a much stronger option than Lundbom's reading of the text as the 'prophet ... in dialogue with himself'. Lundbom, *Jeremiah 1-20*, p. 604.

[154] Polk, *Prophetic Persona*, p. 62.

[155] In Jer. 6.6-7, שֶׁבֶר is paired with חֳלִי and addressed to the city of Jerusalem. Polk points out that this motif is picked up later in the so-called 'Book of Consolation' (cf. Jer. 30.12-17) which 'takes up the earlier depictions of Jerusalem as the adulterous woman ... spurned and assaulted by the foes she had once solicited as lovers ... in order now to proclaim judgment upon the lover-foes and to promise healing'. In Jer. 30.12, we see the same parallel between שֶׁבֶר and נַחְלָה מַכָּתֵ; thus, Jer. 30.15 is an *echo* of 'Jerusalem's pained cries' that are exemplified in Jer. 10.19. Polk, *Prophetic Persona,* p. 67.

reformation'.[156] It is both a *wound*, damage inflicted by another's 'attack' upon Jerusalem's 'body', and an *infection*, a manifestation of corruption already present within.[157] However, whether Jerusalem's 'incurable wound' is a manifestation of God's anger, her own corruption, or both, the nation remains 'at God's mercy'.[158] For our present purposes, though, the most important aspect for consideration is the affective impact of this image of a festering wound, which arouses powerful emotions of 'pity and disgust'.[159]

The shocking nature of this image leads us then to the puzzle of the response. 'Then I, I said to myself: "But this is suffering and I must bear it ...".' Again, the matter of the speaking voice is crucial to understanding this passage. Lundbom sees this as the prophet Jeremiah reminding himself that such suffering is his unfortunate lot to bear.[160] Holladay, who assumes that the people speak these words, feels they express the (false) assumption the wound is not as serious nor as painful as it appears and can be easily remedied.[161] It could also be that the people are admitting their guilt but see the punishment as something that must be borne without complaint.[162]

Again, Polk returns to the issue of the possibility of this being the prophet's voice. He admits that, from a form-critical perspective, this

---

[156] Amy Kalmanofsky, 'Israel's Open Sore in the Book of Jeremiah', *JBL* 135.2 (2016), pp. 247-63 (261).

[157] Thus, the sickness can be seen

either as a wound that results from a divine assault or as an infection ... Both have distinct implications for understanding the rhetorical impact of the image and its theological meaning ... the complexity and potency of the image of the incurable sore come from the integration of the wounded and the infected body in Jeremiah's corporeal rhetoric (Kalmanofsky, 'Israel's Open Sore', p. 254).

[158] 'Afraid that Israel's infection will repel God forever, the prophet employs this image to reveal to Israel its dire condition. Yet God is the healer in the Bible and heals both wounds and infections.' This imagery then simultaneously communicates YHWH's power to punish *and* to heal as well as Israel's own shame *and* estrangement from God. Kalmanofsky, 'Israel's Open Sore', pp. 260-61.

[159] Kalmanofsky, 'Israel's Open Sore', p. 263.

[160] Lundbom, *Jeremiah 1-20*, p. 605.

[161] Cf JB translation: 'And I used to think, "If this is the worst, I can bear it!"' Holladay, *Jeremiah 1*, p. 342. See also Bright, *Jeremiah* (AB 21, Garden City, NJ: Doubleday, 1965), p. 71.

[162] Cf. RSV, NEB, and NJV. Holladay, *Jeremiah 1*, p. 342; Fretheim, *Jeremiah*, p. 73; McKane, *Jeremiah*, p. 231.

nearly *must* be only the voice of the beleaguered city.[163] However, certain literary considerations destabilize this form-focused conclusion. First, in the psalmic 'self-quotations', the irony is self-conscious; that is, the speaker's self-quotation clearly points to the folly of the statement. The persona of Jerusalem in the opening chapters of Jeremiah is incapable of such irony, which is why she finds herself in such a desperate situation.[164] Secondly, nowhere else, including the psalms and the prayers of Hezekiah[165] and Jonah[166] do these 'I said' statements function in quite this way.[167] Finally, the verse is essentially redundant, unless, and *only* unless, it is spoken by a different speaker.[168]

Polk does not *deny* that this is the voice of Jerusalem; rather, he is attempting to demonstrate that we can both logically and theologically hear the voice of the prophet and the voice of the city, for a rare moment, speaking *in concert*. The prophet's voice should not be heard as 'breaking in' and 'taking over' but as 'joining in'. As he says: 'It is not too fanciful that we should hear Jerusalem's voice resonating in [the prophet's] own or that his persona has, as it were, blended into and fused with the persona of Jerusalem'.[169] In this way, Jer. 10.19b, 'Then I, I said to myself: "But this is suffering and I must bear it"', becomes both the prophet's 'self-identification' with and 'commentary' on Jerusalem's condition.[170]

---

[163] He even notes that the disruptive self-quotation formula in v. 19b ('but/and I said …') is not an *automatic* sign of a shift in speaker. 'In fact, when it occurs within the "descriptions of distress" in the lamentations and thanksgiving Psalms, a shift in speakers is not only *not* required but quite inappropriate, since there the formula only marks the Psalmist's recollection of a state of mind.' See, for example, Ps. 30.7. Polk, *Prophetic Persona*, p. 69.

[164] 'Unable to make the connection between her grief and her guilt [cf. 6.15; 8.12; 9.11-13 (12-14); 13.22-27], her laments fall short of genuine confession [cf. 4.13-14, 31; 6.4; 14.7-9] and what ostensible repentance she makes is judged a "pretense" [cf. 3.10; 5.2; 14.10; 34.15-17].' Polk, *Prophetic Persona*, p. 70.

[165] Isaiah 38.10-11.

[166] Jonah 2.4.

[167] Polk, *Prophetic Persona*, p. 70.

[168] 'The redundancy ceases to be redundancy *only* when someone else is speaking it.' Polk, *Prophetic Persona*, p. 71.

[169] In fact, all that has *really* transpired in this passage is a shift in the relative positions of the personae of the prophet and of the city. 'Jerusalem from background to foreground, and Jeremiah from foreground to, if not precisely the background, at least to a parallel position.' Polk, *Prophetic Persona*, p. 69.

[170] Polk further defends this approach: 'The feasibility of such a reading is substantially heightened by the fact that the identification which is the substance of

Polk is assuredly right that the 'and I said' formula that begins v. 19b 'serves to individuate the prophet',[171] giving him his own voice distinct from the voice of the people. This actually *adds* emotive power to the prophet's self-identification with the people; it is a *deliberate* act on the prophet's part. By giving voice to grief, the prophet here *chooses* to be identified with suffering Jerusalem, in much the same way by giving voice to protest, the prophet chose to be identified *over against* YHWH at the time of his call (cf. Jer. 1.6).[172] Though distinct from the people, the prophet here makes himself one of them, inseparable from them.

Perhaps the most important question is *why* the prophet would make such a stunning rhetorical move to identify himself with the idolatrous city, to take upon himself, in a way, their sinful suffering, making the distinction between prophet and community here 'more apparent than real'.[173] Clearly, the community is unaware of her disastrous destiny; however, the prophet clearly knows what the future holds.[174] Operative here is an *emotive* logic that dramatically shapes the hearing of this expression of sorrow and grief.

Carroll describes the imagery of the following passage as 'that of a Bedouin family whose tent has been wrecked and the children taken away',[175] a truly moving image of disaster.[176] However, the reference to '*my* tent/curtains' is probably an oblique reference to the Temple and, by extension, to the city that housed it.[177] This passage also

Jeremiah's commentary has been anticipated by 4.19-21 and even more pointedly by 8.21', which verse is 'in fact identical in thrust'. Polk, *Prophetic Persona*, p. 72.

This seems to be a rather unique feature of Jeremiah MT. McKane comments: 'Sept. distinguishes more clearly between Jeremiah and those for whom he prays. MT leaves us with a more mysterious relation between prophet and community, an identification of prophet and community so complete that no distinction can be enforced'. McKane, *Jeremiah*, p. 233-34.

[171] The prophet is by no means 'dissolved' into the community he represents. Polk, *Prophetic Persona*, p. 73.

[172] To put it precisely: 'Affirming Jerusalem's affliction to be his own, he constitutes himself as her co-complainant and enacts his identity in terms of an identification with her'. Polk, *Prophetic Persona*, p. 73.

[173] McKane, *Jeremiah*, p. 234.

[174] More precisely, the prophet 'knows *and feels* that this is the future which will eventuate'. McKane, *Jeremiah*, p. 231, italics mine.

[175] Carroll, *Jeremiah*, p. 261.

[176] Holladay describes the diction here as 'profoundly emotional and domestic'. Holladay, *Jeremiah 1*, p. 342.

[177] Polk, *Prophetic Persona*, 68. See also F. Kenro Kumaki, 'A New Look at Jer. 4, 19-22 and 10, 19-21', *AJBI* 8 (1982), pp. 113-22 (114).

participates in an important and tragic 'lost sons' motif that links key portions of the book. In Jeremiah 5.7, YHWH addresses Jerusalem as a mother of apostate sons (בָּנַיִךְ עֲזָבוּנִי); here (10.20), Mother Jerusalem weeps for her sons that are 'no more' (בָּנַי יְצָאֻנִי); in Jer. 16.2, the prophet is forbidden to marry, thus his sons never will be; finally, Jer. 31.15[178] personifies the forsaken land as Rachel weeping for her slain sons. There is no greater human grief than the parent's loss of a child.

That the text invites us to hear the voices of *both* Jeremiah *and* Jerusalem crying out over this unimaginable loss creates astounding emotional depth. The boundaries between individual and corporate lament blur, giving the typical language of lament 'special density and depth'.[179] The audience is directed to picture the people as a city ... then to picture the city as a collapsed tent ... then to picture the collapsed tent as the ruined Temple; and only then is all of this corporate tragedy distilled into the 'personal distress of a single individual', [180] a solitary person containing a nation's worth of pain. To put it another way, the literary life of the figural prophet is presented to us as the hermeneutical key to understanding the message of the book. The audience comes to understand what happened to Jerusalem by understanding what happened to Jeremiah.

At v. 21, we arrive at a disputed break: the content shifts (from mourning to accusation) with no apparent accompanying shift in speaker.[181] Allen does find a sort of inclusio in the negative 'sheep metaphors' (v. 21b, 25c) and notes that both subsections end with descriptions of devastation,[182] which seems to me to be sufficient reason separating v. 21 from v. 20 and connecting it to v. 22.

---

[178] Part of the so-called 'Book of Consolation' which clearly functions as 'a reprise of earlier themes and motifs reworked in the context of salvation'. Polk, *Prophetic Persona*, p. 68.

[179] Polk, *Prophetic Persona*, p. 74.

[180] The result is 'a mutual illumination of the condition of each'. Polk, *Prophetic Persona,* p. 74.

[181] I, along with Allen, follow the scholars who see v. 21 as part of a divine response to the lament. See Reventlow, *Liturgie*, 202; John Maclennan Berridge, *Prophet, People and the Word of Yahweh: An Examination of Form and Content in the Proclamation of the Prophet Jeremiah* (BST 4; Zürich: EVZ-Verlag, 1970), p. 176; and Lundbom, *Jeremiah 1-20*, p. 607. Carroll, however, rejects this opinion; see Carroll, *Jeremiah*, p. 261.

[182] Allen, *Jeremiah*, p. 131.

Unfortunately, Polk's detailed exposition of the voicing in this passage ends at v. 21. However, those same interpretive principles are apparently still in play here.[183] Keeping in mind the way we have argued that Jeremiah 'joined' his voice to Lady Jerusalem's, we can hear that same kind of 'joining' of the voice of the prophet to the voice of YHWH. To use Polk's language, it is now the *prophet's* voice in the foreground and YHWH's voice ominously in the background.[184] This would also heighten the emotional tension within the literary figure of the prophet, for he not only empathizes with the distress and terror of the destroyed city but also with YHWH's righteous indignation that has led to this horrific judgment.

The opening 'For' (כִּי) indicates that what follows provides the rationale for the promised and just-described destruction. The blame is clearly placed upon the leadership in most astounding terms.[185] Holladay notes that the verb here, בער niphal means 'become like cattle'.[186] It is not just that they are 'stupid',[187] but the shepherds themselves have become dumb animals in need of shepherding! The coming conquest is YHWH's only option to get this unruly 'herd' of wayward leaders under control. The fall of Jerusalem is therefore necessary and unavoidable.

Because of their stupidity, the leaders (and by extension the people) have not 'prospered'. The only other time this verb is used with the negative (לֹא הִשְׂכִּילוּ) in the book of Jeremiah is in 20.11, part of the final Confession text, as a strong statement of judgment on Jeremiah's persecutors.[188] Over against Holladay, the emotional level of the surrounding verses[189] serves to inform our reading of this statement. Within this accusation of the leader's failure is an implicit *lament* of that failure. There is a bitter irony to the claim that Jerusalem's leaders have not prospered when we consider that her only prospect in this passage is utter destruction at the hands of Babylon. We are

---

[183] Especially since there is no discernible shift in speaker.

[184] Allen observes that this passage 'follows the contours of an oracle of disaster, but is spoken by the prophet rather than Yahweh'. Allen, *Jeremiah*, p. 131.

[185] Carroll, *Jeremiah*, p. 261.

[186] Jeremiah 10.14. Holladay, *Jeremiah 1*, p. 342.

[187] Carroll notes that this makes them like the 'idols and idol makers of vv. 8, 14'. Carroll, *Jeremiah*, p. 262. 'Stupidity here, then, is more than political ineptitude … it is outright religious rebellion!'

[188] Holladay, *Jeremiah 1*, p. 343.

[189] Especially its connection to the Confession text.

not presented here with an austere analysis of socioeconomic and political factors, but with an involved critique of total social collapse.

The styling of v. 22 as an audition report again seems to be rhetorical device aimed at heightening emotive response. That it is *heard* rather than *seen* creates heightened anxiety. Normally, שְׁמוּעָה means 'news' or 'rumor';[190] however, here the parallel with רַעַשׁ גָּדוֹל ('great shaking')[191] justifies the translation 'noise' and refers simultaneously to the 'news and the noise of approaching battle',[192] both sources of great terror. This is rumor become terrifying reality. In many ways, vv. 21-22 serve a similar function to the penultimate ending of the first cycle of poetry in 6.22-26,[193] another deeply emotional narrative. Those verses like these use visual and auditory cues to provide a terrifying description of the invaders' strength and savagery.[194] Finally, and perhaps most importantly, Jeremiah's appeal to the people in vv. 25-26 demands a physical response (e.g mourn bitterly) that conveys the emotional realities of the event.[195] Clearly, the passage before us is an 'echo' of that earlier passage, meant to evoke the horror of the inevitable.

The complexity of the voicing in vv. 19-20 sheds important light upon the prayer in the concluding section of ch. 10. Again, the debate on who is actually speaking is sharp, with vv. 23-24 receiving the most divergent interpretations.[196] The lament is spoken in the first person singular; however, key phrases like 'lest you make me few' in v. 24 and 'for they have devoured Jacob' in v. 25 indicate this is, at root, a corporate prayer of lament.[197] It is not surprising then that this prayer has been described as an intercessory prayer of the prophet for the

---

[190] Cf. Isa. 28.9, 19; 37.7; Jer. 49.14; Ezek. 7.26; 21.12.

[191] This noun 'commonly describe[s] commotion associated with an approaching army … tramping soliders … snorting horses … rumbling chariot wheels'. Lundbom, *Jeremiah 1-20*, p. 608. See Jer. 8.16; 47.3.

[192] Holladay, *Jeremiah 1*, p. 343.

[193] Carroll, *Jeremiah*, p. 262.

[194] Kalmanofsky, *Terror All Around*, p. 121.

[195] She also notes that by adding the phrase 'upon us' to the appeal's conclusion, 'Jeremiah includes himself among the mournful, terrified, and weak people'. Kalmanofsky, *Terror All Around*, p. 121.

[196] Holladay, *Jeremiah 1*, p. 339.

[197] Similar to the cry of anguish in vv. 19-20.

people,[198] a prayer of the prophet for himself,[199] or a prayer of people.[200]

If one chooses to hear this as a prayer of the people, then it assumes an ambiguous, if not an outright ironic, tone. The book's audience has already been forewarned to beware the people's 'lying words' (cf. Jer. 7.4). Holladay, who follows this line of interpretation, finds the prayer a pious pastiche of scriptural phrases.[201] As Polk says:

> The penetrating insight of v. 23 that 'the way of man is not in himself, that it is not in man who walks to direct his steps' … were it to come only from the mouth of the Jerusalem whose people 'have stubbornly followed their own hearts' (Jer. 9.14), would be reduced to a self-serving platitude.[202]

However, if the connection of this passage with the preceding texts means anything, it means that the audience is positioned to hear again the 'blended' voice of Jeremiah/Jerusalem, as the prophet is praying both with and for the wayward people.[203] Thus, the hearer of the book is set up to understand truths about humanity, YHWH, and the operation of divine justice and mercy that completely escape the morally corrupt (i.e. 'stupid') audience within the book. We have reached a moment where the book of Jeremiah not only *reveals* the incorrigible waywardness of Judah/Jerusalem but powerfully calls the audience away from such stubbornness to *true* fidelity and trust in YHWH.

The prayer opens by confessing YHWH's sovereign, providential control of the world of human activity,[204] followed by a plea for fairness.[205] Allen points out that the prayer is *not* for the averting of the

---

[198] So Cornill and Rudolph.

[199] So Hyatt, *IB* V, p. 902 and Bright.

[200] So Condamin.

[201] Verse 23 is an expansion of Prov. 16.9; 20.24; v. 24 is an expansion of Ps. 6.2; cf. 38.2; and v. 25 is a direct citation of Ps. 69.6-7. 'This is scripture … which the people prefer to cite, pious self-exculpation, whining, revenge'. Holladay, *Jeremiah 1*, p. 343.

[202] Polk, *Prophetic Persona*, p. 74.

[203] Thus, Reventlow describes Jer. 10.19-25 as a 'lament liturgy'. Reventlow, *Liturgie*, pp. 196-205.

[204] Allen, *Jeremiah*, pp. 132.

[205] Holladay notes that the verb יסר pi'el is related to the noun מוּסָר usually translated as 'discipline/chastisement'. Holladay, *Jeremiah 1*, p. 344.

punishment.[206] The underlying fear is that YHWH's untrammeled anger would destroy the nation past all hope of survival.[207] Again, our anxiety and fear is heightened as we realize the extent of YHWH's rage. Annihilation is a near certainty. And to think that the 'stupid' leaders do not realize their tenuous position makes the tension nearly unbearable. Yet, even *in extremis*, the justice and grace of YHWH remain visible on the edges of human reality.[208]

In the final verse, the prayer takes an unexpected turn with the cry for divine vengeance upon the nations. Considered as the people's prayer, this plea becomes ironic at several levels. First of all, in light of the satire on the nations' idolatrous ways in Jer. 10.1-16, it must be noted that 'these stupid nations with their stupid little idols have devoured and consumed Jacob'.[209] Also, there is the ironic contrast between vv. 24 and 25; the plea is essentially, 'Do not treat me with your anger … but treat others with that anger'.[210]

The faithful voice of the prophet provides an important overlay to this rather cynical hearing. When heard within the context of the book, this verse forms a fitting conclusion to the first major section. We were informed in the opening call narrative, that Jeremiah has been appointed a prophet to 'the nations' (גּוֹיִם) and that his words would bring, in sequence, destruction then rebuilding. Finally, with the movement from expressions of sorrow to cries for swift divine justice, we are presented with a prayer that sounds very much like Jeremiah's own prayers in the very next section,[211] and are thereby prepared for our encounter with Jeremiah's Confessions.

However, Jer. 10.17-25 is an important passage in another way crucial to the task of the present work. The previous selected

---

[206] 'Jeremiah's choice in reaction to the national crisis was not for a psalm of lament in hope that prayer would change things.' Allen, *Jeremiah*, p. 132.

[207] Carroll reminds that the patriarchal narratives present Israel as 'the fewest of all peoples (cf. Deut. 7.7; 26.5) but became a great nation'. Here, the plea of the prayer is that Israel 'does not return to being too few for survival'. Carroll, *Jeremiah*, p. 264. Holladay notes that Job uses a similar argument in Job 10.8. Holladay, *Jeremiah 1*, p. 344.

[208] The term 'in justice' (בְּמִשְׁפָּט) is also used in Ps. 112.5 in 'the picture of a man who … is generous and gracious'. Holladay, *Jeremiah 1*, p. 344.

[209] Carroll, *Jeremiah*, p. 264. He sarcastically adds: 'So much for the powerlessness of their gods!'

[210] Carroll, *Jeremiah*, p. 264.

[211] Brueggemann, *Commentary on Jeremiah*, pp. 107-108.

passages dealt with emotive tensions present within individual figures, the prophet Jeremiah's tense struggle with accepting and protesting the divine call in ch. 1, YHWH's inner turmoil of love and anger in ch. 2, and the people's own pernicious piety in ch. 7. However, as I have tried to tease out, what is so important about this present passage is the 'blending' of these three key figures. Here we find the whole range of emotions we have already experienced at those other key waypoints. fear, anger, trust, and grief, among others. In his concluding comments on this rather untidy conclusion, McKane says:

> We may not describe the structure of the passage too nicely, but we can say that only an individual who had made the community's brokenness his own could have spoken like this, and that at this level of appreciation the distinction between the voice of Jeremiah and the voice of the community must disappear.[212]

The people cry out, 'My tent is destroyed', but it is *more* than just the people's plaint, for we hear, as well, the wounded voice of the prophet. The prophet thunders, 'For the shepherds are stupid', but it is more than just the grumbling of a rejected outsider, for we hear the ringing indictment of an offended YHWH. We must acknowledge that the fall of Jerusalem would be a world-stopping tragedy for YHWH, the prophet, and the people. Poet-priest Daniel Berrigan is assuredly right when he remarks: 'Yahweh, Jeremiah, Jerusalem: a trinity of anguish and lamentation'.[213] What we hear in the concluding section of Jeremiah 10 can only be described as a kind of 'mutual interpenetration' of these three literary figures in their traumatic experience of Jerusalem's fall.

Therefore, we cannot help but hear a fearful quaver in Jeremiah's voice as he announces to the people YHWH's intention to 'hurl' them (and him too, as far as he knows) out of the land. Lady Jerusalem's 'open sore', the source of both her unbearable pain and YHWH's unstoppable anger, becomes Jeremiah's unending grief.

---

[212] McKane, *Jeremiah*, p. 235.

[213] Daniel Berrigan, *Jeremiah: The World, the Wound of God* (Minneapolis: Fortress Press, 1999), p. 72. Louis Stulman's observation supports this view: 'In character with the dialogical texture of the book, the text probably reflects a combination of individual and collective voices. The prophetic, communal, and divine voices converge in shared anguish and disappointment.' Louis J. Stulman, *Jeremiah* (AOTC; Nashville: Abingdon Press, 2005), p. 109.

Jeremiah's pitiful plea for 'just punishment' becomes the people's cavalier bargaining with YHWH to be punished '"only" in moderation' for the crisis is '"only" a bearable illness'.[214] In calling for justice on 'the nations', the prophet Jeremiah is faithfully fulfilling his commission, while the people, *praying the exact same prayer*, are unwittingly calling down divine judgment and ruin on their heads for their idolatrous ways.

3.3 CONCLUSION

The present chapter has offered an affective hearing of Jeremiah 1-10 in preparation for our encounter with the Confession texts. The emotive impact of the language and imagery we have encountered, even within the brevity of an overview, is striking – even unnerving – in its conflicting range and raw power. Yvonne Sherwood is probably right that a discussion of prophetic rhetoric is possibly a misnomer: 'A more radical description of prophetic "poetics" is needed-something that goes beyond rhetoric and the implicit sense of language in control'. Prophetic images (like the 'festering wound' of Israel's idolatry in Jer. 10.19) 'goes to a place beyond images'.[215] However, those features that place prophetic language in a realm beyond the reach of rhetorical analysis are precisely what we find are key elements for hearing the book of Jeremiah.

> The abjection and trauma of the speaking subject … in prophecy, not only do the figures bleed and release a whole welter of uncontrollable emotions, but the speaking, writing body goes through the same trauma and revolts of being as the national body … the [figure of the prophet is] at times literally beside/against himself. In stark contrast to the composed rhetorical figure of the author-in-control, dispatching servile words to do his bidding, the prophet is the site of a rhetoric that is beyond/above him, a voice and body wielded by another.[216]

---

[214] This is Holladay's reading. Holladay, *Jeremiah 1*, p. 344.

[215] Yvonne Sherwood, 'Prophetic Scatology: Prophecy and the Art of Sensation', *Semeia* 92 (1998), pp. 183-224 (213).

[216] Sherwood, 'Prophetic Scatology', p. 214.

In Jeremiah, unspeakable words *are* spoken; indescribable pain *is* described.

It is not surprising that O'Connor renewed her interpretive insight into the book of Jeremiah through the use of insights from trauma studies.[217] The emotive power of the rhetoric of Jeremiah is itself almost traumatizing, especially for contemporary listeners. However, the most important effect of this traumatic affective overload is how the audience's ear is now transfixed by the voice of the prophet. The narrative space of the prophet's voice is clearly inhabited by the people's grief and YHWH's anger. And this voice that gives voice to others – to their rage and fear and despair and endless grief – becomes the point where the hearer can enter the emotive world of the text and allow the figure of the prophet to give voice to the stirrings of their *own* hearts. Tracing the emotional shifts of these interlocked characters effectively forces the hearer to open up to the text's affective impact and transformative power. Now, when the audience encounters the cries of the prophet in the Confessions, they are powerfully positioned to receive those as expressions – perhaps even 'interpretations' – of their own tumultuous states; the text subtly invites the hearer to *identify* with the outcries of the prophet and thus begins its work of affective transformation in the hearer.

---

[217] See Chapter 1 above.

4

JEREMIAH'S FIRST CONFESSION (11.18-23)

4.1 Introduction

The last chapter presented a broad overview of Jeremiah 1-10, highlighting the key ways in which an affective approach to the book of Jeremiah causes us to 'hear' the book differently. Although limitations of space allowed for only brief analyses of key passages, the survey revealed a developing pattern of deeply contrasting emotions coexisting within the text. Jeremiah 1 reveals to us a prophet both resistant to and yet overwhelmingly compelled by his calling. In Jeremiah 2, we heard YHWH's undying love for Israel and Judah give way to a betrayed lover's grief and deadly rage. In Jeremiah's pronouncement of judgment against the Temple in Jeremiah 7, we quite literally overheard the pious chantings of a faithless, deceptive people who had driven YHWH to heartbreak.[1] Finally, at the very close of the opening section in Jeremiah 10, we find the prophetic voice rise above the emotional cacophony to take up both the grief of the punished people and the righteous anger of their betrayed covenant Lord. Since the figure of Jeremiah has already given voice both to YHWH and to the people, we have been prepared for[2] the voice of the literary figure of the prophet Jeremiah to offer now a way for hearers to voice their own experience of the text.

---

[1] 'The Temple of the Lord, the Temple of the Lord, the Temple of the Lord' (Jer. 7.11).

[2] It might not even be too much of a stretch to claim that the book of Jeremiah affectively leads the hearer to *expect* just such a move.

This hearing of the Confessions will demonstrate two key points. First, we seek to demonstrate that the variety of emotions presented in the Confession texts resonate with the emotions an attentive hearer has *already been experiencing* in their interaction with the book. In effect, the Confession texts provide the hearer with an emotional vocabulary to help articulate the affective impact of the book of Jeremiah. Second, not only do the Confessions help the hearer articulate the *transformational* impact of the book but they also have a profound *formational* impact, teaching us *how* to listen to the book of Jeremiah. In that sense, the careful hearer has been intentionally prepared to experience the Confessions as *both* cathartic *and* constructive. They provide emotional *release,* while simultaneously presenting the hearer with a new sense of *responsibility* to YHWH's word.[3] To use *Pentecostal* language, the hearer should experience the Confessions as a 'primitive' yet 'pragmatic' word; to use *Jeremianic* language, the hearer should experience the Confessions as a word that both 'uproots and pulls down' and 'builds and plants'.[4]

The plan of the present chapter is to offer some introductory comments on the Confessions as a textual corpus and then embark on a detailed exegesis of the first two Confession texts, applying the affective interpretive method outlined in Chapter 2 and already utilized in Chapter 3. As we 'feel' our way through the text,[5] we will highlight the ways in which such an affective hearing brings to the surface interconnections and dimensions of the text that have not heretofore been fully explored. Each 'hearing' will first offer a translation of the text, followed by comments on the overall textual structure, and conclude with a detailed analysis of the text, focusing on affective structures and dynamics.

---

[3] It is precisely at this point that my socio-religious location as a 'Pentecostal' hearer uniquely positions me to offer an analysis of these elements within the text. In the Pentecostal tradition, the Bible is a text that moves the heart as much as it clarifies the mind. I agree with Andrew Davies: '[Pentecostal interpreters] need to reassert our confidence in an ideological approach to reading the biblical text and acknowledge without shame the plain fact that our distinctive preconceptions invite us to a distinctive appropriation of the text – and that our readings are worth hearing by others'. Davies, 'What Does It Mean', p. 222.

[4] Jeremiah 1.10.

[5] E.g. staying alert to how the affective dimension of the rhetoric and characterization in the text work to shape the hearer's response.

4.2 the Confessions of Jeremiah – An Overview

As was demonstrated in the first chapter, the Confessions of Jeremiah are perhaps one of the most-discussed, most-disputed collections of prophetic texts in the entire Hebrew Bible.[6] For over a century of critical study, these texts have continuously generated new insights and new controversies. They have also been something of a bellwether in the field of Jeremiah studies; new approaches and theories are often experimentally applied to the Confession texts and then become mainstreamed in broader Jeremianic scholarship.

Currently, the study of the Confessions is largely dominated by form- and redactional-critical analyses, which have provided us with important and lasting insights into the process of the book's composition as well as its key theological ideas. However, Biddle is likely correct that the reliance on form-critical methodologies[7] have in some ways stunted our ability to appreciate the rhetorical power of Jeremiah's unique language.[8]

---

[6] Leslie Allen, 'Jeremiah: Book of', in Mark J. Boda and J. Gordon McConville (eds.), *Dictionary of the Old Testament Prophets* (Downers Grove, IL: InterVarsity Press, 2012), pp. 423-40 (431-32). Jack R. Lundbom, *Jeremiah Closer Up: The Prophet and the Book* (Hebrew Bible Monographs; Sheffield: Sheffield Phoenix Press, 2010), pp. 75-103.

[7] Especially in their uses as an attempt to 'prove' the Confessions are 'authentic' to the historical prophet.

[8] Biddle, very bluntly says that form-critical categories provide 'no satisfactory original public setting for this private language'. Biddle, *Polyphony and Symphony*, p. 38.

Lewin is even critical of Holladay and Lundbom, who claim to use rhetorical-critical methods in their work on Jeremiah. 'Little attention has been paid to the material as rhetoric in the more precise sense. i.e. *how it develops a persuasive argument* in a situation of controversy.' For example, though both recognize the presence of an inclusio between Jer. 1.4-19 and 20.7-18, 'neither has looked beyond the semantic level to ask how the frame fits the contents or functions within the book as a whole'. Lewin, 'Arguing for Authority', pp. 105-106.

The predominance of historical-critical concerns is still evident in Holladay's *Architecture of Jeremiah 1-20*. He explicitly claims to be applying 'rhetorical' critical methods to the text, 'looking for repetitions, parallels, and contrasts in words, phrases, syntax, and other structures, to see what they can teach us'. Holladay, *Architecture*, p. 21. However, there are some compelling evidences that historical-critical concerns still lead his thinking. Most obviously, Holladay dedicates his final chapter to a discussion of the precise nature of the *Urrolle* mentioned in Jeremiah 36, and the evidence about its nature that can be adduced from his analysis. The most telling sign, though, is Holladay's restricted discussion of the 'rhetoric' of the Temple Semon; he covers Jer. 7.1-8.3 (arguably, one of the most rhetorically-laden

Taken together, the dialogues between YHWH and prophet contrast sharply with YHWH's words to the people. As Biddle states, the YHWH-people interactions reveal 'a distressed, bewildered people and a disconsolate, resigned deity' while the YHWH-prophet interactions reveal 'a resolute angry deity in dialogue with a relatively quiet, yet petulant prophet whose primary contribution to the discussion explores the character and scope of divine justice'.[9] While there can (and should) be some disagreement with Biddle's characterizations of the dialogue-partners, the larger point of the distinctiveness of the dialogues is an important interpretive insight.

For Carroll, the pressing problem is the idea of the Confessions as the historical prophet's personal statements, useful for autobiography or psychological profiling. The issue is that these analyses present Jeremiah as almost-*modern*, a heroic figure struggling mightily with doubts and fears.[10] It is particularly intriguing that Carroll feels compelled to adopt this position precisely because of the surfeit of affective language.[11] However, the affective language is literally unintelligible unless somehow understood on a personal level.[12] Allen, as well, finds the moniker 'confessions' particularly unhelpful, since these texts are neither expressions of personal sin nor expressions of devout faith in God.[13]

---

passages in the book) in a mere *four pages*. Holladay, *Architecture*, pp. 102-105, 169-74.

[9] Biddle, *Polyphony and Symphony*, p. 47.

[10] Jeremiah 'appears as an Augustine or a Rousseau offering his innermost thoughts and feelings as theological commentary on his life and times ... How very modern and existential an image of Jeremiah it [i.e. this reading of the Confessions] produces!' Carroll, *Jeremiah*, p. 277. See also Joe E. Henderson, 'Duhm and Skinner's Invention of Jeremiah', in Else K. Holt and Carolyn J. Sharp (eds.), *Jeremiah Invented: Constructions and Deconstructions of Jeremiah* (LHB/OTS 575; New York. Bloomsbury, 2015), pp. 1-15.

[11] 'There is such an overload of language and emotion in these laments that we cannot reconstruct a biography of the speaker ... to do so would be to diminish them, to reduce them to a particularity which would rob them of significance and render them incapable of serving the whole community.' Carroll, *Jeremiah*, p. 279.

[12] 'The lament is not just a catalogue of woes recorded for private relief or the benefit of an anonymous public; it is a specific complaint addressed to the God who has a history of relationship with the lamenter and may therefore be expected to care.' Lewin, 'Arguing for Authority', p. 111.

[13] 'The traditional label is a misnomer for a series of prayers and outbursts in the style of Psalms of lament, spoken out of situations of distress and adapted to a prophetic setting.' Allen, *Jeremiah*, p. 145.

As usual, Brueggemann's grasp of the essential issues is keen, and he offers a mediating solution. Clearly, the Confession texts are first lament-like personal prayers, similar to the individual laments found in Psalms. However, in Jeremiah, these prophet-associated prayers have become communal – not just individual – texts. Thus, they are preserved in the book of Jeremiah not simply as a record of the historical prophet Jeremiah's personal prayers[14] but as 'a poignant vehicle for Israel's faith'.[15]

For the community, these laments serve two key principles that guide the book of Jeremiah. The first is the book's presentation of the figure of Jeremiah as the 'true prophet'. It is his persecution, witnessed in the Confessions, that differentiates Jeremiah from the larger and more influential group of false prophets.[16] The second and related principle served by the Confessions is that the people's persecution/rejection of the prophet further justifies the book's verdict of destruction for Jerusalem and exile for Judah.[17] The community that rejects Jeremiah suffers 'a double measure of culpability'.[18]

Finally, these texts are bounded by a significant inclusio in Jer. 11.20 and 20.12. The verses are identical except for the descriptions of YHWH, which are nearly so.[19] Both descriptions present YHWH as the one who knows humanity, even their 'innermost' parts – thoughts, motives, feelings, and intentions; both also ask that YHWH

---

[14] Archived in the book in a way similar to a modern university library housing all the 'papers' (letters, memoranda, unpublished articles, journals, etc.) of a famous intellectual.

[15] Brueggemann, *Commentary on Jeremiah,* p. 115.

[16] This group of 'optimistic prophets' (Holladay's phrase) were 'false' precisely because of the group's attempt 'to ingratiate itself to the king and the people by transmitting a positive, soothing message'. Avioz, *'I Sat Alone'*, p. 42.

[17] 'The people ... will not be able to claim that the calamities that befell them were arbitrary. When they read these lamentations, they will understand that the destruction and exile could have been prevented had they listened to Jeremiah and treated him properly'. Avioz, *'I Sat Alone'*, p. 42.

Jeremiah's reactions of pain and utter unease reflect the way the people were treating Yahweh. The confessions are variously keyed into their individual contexts to show that corporate rejection of Jeremiah as Yahweh's prophetic messenger meant nothing less than spurning the divine message and will for the covenant people (Allen, *Jeremiah*, p. 145).

[18] Jeremiah 7.25-26 'laid down this theological axiom in respect to the prophets, after a torah reference in 7.24, and it is recapitulated in 25.4'. Allen, *Jeremiah*, p. 145.

[19] In 11.20, YHWH is שֹׁפֵט צֶדֶק, the 'Righteous Judge'; and in 20.12, YHWH is בֹּחֵן צַדִּיק, 'one who tests the righteous'.

take 'vengeance' (נְקָמָה) upon the prophet's enemies. The language also harks back to Jeremiah's own call narrative, which opens with YHWH's announcement that before Jeremiah was born, YHWH 'knew' him (יְדַעְתִּיךָ, Jer. 1.5).

Thus, the Confession texts are both rhetorically and affectively linked to the call narrative. In fact, to consider the Confessions as reflections on Jeremiah's calling is perhaps the most direct interpretive approach. We learn in the Confessions that YHWH's knowledge of Jeremiah includes not simply comprehension of Jeremiah's destiny or purpose in YHWH's plans for 'the nations' but knowledge of the prophet's 'inner self'.[20] Jeremiah's identity, relationship with YHWH, mission, and emotions all come into play within and across these texts, usually in very surprising ways.

4.3 Hearing the First Confession

4.3.1 Text & Translation

Hebrew (MT) Text	English Translation
וַיהוָה הוֹדִיעַנִי וָאֵדָעָה	[11.18] *Jeremiah*: 'And YHWH[21] made me to know and I knew,[22]
אָז הִרְאִיתַנִי מַעַלְלֵיהֶם	Then he showed me[23] their deeds.[24]

---

[20] It is important to reiterate here my agreement with Carroll's hesitancy at using the Confessions to reconstruct a biography or psychological profile of the historical prophet. This study deals strictly with the literary figure of the prophet, what Kessler called the 'Jeremiah of the Scriptures'. However, it cannot be denied that the Confession texts give us a glimpse of the character Jeremiah's 'inner life'; they are presented to us as *prayers* – private, interior dialogues. Any understanding of the function of the literary figure of Jeremiah within the book must take these texts into serious account as part of that figure's presentation.

[21] LXX and S read וַיהוָה as a vocative. See Holladay, *Jeremiah 1*, p. 363, against Baumgartner, who maintains, 'The "and" that opens the verse in the MT is to be deleted … this was intended to facilitate the transition from what came before, with which there is originally no connection at all.' Baumgartner, *Jeremiah's Poems of Lament*, p. 40. The MT, however, 'understands this verse as a simple statement of fact'. Craigie, Kelley, and Drinkard, Jr., *Jeremiah 1-25*, p. 177.

[22] MT vocalizes וָאֵדָעָה, following the previous verb: 'and I knew'. See Holladay, *Jeremiah 1*, p. 363.

[23] LXX reads εἶδον, 'I saw their deeds', probably from רָאִיתִי, qal, 'I saw'. This 'does away with the shift to the second person' and with 'a revelation to the prophet by some confidant'. Lundbom, *Jeremiah 1-20*, p. 636. Holladay also notes if we read גִּלִּיתָ 'you revealed' in v. 20, then MT should be preferred here. Holladay, *Jeremiah 1*, p. 363.

[24] 'The whole verse may be translated in one of the following ways: (1) 'It was the LORD who informed me of the evil some people were doing, so I knew it';

וַאֲנִי כְּכֶבֶשׂ אַלּוּף	11.19 I[25] was like a trusting[26] lamb[27]
יוּבַל לִטְבוֹחַ	Led[28] to the slaughter.[29]
וְלֹא־יָדַעְתִּי כִּי־עָלַי	I did not know that against me[30]
חָשְׁבוּ מַחֲשָׁבוֹת	They had schemed schemes.[31]
נַשְׁחִיתָה עֵץ בְּלַחְמוֹ	'Let us destroy[32] the tree with its sap!'[33]

---

(2) 'The LORD informed me, so I knew what the evil people were doing'; (3) 'I knew about the evil some people were doing; it was the LORD who showed me'. Newman and Stine, *Handbook on Jeremiah*, p. 305.

[25] In the emphatic position. Holladay suggests paraphrastically, 'I, for my part, was like …' Holladay, *Jeremiah 1*, p. 372.

[26] The adverb 'trusting' (אַלּוּף) can also mean 'familiar [e.g. tame]'. See *CHALOT*, s.v. 'אַלּוּף I'; Clines suggests 'obedient', *CDCH*, s.v. 'אַלּוּף III'. The point of the image is to convey Jeremiah as 'unsuspecting … One thinks instinctively of the pet lamb in Nathan's parable (2 Sam. 12.3).' Lundbom, *Jeremiah 1-20*, p. 636. See Ps. 55.14 [13].

[27] The word for lamb, כֶּבֶשׂ typically refers to a *sacrificial* lamb. Noting Cornill, Baumgartner says: 'No fewer than 111 of the 116 OT passages that speak of the כבש, the reference is to sacrifice'. Baumgartner, *Jeremiah's Poems of Lament*, p. 43; see Lundbom, *Jeremiah 1-20*, p. 636.

[28] 'H-stem passive יוּבַל means "led along" or "brought as a sacrifice"'. Lundbom, *Jeremiah 1-20*, p. 636. Cf. Ps. 44.12, 23 [11, 22]; Isa. 53.7; Acts 8.32-35 for other uses of the imagery of sheep led to slaughter.

[29] This is 'not the normal verb for sacrifice (זבח) but the one that ordinarily refers to domestic slaughter (טבח)'. Holladay, *Jeremiah 1*, p. 372.

[30] Again in the emphatic position, like 'I' in the first colon. Holladay, *Jeremiah 1*, p. 372.

[31] Lundbom translates 'planned plans', noting it is 'likely a wordplay'. Lundbom, *Jeremiah 1-20*, p. 636. The term is 'itself neutral'; however, 'the context definitely points to something negative and evil'. Newman and Stine, *Handbook on Jeremiah*, p. 306. I thus chose the more nefarious term 'scheme'.

[32] נַשְׁחִיתָה is intended to offer assonance with 'made plans' (חָשְׁבוּ מַחֲשָׁבוֹת) in the prior verse, acting as a kind of poetic 'revelation' of the enemies' plot. Cf. Jer. 18.18 for the same type of word-play. See Holladay, *Jeremiah 1*, p. 372.

[33] Perhaps the most difficult phrase in this passage. T has 'Let us cast deadly poison into his food'. LXX [also V] has, 'Let us put wood (ξύλον) into his food', reading the verb as נָשִׂיתָה, נַשְׁלִיכָה, or נִשְׁלְחָה. Holladay says T's translation is 'logical but evidently only a guess'. Holladay, *Jeremiah 1*, p. 363. Burkitt and Houberg accept the verb in LXX/V, נָשִׂיתָה, and then redivide to לַחְמוֹ עֵצֶב: 'Let us make trouble in his bread'. See Francis C. Burkitt, 'Justin Martyr and Jeremiah xi 19', *JTS* 33.132 (1931-32), pp. 371-73; R. Houberg, 'Note sur Jérémie xi 19', *VT* 25.3 (1975), pp. 676-77. Furthermore, Hitzig, Duhm, Giesebrecht, Cornill, Condamin, Rudolph all emend בְּלַחְמוֹ to בְּלֵחֹה 'in its freshness, sap' (cf. Deut. 34.7). However, Lundbom claims the emending the text is unnecessary to arrive at this translation 'if we assume an enclitic *mem* and simply repoint'. Lundbom, *Jeremiah 1-20*, p. 636. See also Allen, *Jeremiah*, p. 143, note a; Bright, *Jeremiah*, p. 84; McKane, *Jeremiah*, p. 253, 257. Newman and Stine suggest the essential meaning is 'while it is still healthy'. Newman and Stine, *Handbook on Jeremiah*, p. 306.

וְנִכְרְתֶנּוּ מֵאֶרֶץ חַיִּים   Let us cut him off from the land of the living

וּשְׁמוֹ לֹא־יִזָּכֵר עוֹד: That his name be remembered no more!'[34]

וַיהוָה צְבָאוֹת שֹׁפֵט צֶדֶק   11.20 [But][35] Yahweh of hosts, who judges righteously,[36]

בֹּחֵן כְּלָיוֹת וָלֵב   Who tests the innermost being[37] and the
heart,

אֶרְאֶה נִקְמָתְךָ מֵהֶם   Let me see your vengeance upon them

כִּי אֵלֶיךָ גִּלִּיתִי אֶת־רִיבִי: [For] to you[38] I have revealed[39] my case!'

---

[34] 'The theme of "seeking to take one's life" appears often in the Psalms'.
Lundbom, *Jeremiah 1-20*, p. 637. See, for example, Pss. 35.4; 38.13 [12]; 40.15 [14];
54.5 [3]; 63.10 [9]; 70.3 [2]; 86.14.

[35] Baumgartner argues the ו, though missing in LXX, is present in the Vulgate
and Symmachus and is 'indispensable on account of the contrast to what comes
before'. Baumgartner, *Poems of Lament*, p. 41. The adversative is implied in the text
itself; the addition or subtraction of the ו does not really seem to affect the overall
meaning or structure. See Hubmann, *Untersuchungen*, pp. 78-79, 95.

[36] Literally 'what is righteous'. So Lundbom, *Jeremiah 1-20*, p. 637. For adverbial
use of צֶדֶק, see Ps. 119.138.

[37] Literally 'kidneys'.

[38] Baumgartner reads עליו instead of אליך, following Ps. 37.5. Baumgartner, *Jeremiah's Poems of Lament*, p. 41. Holladay finds the appearance of אֵלֶיךָ 'to you' in the
emphatic position odd: '"For you are the one to whom I have committed my cause"
is not what one would expect – one would respond, "pray, to whom else?"' Instead,
'one might have expected גִּלּוֹתִי אֵלֶיךָ כִּי רִיבִי ["I have committed my adversaries to
you"]'. Holladay, *Jeremiah 1*, p. 374.

[39] Baumgartner calls this MT phrase 'meaningless'. Baumgartner, *Jeremiah's Po-
ems of Lament*, p. 41. Holladay reads אֵלַי גִּלִּיאת יְרִיבַי for MT's אֵלֶיךָ גִּלִּיתִי אֶת־רִיבִי 'to
you I have revealed my (legal) case', translating instead: 'for to me you have revealed
my adversaries'. He argues: 'The verb "I have revealed" does not fit the object'.
Holladay, *Jeremiah 1*, p. 363. Most commentators (e.g. Duhm, Baumgartner, Cornill,
Volz, Condamin) accept Hitzig's revocalization גִּלּוֹתִי (גלל qal) 'I have entrusted' (cf.
Pss. 22.9; 37.5). Even Holladay calls this 'an attractive possibility', though he prefers
his translation on the basis of 'unity of diction'. Holladay, *Jeremiah 1*, p. 363.

However, a primary goal of this work is to avoid emendation of the MT text
if at all possible because it opens up the possibility of manipulating the affective
dimension of the words to fit a pre-determined interpretive end. Therefore, if the
MT *can* be read intelligibly, then we are required to follow that sense, even if it is
sometimes puzzling. Understanding Jeremiah's revelation to YHWH here as an
emotive revelation helps to clarify the function of v. 19 within the Confession. Furthermore, LXX reads ἀπεκάλυψα, 'I have revealed', which supports MT. See comments below in the interpretation for further explanation.

לָכֵן כֹּה אָמַר יְהוָה עַל־אַנְשֵׁי
עֲנָתוֹת הַמְבַקְשִׁים אֶת־נַפְשְׁךָ
לֵאמֹר לֹא תִנָּבֵא בְּשֵׁם יְהוָה
וְלֹא תָמוּת בְּיָדֵנוּ:
לָכֵן כֹּה אָמַר יְהוָה צְבָאוֹת
הִנְנִי פֹקֵד עֲלֵיהֶם
הַבַּחוּרִים יָמֻתוּ בַחֶרֶב
בְּנֵיהֶם וּבְנוֹתֵיהֶם יָמֻתוּ בָּרָעָב:

11.21 *YHWH*[40]: 'Therefore,[41] thus YHWH has said concerning the men of Anathoth who are seeking your life[42] and saying to you: 'You shall not[43] prophesy in the name of YHWH or you will surely die by our hand.'

11.22 Therefore thus YHWH of hosts has said:[44]

'Look, I will reckon with them.

The chosen ones[45] will die by the sword;[46]

Their sons and their daughters will die by famine.

---

[40] Since the phrase introduces a divine word and such introductions are typically narrative, Baumgartner judges v. 21 to be not poetry, but 'rhythmic prose'. Baumgartner, *Jeremiah's Poems of Lament*, p. 42. Holladay asserts: 'These words are redactional, contradicting the context of conspiracy in vv. 18-20'. Holladay, *Jeremiah 1*, p. 364.

[41] 'Since a new song clearly commences ... I delete לכן as a redactional link'. Baumgartner, *Jeremiah's Poems of Lament*, p. 41.

[42] LXX reads ψυχήν μου, 'my life'. In the MT, the phrase 'concerning the men of Anathoth' appears to begin YHWH's words. However, LXX apparently understands 'concerning the men of Anathoth' to be a continuation of the introduction of YHWH's words and has corrected the text. See Holladay, *Jeremiah 1*, p. 364; Lundbom simply states: 'The LXX's "my life" cannot be correct'. Lundbom, *Jeremiah 1-20*, p. 638.

[43] לא is an apodictic prohibition: 'Never prophesy in the name of YHWH!' Holladay, *Jeremiah 1*, p. 375; see John Bright, 'The Apodictic Prohibition: Some Observations', *JBL* 92.2 (1973), pp. 185-204 (197). Lundbom suggests it is to be read as an 'asseverative, which makes the words more a threat'. Lundbom, *Jeremiah 1-20*, p. 638.

[44] Phrase is missing in LXX. Given their prior appearance in v. 21, Holladay, calls its appearance in MT 'dittographic' or perhaps representative of a 'conflate text, if there was a text tradition in which the messenger formula was missing at the beginning of v 21'. Holladay, *Jeremiah 1*, p. 364. Allen likewise deletes, saying it represents 'a wrongly incorporated marginal reading supplying the variant and cue words'. Allen, *Jeremiah*, p. 144. See also Baumgartner, *Jeremiah's Poems of Lament*, p. 41.

[45] Holladay thinks הַבַּחוּרִים יָמֻתוּ בַחֶרֶב disrupts the poetic pattern because בָּנִים is a standard parallel to בַּחוּרִים (see Jer. 6.11; 9.20); thus, בְּנֵיהֶם 'their sons' should be reinterpreted as 'their children'. Holladay, *Jeremiah 1*, p. 364. However, Baumgartner points out: 'Since הבחורימ is never found with בנות but always with בתולות הבחורימ must be taken as the original reading'. Baumgartner, *Jeremiah's Poems of Lament*, p. 42. Therefore, changing the normal translation of בָּנִים seems a bit unnecessary. I follow Lundbom's suggestion that הַבַּחוּרִים is a reference to 'the elite fighting men of Judah'. Lundbom, *Jeremiah 1-20*, p. 639; see McKane, *Jeremiah*, p. 258.

[46] Note the word-play of בַּחוּרִים and חֶרֶב. Holladay, *Jeremiah 1*, p. 375.

וּשְׁאֵרִית לֹא תִהְיֶה לָהֶם

11.23 And there shall not be a remnant of them.[47]

כִּי־אָבִיא רָעָה אֶל־אַנְשֵׁי עֲנָתוֹת

For I shall bring disaster to the men of Anathoth,

שְׁנַת פְּקֻדָּתָם׃

The year of their visitation.'

4.3.2 Structure[48]

The structure of Jer. 11.18-23 largely follows the typical structure of an individual psalm of lament,[49] invocation (v.18),[50] complaint (v. 19), prayer (v. 20), and divine response (vv. 21-23).[51] The divine response is not problematic, containing all the typical elements of a judgment oracle.[52] However, even Diamond admits that 11.18-23 does not *exactly* fit the mold of an individual lament.[53]

---

[47] Some translators have understood this phrase 'to refer only to the children. It seems more likely, however, that it refers to all the people of Anathoth, as in "And none of those people will be left [alive]"'. Newman and Stine, *Handbook on Jeremiah*, p. 309.

[48] The present work is not as concerned with matters of 'form' or 'setting', though those matters at points do impinge upon decisions about the structure of the text. As Holladay says: 'Details of text, redaction, structure, form, and setting … interact, so that one's decision on one has consequences for the others'. Holladay, *Jeremiah 1*, p. 365.

Diamond, for example, thinks the most appropriate 'form' to define 11.18-23 is the 'well-attested prophetic liturgy which has incorporated elements from national lament and divine oracle into a single structure'. Diamond, *Confessions in Context*, p. 24. See, for example, Hos. 6.1-6; 14.2-9; Jer. 3.21-4.2; 14.1-10; 14.17-15.4. However, Diamond later cautions the exegete to remember: 'Once the transfer and borrowing of genres from one setting to another is recognized, a given genre of text can no longer be taken as providing immediate indication of its setting within the prophetic mission'. Though a genre may have a 'primary' usage, that does not preclude 'secondary' usages. Diamond, *Confessions in Context*, p. 4.

While form-critical observations will inform the discussion here, they will by no means dictate outcomes. More interpretive weight will be granted to the text's individuality than to its commonality with other texts.

[49] Diamond calls it 'preferable' to approach the confessions as 'editorial compositions employing pre-existing lament Psalms, placed on Jeremiah's lips, and interpreting the prophet in relation to their own needs and problems'. Diamond, *Confessions in Context*, p. 32. Cf. 1 Sam. 2.1-10 and Jon. 2.3-10.

[50] The invocation has been modified here; see translation above.

[51] See Craigie, Kelley, and Drinkard, Jr., *Jeremiah 1-25*, p. 176.

[52] E.g. messenger formula, accusation, messenger formula, pronouncement of judgment. Diamond, *Confessions in Context*, p. 23.

[53] 'At least for this confession a certain allowance for the employment of authentic material or even reworking of pre-existing Jeremianic units would have to be made.' Diamond, *Confessions in Context*, p. 32.

The real obstacle to identifying the prayer's structure is found in vv. 18-20, which seems to jumble elements of *both* psalms of lament *and* psalms of thanksgiving (cf. Ps. 40). While vv. 19-20 follow the lament pattern,[54] v. 18 is *not* an invocation and introductory petition. It is rather a report of past divine activity, which is a common feature of psalms of thanksgiving.[55] At the same time, the prayer also refers to personal suffering and the work of enemies,[56] common features of lament.

Even as a report, however, v. 18 is still anomalous. Usually, in a psalm of thanksgiving, the worshiper is fully aware of the (past) trouble and has cried out to YHWH for aid; however, here, Jeremiah is unaware of the trouble until YHWH reveals it to him.[57] This leads Diamond to conclude, based on the obvious close relationship between lament and thanksgiving that we have here in Jer. 11.18-23 a 'borderline case' that includes *both* elements of lament and elements of thanksigiving.[58] Baumgartner, however, thinks v. 18, falling outside the schema of the lament, is the prophet's 'tell-tale mark', his adaptation of a common genre for his own prophetic purpose.[59]

These divergences from known genres encourage attentiveness to this text's particular structure indicated by the disjunctive markers and the unique shift from present to retrospect to prospect.[60] Furthermore, vv. 18 and 20 form a verbal inclusion: in v. 18, YHWH

---

[54] Lament (v. 19), expression of trust (v. 20a), petition (v. 20b). Diamond, *Confessions in Context*, p. 32.

[55] Cf. Ps. 118.5. Allen, *Jeremiah*, p. 146. This is enough for Reventlow to categorize 11.18-23 as a Psalm of thanksgiving rather than lament. See Diamond, *Confessions in Context*, p. 23.

[56] 'The vague references to "their", "they", and "them" … are consistent with the broad language that can appear in the lament (cf. Ps. 142.4 [3]; Jer. 17.15).' Allen, *Jeremiah*, p. 146.

[57] YHWH is 'the initiator of aid to an individual oblivious of his danger'. Diamond, *Confessions in Context*, p. 23.

[58] Which, given the logical relationship of both forms, is not all that surprising. 'The typicalities of both genres affect the tone of the piece, since it reverberates between confident expectation and alarmed plea.' Diamond, *Confessions in Context*, p. 24. This is the type of interpretive conundrum that generated Muilenburg's push to supplement form-critical analysis with rhetorical analysis. For further discussion of the limitations of form criticism, see David Greenwood's response to Muilenburg's proposal. David Greenwood, 'Rhetorical Criticism and *Formgeschichte*: Some Methodological Considerations', *JBL* 89.4 (1970), pp. 418-26.

[59] Baumgartner, *Jeremiah's Poems of Lament*, p. 45.

[60] Diamond, *Confessions in Context*, p. 25.

'reveals' (ראה) the enemies' plot; in v. 20, Jeremiah requests to 'see' (ראה) YHWH's vengeance upon them because Jeremiah's (innocent) heart stands revealed to YHWH. The effect then is to make v. 19 the center of the prophet's prayer.[61]

O'Connor agrees with Baumgartner's assessment that this is a creative adaptation of lament for a specified purpose.[62] Specifically, she thinks the admixture of lament and thanksgiving elements expresses the conflict between Jeremiah's trust in YHWH and YHWH's apparent failure to protect the prophet's life and mission; she concludes that this first confession ends in 'paradox'.[63]

What seems to be noticeably left to the side in this discussion is the emotive impact of such a mixing of genres. In the prayer, the prophet is not simply encountering an intellectual conflict but a deeply emotional crisis: though YHWH has revealed the enemies' plans, YHWH has done nothing yet (apparently) to stop them. The enemies' threats continue to hang over him, producing powerful emotions of confusion, disappointment, and even despair.

Though the divine response (vv. 21-23) is more typical than Jeremiah's prayer, it does have a similar structure. The doubled messenger formulas[64] actually mark the oracle's divisions, and the phrase 'men of Anathoth' (אַנְשֵׁי עֲנָתוֹת) forms an inclusio (vv. 21, 23).[65]

---

[61] More precisely, the inclusio forms the prayer into a chiastic structure:

A Begins with וַיהוָה ... uses the verbal root ראה and closes with כִּי עָלַי (vv. 18-19bα).

B Quotation of the plotters (v. 19bβ)

A' Begins with וַיהוָה ... uses the verbal root ראה and closes with כִּי אֵלֶיךָ (v. 20). Holladay, *Jeremiah 1*, p. 367.

[62] 'Jeremiah plays with the lament form, creatively adapting it to the content of his message.' O'Connor, *Confessions of Jeremiah*, p. 25.

[63] O'Connor, *Confessions of Jeremiah*, p. 25.

[64] See note on translation of 11.22 above.

[65] Diamond, *Confessions in Context*, p. 25. Baumgartner, who thinks this is an entirely separate piece, calls vv. 22-23 'quite different' than vv. 18-21. It is a divine oracle of judgment directed to the men of Anathoth. The prospect is 'severe punishment, even total annihilation, for their persecution of Jeremiah'. In fact, Baumgartner claims the song 'is purely prophetic in form ... it does not belong to the "poems of lament" at all'. He only addresses the passage along with Jer. 11.18-20 'because of its relatedness in terms of situation and ideas'. The passage cannot be considered (as is usual) 'the continuation and conclusion of the preceding one'. First of all, there is the wordy introduction of v. 21a, but more tellingly, v. 21b contradicts v. 19; v. 21b complains of 'secret assassination plans' whereas v. 19 laments 'an open threat'. Baumgartner, *Jeremiah's Poems of Lament*, pp. 45-46.

What Baumgartner seems to fail to consider is the implication of v. 18 that, in some undefined way, YHWH has given Jeremiah access to knowledge of his

Diamond also deduces other points of connection. First, the use of
לָכֵן invites the reader to connect the sections logically; Jeremiah's
prayer ended with a petition, clearly confident than an answer would
be forthcoming. Both sections refer to the enemies merely as
'they/them'; in fact, the ambiguous reference of vv. 18-20 is *only* resolved by vv. 21-23 where 'they' are identified as 'men of Anathoth'.
Finally, there is a poetic correspondence between the enemies'
threats and YHWH's promised judgment.[66]

4.3.3 Interpretation

In the immediately prior section (Jer. 11.1-17), Jeremiah accused the
people, on YHWH's behalf, of having 'broken my covenant' (בְּרִיתִי-
אֶת ... הֵפֵרוּ); there was a glancing mention of Jeremiah's prophetic
ministry (v. 7), but Allen is right that this prior section, especially vv.
2-10, effectively defined Jeremiah's prophetic task 'in terms of reaf-
firming the torah covenant's accountability'.[67] This segues nicely into
the first confession, which is focused on Jeremiah's prophetic role.[68]
As was briefly noted above, the exchange here between prophet and
YHWH has a 'complex tone ... of confident certainty, urgent plea,
assurance, and threat'.[69]

Jeremiah's Prayer (11.18-20)

It should be kept in mind that the goal of the plaintive prayer is to
describe the trouble/crisis in a manner that will provoke a swift divine reaction.[70] The center of the prayer clarifies that the prophet's
enemies are bent on his destruction. That this is presented as a direct

---

enemies' plans. It could be that Jeremiah is here claiming knowledge of a private
conversation amongst the conspirators. He later acknowledges that breaking vv.
21-23 away from vv. 18-23 would mean 'the first song does lose its only concrete
datum [e.g. connection to Anathoth] ... which would have been so valuable for our
understanding of [the historical prophet Jeremiah]'. Baumgartner, *Jeremiah's Poems
of Lament*, p. 46.

[66] In vv. 19 and 21 'the intentions of the opponents are articulated with three
members – two positive, one negative – as also the pronouncement of judgment'
in vv. 22b-23a. These statements in v. 19bβ and vv. 22b-23a form the '"midpoint"
of Jeremiah's lament and YHWH's response'. Diamond, *Confessions in Context*, p.
26.

[67] Allen, *Jeremiah*, p. 145.
[68] This is made clear in YHWH's disclosure in v. 21.
[69] Diamond, *Confessions in Context*, p. 34.
[70] Brueggemann, *Commentary on Jeremiah*, p. 115.

quote indicates both the certainty and enormity of the now-perceived threat.

The opening of the confession וַיהוָה is translated above 'And YHWH', though several versions translate it as a vocative: 'O YHWH', in parallel with v. 20.[71] However, especially given the proximity to v. 20, it seems possible here to hear *both* an introduction to a report *and* an opening to a prayer. This then becomes a story that is *more* than a story, spoken not just to the book's audience but also addressed to YHWH. Such intentional ambiguity serves to increase the text's emotive power and impact on the audience.

This ambiguity creates an introduction that is strangely disruptive. Nothing in the prior verses leads us to expect Jeremiah to offer up a prayer to YHWH or to relate a report to the audience. Furthermore, the narrative Jeremiah relates begins in the middle of the story. Most particularly, there is no identifiable antecedent for 'their deeds' (מַעַלְלֵיהֶם).[72] This introduction is both puzzling and evocative,[73] quite frankly leaving the hearer as clueless as Jeremiah was until the moment of YHWH's revelation.[74] In effect, the confession becomes the listener's moment of revelation. This abruptness[75] is clearly a poetic device that draws the listener into the poem.[76] It heightens suspense and leaves the listener feeling wary, wondering: 'What revelation? What 'deeds'?'

Although the hearer may lack information, Jeremiah assures us that YHWH made him know[77] and now he knows.[78] In fact, Jeremiah

---

[71] See translation note on 11.18 above.

[72] McKane, *Jeremiah,* p. 254.

[73] O'Connor, *Confessions of Jeremiah,* p. 16.

[74] The poem's opening 'could also reflect the prophet's initial lack of awareness concerning the plot'. Craigie, Kelley, and Drinkard, Jr., *Jeremiah 1-25,* p. 177.

[75] However, some introductions to other laments are likewise abrupt; e.g. Ps. 13.1; 28. Craigie, Kelley, and Drinkard, Jr., *Jeremiah 1-25,* p. 177.

[76] O'Connor, *Confessions of Jeremiah,* p. 16.

[77] Bright argues that 'deeds' in v. 18 is a reference to Jeremiah's family's plot to assassinate him in 12.6. See Bright, *Jeremiah,* pp. 89-90, leading him to completely rearrange the text (see below on the structure of 12.1-13). Lundbom questions Bright's judgment and especially finds the textual transposition 'not necessary'; Jeremiah's 'knowledge' of the plot could have 'come in a moment of God-given insight ... [or] some other means'. Lundom, *Jeremiah 1-20,* p. 636.

[78] This doubled occurrence of the same root in immediate succession is known as *multiclimatum* in classical rhetoric; it appears to be a signature construction of the prophet Jeremiah; cf. Jer. 15.19; 17.14 (2x); 20.7, where the 'figure [also] begins a confession, as here'; 31.4, 18 (2x); 30.16. Lundbom, *Jeremiah 1,* p. 636.

reports that YHWH 'showed me' their deeds, the hiphil ראה balanc-
ing the hiphil ידע in the first line. Although the specific dangerous
circumstances are not yet clear,[79] the term 'their deeds' (מַעַלְלֵיהֶם) generally has a 'bad sense' in the book of Jeremiah;[80] even when the term
is technically neutral,[81] Holladay says it still has a 'bad odor', so the
audience should already have an inkling that 'what they are doing is
bad news for Jeremiah'.[82]

In v. 19, it remains uncertain if we are listening to a prayer or a
report.[83] The effect is that this verse can potentially be read as addressed *both* to YHWH *and* to the listeners. That makes the pathetic
statement: 'I was like a trusting lamb led to the slaughter', a *plea for
sympathy* from both YHWH and the audience. Jeremiah views himself
as a docile (pet?) lamb naively following someone to its death. The
image emphasizes the feelings of trust and innocence,[84] or even
'blissful ignorance'.[85] It is a simile of helplessness.[86] Not far in the
background is Nathan's parable of the 'pet lamb'. McKane notes that,
as a 'family pet', the lamb would have been *less* able to care for itself
than a lamb raised in the field, even further magnifying Jeremiah's
vulnerability and innocence.[87] This image sharply contrasts Jeremiah
and his enemies, highlighting Jeremiah's trusting innocence and righteousness against the backdrop of the enemies' evil plotting,[88] evoking
both YHWH (and the listener's) empathy for Jeremiah and rising anger against his enemies.

The second line begins by reiterating Jeremiah's lack of
knowledge. This deliberate pick-up of the verb ידע from v. 18a

---

[79] Holladay, *Jeremiah 1*, p. 365.

[80] Jeremiah 4.4, 18.

[81] Jeremiah 7.3, 5.

[82] Holladay, *Jeremiah 1*, p. 365.

[83] Allen notes the presence of key elements of an 'autobiographical report': a
revelatory intervention (v. 18), a summary of the background (v. 19), and a divine
response to the prophet's request (v. 21). Allen, *Jeremiah*, p. 146.

[84] Baumgartner, *Jeremiah's Poems of Lament*, p. 43.

[85] Carroll, *Jeremiah*, p. 276.

[86] Holladay, *Jeremiah 1*, p. 368, who mentions other such similes found in Psalms:
'I am poured out like water'; 'my heart is like wax'; 'my strength is dried up like a
potsherd'. See e.g. Pss. 22.15-16; 104.4-12.

[87] The lamb's 'instincts of self-preservation are undeveloped and he is unable
to envisage the moves which are being made against him, fare less to take steps to
ensure his safety in a dangerous world'. McKane, *Jeremiah*, p. 256.

[88] Allen, *Jeremiah*, p. 146.

contrasts Jeremiah's 'not-knowing' with YHWH's 'all-knowing'.[89]
The use of עָלַי makes it abundantly clear that these enemies are Jeremiah's *personal* enemies plotting against *him*;[90] he is not simply an un-
intended victim or collateral damage-Jeremiah is the primary target.
The reference here to 'scheming schemes' is even more interesting
when one considers that, earlier in the chapter, YHWH had revealed
to Jeremiah that there was a 'conspiracy' (קֶשֶׁר)[91] among the Judeans
to turn away from YHWH and to serve other gods (see Jer. 11.9-10).
The suddenness of threat to Jeremiah in 11.19 reinforces the likeli-
hood of a connection between the people's 'conspiracy' (קֶשֶׁר) against
YHWH and the 'schemes' (מַחֲשָׁבוֹת) against Jeremiah. The people (including the men of Anathoth apparently) are 'joining together in an
unholy alliance, forsaking the Lord, and throwing off their covenant
commitments in the most overt, despicable way'. It is quite literally
an 'act of corporate treason'.[92] By standing with YHWH, Jeremiah
has become the unwitting target of their animosity, ultimately directed at their rejected covenant Lord. It is even worse than this, for
now Jeremiah shares the enemies' precise *words*. Not only does he
know that he is the object of a plot but also he knows precisely what
the plot is.[93] By *quoting* his enemies, Jeremiah is subtly reiterating his
claim that the plot was somehow revealed by YHWH.[94]

The opening phrase of the enemies' words, 'Let us destroy the
tree with its sap', has generated near endless debate and very little
substantive agreement,[95] particularly because the versions offer very
different interpretations. The most literal reading of the Hebrew is:
'Let us destroy the tree *with its bread* (בְּלַחְמוֹ)', a clearly difficult phrase.
לֶחֶם clearly has to be understood as a metaphorical reference either
to the tree's produce (e.g. its 'fruit') or to the tree's sustenance (e.g. its

---

[89] Holladay, *Jeremiah 1*, p. 372.

[90] Holladay, *Jeremiah 1*, p. 372.

[91] A pretty-apparent wordplay on the catchword שֶׁקֶר, translated 'falsehood'. See comments in ch. 3 on Jer. 7.

[92] Michael L. Brown, 'Jeremiah', in Tremper Longman and David E. Garland (eds.), *Expositor's Bible Commentary* (rev. ed.; Grand Rapids: Eerdmans, 2006), VII, p. 205.

[93] Baumgartner notes that such a 'verbatim citation of the evil plan' is found in the Psalms; see e.g. Pss. 71.11; 74.8. He also notes that the 'last line of v. 19 reap-pears almost word for word in … Ps, 83.5'. Baumgartner, *Jeremiah's Poems of Lament*, p. 44.

[94] Holladay, *Jeremiah 1*, p. 372.

[95] See translation notes above.

'roots').[96] There might also be a connection here to Jeremiah's announcement to the Judeans that the foe from the north will 'devour
(אָכַל)…your *bread* (לְחְמֶךָ) as well as 'your harvests' (קְצִירְךָ) and 'your
sons and daughters' (בָּנֶיךָ וּבְנוֹתֶיךָ).[97] The conspirators, then, would be
planning to do to Jeremiah as Jeremiah declared would be done to
them.[98]

However, the point of the image of felling a sap-filled tree is perhaps more obvious. Jeremiah's enemies desire to 'cut him down' in
his prime/youth; that is, they wish to *fell* the tree, destroying *every part
of it*.[99] That the tree is young and flourishing[100] will make its sudden
demise all the more a shocking surprise.[101] The enemies' use of this
imagery for their assassination plot is hardly coincidental.[102] Earlier,
the prophet had announced that Judah, because of her disobedience,
would be like a green (e.g. young) olive tree destroyed in a storm (Jer.
11.16). In effect, Jeremiah had pronounced a covenant curse over
Judah; now, these plotters 'intend that he will receive the judgment
he announced'.[103] This blatant vengefulness, though, only proves the
point of the earlier section. Judah refuses to listen to YHWH or
YHWH's appointed messenger.[104]

The next line of the threat, 'Let us cut him off from the land of
the living', carries over the tree imagery of the first line.[105] The last

---

[96] Such metaphorical use of לֶחֶם, though unusual, is not unknown. See for example, Prov. 31.14, where 'bread' (לֶחֶם) is a metaphor for a ship's cargo, and Eccl.
11.1, where the term is a metaphor for capital investment.

[97] Jeremiah 5.17.

[98] Although it should be noted they threaten to 'spoil' (שָׁחַת) rather than 'devour'
(אָכַל) Jeremiah.

[99] Lundbom, *Jeremiah 1-20*, p. 637.

[100] If there is any allusion here (e.g. the use of לֶחֶם) to the idea of fruit-bearing
tree, this makes even the *description* of the enemies' plan a violation of Torah (Deut.
20.19), which explicitly forbade the 'destroying' (hiphil שׁחת) of a fruit tree by
'felling' (כרת) it when they had besieged a city; that is, they could not use live fruit-
trees to construct siege-works. Holladay, *Jeremiah 1*, p. 372.

[101] Carroll, *Jeremiah*, p. 276.

[102] Rather than say, something to the effect of, 'Let's slaughter him like a sheep!'
which the listener might have reasonably expected from the earlier imagery.

[103] This reinforces the possibility that לֶחֶם is used in this text to create an inter-
textual echo with Jer. 5.17. John W. Bracke, *Jeremiah 1-29* (Westminster Bible Companion; Louisville, KY; Westminster/John Knox Press, 1999), p. 110. See also Craigie, Kelley, and Drinkard, Jr., *Jeremiah 1-25*, p. 178.

[104] Jeremiah 11.3, 8, 10, 11.

[105] Holladay, *Jeremiah 1*, p. 373.

phrase 'land of the living' (נִכְרְתֶנּוּ מֵאֶרֶץ חַיִּים) is only found here in the
book of Jeremiah.[106] Clearly, it is meant to contrast with the 'land of
the dead'.[107] The enemies' ultimate intent, though, is not simply to
murder Jeremiah; the threat concludes 'that his name be remembered
no more!' As Allen so succinctly puts it: 'The vehemence of the death
wish is expressed in terms of the obliteration of Jeremiah's very name
from human memory'.[108] Just as Judah and Jerusalem wish to forget
YHWH, these schemers wish to forget YHWH's prophet.

The language here could not be more extreme or violent.[109] Diamond notes that in the Psalms, the removal of a name and banish-
ment from 'the land of the living' (i.e. the 'sphere of blessing for the
righteous')[110] is meant to be the fate of wicked persons.[111] What
YHWH has threatened to do to them, they now threaten to do to
Jeremiah.[112] Jeremiah is at a point of unequalled personal danger;
there is no hope that these plotters will suffer a sudden pang of conscience and decide to scrap their plot. They are covenant-breakers
and ignorers of YHWH and YHWH's prophets, the lot of them! The
scheme has clearly already been planned out; all that awaits now is its
final execution. It is requisite that the listener pause a moment to
realize fully the emotive impact of the text's sense of imminent and
inevitable doom for the prophet. Jeremiah stands at the brink of
death for nothing more than faithfully following YHWH's own calling. YHWH's revelation of the plot has not quieted but rather created
unparalleled angst and turmoil.

Though the seriousness of the threat is fully conveyed by the tight
cluster of powerful Hebrew words,[113] there is a bit of an ironic touch
here as well. The idea of eradicating someone's name usually was associated with not having any children. Lundbom suggests that the
enemies may have been plotting to murder the young Jeremiah

---

[106] Thirteen other times in the OT.

[107] Elsewhere in the book, 'Jeremiah sees his opponents the prophets and
priests going off to "the Land", that is, the land of the dead [cf. e.g. Jer. 14.18]'.
Holladay, *Jeremiah 1*, p. 373.

[108] Allen, *Jeremiah*, p. 147.

[109] 'We can imagine that Jeremiah had powerful enemies who wanted to silence
such a treasonable voice'. Brueggemann, *Commentary on Jeremiah*, p. 115.

[110] See, e.g. Pss. 27.13; 116.9; 142.6.

[111] Diamond, *Confessions in Context*, p. 34.

[112] Carroll, *Jeremiah*, p. 279.

[113] E.g. 'Destroy' (שׁחת), 'cut off' (קרת), 'not remember' (לֹא־זכר).

before he had a chance to marry and have children.[114] However, in Jer. 16.1-2, YHWH forbids Jeremiah to marry or have children, effectively accomplishing what Jeremiah's enemies wished to do.[115]

In light of this astounding threat, Jeremiah now plainly makes his petition to YHWH in v. 20. The 'and YHWH' (וַיהוָה) matches the 'and I' (וַאֲנִי) of v. 19, marking an important transition.[116] His choice to describe YHWH as the one who 'judges righteously'[117] is clearly intentional. Blank has argued that this should also be considered legal language.[118] Baumgartner, however, sees the language here as still belonging to the common lament motif of 'trust and innocence'.[119] As 'Judge', YHWH is trusted to perceive correctly both innocence *and* guilt.[120]

The reason that YHWH's perceptions of guilt and innocence can be trusted is explained in the next appellation; YHWH is also the one who 'tests the innermost being and the heart'. This language is also quite common in the Psalms.[121] The verb 'test' (בֹּחֵן) is used at two other significant prior points in the book. In Jer. 6.27, Jeremiah is called upon by YHWH to 'test' the people; later, in 9.6 [7], it is YHWH who 'tests' the people.[122] The verbal root means 'examining to determine essential qualities'.[123] Typically, *God* is the subject of

---

[114] Lundbom, *Jeremiah 1-20*, p. 647.

[115] Holladay, *Jeremiah 1*, p. 373.

[116] Cf. Ps. 22.3, 6, 19. Baumgartner, *Jeremiah's Poems of Lament*, p. 44.

[117] Or as 'YHWH, Righteous Judge'. The phrase שֹׁפֵט צֶדֶק [lit. 'judge of righteousness'] is paralleled in 20.12 by בֹּחֵן צַדִּיק [lit. 'righteous tester' or 'tester of the righteous man']. See comments on structure in Holladay, *Jeremiah 1*, p. 373.

[118] Cf. Jer. 12.1. Following on this, Wimmer thinks the confession genre is actually defined by an admixture of lament and formal complaint (רִיב) genres. See Donald H. Wimmer, 'The Sociology of Knowledge and "The Confessions of Jeremiah"', in Paul J. Achtemeier (ed.), *SBL Seminar Papers, 1979* (SBLSP 15; Missoula, MT: Scholars Press, 1978) I, pp. 399-403.

[119] 'Jeremiah has a strong source of comfort; however, much people misunderstand and persecute him, the divine Judge exercises justice and is not deceived by appearances'. Baumgartner, *Jeremiah's Poems of Lament*, p. 44.

[120] Baumgartner, *Jeremiah's Poems of Lament*, p. 44.

[121] See Pss. 7.10 [9]; 17.3; 26.2; cf. also Prov. 17.3; 21.2.

[122] Lundbom, *Jeremiah 1-20*, p. 637. Among the prophets, בחן is something of a Jeremianic 'signature term', being used 6 times and only twice in all other prophetic books. M. Tsevat, 'בחן', *TDOT*, II, pp. 69-72.

[123] The term is actually a 'middle' verb between נָסָה 'to put to the test, tempt', and צָרַף 'to smelt, refine'. Bruce K. Waltke, 'בָּחַן', *TWOT*, I, p. 100.

בֹּחֵן;[124] the term is used 'almost exclusively' in reference to spiritual matters[125] and is also used quite specifically in reference to people.[126]

'Innermost being' translates the term כְּלָיוֹת (literally, 'kidneys'). These organs were regarded by the Israelites as predominantly organs of feeling.[127] In fact, the kidneys are associated with all manner of emotional states, from joy (Prov. 23.15-16) to agony (Ps. 73.21).[128] In fact, when Job and the author of Lamentations are overcome by their sorrow, they state that YHWH has pierced their 'kidneys' with an arrow.[129] Perhaps most fascinating for our consideration is how the psalmist specifically mentions the kidneys in the recounting of his 'personal creation story' in Ps. 139.13-14: 'You formed my kidneys; you knit me together in my mother's womb'. It cannot escape notice here how incredibly close the *last* cola of the verse (תְּסֻכֵּנִי בְּבֶטֶן אִמִּי כִּי־אַתָּה קָנִיתָ כְלְיֹתָי) is to the *opening* cola of Jer. 1.5 (אֶצָּרְךָ בַבֶּטֶן יְדַעְתִּיךָ בְּטֶרֶם).

More than just 'organs of feeling', however, the 'kidneys' are the seat of the individual's 'innermost being'[130] and seem to function as

---

[124] Which makes Jer. 6.27 something of a novelty.

[125] Waltke, 'בָּחַן', p. 100.

[126] Tsevat, 'בחן', p. 71.

[127] Job 19.27; Prov. 23.16. Lundbom, *Jeremiah 1-20*, p. 637. Andrew Bowling gives a helpful (partial) list of feelings attributed to the 'heart' in the OT: joy (1 Sam. 2.1); loyalty (2 Sam. 15.6); gladness (Gen. 45.26); grief (Neh. 2.2, 'sadness of heart'); regret (1 Sam. 24.6; cf. 2 Sam. 24.10; Gen. 6.6); contempt (2 Sam. 6.16); envy (Prov. 23.17); anger (Prov. 19.3); and fear (Gen. 42.28, the heart 'left'; 1 Sam. 17.32, the heart 'fell'; Josh. 14.7, the heart 'melted'). In fact, 'the whole spectrum of emotion is attributed to the heart'. Andrew Bowling, 'לֵבָב', *TWOT*, I, pp. 466-67.

[128] 1 Maccabees 2.24 records that Mattathias became so angry at witnessing an apostate Jew offering pagan sacrifice that 'his kidneys trembled'. D. Kellerman, 'כְּלָיוֹת', *TDOT*, VII, pp. 178-82.

[129] See Job 16.13; Lam. 3.13. Robert B. Chisholm, 'כִּלְיָה', *NIDOTTE*, II, pp. 656-57. On this, Oswalt makes an interesting point: 'If a near eastern warrior could be fired on from the rear, he was very vulnerable'. In both the Job and Lamentations passage, it is clear the speakers 'are claiming that God has surrounded them and overcome them with … superior strength'. John N. Oswalt, 'כלה', *TWOT*, I, pp. 440-41.

[130] Oswalt thinks this may have something to do with the practice of animal sacrifice in the Israelite cult since, in the required dismemberment of the animal, the kidneys were the last organ to be reached and were also encased in protective fat. Oswalt, *TWOT*, I, p. 441.
In fact, the kidneys were of special significance in the Hebrew cult. Of the 31 occurrences of the term, 16 'relate to sacrificial practices'. Oswalt thinks the most obvious reason is that fat was considered a 'special delicacy reserved for God'.

a metonymy for a person's moral character.[131] In fact, it is not too great a stretch to claim that the 'kidneys', in ancient Israelite anthropology, functioned as the *seat of the affections*,[132] those 'controlling loves' that define our truest self, effectively dictate our actions and reactions, and ultimately determine our final destiny.[133]

Yet YHWH is not simply the 'Tester of Kidneys'; rather, YHWH is the one who tests 'the kidneys *and* the heart'. If there is any Hebraic anthropological term more important than כְּלָיוֹת, it may be the term לֵב. Intriguingly, the term 'heart' (לֵב) is rarely used with reference to the actual physical organ.[134] In Hebraic anthropology, the 'heart' actually functions in every dimension of human existence and in all

---

Since the kidneys were usually encased in fat, they were therefore sacred. Oswalt, *TWOT*, I, p. 440; see also R.K. Harrison, 'Kidneys', *ISBE*, III, p. 13.

[131] Chisholm, *NIDOTTE*, II, p. 656.

[132] 'As the protected, inmost organ, the kidneys signify the deepest aspects of the character.' Holladay, *Jeremiah 1*, p. 373.

[133] I am here using the term 'affections' as a precise theological term, in the sense described by Steven Jack Land. Land writes, 'If the heart is understood to be the integrative center of the mind, will, and emotions then it is clear that affections are more than mere feelings and … are meant to characterize a person's life'. In Land's definition, 'affections' have three key characteristics. First, they are objective; that is, they are to be found in God, whose character is the 'source of correlative affections in the believer'. Second, they are relational, and religious practice, especially Christian religious practice, is designed to both shape and express the affections. Finally (and most importantly for our use of the term here), affections are 'dispositional', which is the natural result of their being objective and relational. This means that 'affections' have more to do with a person's *character* than with their *emotions*. He describes the difference with this example. 'One might, with adrenalin flowing, heart pumping, and mood considerably elevated, breathe a silent thanks after a near miss on the highway. But this does not mean that one is a grateful person, much less a thankful Christian.' That is, 'giving thanks' is an act of *emotion*, but 'being thankful' (especially in trying circumstances, for example) is an *affection*.

As 'orientations' of our basic character, our 'affections' shape how we construe the world. They motivate our behavior and become, over time, the 'reasons' for our behaviors. Affections thus serve to 'integrate', not just 'balance', individual thoughts and feelings and become the 'core' that links the heart to the mind. Steven Jack Land, *Pentecostal Spirituality*, pp. 128-32.

[134] Also, the term is used almost exclusively in reference to humans; the idea that animals had a לֵב appears to have been 'largely unknown to the OT'. H.-J. Fabry, 'לֵב', *TDOT*, VII, pp. 399-437.

aspects of the person,[135] so much so that Fabry declares it nearly identical with the term נֶפֶשׁ.[136]

It is important to remember, too, that, while Hebraic thought *did* consider the human person a 'composite', analyzing and compartmentalizing that composite structure was never a central issue. The OT seeks to present humans not as beings-comprised-of-separable-components but as beings-in-relation-to-God.[137] Thus, לֵב became a deeply rich term for the immaterial nature; the לֵב may be thought of as 'an inner reflection of the outer [person]'.[138]

There is one final aspect to consider, the OT presentation of YHWH's heart. Fabry notes that of the 26 OT texts that mention YHWH's heart, the book of Jeremiah contains the most references.[139] Most intriguingly, YHWH's heart functions in much the same way as the human heart. YHWH's 'heart' is the source of YHWH's emotions,[140] recognition and memory,[141] and will and forethought.[142]

Thus, the 'heart' is, in some way, a shared divine-human nexus, a way in which humanity 'images' their Creator. As the 'core' of each individual, the heart is 'the point where Yahweh impinges on human existence'.[143] As Creator of the לֵב, YHWH is the one who ultimately

---

[135] E.g. 'vital, affective, noetic, voluntative'. Fabry, 'לֵב', p. 412.

[136] Fabry, 'לֵב', p. 413. In fact, in some texts, the term לֵב can almost replace the personal pronoun. See Friedrich Stolz, 'לֵב', *TLOT* II, pp. 638-42. See, for example, Psalm 27: 'If an army should encamp against me, my heart (לִבִּי) does not fear; if a battle arises around me, in this I (אֲנִי) am confident'. Clearly, לֵב and אֲנִי are paralleled.

[137] Cf. Ps. 8.5 [4]; 144.3; Job 7.17. Fabry also points out that the 'primary point' of the linguistically differentiated accounts of the creation of humanity in Gen. 1.27 and 2.7 'is the relationship of the human individual to God the creator rather than the structure of the person'. Fabry, 'לֵב', pp. 412-13.

[138] Bowling, *TWOT*, I, p. 466.

[139] Jeremiah 3.15; 7.31; 8.18; 19.5; 32.35 (cf. 7.31); 32.41; 44.21; 48.36. Fabry, 'לֵב', p. 426; Stolz, 'לֵב', p. 642. Lundbom points out that the book of Jeremiah uses the term 'heart' 57 times. Lundbom, *Jeremiah 1-20*, p. 637.

[140] Genesis 6.6, concern; Hos. 11.8, compassion.

[141] 1 Kings 9.3; Jer. 44.21. Particularly in that last text, Judah's continued worship of the 'Queen of Heaven' has 'gone to the heart' (וַתַּעֲלֶה עַל־לִבּוֹ) of YHWH. Fabry, 'לֵב', p. 435.

[142] Genesis 8.21; Jer. 7.31. Stolz, 'לֵב', p. 642.

[143] Though the OT does not have a word close to the English concept of 'conscience', the Israelites 'were commanded constantly to follow the Torah and shape their לֵב in obedience to God's word [Deut. 30.14, 17; Jer. 31.33; Ezek. 36.26-27]. The לֵב as the organ of knowledge notes deviations from God's will.' Fabry, 'לֵב', p. 426.

governs it, and the לֵב of YHWH provides the norm for human conduct.[144]

Given the recurrence of the combined phrase, Kellerman claims
that 'the heart and the kidneys' is an OT merism for the entire person.[145] To satisfy our Western analytical compulsions, Lundbom suggests that the 'kidneys' represent our feelings and the 'heart', though
not disconnected from our feelings, is more representative of the
mind and will.[146] However, just as the 'heart' connects YHWH and
the individual person,[147] so it appears the idea of 'emotions' or 'feelings' is the shared commonality of the OT conceptions of the 'kidneys' and the 'heart', further supporting the above suggestion that
the 'kidneys' could be described as the seat of human affections.

By framing his petition to YHWH in this very particular manner,
Jeremiah is clearly making assertions about YHWH that lead to a specific set of expectations. What is surprisingly *unclear* yet is precisely
whose heart and kidneys righteous YHWH is supposed to test! Is
Jeremiah requesting YHWH to test *his* heart or his *enemies'* hearts?[148]
The ambiguity on this point may indicate the language is not just language of *intimacy* but also language of *vulnerability*. YHWH's scrutiny,
then, has both constructive and destructive aspects, as does YHWH's
Word. It is a positive, comforting reality for Jeremiah[149] and a negative, discomfiting reality for Jeremiah's enemies (or, at least, it *should*
be).

With this identification of YHWH in place and with the revelation of the plot against Jeremiah, the attentive listener might pause to

---

[144] 1 Samuel 2.34; 13.14. Fabry, 'לֵב', p. 435.

[145] The phrase was 'presumably meant to characterize the total person by referring to an especially important organ in each of the two major portions of the
body: the heart in the chest cavity above the diaphragm and the kidneys representing the abdominal cavity extending below the diaphragm.' Kellerman, *TDOT*, VII,
p. 181.

[146] Lundbom, *Jeremiah 1-20*, p. 637; Kellerman, *TDOT*, VII, p. 181.

[147] That is, each person and YHWH both have a 'heart', in the metaphorical
sense predominant in the OT.

[148] See Holladay, who suggests that the phrase 'on them' (מֵהֶם) in 11.20c indicates that Jeremiah is requesting the test be conducted on his enemies. Holladay,
Jeremiah 1, p. 373.

[149] Baumgartner suggests that even though the phrase is grammatically a petition (e.g. 'May I see …'), practically and functionally it could perhaps also be
thought of as an expression of assurance (e.g. 'I *will* see …'.). Baumgartner, *Jeremiah's Poems of Lament*, p. 44.

wonder what kind of request Jeremiah will make of YHWH. As we
have seen, the plot is in motion and the threat of death appears imminent. Requesting YHWH's *protection* from the threat would seem
to be a very logical choice.[150] What we find instead is the angry-
sounding: 'Let me see your vengeance upon them'. Jeremiah's terror
has given way to vengeful anger.[151]

Long ago, Baumgartner had already noted that this 'passionate
desire for revenge' was a problem for most exegetes, who attempted
to reread it as a zealous desire for YHWH's cause. However, Baumgartner allows no such quibbling, noting that נִקְמָתְךָ simply (only)
means 'the vengeance that comes from thee'.[152]

However, the problem persists among contemporary interpreters.[153] So it is fair and important[154] to ask what exactly Jeremiah is
requesting when he asks for 'vengeance' (נְקָמָה). Sauer notes that, in
its origin, the term was probably legal language. In the Israelite legal
system, a punishment was thought to rectify or cancel out an injustice.[155] Thus, the concepts of legitimacy and authority inhere in the
concept of vengeance;[156] this is perhaps best expressed in Deut.

---

[150] In the book of Psalms, for example, the language of YHWH as a 'refuge' is
one of the 'broadest metaphorical schemas ... in which a host of particular images
and iconic metaphors have their home'. William P. Brown, *Seeing the Psalms: A Theology of Metaphor* (Louisville, KY: Westminster/John Knox Press, 2002), pp. 15-16.
Brown offers as an example (Ps. 18.1-2) where 'refuge' metaphors abound:
I love you, YHWH, my strength (חִזְק)
YHWH is my crag (סֶלַע), my stronghold (מְצוּדָה),
    And my deliverer.
My God is my rock (צוּר), in whom I take refuge (אֶחֱסֶה),
    My shield (מָגֵן), and the horn of my salvation,
    My secure height (מִשְׂגָּב).
[151] Carroll sees Jeremiah's appeal for divine vengeance *as* a request for 'protection'. Carroll, *Jeremiah*, p. 276.
[152] The wording gives 'no indication' of allusion to YHWH's 'cause'. Baumgartner, *Jeremiah's Poems of Lament*, p. 44.
[153] For example, Lundbom is insistent that Jeremiah is not seeking 'personal
vengeance, rather the vengeance of YHWH', that is, 'appropriate punishment for
wrongdoing'. Lundbom, *Jeremiah 1-20*, p. 638. See H.G.L. Peels, *The Vengeance of
God* (*OtSt* 31; Leiden: Brill, 1995), pp. 224-33.
[154] 'More than half of the 79 occurrences of the root [נקם] are in the Prophets
... and the root occurs most in Jeremiah (18x).' G. Sauer, 'נקם', *TLOT*, II, pp. 767-
69.
[155] Sauer, *TLOT*, II, p. 768.
[156] H.G.L. Peels, 'נקם', *NIDOTTE*, III, pp. 145-56.

32.35, where YHWH lays claim to נְקָמָה as solely a divine prerogative.[157]

Peels argues that, contra its modern connotations, the OT concept
of 'vengeance' is a *positive* concept, having to do with 'lawfulness, justice, and salvation'.[158] While it is most certainly punitive, it represents
YHWH as sovereign King, standing up against injustice and evil to
vindicate YHWH's name, maintain justice, and intervene to save
YHWH's people.[159] But divine vengeance is not only directed against
non-Israelites. It is true that YHWH becomes Israel's Champion
when she is faced by an enemy, but it is also true that YHWH, as the
covenant God, punishes all who break covenant.[160]

So far, Peels' explanation is insightful and helpful. However,
when he specifically addresses the imprecatory psalms and Jeremiah's
Confessions, his interpretation becomes more difficult to accept. In
these texts Peels says that we see:

> An abandonment of private revenge and a total surrender to him
> who judges righteously. In no instance is the satisfaction of feel-
> ings of hatred of embittered people at stake. The prayer for
> vengeance is the prayer for victory of lawfulness and the revela-
> tion of the God of the covenant, who, while judging, keeps his
> word[161] … The imprecation, *in its deepest intention*, is a cry for the
> breakthrough of God's kingdom in liberation and vengeance.[162]

In this observation, Peels has effectively gutted the imprecatory
psalms and the confessions of any authentic emotive content. That
this is Peels' conclusion is even more puzzling because he had already

---

[157] In about '85 percent' of the occurrences, 'God is the subject, either directly
or in a derivative sense. In the OT, נקם is normally God's prerogative, or that of the
people used by him as instruments (judge, king, court, people) … Metaphors like
God as King, God as Judge, and God as Warrior play a great part in נקם-texts'.
Peels, *NIDOTTE*, III, p. 154.

[158] Which is why 'vengeance' is such an important theological category for the
prophets, especially Isaiah, Jeremiah, and Ezekiel. Peels, *NIDOTTE*, III, p. 154.

[159] Peels, *NIDOTTE*, III, p. 154. נְקָמָה 'is a command that the sovereign authority of Yahweh should be placed in action in order to punish/redress an action that
is incompatible with the sovereignty of that same ultimate authority'. George E.
Mendenhall, *The Tenth Generation: The Origins of the Biblical Tradition* (Baltimore:
Johns Hopkins University Press, 1973), p. 91.

[160] Cf. Ps. 94; Lev. 26.24-25. Elmer B. Smick, 'נקם', *TWOT*, II, pp. 598-99.

[161] See Pss. 58.11; 79.10; 94.1; 149.7.

[162] Peels, *NIDOTTE*, III, p. 155, italics mine.

described the notion of divine vengeance as 'no foreign element in the OT revelation of God'.[163]

Sauer affirms the inclusion of an emotive element in the concept of נקם. While noting that Lev. 19.18 is an explicit warning against human vindictiveness, he observes that 'emotionally laden action often assumes the foreground and largely determines the meaning of נקם'.[164] Furthermore, to admit the presence of an emotive element in the OT concept of vengeance does not equate to denying its roots in the concept of justice nor its ownership by YHWH. It does, however, affirm that, in the OT, 'crying out to God for vengeance' is *both* a petition for justice *and* an emotional catharsis.[165]

Brown's interpretation of this phrase likewise seems to be particularly unhelpful and confusing, especially his distinction between 'righteous' emotions[166] and 'earthly' emotions that are (both) seen in the Confessions.[167] He cautions: 'While the prophet's humanity may be a tool in God's hands … his sinfulness must be bypassed when a word from heaven is being delivered'.[168] Apparently, then, in certain of the Confession passages, Brown must assume that Jeremiah is speaking sinfully. Also, Brown seems to assume that YHWH is capable of using every aspect of the human to communicate YHWH's Word except for human emotions.

Allen's comments are bit more helpful. He does not find this climactic request surprising; in fact, he calls it 'appropriate'.[169] This is not simply a request that YHWH carry out vengeance; more

---

[163] Peels, *NIDOTTE*, III, p. 155. That there most certainly *is* an emotive element attached to the idea of 'vengeance' is evident, it seems, just from Ps. 94, to use one of Peels' own examples. *Twice* in the opening verse of the Psalm, YHWH is addressed as אל־נקמות – literally, 'God of vengeance'. Not only that, but the *closing verse* (Ps. 94.23) twice reiterates the request: 'Annihilate them (יצמיתם) through their wickedness; annihilate them (יצמיתם), YHWH our God'. It is difficult to see this as an 'unemotional' petition for justice, especially with the use of such drastic language.

[164] For an especially good example, see Prov. 6.34. Sauer, *TLOT*, II, p. 768.

[165] I find it interesting that in Peels' definition of imprecation as 'a cry for the breakthrough of God's kingdom' (see above), he seems to miss the fact that it still is, first of all, a 'cry'.

[166] E.g. 'emotions that long for justice to prevail and for the Lord to be honored among his people'. Brown, *Expositor's Bible Commentary*, VII, p. 210.

[167] Esp. Jer. 12.1-4; 15.10; 20.14-18. Brown, *Expositor's Bible Commentary*, VII, p. 210. Brown does not provide any detailed criteria for distinguishing a 'righteous' emotion from an 'earthly' emotion.

[168] Brown, *Expositor's Bible Commentary*, VII, p. 210.

[169] Allen, *Jeremiah*, p. 147.

precisely, it is a request that YHWH carry out vengeance for an offense committed against *YHWH*, i.e. the plot to assassinate YHWH's appointed messenger.[170] Thus, the request reinforces the identity of Jeremiah with YHWH and YHWH's Word.

Finally, Jeremiah follows the petition with a motivational clause, the reason why he is requesting YHWH's 'vengeance' upon the plotters: 'For to you I have revealed my cause'. Just as Jeremiah had willingly placed himself under YHWH's scrutiny at the beginning of the verse, he now willingly 'turns his case over' to YHWH to prosecute. It seems that the emphatic 'to you' (אֵלֶיךָ) of the appeal here balances the equally emphatic 'against me' (עָלַי) of the schemers' scheme in the prior verse.

The verb 'revealed' (גִּלִּיתִי)[171] literally means to 'uncover'. However, this seems to introduce a contradiction into the first confession. Jeremiah is claiming now that *he* has 'revealed' this to YHWH; in v. 18, Jeremiah stated that *YHWH* had been the agent of revelation to *the prophet*. The emendation of גִּלִּיתִי ('I have revealed') to גִּלּוֹתִי ('I have entrusted') presented an easy solution to the apparent contradiction in the direction of revelation.

However, Jeremiah does not claim that he revealed *the plot* (מַעַלְלֵיהֶם);[172] rather, he claims to have revealed 'my case' (רִיבִי). Thus, the real interpretive issue here is not so much the verb but rather the *object* of the verb. What is Jeremiah's 'case'? Above, we noted that Jeremiah's actual petition to YHWH does not begin until 11.20; 11.19 is often treated simply as a summary explanation of what YHWH revealed to Jeremiah at the beginning of 11.18. However, notice that Jeremiah does *not* say: 'YHWH told me, "You are being led like a lamb to the slaughter"'. Those are Jeremiah's *own* words *to* YHWH (and to the listener).

What Jeremiah, then, has 'revealed' to YHWH – his 'case' (e.g. defence) against the enemies' plot – is his own *innocence* and *vulnerability*, couched in one of the most powerful emotive images in the

---

[170] Cf. Jer. 15.15. In these texts, then, the listener is 'invited to hear an echo of Yahweh's national commitment to vengeance in the refrains of 5.9, 29; 9.9 [8]'. Allen, *Jeremiah*, p. 147.

[171] I do not follow Hitzig's popular suggestion that verbal root is נלל ('to trust') rather than נלה ('to reveal/uncover'). See notes on translation above.

[172] E.g. 'their deeds' (Jer. 11.18).

Confessions. The core of Jeremiah's 'case', then, is both his *righteous-ness*[173] and his *emotional state*.[174]

It is important to note as well, especially given the attention to the *legal* vocabulary in this statement, that the term גָּלָה is a significant term in *prophetic* literature. In particular, in his classic definition of the role of the prophet, Amos asserts that YHWH does not act unless YHWH 'reveals' (גָּלָה) YHWH's 'counsel' (סוֹד) to the prophets.[175] A key reason that Jeremiah can be confident that YHWH knows/sees/tests his innermost being and heart is that Jeremiah has *revealed* that to YHWH ... *in the same way that YHWH has revealed YHWH's will and word to him*! It appears then that prophetic revelation in Jeremiah works *both* ways, with YHWH revealing YHWH's counsel and will to the prophets, and the prophets likewise revealing their hearts to YHWH.

The choice of this term here in the final cola of Jeremiah's request perhaps could be, then, a quite dramatic summary of the various emotive dimensions we have been exploring. Jeremiah is revealing his cause to YHWH, exposing all the fear and anger residing in his heart. Such exposure is an act of ultimate trust; one would only express such innermost feelings to a trusted confidant. As was mentioned, YHWH the Righteous Judge is very much a double-sided image of YHWH. YHWH's perception gives great hope to the (truly) righteous but should strike fear into the hearts of the wicked and rebellious. It seems clear that Jeremiah makes his request for examination and final verdict not simply because he is confident in his innocence before and intimacy with YHWH but also because he wishes to expose his enemies to YHWH's scrutiny and subsequent judgment. There is perhaps a sense of poetic justice here. Jeremiah's enemies have been going 'behind his back', plotting his early demise; so Jeremiah now requests that *YHWH* go 'behind *their* backs'[176] to reveal the evil of their secret thoughts and judge them accordingly.

---

[173] Expressed as a claim to innocence.

[174] Expressed in the language of vulnerability.

[175] Amos 3.7. The term is not a 'technical term for God's revelation' since 'it is used of men as well as of God'. For use with a human subject, see 1 Sam. 20.2, 12-13; 22.8, 17; Ruth 4.4; for use with the divine subject, see 1 Sam. 9.15; 2 Sam. 7.27=1 Chron. 17.25; also Job 33.16; 36.10. Waltke, however, admits: 'Though not a technical term for divine revelation, the verb ... *frequently conveys this meaning*'. Bruce K. Waltke, 'גָּלָה', *TWOT*, I, pp. 160-61, italics mine.

[176] E.g. the location of the 'kidneys'.

Brueggemann, sees the same dynamic at work in the text's foren-sic language. The petition here is simultaneously a 'suit for acquittal' and a 'countersuit for conviction'.[177] Though this is clearly an emo-tionally-laden request, it is not a hysterical cry for revenge. Certainly, fear and anger are present and are deeply felt, yet Jeremiah's petition remains a justified legal claim.[178] In fact, Jeremiah *must* make the pe-tition because, at this precise moment, the unrighteous (e.g. those who plot against Jeremiah) appear to be winning against the righteous (e.g. the prophet himself), threatening not just the death of the prophet but the 'uprooting' and 'overthrowing' of the moral order of YHWH's world if they are allowed to succeed.

Already, the careful listener hears, stirring just beneath the sur-face, powerful and conflicting/shifting emotions that move the text in surprising directions and open new possibilities. The most obvious shift presented to us here is found in Jeremiah's feelings toward the plotters. At the *very* beginning (e.g. *before* YHWH's revelation), Jere-miah's relationship with this still-unidentified group was at least am-icable.[179] However, as soon as the plot is revealed in the beginning of the text, that immediately falls away to be replaced by fear and per-haps even a sense of impending doom. It seems important to remem-ber that YHWH has *only* revealed that a plot was afoot and has said not a word about any plans to thwart it and/or protect the prophet. As Jeremiah petitions YHWH for help, that fear clearly and quickly gives way to a cry for vengeance against his enemies whose angry, un-prophet-like tones still trouble listeners today. Then, in the prayer's very last phrase, trust in YHWH returns to the fore. That trust does not cancel the fear and anger of the prior lines but rather seems to envelop it in the central affection that orients the prophet's life with YHWH.

YHWH's Reply (11.21-23)

In v. 21, we come to the second half of the first Confession text. YHWH's response to Jeremiah's prayer. YHWH's answer to Jere-miah's prayer is framed as a disaster oracle proclaimed against the

---

[177] Brueggemann, *Commentary on Jeremiah*, p. 116.
[178] Brueggemann, *Commentary on Jeremiah*, p. 116.
[179] The depth of Jeremiah's reactions may indicate that the relationship was even closer.

plotters.[180] However, this is an odd sort of oracle because, clearly, it is not to be proclaimed. YHWH is simply informing the prophet about the impending judgment soon to fall upon them.[181] In a way, YHWH's answer to the plot of Jeremiah's enemies is to hatch a counter-plot of YHWH's own involving Jeremiah!

Verse 21 should be understood as the introduction to the oracle rather than the oracle proper.[182] The repetition of the messenger formula, though disruptive, serves to keep the enemies' words separate from YHWH's.[183] Most importantly, in the oracle itself, YHWH's promised intervention is presented in tricolic form, matching the form of the description of the plot against Jeremiah in v. 19b. This poetic balance emphasizes that YHWH's planned punishment matches the enemies' planned assassination; in effect, 'the threat of death in v. 21 becomes a boomerang'.[184] Another effect of YHWH's reply is to align the prophet firmly with YHWH and Jeremiah's enemies with the rebellious people of Israel.[185] Thus, Jeremiah and the plotters are revealed now to be representatives of a much larger drama. The issue here no longer is simply Jeremiah's contention with those who seek his life; that conflict is now caught up into YHWH's ongoing struggle with the entire rebellious people.[186]

What is perhaps most intriguing about the introduction to YHWH's answer is how *it* reveals the identity of the plotters before YHWH even speaks. The listeners' fear has been building across the opening verses because of the prolonged anonymity of the conspirators; it is natural to expect the revelation of their identity to relieve the dramatic tension. Instead, the listener is subjected to a

---

180 Allen, *Jeremiah*, p. 147.

181 McKane, *Jeremiah*, p. 258.

182 For a similar format, see Jer. 7.15. As there, Jer. 11.21 contains a 'messenger formula, a word about the individuals for whom the oracle is intended, and a summary of what these individuals have said'. The key difference is that Jer. 7.15 offered a 'summary statement' of the oracle; Jer. 11.21 does not. Lundbom, *Jeremiah 1-20*, p. 633.

183 'Formula redundancies occur in introductions, not at the beginning of oracles'. Lundbom, *Jeremiah 1-20*, p. 634.

184 Allen, *Jeremiah*, p. 147.

185 O'Connor, *Confessions of Jeremiah*, pp. 18-19.

186 The use of highly rhetorical language to describe the men of Anathoth's punishment 'may indicate that they represent all the people who, like them, reject the word of the prophet'. O'Connor, *Confessions of Jeremiah*, p. 19.

tremendous shock: the plotters are 'the men of Anathoth'. To put it perhaps too colloquially, the plotters are Jeremiah's 'home-town friends'.

The effect of this revelation, which the listener only receives second-hand,[187] is simply awful. Baumgartner, with rather uncharacteristic feeling, calls it 'a terrible message, considering the strong love for home that people of antiquity had. What raging anger must have filled the prophet.'[188] The audience already knew that the conspirators were out to murder Jeremiah from the prophet's prayer, but now we hear the threat straight from them, confirming Jeremiah's report and the listener's worst fears for the prophet. 'You shall not prophesy in the name of YHWH or you will surely die by our hand.'

This verse has been something of an interpretive puzzle. Many commentators have found a conflict between this report and the description of the situation provided in Jer. 11.18-20, where the plot is hidden. Suddenly, a hidden plot appears to be an open threat. One solution would be to keep in mind that the *means* of YHWH's revelation of the plot were never fully explained, only assumed, in Jer. 11.18; perhaps it was at the moment of an utterance such as this (which YHWH has clearly overheard and recorded) that YHWH chose to reveal to Jeremiah the entirety of the plot against him. Again, Jer. 11.21 appears to function more as a revelation for the *listener* than for the figure of the prophet, leading us on the same horrifying journey Jeremiah has just undergone.

The men of Anathoth's threat is a categorical demand, an absolute prohibition like the Ten Commandments.[189] The sense of it is 'Absolutely not' or 'Under no circumstances'. To be clear, they are not demanding Jeremiah take a vow of silence; it is a particular kind of speech that is prohibited, prophecy 'in the name of YHWH'. Read another way, the threat here implies that if Jeremiah *will* cease to prophesy in YHWH's name, the death threat will be lifted.[190] YHWH

---

[187] Perhaps Jeremiah could not actually bring himself to 'say it'? It seems safe to assume that the prophet already knew this about the identity of the plotters from the revelatory moment reported in Jer. 11.18; the shock that the prophet felt then is now shared by the audience.

[188] Baumgartner, *Jeremiah's Poems of Lament*, p. 45.

[189] Exodus 20.1-17; Deut. 5.6-21.

[190] Carroll, *Jeremiah*, p. 280.

has compelled Jeremiah to speak the Word;[191] the men of Anathoth are here trying to compel Jeremiah to silence. Attentive listeners should sense the prophet's unbearable emotional strain.

Lundbom notes that, as with humans, the name of YHWH is the embodiment of YHWH's essential character.[192] There appears to be a fascinating recognition at work here among Jeremiah's enemies: even in their threatening, they are admitting (wittingly or unwittingly is harder to say) that the word Jeremiah speaks actually embodies YHWH's character. That is, their prohibition testifies that Jeremiah's word is the *true* prophetic word that should be obeyed.[193] The men of Anathoth would simply rather not listen and obey. In Jer. 11.10, the first mark of the conspiracy against YHWH was that the people 'refused (מאן)[194] to hear (שמע) my word (דבר)' and thereby have broken the covenant.[195] Furthermore, this prohibition against speaking 'in YHWH's name' is linked to their plan to obliterate Jeremiah's 'name' from the social memory. Given the identification of Jeremiah as *YHWH's* spokesman, the removal of Jeremiah's name is tantamount to the removal of YHWH's name from Israel.[196]

If Jeremiah refuses to cease preaching in the name of YHWH, the men of Anathoth have a promise of their own to him: 'You will surely die by our hand'. The personal nature of the threat – these are men that Jeremiah knows well – makes it even more threatening.[197] It also makes clear the depth of deception operative in the Judah of

---

[191] Jeremiah 20.9.

[192] Lundbom, *Jeremiah 1-20*, p. 638.

[193] Holladay, *Jeremiah 1*, p. 375.

[194] This root appears 12x in the book of Jeremiah: nearly all occurrences are a refusal to obey YHWH; the only exceptions are Jer. 15.18 (where the prophet's wound 'refuse" to heal), 31.15 (where Rachel 'refuses' comfort for her lost children); and 50.33-34 (where YHWH announces the intention to rescue Israel from captivity since her captors 'refuse' to let her go). Jeremiah 50.33 appears to be the only place in Jeremiah where the term is used in a positive way.

[195] Clements comments: 'Jeremiah's declaration that Israel had broken its covenant relationship with God … in [an] irremedial way set the prophet in a new role. From being mediator within the covenant Jeremiah had effectively stepped outside its range to declare that the covenant itself had suffered a mortal blow.' Jeremiah, however, retains his position as 'go-between, mediating between God and a godless nation', and it 'was tearing apart his own inner being. His message-bearing task imposed on him a tension between wanting to defend the people against God and wanting to defend God against the misunderstandings of the people.' R.E. Clements, *Jeremiah* (IBC; Louisville, KY; Westminster/John Knox Press, 1989), p. 79.

[196] O'Connor, *Confessions of Jeremiah*, p. 19.

[197] Craigie, Kelley, and Drinkard, Jr., *Jeremiah 1-25*, p. 178.

Jeremiah's day. These men felt free to issue a death threat against Jeremiah *because they considered him a false prophet*.[198] This may well be one of the most tragic ironies in the book. They have justified their animosity toward YHWH's prophet and the Word that he bears by denying that he is a prophet at all. No matter what Jeremiah says to them now, they will not believe him. There is, therefore, no chance for these plotters to repent. They have not simply stopped listening to YHWH's Word; worse, they have lost all ability to hear it *as* YHWH's Word. Their prospects are frightening, as YHWH's response bears out.

The second messenger formula effectively reinserts YHWH into the argument between the men of Anathoth and the prophet Jeremiah. 'Therefore, thus YHWH of hosts has said ...' The effect of the perfect verb (אָמַר) here is to emphasize the 'decidedness' of what is now decreed; YHWH's decision has been finalized and there will be no going back. In continuity with the legal language so liberally sprinkled throughout Jeremiah's prayer, YHWH has issued the indictment and is now passing sentence on the conspirators.

That sentence is effectively summarized in the main verb of the first colon: 'Look, I will reckon (פֹּקֵד) with them'. The most literal translation is 'visit',[199] though the term's modern connotations are much more congenial than its Hebraic sense. Hamilton suggests its most basic meaning is 'to exercise oversight over a subordinate'.[200] The idea here is of a close inspection.[201] When the term is used specifically of YHWH, פקד often has a sense of being called to accountability or responsibility, especially for wrongdoing.[202] And the men of

---

[198] 'According to their viewpoint, Jeremiah predicts prophecies of retribution of his own plotting and [then] attributes these prophecies to God.' Such an accusation had some measure of credibility 'since Jeremiah's prophecies had not yet been realized'. Avioz, *'I Sat Alone'*, p. 36.

[199] *CDCH*, s.v. 'פקד'; *BDB*, s.v. 'פקד'.

[200] Victor P. Hamilton, 'פָּקַד', *TWOT*, II, pp. 731-33.

[201] See W. Schottroff, 'פקד', *TLOT*, II, pp. 1018-31, that this 'obvious meaning' extends to mean 'to see attentively or in an examining manner'. Cf. 1 Sam. 14.17; 20.6; 2 Sam. 3.8; 2 Kgs. 9.34; Isa. 27.3 for examples of 'visitation' with a negative purpose. 'God entrusts people with a job to be done, and the day comes when he visits to call them to account. If they have been unfaithful or unwise in their stewardship, [God] punishes'. Lundbom, *Jeremiah 1-20*, p. 382.

[202] Schottroff also suggests that when the absolute is used with the preposition עַל (as here), that it emphasizes the idea of 'vengeance for (already well-known) transgression'. Schottroff, *TLOT*, II, p. 1025. For this construction, see, for

Anathoth are guilty of attempting to *silence* YHWH's prophet, a 'scandalous' offense because 'prophets are constitutive of communal life'.[203] Their attempt to hush Jeremiah threatens to rip apart the socio-theological fabric of the covenant community.

Thus, it is easy to see the appropriateness of the term to this context. Jeremiah's plea for retribution (נִקְמָה) is answered by YHWH's visitation (פקד).[204] In further proof of Jeremiah's status as the 'true prophet', YHWH is doing exactly as Jeremiah has asked. YHWH is 'looking into' the plot of the men of Anathoth, proving both Jeremiah's *relatedness* to YHWH and his *righteousness* in YHWH's sight.

The precise (and terrifying) nature of this divine 'visitation' is the central part of YHWH's response. As was noted above, the tricola here matches blow-for-blow the plot's description in Jer. 11.19:

> Their chosen ones will die by the sword,
> And their sons and daughters will die by famine.
> And there shall not be a remnant of them.

Here, YHWH adapts a Jeremianic catch-phrase, 'by sword, and by famine, and by pestilence' (בַּחֶרֶב וּבָרָעָב וּבַדֶּבֶר)[205] used to describe the utter destruction of Jerusalem.[206] It is important to note that the punishment declared on the men of Anathoth is applied to the whole people in other places.[207] This connection accomplishes some significant things. First of all, it again reinforces the idea that this seemingly minor conflict between a prophet and his fellow-villagers is, in reality, the *national* conflict between the people of Israel and YHWH writ small.[208] This also solidifies Jeremiah's position as YHWH's true

---

example, Isa. 24.21; 27.1; Jer. 9.24; 21.14; 23.34; 27.8; 29.32; 44.13, 29; 46.52; 51.44, 47, 52; Hos. 12.3; Amos 3.14b; Zeph. 1.8-9, 12; Zech. 10.3a.

[203] Amos 2.12; 7.1; Jer. 26.18-19. Brueggemann, *Commentary on Jeremiah*, pp. 116-17.

[204] Holladay, *Jeremiah 1*, p. 375.

[205] Sometimes shortened to 'sword and famine' as here. See also 14.12-13, 15-16; 16.4; 21.7, 9; 24.10; 27.8, 13; 29.18; 32.24, 36; 34.17; 38.2; 42.16-17, 22; 44.12-13, 18, 27.

[206] It appears to be an adaptation from the Song of Moses in Deuteronomy, where YHWH promises to send the 'sword' and 'famine' among other disasters upon a rebellious people (see Deut. 32.24-25). Lundbom, *Jeremiah 1-20*, p. 390.

[207] Jeremiah 6.11. Holladay, *Jeremiah 1*, p. 375. Furthermore, the term 'remnant' (שְׁאֵרִית) is also applied to Israel as a whole in Jer. 6.9.

[208] As Craigie notes, the punishment here sounds so extreme that 'it is difficult to escape the conclusion that this lament concerns more than just the fortunes of one man'. Craigie, Kelley, and Drinkard, Jr., *Jeremiah 1-25*, p. 179.

representative; the rejection and resistance he is experiencing – more importantly, the *mixed emotions* Jeremiah feels – match and mirror YHWH's *own* experience within the narrative world of the book.[209]

Second, these clear references to coming destruction of Jerusalem indicate that YHWH is promising that 'Anathoth would be caught up in the destruction that was to befall the community at large'.[210] This sounds like an amazing reassurance. the wicked men of Anathoth will be destroyed without remedy. As Carroll says: 'Thus those who set out to kill one of the sons of Anathoth must bear as their punishment the death of all the children of Anathoth (bar one!)'.[211]

Edited to here. YHWH continues the declaration of judgment in 11.23, 'For I shall bring disaster to the men of Anathoth, the year of their visitation'. Again, the judgment, like the threat, is couched in emotively powerful terms. 'Disaster' (רָעָה) has also been translated 'evil' (KJV, RSV, JPS).

Perhaps the most important indicator of the magnitude of the term is how the OT presents רָעָה as the opposite of טוֹב ('good'), most famously in Moses' challenge to Israel in Deuteronomy: 'See I set before you today life and what is good (טוֹב), death and what is evil (רָע)'.[212] The parallel here between life/good and death/evil confirms Baker's core definition of רעע as 'an action or state that is detrimental to life or its fullness … a departure from that which is ideal and desired for fullness and enjoyment of life'.[213] A key indicator of the term's relative importance to the present project is provided by an analysis of the distribution of the root רעע in all its various forms. For the sake of brevity, only the top three are included in ascending order: third, Proverbs (75x); second, Psalms (80x); first, Jeremiah (146x).[214] Most important, the feminine nominative form is used to describe people,[215] their deeds, and the *results* of those deeds.[216]

---

[209] As we shall soon see; cf. Jer. 12.7-13.

[210] Allen, *Jeremiah*, p. 148.

[211] Carroll, *Jeremiah*, p. 280.

[212] Livingston's translation of Deut. 30.15. See G. Herbert Livingston, 'רָעַע', *TWOT*, II, pp. 854-56. The verb רעע is the root of the noun forms רָעָה and רַע.

[213] David W. Baker, 'רעע', *NIDOTTE*, III, pp. 1154-58.

[214] See C. Dohmen, 'רעע', *TDOT*, XIII, pp. 560-88.

[215] Cf. Num. 14.17, 35; Jer. 8.3. Livingston, *TWOT*, II, p. 856.

[216] Baker, *NIDOTTE*, III, p. 1155.

The threat here in 11.23 is an almost exact replica of the threat made against the nation in Jer. 11.11, the declared consequence of the 'broken covenant' of v. 10.[217] The main distinction it seems is, as one would expect, the *specificity* of the threat. Jeremiah 11.11 simply says 'upon them' (אֲלֵיהֶם), for which Jer. 11.23 substitutes 'men of Anathoth' (אַנְשֵׁי עֲנָתוֹת). Again reinforcing the relationship of this domestic drama to the unfolding national drama, the connections here show that this coming disaster is not simply the unwarranted attack of an unjustly-angered deity. Rather, it is the precise consequence of their own deeds. The men of Anathoth will be judged because they plotted to kill YHWH's prophet just as the entire nation will be judged because they have killed YHWH's covenant by serving other gods. Their punishment only fits their crime. The final phrase 'year of their visitation' provides a nice inclusio, using the root פקד from 11.22a. The image of YHWH here is that of a 'great king who from time to time holds a review of his lands'.[218] YHWH is coming as YHWH's prophet has both predicted and requested ... coming to judge the evildoers.

4.3.4 Summary

What is perhaps most surprising here is the issue of how this confession resolves itself. On the surface, Jeremiah has received his needed word of assurance. YHWH has promised that the wicked plotters will be themselves disposed of. Given the erratic emotive journey of Jeremiah's prayer (from fear to anger to vengeance to trust), listeners might be easily persuaded to assume YHWH's reassuring reply simply reinforces Jeremiah's decision to entrust his case to YHWH's care. Yet, jumping to such a conclusion may actually blind us to perhaps the most obvious fact of the *delay* of YHWH's predicted judgment on the men of Anathoth.

To paraphrase badly YHWH's rather beautiful judgment speech, YHWH assures the prophet: 'The men of Anathoth will be destroyed when I destroy Jerusalem and Judah'. But that day has not yet come.[219] And YHWH has *not* (yet) specifically promised to protect Jeremiah from this assassination plot but only to bring judgment

---

[217] Both phrases use the verb 'bring' (hiphil בוא).

[218] Baumgartner, *Jeremiah's Poems of Lament*, p. 23.

[219] Let it not escape the listener that, even after YHWH's reassuring answer, *the assassination plot is apparently still active.*

(eventually) upon the conspirators. This is an important point to make as a reminder that the *emotive* ending of a text is sometimes quite different than its formal characteristics might suggest. Clearly, the text has technically concluded. And yet the attentive listener, like the prophet Jeremiah, should remain uneasy, with bits of fear and unresolved anger and a stinging sense of treacherous betrayal lingering on, for the Confessions have only just begun to show us how to 'hear' the prophet's words.

5

JEREMIAH'S SECOND CONFESSION (12.1-13)

We now come to the second confession text. It is important to keep in mind that the emotive journey begun in the first confession continues on into this text, especially given the lack of affective resolution. However, the openness of the ending of the first confession compels the audience to keep listening.

5.1 Text & Translation

Hebrew (MT) Text	English Translation
צַדִּיק אַתָּה יְהוָה כִּי אָרִיב אֵלֶיךָ	[1]*Jeremiah:* 'Innocent are you, YHWH, when I accuse you,
אַךְ מִשְׁפָּטִים אֲדַבֵּר אוֹתָךְ	Nevertheless[1] I will speak judgments upon you.
מַדּוּעַ דֶּרֶךְ רְשָׁעִים צָלֵחָה	Why[2] does the way of the wicked prosper?

---

[1] אַךְ 'introduces an idea of contrariness'. Lundbom, *Jeremiah 1-20*, p. 643. Holladay suggests a 'nuance of "but just let me …"'. Holladay, *Jeremiah 1*, p. 376.

[2] 'Why?; is a frequent question in laments but the more common word is לָמָה (cf. Hab. 1.3; Pss. 10.1; 22.2; 43.2), not מַדּוּעַ as here. Since 16 of the 61 OT occurrences of מדוע are found in the book of Jeremiah, Holladay describes this as Jeremiah's 'preferred term' and suggests it may carry a 'reproachful tone'. Holladay, *Jeremiah 1*, pp. 368-69.

שָׁלוּ כָּל־בֹּגְדֵי בָגֶד: Why are the faithlessly faithless[3] at ease?[4]

נְטַעְתָּם גַּם־שֹׁרָשׁוּ ²You have planted them; they are even rooted!

יֵלְכוּ גַּם־עָשׂוּ פֶרִי They spread forth shoots;[5] they are even fruitful!

קָרוֹב אַתָּה בְּפִיהֶם You are near in their mouth,

וְרָחוֹק מִכִּלְיוֹתֵיהֶם: But far from their innermost being.[6]

וְאַתָּה יְהוָה יְדַעְתָּנִי תִּרְאֵנִי ³'But you, O YHWH,[7] you know me, you see me,[8]

וּבָחַנְתָּ לִבִּי אִתָּךְ You test my heart toward you.[9]

_____

[3] Lundbom's translation. The noun בֶּגֶד only appears here and in Isa. 24.16. Most translations prefer the word 'treachery', another possible meaning, derived from the verbal form used in 12.6 (see below). See Lundbom, *Jeremiah 1-20*, pp. 644-45. Carroll suggests the term means 'really treacherous'. Carroll, *Jeremiah*, p. 285.

Other scholars have argued the root is connected with בֶּגֶד, 'clothing'. Erlandsson notes one could possibly see then a 'transferred figurative meaning', perhaps 'to behave secretively' or 'to do something veiled', i.e. deceptively. See Seth Erlandsson, 'בָּגַד', *TDOT*, I, pp. 470-73.

[4] 'Can also be expressed as "do well" or "have [all] things go their way"'. Newman and Stine, *Handbook on Jeremiah*, p. 311.

[5] For this sense, see BDB, s.v. 'הָלַךְ', esp. Hos. 14.7. Volz reads יֵלְהוּ, 'they are fresh (i.e. "sappy")'. See Carroll, *Jeremiah*, p. 283. The LXX reads it as יָלְדוּ, 'they have children'; see Isa. 65.23; so Lundbom, *Jeremiah 1-20*, p. 645. Baumgartner, however, notes the MT is to be preferred because 'the imagery of the tree continues'. Baumgartner, *Jeremiah's Poems of Lament*, p. 63.

[6] 'From their kidneys', i.e. 'their true feelings'; cf. Jer. 11.20; 20.12a. Carroll, *Jeremiah*, p. 283.

[7] Rudolph proposed reading simply אתה, 'you', and omitting 'O YHWH', on the 'basis of meter, but there is no textual support for this'. Craigie, Kelley, and Drinkard, Jr., *Jeremiah 1-25*, p. 175.

[8] 'No reason to omit "you see me" with the LXX. The loss can be attributed to haplography'. Lundbom, *Jeremiah 1-20*, p. 645.

[9] אִתָּךְ is rather odd here. Bright has suggested: "Thou dost examine my thoughts toward thyself'. Bright, *Jeremiah*, p. 83; Rudolph, 'You test my heart, how it is inclined toward you'. Holladay suggests that Joseph's request to the cupbearer in Gen. 40.14 is the closest parallel. כִּי אִם־זְכַרְתַּנִי אִתְּךָ ('For if you remember to you/yourself'), and suggests that it is Jeremiah's affirmation that his heart is (still) 'with' YHWH. Holladay, *Jeremiah 1*, p. 378.

הַתִּקֵם כְּצֹאן לְטִבְחָה   Tear them out[10] like sheep for the slaughter![11]

וְהַקְדִּשֵׁם לְיוֹם הֲרֵגָה: Set them apart[12] for the day of killing! [13]

עַד־מָתַי תֶּאֱבַל הָאָרֶץ   4 'How long will the land mourn[14]

וְעֵשֶׂב כָּל־הַשָּׂדֶה יִבָשׁ   And the grass[15] of every field wither?

מֵרָעַת יֹשְׁבֵי־בָהּ   Because of the evil of the inhabitants,

סָפְתָה בְהֵמוֹת וָעוֹף   Beast and bird are swept away.[16]

כִּי אָמְרוּ   For they thought *to themselves,*[17]

לֹא יִרְאֶה אֶת־אַחֲרִיתֵנוּ:   'He[18] will not see our latter end.'

כִּי אֶת־רַגְלִים רַצְתָּה וַיַּלְאוּךָ   5 *YHWH*: 'If you have raced with men and they have wearied you,

וְאֵיךְ תְּתַחֲרֶה אֶת־הַסּוּסִים   How then will you challenge[19] horses?

---

[10] Baumgartner notes the only attested meanings of the verb are 'tear off' or 'cut off'. He calls התקם 'suspicious' because it remains unclear *where* these sheep are to be taken from; he prefers to read תְּקֵם, 'carry them off', because 'it is by no means rare for an imperfect (jussive) to stand in parallel to the imperative'. Pss. 10.15; 17.8; 51.13, 19 [14, 20]; 54.2 [3]; 59.1 [2]; 64.1 [2]; 71.2; 142.1-4 [2-5]'. Baumgartner, *Jeremiah's Poems of Lament*, p. 62.

[11] LXX omits.

[12] Or literally, הַקְדִּשֵׁם 'sanctify them'. As Lundbom notes: 'Sanctimonious deaths make for bitter irony'. Lundbom, *Jeremiah 1-20*, p. 645.

[13] LXX does not have 'you see me' or 'pull them out like sheep for the slaughter'. Carroll, *Jeremiah*, p. 283.

[14] Or 'be dry'. See Katherine M. Hayes, *The Earth Mourns: Prophetic Metaphor and Oral Aesthetic* (AcBib 8; Society of Biblical Literature, 2002), pp. 12-18.

[15] 'Grass, plants, and herbage in general'. Lundbom, *Jeremiah 1-20*, p. 646.

[16] ספה means 'sweep away'. Lundbom, *Jeremiah 1-20*, p. 646, in the sense of 'have perished' or 'died'. Newman and Stine, *Handbook on Jeremiah*, p. 313. Holladay, however, follows J.D. Michaelis and revocalizes MT's third singular feminine סָפְתָה as 2nd-person masculine סָפִתָה 'you have swept away beast and bird'. Holladay, *Jeremiah 1*, p. 364.

[17] The verbal root of אמרו usually means 'to speak' but can mean (as here) 'to say to oneself', i.e. 'to think'. See Lundbom, *Jeremiah 1-20*, p. 646; cf. Jon. 4.2.

[18] 4QJer has 'Yah'; LXX supplies 'God'. Lundbom, *Jeremiah 1-20*, p. 646. Also, LXX has οὐκ ὄψεται ὁ θεὸς ὁδοὺς ἡμῶν '"god will not see our ways"', thus providing a non-ambiguous subject for "he will see"'. Carroll, *Jeremiah*, p. 283.

De Waard notes: 'Although a majority of commentators advocate the view that God is the implicit agent ... a minority of exegetes since Joseph Qara have considered Jeremiah the implicit subject of the verb'. De Waard points to the CEV translation: 'Jeremiah won't live to see what happens to us', as a model of this alternative translation. Jan de Waard, *A Handbook on Jeremiah* (ed. Harold P. Scanlin; TCT 2; Winona Lake, IN: Eisenbrauns, 2003), p. 61.

[19] The term תְּתַחֲרֶה is a Tiph'el of חרה 'be hot' (GKC §55h), 'meaning something like "hotly compete"'. Lundbom, *Jeremiah 1-20*, p. 647. Wood suggests the imagery of 'burning to outrace'. Leon J. Wood, 'חָרָה', in *TWOT*, I, p. 736. It has been argued, however, that it derives from תחרה, 'quarrel' (HALOT, p. 351).

וּבְאֶרֶץ שָׁלוֹם אַתָּה בוֹטֵחַ   And if[20] in a safe land[21] you are collapsing,[22]

וְאֵיךְ תַּעֲשֶׂה בִּגְאוֹן הַיַּרְדֵּן: How will you do in the jungle of the Jordan?[23]

כִּי גַם־אַחֶיךָ וּבֵית־אָבִיךָ   [6]For even your brothers and the house of your father

גַּם־הֵמָּה בָּגְדוּ בָךְ   Even they have dealt faithlessly[24] with you

---

[20] The כִּי ('if') from the first cola of the first line 'does double-duty for the first colon in this line'. Lundbom, *Jeremiah 1-20*, p. 647.

[21] Literally, 'land of peace'. 'There is no exact parallel to the phrase אֶרֶץ שָׁלוֹם ... Isa. 32.18 has נְוֵה שָׁלוֹם "dwell in peace", as the closest proximation.' Holladay, *Jeremiah 1*, p. 380.

[22] Literally, 'and in a peaceful land you are ... confident'. Carroll, *Jeremiah*, p. 283. The verb בטח is usually translated 'trust', *BDB*, s.v. בָּטַח I'. However, Holladay and Lundbom read בטח as 'to fall down'; see *CDCH*, s.v., 'בטח II', which is apparently a 'homonymous verb'. Holladay, *Jeremiah 1*, p. 380; Lundbom, *Jeremiah 1-20*, p. 647; also Solomon L. Skoss, 'The Root בטח in Jeremiah 12.5, Psalms 22.10, Proverbs 14.16, and Job 40.23', in Salo W. Barron and Alexander Marx (eds.), *Jewish Studies in Memory of George A. Kohut, 1874-1933* (New York: Alexander Kohut Memorial Foundation, 1935), pp. 549-53. Thus, the line can logically be rendered in two distinct ways: 'If in a land of peace you are trusting...' and 'If in a safe land you are collapsing...' See exegesis for a more detailed discussion.

[23] Literally 'in the majesty of the Jordan'. V's *superbia* is 'a reference to the "swell" of the Jordan', e.g. a reference to the well-known seasonal *flooding* of the Jordan River; however, McKane says this interpretation is 'decidedly' disproven because the phrase 'cannot mean "swelling current of the Jordan" in the other places where it occurs (Jer. 49.19; 50.44; Zech. 11.3)'. McKane, *Jeremiah*, pp. 264-65.

It is best to regard the phrase as referring to the lush vegetation on the Jordan's banks, 'the green and shady banks, clothed with willows, tamarisks, and cane, in which the lions made their covert [cf. Jer. 49.19; 50.44; Zech. 11.2] ... and therefore dangerous [cf. Jer. 12.5]'. Carroll, *Jeremiah*, p. 283; see BDB, s.v. 'גָּאוּת'. The lowest spot in the Jordan Rift is actually known as the 'Pride of the Jordan'. Menashe Har-El offers this description of that area:

> Living conditions at the Pride were unbearable for both man and beast; the soil, plants, water and climactic conditions rendered it a 'land which devoureth its inhabitants'. In winter and spring there are destructive floods which endanger the lives of all living things; there are quicksand marshes along the banks which breed malarial mosquitoes ... the heat of summers is unbearable and during the *hamsin* the thick forests are suffocating.

See Menashe Har-El, 'The Pride of the Jordan: The Jungle of the Jordan', *BA* 41.2 (1978), pp. 65-75 (71-72).

[24] See Jer. 12.1.

גַּם־הֵמָּה קָרְאוּ אַחֲרֶיךָ מָלֵא   Even they[25] cry out behind you, 'Assemble!'[26]

אַל־תַּאֲמֵן בָּם   Do not believe in them[27]

כִּי־יְדַבְּרוּ אֵלֶיךָ טוֹבוֹת: When they speak to you good things. [28]

---

[25] Baumgartner finds the verse 'overloaded' and argues for deletion of גַּם־הֵמָּה. Baumgartner, *Jeremiah's Poems of Lament*, p. 64. Holladay, however, finds the phrase necessary, pointing out that it is used twice in Nah. 3.11, 'but an appearance three times is highly unusual and indicates extreme emphasis'. Holladay, *Jeremiah 1*, p. 380.

[26] Carroll points to Jer. 4.5: 'They cry aloud after you'. *BHS* follows Volz's reading: 'They have all conspired after you'. This is similar to the LXX's ἐπισυνήχθησαν, 'they have conspired against [you]'. Carroll, *Jeremiah*, p. 283. Baumgartner notes: 'When Jeremiah's relatives call after him at the top of their voices ... he hears it too and has no need to be warned'. So he suggests, following Gunkel, that we read כְּלִמָּה 'disgrace'. See Ezek. 34.29, where the term is variously translated 'taunts' (NJPS), 'insults' (NET/NRSV), and 'scorn' (NIV); see also Ezek. 36.6 -7, 14; Ps. 89.50b [51b].

Diamond sees the same issue as Baumgarter because normally this word is taken 'in an adverbial sense' rendering 'cry aloud' or 'cry with a loud voice', which would render a divine warning useless. The solution, he finds, is to offer an alternative nuance for the root מלא, which, when taken as a piel singular imperative or infinitive absolute, could be 'viewed as a one-word citation ["Assemble!" or "Help!"] ... with the implicit connotation for mutual help or defence'. Diamond, *Confessions in Context*, pp. 49, 217, n. 76.

Diamond is here following the suggestion of D.W. Thomas, who repointed מלא and argued the expression here (as in Jer. 4.5) was a military idiom to be rendered 'mass' or 'multitude' or 'muster'. See, as well, Jer. 51.11; Job 16.10, Gen. 48.19; Isa. 31.4. D.W. Thomas, 'מלאו in Jeremiah IV,5. A Military Term', *JJS* 3.2 (1952), pp. 47-52 (47).

Holladay, however, goes in a completely different direction, suggesting the word be translated, 'Drunk!', making it a taunt or a rumor instigated by his antagonistic family. Holladay chooses the translation 'drunk' for the following reasons. First, Jeremiah describes himself 'like a drunken man, like a fellow overcome by wine' (23.9). Also, Jeremiah describes himself as 'filled' (מלא) with Yahweh's wrath (6.11; 15.17). This leads Holladay to surmise: 'One may conclude that Jeremiah describes himself as "filled with Yahweh's words" and that on occasion he feels (or acts) drunken'.

Third, Holladay notes that Jer. 13.12-14 uses מלא in connection with drunkenness, which might be associated with Jer. 12.6 on the basis of this shared terminology. Fourth, in both the OT and NT, people who exhibit deep religious emotion are considered drunk, e.g. Hannah (1 Sam. 1.12-15) and the 120 in the upper room on the Day of Pentecost (Acts 12.13). Finally, in many languages, the terms 'full' or 'loaded' are idioms for drunkenness (e.g. French *plein*, German *voll*). 'None of these considerations is conclusive, but they are all suggestive.' Holladay, *Jeremiah 1*, p. 381.

[27] Baumgartner, *Jeremiah's Poems of Lament*, p. 64, also deletes אַל־תַּאֲמֵן בָּם.

[28] 'This verse is transposed to between 11.18 and 19 by Rudolph ... other scholars (e.g. Reventlow, Berridge) treat v. 6 separately from 11.18-12.5'. Carroll, *Jeremiah*, p. 283. In fact, Bright, following Cornill places 12.1-6 before 11.18-20. See comments on structure below.

עָזַבְתִּי אֶת־בֵּיתִי   [7] 'I have forsaken my house,[29]

נָטַשְׁתִּי אֶת־נַחֲלָתִי   I have abandoned my heritage,

נָתַתִּי אֶת־יְדִדוּת נַפְשִׁי   I have given the beloved of my soul[30]

בְּכַף אֹיְבֶיהָ׃   Into the hand of her enemies.

הָיְתָה־לִּי נַחֲלָתִי   [8] My heritage has become to me

כְּאַרְיֵה בַיָּעַר   Like a lion in the forest!

נָתְנָה עָלַי בְּקוֹלָהּ   She has set her voice against me,

עַל־כֵּן שְׂנֵאתִיהָ   For which reason I hate her.

הַעַיִט צָבוּעַ נַחֲלָתִי לִי   [9] Is my heritage to me[31] a hyena's den?[32]

הַעַיִט סָבִיב עָלֶיהָ לְכוּ   Are birds of prey[33] circling around her?

אִסְפוּ כָּל־חַיַּת הַשָּׂדֶה   Let[34] the wild beasts assemble!

---

[29] T has 'I have forsaken the house of my sanctuary'. Lundbom, *Jeremiah 1-20*, p. 653.

[30] The full phrase is אֶת־יְדִדוּת נַפְשִׁי. The Hebrew term יְדִדוּת is a *hapax legomenon*, 'equivalent to the term used in 11.15'. Newman and Stine, *Handbook on Jeremiah*, p. 317; cf. Lundbom, *Jeremiah 1-20*, p. 654.

[31] MT has לִּי 'to me'; *BHS* reads as כִּי, 'for'. Carroll, *Jeremiah*, p. 289.

[32] Cf. *CDCH*, s.v. עיט II'. LXX μὴ σπήλαιον ὑαίνης "a hyena's cave" seems to be a correct interpretation of הַעַיִט צָבוּעַ … There is wordplay with the next colon, where עַיִט … is a homonym meaning "birds of prey"'. Allen, *Jeremiah*, p. 151. Note also that Volz 'omits the first occurrence of הַעַיִט as a dittography or a marginal note'. Carroll, *Jeremiah*, p. 289. The real problem is the *hapax legomenon* צָבוּעַ. De Waard finds no problem with the term meaning 'hyena' and asserts 'the problem is not of a textual but of an exegetical nature'. De Waard, *Handbook on Jeremiah*, p. 61.

[33] הַעַיִט also occurs here, leading to the temptation to translate both occurrences in the same manner. De Waard argues this is 'intentional play on two homonyms by the writer, the first having the meaning "lair, den", the second, "bird of prey"'. Though this interpretation is 'rarely represented in translation', it is still 'more likely'. De Waard, *Handbook on Jeremiah*, p. 62; see G.R. Driver, 'Birds in the Old Testament', *PEQ* 87.1 (1955), p. 13 and James Barr, *Comparative Philology and the Text of the Old Testament* (Oxford: Clarendon, 1968), p. 128.

[34] MT has אִסְפוּ, qal imperative masculine form of 'gather' *BHS*'s passive הֵאָסְפוּ, i.e. 'let [the beasts] be gathered', follows V and is preferred by Cornill. Carroll, *Jeremiah*, p. 289. Holladay notes: 'Reading niphal (intransitive) הֵאָסְפוּ with V for the qal אִסְפוּ "gather (the beasts)" …brings the verb into consistency with the imperative in the fourth colon'. Holladay, *Jeremiah 1*, p. 383.

הֵתָיוּ לְאָכְלָה   Bring them[35] to consume her![36]

רֹעִים רַבִּים שִׁחֲתוּ כַרְמִי   [10] 'Many shepherds have destroyed my vine-
                                 yard.

בֹּסְסוּ אֶת־חֶלְקָתִי   They have trampled[37] my portion,[38]

נָתְנוּ אֶת־חֶלְקַת חֶמְדָּתִי   They have given over[39] my pleasant portion

לְמִדְבַּר שְׁמָמָה: To be a desolate[40] wilderness.

שָׂמָהּ לִשְׁמָמָה   [11] They[41] have turned her[42] [into] a desolation!

אָבְלָה עָלַי שְׁמֵמָה   Desolate, it mourns to me.[43]

נָשַׁמָּה כָּל־הָאָרֶץ   The whole land is laid desolate

כִּי אֵין אִישׁ שָׂם עַל־לֵב: For[44] no one turns their heart.[45]

---

[35] Cornill, Volz, Condamin, and Rudolph, read 'Come to devour!' following V and 3 MSS, preferring אֱתָיוּ (qal) for MT's הֵאתִיוּ hiphil ('bring them').

[36] Vocalizing לָאָכְלָה for MT's לְאָכְלָה, which 'has been construed either as an alternative infinitive construct without personal suffix ... or as a noun, "for eating"'. Holladay, *Jeremiah 1*, p. 383.

[37] The only occurrence in Jeremiah of 'trample' בוס po'lel. Holladay, *Jeremiah 1*, p. 388.

[38] Volz and Rudolph, following some MSS that substitute נַחֲלָתִי 'my possession', the term used in vv. 7, 8, and 9. However, Holladay points out: 'No Version reflects it, and MT חֶלְקָתִי is to be preferred because it preserves the poetic repetition'. Holladay, *Jeremiah 1*, p. 383; see also Carroll, *Jeremiah*, p. 290.

[39] Following Lundbom, trying to 'preserve the repetition of the verb נחן from vv 7 and 8'. Lundbom, *Jeremiah 1-20*, p. 657.

[40] 'Bell-like, the term "desolate" tolls at the end of three successive cola and at the start of the fourth.' Allen, *Jeremiah*, p. 153.

Nominal phrases using the root שמם are 'uncommon'. I. Meyer, 'שָׁמַם, שָׁמֵם, שְׁמָמָה, יְשִׁמוֹן/יְשִׁימוֹן, שְׁמָמָה, מְשַׁמָּה, שִׁמָּמוֹן', *TDOT*, XV, pp. 238-48. The two most common are מִדְבַּר שְׁמָמָה ('desolate wilderness'; here, also Joel 2.13) and שְׁמָמָה עַד־עוֹלָם ('everlasting desolation'; cf. plural form in Jer. 51.26, 62; Ezek. 35.9).

[41] Reading with all commentators (except Lundbom, *Jeremiah 1-20*, p. 657) and V, S, and T שָׂמֻהָ for MT's שָׂמָהּ 'he has made her'. 'The Hebrew indefinite singular verb is more naturally pointed as plural [שָׂמוּהָ].' Allen, *Jeremiah*, p. 152; see Carroll, *Jeremiah*, p. 290.

[42] Cf. Isa. 23.13, where שָׂמָהּ is translated 'turned' by NJPS, NET, NIV, NLT.

[43] 'S.R. Driver says עָלַי ("to me/upon me") means "to my sorrow"'; cf. Gen. 48.7. Lundbom, *Jeremiah 1-20*, p. 657. Holladay, who thinks the cola are wrongly divided, construes עָלַי with the verb שמם rendering, 'The land is desolate *on my account* [cf. Ps. 44.23]'. Holladay, *Jeremiah 1*, p. 388.

[44] Duhm, Cornill, and Rudolph read וְ 'and' for MT's כִּי 'for' (see Isa. 57.1).

[45] Attempting, like Lundbom, to preserve the repetition of שִׂים from the first colon. The idiom here שָׂם עַל־לֵב means 'something like the English, "take to heart"'. Lundbom, *Jeremiah 1-20*, p. 657. See Isa. 57.1; cf. 42.25; 57.11.

BDB notes the preposition עַל suggests 'the substratum upon which an object in any way rests, *or on which an action is performed*'. BDB, s.v. 'עַל, עַל II', italics mine.

עַל־כָּל־שְׁפָיִם בַּמִּדְבָּר [12] 'Upon all the bare heights[46] in the desert,

בָּאוּ שֹׁדְדִים Spoilers have come.

כִּי חֶרֶב לַיהוָה אֹכְלָה Indeed,[47] a sword of YHWH consumes[48]

מִקְצֵה־אֶרֶץ וְעַד־קְצֵה הָאָרֶץ From one end of the land to the other –

אֵין שָׁלוֹם לְכָל־בָּשָׂר׃ No peace for all flesh.

זָרְעוּ חִטִּים [13] 'They have sown[49] wheat,

וְקֹצִים קָצָרוּ And thorns they have reaped.

נֶחְלוּ לֹא יוֹעִלוּ They have wearied themselves[50] to no avail.[51]

---

[46] 'The precise meaning of the Heb. שְׁפָיִם is uncertain [cf. Jer. 3.21; 4.11; 7.29; 12.12; 14.6; Isa. 41.18; 49.9]', and suggests the translation 'open country', pointing to McKane, whom he says has demonstrated 'clearly that "hill tops, high places" is an inappropriate translation'. Craigie, Kelley, and Drinkard, Jr., *Jeremiah 1-25,* pp. 49-50; see W.A. McKane, 'SPY(Y)M with Special Reference to the Book of Jeremiah', in A Caquot and M. Delcor (eds.), *Mélanges bibliques et orientaux en l'honner de M. Henri Cazelles* (AOAT 212; Neukirchner-Vluyn: Neukirchener Verlag, 1981), pp. 319-35.

[47] Following the pattern of Jer. 25.30-37 (esp. vv. 30, 31, 36b-37). Holladay, *Jeremiah 1*, p. 385.

[48] Because Jer. 12.12 has 5 cola, commentators have tried to excise phrases to provide better poetic balance. Duhm excised 'the sword of Yahweh devours' to reduce the verse to 4 cola and make it fit better with v. 13. Volz omits all of 12b: 'For the sword of Yahweh devours from one end of the land to the other; no flesh has peace'. Bright omits 'from one end of the land to the other'.
Holladay, however, argues for authenticity of the entire verse, countering the various excisions. Against Duhm and Volz, he notes that חֶרֶב לַיהוָה ('sword of YHWH') occurs in Jer. 47.6, an undisputed authentic passage; against Volz and Bright, he notes that the phrase מִקְצֵה־אֶרֶץ וְעַד־קְצֵה הָאָרֶץ ('from one end of the land to the other') is found in Jer. 25.33, another authentic oracle and here balances 'the first colon, which likewise is an adverbial phrase of location'. Holladay, *Jeremiah 1*, p. 385.

[49] LXX uses imperatives for MT perfects: 'Sow ... reap'. See Carroll, *Jeremiah*, p. 290.

[50] This verb is 'frequent in Jeremiah with the N-stem participle נַחְלָה ("incurable") a veritable signature term in the poetry of 10.19; 14.17; and 30.12'. Lundbom, *Jeremiah 1-20*, p. 658.
The LXX οἱ κλῆροι αὐτῶν οὐκ ὠφελήσουσιν αὐτούς ('their inheritance shall not profit them') is 'doubtless a misreading of נָחֲלוּ ("they inherited")'. NEB/REB's rendering 'they sift' is based on a 'revocalization by G.R. Driver said to derive from a Semitic root, נחל but which is unattested in the OT despite Driver's claim for Ps. 82.8. The reading of the MT should be retained.' Lundbom, *Jeremiah 1-20*, p. 658.

[51] V and S 'insert וְ ("and"/"but") before "not" and the verb. It is a possible reading but by no means a necessary one'. Holladay, *Jeremiah 1*, p. 384.

וּבֹשׁוּ מִתְּבוּאֹתֵיכֶם Be ashamed[52] of your harvests[53]

מֵחֲרוֹן אַף־יְהוָה: Because of the burning anger of YHWH'.[54]

5.2 Structure

The above translation has already raised two important questions for most readers who have even slight familiarity with the study of Jeremiah's Confessions. The first question relates to the *division* of Jer. 12.1-6 from Jer. 11.18-23; the second relates to the *addition* of Jer. 12.7-13 to 12.1-6. Thus, this segment on the structure of the chosen passage will address the concerns raised by these interpretive moves as well as describe the structure of the identified textual section. We will begin with the issue of whether 11.18-12.6 should be treated as one text or two, then move to discuss the structure of 12.1-6, and conclude with an argument for the inclusion of 12.7-13 as part of YHWH's reply to Jeremiah's complaint.

Jeremiah 12.1-6 is quite often read simply as a continuation of sorts of Jer. 11.18-23.[55] Canonically speaking, this makes good sense since this text does immediately follow.[56] However, Baumgartner was convinced there could be no direct connection as the textual order might be taken to imply. He pointed out that, at minimum, there would have to be a significant *temporal* gap as Jeremiah waited for YHWH's promised annihilation of the conspirators ... enough time that his waiting became annoyed exasperation and even anger.[57] For Baumgartner, Jer. 12.1 'gives *no hint at all* of a preceding promise or of any disappointment at its failure to be realized'.[58] I find this judgment rather surprising given that Jeremiah's prayer directly accuses

---

[52] 'The people are now spoken to directly, which is common at the end of Jeremianic discourse [Jer. 2.9; 8.17; 16.9] ... the imperatives therefore should not be emended to a perfect form ... nor also the second-person suffix on "your harvests" to a third-person suffix, "their harvests"'. Lundbom, *Jeremiah 1-20*, p. 658.

[53] Against Holladay who reads מִתְּבוּאֹתֵיהֶם for MT's מִתְּבוּאֹתֵיכֶם 'your harvests'. Holladay, *Jeremiah 1*, p. 384.

[54] '*BHS* omits ... as an eschatological expansion.' Carroll, *Jeremiah*, p. 290.

[55] Carroll, *Jeremiah*, p. 276.

[56] And it does so in *both* the MT and LXX versions of Jeremiah, indicating that this textual order is established quite early in the textual history of the book.

[57] Because, to Baumgartner's way of thinking, 'Jeremiah waited in vain for the judgment announced in 11.22f to come about'. Baumgartner, *Jeremiah's Poems of Lament*, p. 70.

[58] Baumgartner, *Jeremiah's Poems of Lament*, p. 70, italics mine.

YHWH of protecting – even prospering! – the ungodly; it is difficult to conceive how that is *not* an expression of deep disappointment.

Holladay as well offers up several long-standing reasons why Jer. 11.18-12.6 cannot be considered an organic unity. First of all, the vocabulary of Jer. 11.21 not only is a poor fit in its present context but also is a poor fit in *any* poetic context of Jeremiah; the verse is clearly redactional. So also is Jer. 12.6, given the paucity of verbal links with 12.1-4.[59] Secondly, Holladay argues there can be no dramatic heightening of a murder plot; there is no greater physical threat than death.[60] While this is of course true (a person can only be killed once), there most certainly can be an *emotive* heightening of the plot when it is revealed to Jeremiah that *his own family* is involved with the other villagers' plot against him.[61]

However, the above reasons are not Holladay's main reasons for arguing for two originally separate texts. For Holladay, the real contrast between Jer. 11.18-23 and 12.1-6 is their divergent theodicies. For Holladay, in Jer. 11.18-23, the prophet 'continues to function within the framework of Deuteronomic theology'.[62] By the end of Jer. 12.1-5, especially given YHWH's less-than-reassuring answer, those controlling theological assumptions have 'collapsed'.[63]

Though a good number of commentators regard 11.18-12.6 as a single textual/interpretational unit, a good many of them do not *think* of it as such, which leads to valiant attempts to rearrange the text into a better order. In fact, O'Connor can only identify a two-point consensus about Jer. 11.18-12.6 among commentators. First, nearly all commentators find the text is difficult because 'its contents appear disorderly and incohesive'; secondly and subsequently, nearly all commentators assume 'radical surgery is required to restore the text to its orderly condition'.[64] The upshot has been widely-varying proposals on the text's basic components and their proper

---

[59] The *only* link is the verb 'betray' (בגד). Holladay, *Jeremiah 1*, p. 366.

[60] Jeremiah 12.6 'can offer nothing more dangerous'. Holladay, *Jeremiah 1*, p. 366.

[61] From the perspective of an affective reading, this reason cannot count as a critical argument against the unity of the text.

[62] Holladay, *Jeremiah 1*, p. 367.

[63] Holladay, *Jeremiah 1*, p. 367.

[64] O'Connor, *Confessions of Jeremiah*, p. 15. The key issue that sparks many of these textual rearrangements is 'the rather abrupt manner in which [Jer. 11.18] begins'. Craigie, Kelley, and Drinkard, Jr., *Jeremiah 1-25*, p. 176.

interpretation.[65] One problem with this kind of interpretive solution is that the exegete must either assume the present text was *accidentally* disarranged or *deliberately* restructured into a nonsensical form.[66] Holladay is certainly right that 'the solution to the problems should be sought for in other ways than large-scale displacement'.[67]

Bright's attempt at restructuring is by far the most drastic and demonstrates well the difficulties of this approach. Bright, noting how abruptly the text begins and how absurdly it ends,[68] simply places Jer. 12.1-6 *before* 11.18-23, both textually *and* chronologically. YHWH's revelation in 11.18, then, is that Jeremiah's own family has turned against him and cannot be trusted. For Bright, such a solution is 'manifest' and 'yields an excellent sense'.[69]

The most significant problem with Bright's rearrangement is found in that last term, 'sense'. Of course, all the proffered rearrangements are presented as attempts to give the text a better (i.e., more complete or orderly) sense. However, it can be debated whether rearranging a text per modern Western conventions of chronology and good narrative is more of a *violation* of the text than an *interpretation* of it. The issue here is not so much the actual textual arrangement, but the exegete's *a priori* assumption that a 'good' text must first be chronologically ordered.[70] Given the solidity of this textual

---

[65] O'Connor, *Confessions of Jeremiah*, p. 15.

Craigie, *et al.* offers a helpful representative list of the various textual rearrangements that have been suggested:
  1) Cornill: 12.1-2, 4-6, 11.18-23; delete 12.3
  2) Bright, Peake, Reventlow: 12.1-6; 11.18-23
  3) Rowley: 11.18; 12.6; 11.19-20; 12.1-3; 11.21-23 (12.4-5)
  4) Rudolph, Volz: 11.18; 12.6; 11.19-20a; 12.3; 11.20b-23; 12.1-2; 12.4b-5
  5) Thiel: 11.18; 12.6; 11.19-23; 12.1-4a; 12.5
Craigie, Kelley, and Drinkard, Jr., *Jeremiah 1-25*, p. 176; See Hubmann for a thorough critical review of all the proposals. Hubmann, *Untersuchungen*, pp. 30-41. Holladay says the Rudolph/Volz proposal is the 'most widely accepted'. Holladay, *Jeremiah 1*, p. 365.

[66] Holladay finds both options difficult to imagine, especially since redactors typically only *expand* texts but do not appear to have often *rearranged* them entirely. Holladay, *Jeremiah 1*, p., 365.

[67] Holladay, *Jeremiah 1*, p. 365.

[68] The text 'ends ... with Jeremiah being apprised of the plot against him – which is just what he knew at the beginning!' Bright, *Jeremiah*, p. 89.

[69] Bright, *Jeremiah*, p. 89.

[70] Carroll also questions whether 'Western standards of sense and intelligibility are adequate warrants for changing the text around' and goes on to point out that 'such changes are themselves an interpretative move'. Carroll, *Jeremiah*, p. 277.

arrangement across the ancient versions, it seems unwise to assume that modern textual rearrangements make better or more sense than the present shape.[71]

However, Bright's exegetical move cannot only be critiqued from a hermeneutical viewpoint; it also is *not* all that helpful for making sense of the text. Bright's suggested rearrangement would effectively mean that Jeremiah does not know about the murder plot until *after* he has already complained to YHWH. If the revelation of the family's plot against Jeremiah happens before the complaint of 11.18-23, that *still* leaves Jeremiah's 'case' (רִיב) against YHWH in 12.1 'without any clear cause'.[72] In fact, the text is better understood the other (original) way around; his complaints about the wicked and his prayers for their judgment in 12.1-3 presuppose the persecution described in Jer. 11.19-21.[73]

In part, then, the move to break apart Jer. 11.18-23 and 12.1-6 for affective examination is, in equal parts, a move to extricate the text from the pressure of modernistic assumptions, to listen respectfully to the text as it stands, and to insist that the presented text *does* have a comprehensible sense all its own. At some point, every exegete must come to grips with the reality that finding an overarching structure or theme or intention in the book of Jeremiah might be a very difficult task. Ancient books are not Western books and must be approached, at some level, on their own terms. Clearly, the assumption that texts make sense is the basis of *all* hermeneutics;[74] but, as texts can (and do) make very different *kinds* of sense,[75] their established structure and order should be deeply appreciated not deprecated.

---

[71] Craigie, Kelley, and Drinkard, Jr., *Jeremiah 1-25*, p. 176.

[72] David P. Melvin, 'Why Does the Way of the Wicked Prosper? Human and Divine Suffering in Jeremiah 11.18-12.13 and the Problem of Evil', *EvQ* 83.2 (2011), pp. 99-106 (101).

[73] 'As is also the case with Job, the question of the lots of the righteous and of the wicked does not arise until the righteous individual find[s] himself suffering without apparent cause'. Melvin, 'Why Does the Way of the Wicked Prosper?', p. 101.

[74] If texts are doing something other than making sense, to what purpose 'reading' or 'hearing' them?

[75] Perhaps the best (and most overused) example of this hermeneutical principle would be the contrast between the description of a rose in a biology textbook and the description of the same rose in a poem. We would certainly claim both as 'true' descriptions of the rose and that both descriptions make 'sense'.

The making sense of oddly-arranged ancient texts is a key part of the adventure and the challenge that is biblical hermeneutics.

Having, however, 'overthrown' the assumption that Jer. 11.18-12.6 must be thought of as a single text, it seems incumbent that we now 'build' some connections, for there are links aplenty between Jer. 11.18-23 and 12.1-6. That the Confessions have been purposefully arranged perhaps requires no other proof than the fact that Jer. 20.12, a key verse in the *last* Confession text is almost an exact replica of 11.20, a key verse in the *opening* Confession text.[76] Also, Jer. 11.18-23 and 12.1-6 follow the same pattern of a kind of generality in the prayers of Jeremiah about the identity of his opponents, followed by a specific identification of those enemies in YHWH's replies.[77]

Allen also sees a thematic frame in the motif of 'naïve, misplaced trust'[78] and the polarization of the plotters' bad fate in 11.23 and the family's deceptive smooth-talk in 12.6.[79] This frame is filled in, then, with several key allusions. In 12.2, Jeremiah describes the wicked as a planted, fruitful 'tree'; in 11.19, the conspirators had described Jeremiah as a 'tree' they wished to 'cut down'. Again, in 12.3, Jeremiah prays: 'But you, O YHWH … you test my heart toward you'; in the prior prayer in 11.20, Jeremiah had addressed YHWH as the one 'who tests the innermost being and the heart'. Finally, in 12.3, Jeremiah asks YHWH to remove his enemies 'like sheep for the slaughter'; in 11.19, Jeremiah had described himself as a 'lamb led to the slaughter'.[80] There are other similarities as well. Both texts make

---

[76] Carroll, *Jeremiah*, p. 275.

[77] 'The divine answers … specifically identify the adversaries left suspsensefully undefined in Jeremiah's prayers'. Allen, *Jeremiah*, pp. 144, 148.

[78] In 11.19, Jeremiah says, 'I was like a lamb led to the slaughter; I did not know that against me they had schemed schemes'; in 12.6, Jeremiah is chided by YHWH for such naïveté. 'If in a safe land you are collapsing, how will you fare in the jungle of the Jordan?' (Jer. 12.5b).

[79] Allen says the MT 'has artistically linked the units by importing two new parallels in 12.3, the reference to seeing matching the "know/see" pair in 11.18 and the sheep simile to match the one in 11.19'. Allen, *Jeremiah*, p. 144. It is important to note the assumptive use of 'importation' language. Though Allen is right to see the textual links, this is more about an ordered structure being *imposed* on the texts rather than *discovered* within them.

[80] Melvin, 'Why Does the Way of the Wicked Prosper?', p. 100; see also Craigie, Kelley, and Drinkard, Jr., *Jeremiah 1-25*, p. 179.

extensive use of forensic terminology, and both end with a petition for vengeance against enemies.[81]

Perhaps the most convincing evidence of all that 11.18-23 and 12.1-6 are connected texts is provided by Lundbom, who notes that the 'key words in each poem – which double as catchwords – make a large chiasmus'.[82] This yields the following pattern:[83]

Jeremiah 11.18-20

A YHWH … and I knew
   Then he showed me
   Like a lamb … to the slaughter

    B YHWH … who judges righteously
   The innermost being
   For to you … my case

Jeremiah 12.1-3

    B' Innocent[84] … YHWH
   When I accuse[85] you
   Judgments[86]
   Their innermost being[87]

A' YHWH, you know[88] me
   You see[89] me
   Like sheep[90] to the slaughter[91]

Though 11.18-23 and 12.1-6 show potent and numerous linguistic and structural affinities, that only proves that the texts are artistically

---

[81] Apparently, both texts 'are intended to invoke Yahweh's vengeance upon Jeremiah's enemies'. O'Connor, *Confessions of Jeremiah*, p. 17.

[82] For Lundbom, this feature alone removes the need 'to reverse the poems in the text … or rearrange portions of them'. Lundbom, *Jeremiah 1-20*, p. 634.

[83] I have adapted Lundbom's chiastic structure to the translation given above.

[84] Both the adjective 'righteously' in 11.20a and the description 'innocent' in 12.1a share the same Hebrew root צדק, 'righteous'.

[85] The term 'my case' in 11.20d and 'accuse' 12.1b are the same Hebrew word, ריב, 'dispute/case'.

[86] The verb 'judges' in 11.20a and 'judgments' in 12.1c share the same Hebrew root, שׁפט, 'to judge'.

[87] Literally, in both 11.20b and 12.2d, the term is כְּלָיוֹת, 'kidneys'. See interpretation below.

[88] The verb ידע is used twice in 11.18a; only one instance is noted here because both occurrences are in the qal stem.

[89] The verb 'showed me' in 11.18b and 'you see' in 12.3a share the same Hebrew root, ראה, 'to see'.

[90] Actually, *different* Hebrew words are used here (כֶּבֶשׂ in 11.19a; צֹאן in 12.3c); however, the imagery of the lines clearly parallels.

[91] The terms for 'slaughter' derive from the same Hebrew root, טבח, 'slaughter/butcher'.

linked and is still not enough to prove beyond doubt if they existed originally as one or separate texts. It is interesting to note that Kathleen O'Connor and A.R. Diamond, two scholars who have done some of the most extensive work on the Confession texts, land on opposite sides of this very issue.[92]

Lundbom, perhaps, takes the best possible approach to such an intractable question: he describes 11.18-20 and 12.1-3 as 'companion' poems;[93] Holladay also refers to them as 'parallel' pieces and concludes simply: 'Confessional material beings at 11.18 and closes at 12.6'.[94] Craigie takes a very similar approach, addressing both texts as a pair of laments that follow the same structure.[95]

What our outlined affective approach contributes to this debate is the important way in which it helps us move beyond the impasse. Listening for emotive shifts can happen both within and across texts without invalidating the method. Whether the texts were originally one text or two does not change their *emotive* shape. Furthermore, demonstrating the existence of affective patterns or progressions might prove to be a very good way to explore different kinds of

---

[92] O'Connor argues 'against theses prevailing views to claim that the first confession is a literary unity … the poem presents a cohesive and logical argument regarding Jeremiah's role as a prophet'. However, even she admits such unity might not be 'original'. O'Connor, *Confessions of Jeremiah*, p. 15.

Diamond, who treats the issue at greater length, notes the 11.18-20 prayer had more affinities with lament and thanksgiving genres (see above discussion of the structure of 11.18-23), while, in 12.1-4, 'the balance shifts … to a blend of lament and legal speech forms to the total exclusion of thanksgiving'. Insisting that 11.18-23 be analyzed as 'an integrated and well-rounded composition', i.e. as a *complete* and *independent* literary unit, 'necessarily conditions the approach to 12.1-6. Problems arise from the common practice of removing verses from the latter (esp. v. 3b) to insert into the former'. Diamond, *Confessions in Context*, p. 37.

Amusingly, Diamond and O'Connor published these works within a year of each other (1987 and 1988, respectively); this gives some sense of the continuing nature of this discussion.

[93] Cf. Jer. 6.1-7, 8-12. Lundbom, *Jeremiah 1-20*, p. 634.

[94] Though he does think they were originally separated pieces, they have coexisted as they are, in his best judgment, 'since the earliest redaction'. Holladay, *Jeremiah 1*, p. 366.

[95] That structure is.
    1) Invocation (11.18; 12.1a)
    2) Complaint (11.19; 12.1b, 2)
    3) Prayer (11.20; 12. 3-4)
    4) Divine response (11.21-23; 12.5-6)
Craigie, Kelley, and Drinkard, Jr., *Jeremiah 1-25*, p. 176.

overarching structure and textual coherence.[96] Finally, and perhaps most happily, our affective method allows the hearer to draw on the rhetorical insights of *both* O'Connor *and* Diamond without having to preclude one or the other because of their theory of the text's compositional history; rather than closing off avenues of textual exploration, an affective method allows us to listen to the text with a broader collection of scholarly voices.

The structure of Jer. 12.1-6 as described first by Baumgartner is relatively straightforward and again appears to imitate the laments of the Psalms:[97]

12.1a. Introduction
12.1b-2. Question and reproach
12.3a. Innocence motif
12.3b. Request for vengeance
12.4. Complaint
12.5-6. Answer in divine speech form[98]

In this structure, v. 3 is clearly central,[99] demarcated by the use of the disjunctive וְאַתָּה ('but you'). Also, the questions vv. 1b-2 and 4 are formulated in parallel.[100]

	First Question (Jer. 12.1b-2)	Second Question (Jer. 12.4)
Question	Why [מַדּוּעַ] does the way of the wicked prosper? Why are the faithlessly faithless at ease? (1b)	How long [עַד־מָתַי] will the land mourn and the grass of ever field wither? (4a)

---

[96] Or it could very well expose 'disjunctures' and 'incoherences'.

[97] Allen describes 12.1-6 as an 'intensification of a Psalm of lament, now become a complaint', using the 'telltale questions in vv. 1 and 4, "Why?" and "How long?"' However, this text is 'marked by a shrillness that is absent from the typical lament. The closest parallel is Ps. 35, a complaint that is a cry for justice, which asserts the Psalmist's innocence (vv. 7, 19), asks, "How long?" (v. 17) and appeals to Yahweh's righteousness (v. 24).' Allen, *Jeremiah*, p. 148. See also Craig C. Broyles, *The Conflict of Faith and Experience in the Psalms: A Form-Critical and Theological Study* (JSOTSup 52; Sheffield: JSOT Press, 1988), pp. 48, 193-96.

[98] Baumgartner, *Jeremiah's Poems of Lament*, p. 70, followed by Diamond, *Confessions in Context*, p. 38; cf. Craigie, Kelley, and Drinkard, Jr., *Jeremiah 1-25*, p. 176.

[99] Holladay, *Jeremiah 1*, p. 368; see Hubmann, *Untersuchungen*, p. 368.

[100] The 'if … how' structure of the questions in the divine answer (vv. 5-6) seem to be paralleled to these two question-problems. Diamond, *Confessions in Context*, p. 39.

Elaboration	You have planted them; they are even rooted! They spread forth shoots; they are even fruitful! (2a)	Because of the evil of those who dwell in *the land*, Beast and bird are swept away (4b)
Theological Basis	You are near in their mouth but far from their innermost being (2b)	For they thought to themselves: 'He will not see our latter end' (4c)

Holladay notes as well the contrast between the vocabulary of fertility (v. 2a) and the imagery of drought (v. 4a); also, the 'planting' of the wicked (v. 2a) has resulted in the 'sweeping away' of beast and bird (v. 4b).[101] The final contrast is that the first question interrogates YHWH's treatment of a group of persons (e.g. 'the wicked'), while the second question interrogates that group's impact on/treatment of the land.[102] The inquiry moves from the prophet's *personal* conflict with 'the wicked' to the *national conflict* between YHWH and 'the land'.[103]

Within this elaborate structure, there are two other important features: the high concentration of forensic language and the theme of the 'prosperity of the wicked'. Jeremiah here highlights themes from the wisdom psalms (e.g. Pss. 37; 49; 73), but Diamond quickly notes that no lament in Psalms 'opens in a way similar to vv. 1-2'. Even the wisdom psalms, that deal as well with the problem of the wicked prospering 'draw back from explicit accusation of Yahweh',[104] something Jeremiah is clearly unwilling to do.

Also, the text's use of forensic language[105] is actually rather shocking. The phrase צַדִּיק אַתָּה ('Innocent are you') is a formulaic statement of acquittal, but here it is *Jeremiah* pronouncing *YHWH* acquitted, and that *before the trial ever begins*. Then Jeremiah uses the legal phrase

---

[101] Holladay, *Jeremiah 1*, p. 368.

[102] E.g. the wicked 'prosper' and even are 'fruitful', while the land 'mourns' and 'withers' because of them.

[103] Jeremiah 12.1-6 is a 'microcosm of the national failing'. Allen, *Jeremiah*, p. 148.

[104] Diamond, *Confessions in Context*, p. 38.

[105] Reclassifying Jer. 12.1-6 as a 'lawsuit' text most helpfully illuminated by the 'courtroom scene' has been attempted. Diamond, *Confessions in Context*, p. 38. Blank says: 'The pattern of the confessions ... strongly suggests the *law court* as its source ... we observe a man claiming the right to appear before a higher authority and present his case...condemning his adversaries and protesting his innocence ... Then he appears to await the verdict'. Sheldon H. Blank, 'The Confessions of Jeremiah and the Meaning of Prayer', *HUCA* 21 (1948), pp. 331-54 (331-32). See also Reventlow, *Liturgie*, pp. 243, 246-47.

אָרִיב אֵלֶיךָ ('make/bring a case to/against you'), now addressing YHWH as the *Judge* who adjudicates the case. Finally, Jeremiah announces his intention to מִשְׁפָּטִים אֲדַבֵּר ('speak/pronounce judgments') *against YHWH*. In one statement, YHWH has gone from being the defendant to the judge to the one condemned; Jeremiah, likewise has gone from being the prosecutor to the petitioner to the judge. Diamond's comment: 'It does not seem that a trial process pattern actually exercises a controlling influence upon the text', seems rather an understatement of the case.[106] In fact, such radical inverting of a typical form has powerful emotive effects. The text is simply all wrong; it jars, upsets, and perhaps even frustrates the listener.[107] Just as the abrupt opening of 11.18-23 created a sense of wariness in the listener to match the prophet's own fear, so we find here that the textual opening, with this near abuse of forensic language, once again seems intentionally designed to evoke within the audience the feelings expressed by the prophetic figure.

These surrounding themes of the unjust prosperity of the wicked and the terrible plight of the land serve to highlight Jeremiah's claim of unique covenant relationship with YHWH. YHWH both 'knows' and 'sees' him; YHWH has 'tried' Jeremiah's heart and (apparently) found it to be true. In stark relief to the surrounding wickedness and disaster, Jeremiah is the one righteous man left who thinks to cry out to YHWH. And, yet, when he *does* cry out, Jeremiah says the most unthinkable things. Jeremiah effectively accuses YHWH of committing a crime, and it is *not* the crime of allowing the wicked to attack the prophet. No, it is the crime of *allowing the wicked to exist!* YHWH is implicated in injustice by the *very existence* of the wicked; it is almost as if Jeremiah is accusing YHWH of being a conspirator with the

---

[106] Diamond had earlier argued that exegetes must be willing to consider 'the possibility of discerning some other genre [besides lament] which has been more constitutive in the structuring of this text'. However, he then notes that the forensic terms in this text have been 'strained to the breaking point'. Diamond, *Confessions in Context*, pp. 38-39. So, one is left to wonder, what kind of genre *is* Jer. 12.1-6 if it is neither a lament nor a court proceeding. This highlights the weakness of form criticism to deal with texts that appear to replicate or imitate *multiple* forms.

[107] 'The complex structure of the poem develops much of its potency around the idea of tension/contradiction. In the poem, nothing is right. Matters are not what they seem, and normal values and expectations are turned on their head.' Diamond, *Confessions in Context*, p. 43.

wicked like the men of Anathoth who had planned Jeremiah's assassination!

Keeping in mind the shocking nature of Jeremiah's speech to YHWH is important as we turn to the issue of YHWH's reply, which has consistently puzzled commentators. Clearly, there is some sort of challenge to Jeremiah in the divine reply of 12.5-6, but a challenge of what sort? And, more importantly to our present concerns, is that *all* that YHWH says to Jeremiah's outburst?

We come now to the point most appropriate to address the addition of Jer. 12.7-13 as a *continuation* of YHWH's reply to Jeremiah's complaint in 12.1-4. It is now broadly accepted that 12.7-13 represents the words of YHWH; however, not many see YHWH's words in these verses as connected to YHWH's two-question reply in 12.5-6.[108]

Rudolph offered two different suggestions to explain the placement of vv. 7-13 after vv. 5-6. The passage could be an example of the ways in which the people have conspired against YHWH.[109] Or the passage could have been placed here because it was mistakenly thought to be the words of *Jeremiah* in reply to YHWH's brusque dismissal of his complaint.[110] However, McKane also points out that Weiser thought YHWH's lament (vv. 7-13) was somehow a reply to Jeremiah's complaint (vv. 1-5).[111]

Other commentators have followed Weiser and noted other significant links. Holladay, for example, notes the use of בַּיִת as a catchword in vv. 6 and 7.[112] Carroll, who can always be counted on to present an original position on any debated topic, thinks that v. 6 actually fits *better* with vv. 7-13 than with vv. 1-5.[113] Furthermore, he thinks

---

[108] Lundbom, for example, does *not* treat 12.7-13 as part of YHWH's reply to Jeremiah, noting the presence of *setumahs* before v. 7 and after v. 13 indicates an 'independent unit'. Lundbom, *Jeremiah 1-20*, p. 651. However, he also notes the presence of *setumahs* before 11.18 and 11.20 but does *not* treat them as marking an independent unit. Lundbom, *Jeremiah 1-20*, p. 633.

[109] Cf. Jer. 11.10.

[110] See McKane, *Jeremiah*, p. 269.

[111] These verses (Jer. 12.7-13) 'disclose the tension in God's inner life, conflicts of love and hate, justice and mercy, election and judgment'. McKane, *Jeremiah*, p. 269.

[112] Holladay, *Jeremiah 1*, p. 366.

[113] When v. 6 is connected to 12.1-5, 'it can distort the different meanings of the pieces that make up that unit', making it 'parallel 11.21-23, i.e. an identification of the conspirators against Jeremiah [as] his own family', a reading he rejects. Carroll, *Jeremiah*, p. 287.

that Jer. 12.6-13,[114] which uses the motifs of 'house' and 'beloved' should be most directly connected with Jer. 11.15, except for the unfortunate interruption 'by the build up of units now constituting 11.18-12.6'.[115]

Lalleman most closely follows Weiser's original suggestion. In their present canonical context, Jer. 12.7-13 is a 'counterpart' to Jeremiah's lament in 12.1-4. This is revealed by the fact that vv. 4 and 11 are correlated descriptions of the desolation of the land.[116] Fretheim also keys in on this land connection to present 12.7ff as a continuation of YHWH's response to Jeremiah's lament.[117]

Furthermore, it is also possible to extend Diamond's observations about the tri-partite structure of Jeremiah's questions in 12.1b-2, 4 to YHWH's reply in 12.5-13, yielding something like the following:

	First Question (Jer. 12.1b-2)	Second Question (Jer. 12.4)	YHWH's Reply (Jer. 12.5-13)
Question	Why ... at ease? (1b)	How long ... wither? (4a)	If you have raced ... challenge horses? (v. 5)
Elaboration	You ... fruitful! (2a)	Because ... swept away (4b)	For (כִּי) even your brothers ... For (כִּי) no one turns their heart (v. 6-11)
Theological Basis	You ... innermost being (2b)	For they thought ... latter end (4c)	Upon all the bare heights of the desert spoilers have come ... because of the burning[118] anger of YHWH (vv. 12-13)

YHWH's questions in v. 5 reveal the problem of Jeremiah's apparent weakness, especially in light of what is coming next. The veiled threat is elaborated in vv. 6-11 in terms of *both* the personal

---

[114] See also Berridge, *Prophet, People, and Word of Yahweh*, p. 127.

[115] Carroll, *Jeremiah*, p. 288.

[116] 'After Jeremiah's lament comes God's lament ... Their sufferings are connected, because both are the result of disobedience by the covenant people'. Lalleman, *Jeremiah and Lamentations*, p. 142.

[117] 'Jeremiah brings his lament to a climax in v. 4, not with a concern about himself (though that concern remains), but with an appeal on behalf of the land and its creatures ... God does not respond simply to Jeremiah's more personal issues (vv. 5-6); God also engages Jeremiah's concern about the present situation of the *land* (vv. 7-13) and its future (vv. 14-17)'. Fretheim, *Jeremiah*, p. 191, italics original.

[118] Both 'challenge' in v. 5 and 'burning' in v. 13 share the same verbal root, חָרָה, 'to be kindled, burn'. See interpretation below.

consequences that Jeremiah will face (e.g. threats from his own family) *as well as* the consequences to the entire nation/land (e.g. imminent desolation). In reality, the theological basis for this looming tragedy is found in the very last (and often excised) line: 'Because of the
burning anger of YHWH', which will be discussed in some detail
below.

Melvin has dealt with this issue at some length. Choosing to leave
the text as it stands[119] creates an almost-irreconcilable contrast to
YHWH's reply to the previous lament in 11.21-23.[120] In that text,
YHWH promises to punish Jeremiah's enemies, in fact, to annihilate
them completely. In 12.5-6, YHWH offers no comfort and certainly
no promise of exacting vengeance. The real issue is that YHWH's
reply in 12.5-6 'only addresses Jeremiah's immediate situation, but not
the more universal question that Jeremiah poses in 12.1-2'.[121]

Clearly, what we have in Jer. 12.7-13 is YHWH's own description
of the abandonment of YHWH's chosen people; what is so surprising is how this description is *loaded* with 'terms of endearment and
intimacy'.[122] Notice the repetition of personal possessives in
YHWH's speech: '*my* house' (בֵּיתִי) in v. 7; '*my* inheritance' (נַחֲלָתִי) in
vv. 7, 8, and 9; '*my* vineyard' (כַּרְמִי) and '*my* field/delightful field' (חֶמְדָּתִי
חֶלְקָתִי) in v. 10. These wonderful reiterations of Israel's position as
YHWH's unique possession are frighteningly attached to powerful
verbs of destruction: 'abandon' (עָזַב) … 'desert' (נָטַשׁ) … 'give (over)'
(נָתַן) … 'destroy' (שָׁחַת) … 'trample' (בּוּס).

This clashing terminology makes the point that, while it is certainly YHWH who is responsible for the coming complete destruction, 'it is readily apparent that doing so causes … immense pain and
suffering'. YHWH grieves not just that YHWH's people will be punished but that they will be punished *by YHWH's own hand.*[123]

YHWH's grief, however, reveals an inner logic at work that links
12.7-13 with the preceding text. Our examination of the first confession (Jer. 11.18-23) demonstrated that Jeremiah's sufferings were the

---

[119] That is, with YHWH's reply to Jeremiah's complaint in 12.1-4 ending at 12.6.
[120] Melvin, 'Why Does the Way of the Wicked Prosper?', p. 101.
[121] Melvin, 'Why Does the Way of the Wicked Prosper?', p. 103.
[122] Melvin, 'Why Does the Way of the Wicked Prosper?', p. 103.
[123] Melvin, 'Why Does the Way of the Wicked Prosper?', pp. 103-104.

direct result of and even integral to his prophetic calling.[124] And even though YHWH promises to punish those who persecute YHWH's prophet (11.21-23), Jeremiah is not released from the experience of suffering.[125] Rather, the *people's* suffering will become *his* suffering because, as the people's prophet,[126] Jeremiah's fate is inextricably bound up with theirs (12.5-6). Then YHWH reveals to Jeremiah YHWH's *own* suffering at the fate of Jerusalem and Judah (12.7-13). The suffering of Jeremiah *not only* mirrors the pain of the people *but also* – and equally – mirrors the pain of YHWH.[127] From an affective perspective, Jer. 12.7-13 is *integral* to this confession because, without it, the audience's picture of the full meaning of Jeremiah's suffering remains woefully incomplete. Thus, Jer. 12.7-13 is treated here as the final section of YHWH's response to Jeremiah's complaint in 12.1-4. It comprises two additional units, YHWH's *own* description of the coming disaster in the form of a divine lament (vv. 6/7-11),[128] followed by a brief announcement of the disaster (vv. 12-13).[129]

---

[124] That such suffering was 'part of Jeremiah's calling as a prophet' is even 'indicated in Yahweh's words to Jeremiah at his call (Jer. 1.17-19)'. Melvin, 'Why Does the Way of the Wicked Prosper?', p. 103.

[125] See the summary of my exegesis of 11.18-23 above.

[126] This may be the most distinctive element of the presentation of the office of the prophet in the book of Jeremiah. As prophet, Jeremiah 'belongs' just as much to *the people of Judah* as he belongs to YHWH. Cf. Lee Roy Martin, 'Fire in the Bones: Pentecostal Prophetic Preaching', in Lee Roy Martin (ed.), *Toward a Pentecostal Theology of Preaching* (Cleveland, TN: CPT Press, 2015), pp. 38-39, 56-57.

[127] Melvin sees 'a three-way causal relationship here'. The people cause Jeremiah to suffer, therefore YHWH punishes the people, which causes Jeremiah to suffer *more*. Yet YHWH *must* punish the people for their sin (symbolized by their persecution of the prophet), which causes YHWH even more grief. Melvin, 'Why Does the Way of the Wicked Prosper?', p. 104.

[128] Following Carroll's suggestion above and treating v. 6 as a kind of 'Janus-structure' that *ends* YHWH's 'answer' to Jeremiah's complaint and *begins* the elaboration of the 'worse things to come' that YHWH will bring about.

[129] Allen suggests that vv. 7-11 is an 'oracle of disaster spoken in Yahweh's name'. However, there is no indication of a 'change of speaker' between vv. 6 and 7. The plain reading of the text would be that this is a description of the disaster spoken *by YHWH*. Allen, *Jeremiah*, p. 152.

5.3 Interpretation

From the outset, the text of 12.1-13 has a different, sharper, tone than 11.18-23.[130] In the prior confession, the central theme was certainly *not* a conflict between the prophet and YHWH; rather, they are presented as being in perfect solidarity.[131] However, that has gone topsy-turvy here. As Miller says, 'The case that is presented *to* the Lord in 11.20 ... becomes a case *against* the Lord in 12.1'.[132]

In fact, the tone here is *such* a deviation from the prior text that Baumgartner reminds his readers that Jeremiah is not speaking here as a prophet but as 'an individual pious man who has difficulty with certain experiences he is having to face'.[133] Baumgartner seems to forget that the primary impact of Jeremiah's call as a prophet 'from birth' (Jer. 1.5) is that Jeremiah's *life* is inextricably linked to his calling. Jeremiah can no more 'not be a prophet' and speak only as a pious man than he can force his heart 'not to beat'![134] What is at stake here in this confession is the most profound question of biblical faith: YHWH's faithfulness to the covenant promises. YHWH's righteousness (i.e., ability to keep promises) is the single most important cornerstone of biblical theology.[135]

5.3.1 Jeremiah's First 'Judgment' (12.1-2)

Jeremiah's complaint, like the last, opens with an address to YHWH. Initially, the listener would hear this as a simple declaration. 'You are righteous.'[136] However, the rest of Jeremiah's statement turns this

---

[130] 'The emotional level is comparable to that in 2.35, where Yahweh accuses Israel in spite of her protestations of innocence.' Holladay, *Jeremiah 1*, p. 368.

[131] There, Jeremiah is 'an innocent litigant who is wrongly threatened. It is only natural that Yahweh, who is just and the proper judge of men, will side with such a one'. In fact, 'from the outset it is the prophet's God who has taken steps to warn and protect him and who ultimately will destroy his persecutors'. Diamond, *Confessions in Context*, p. 35.

[132] Patrick D. Miller, 'Jeremiah: Introduction, Commentary, and Reflections', in Leander E. Keck (ed.), *New Interpreter's Bible* (Nashville: Abingdon, 2001), VI, pp. 553-926 (675).

[133] Baumgartner, *Jeremiah's Poems of Lament*, p. 65.

[134] In fact, Jeremiah once tried to 'resign' his prophetic office, with personally disastrous results (Jer. 20.8-9). As was mentioned above, YHWH had informed Jeremiah from the moment of his call that resistance, suffering, and persecution were an integral part of the prophetic office (Jer. 1.17-19).

[135] 'It means that the God who makes promises will keep them and will intervene in powerful ways when the promise runs amok.' Brueggemann, *Commentary on Jeremiah*, p. 118.

[136] Psalm 119.137. Holladay, *Jeremiah 1*, p. 375.

assumption immediately on its head: it makes no sense for the prophet to say to YHWH, 'You are righteous … when[137] I accuse you'. Suddenly, this simple opening becomes either a declaration that YHWH is innocent of wrongdoing or (worse) a sarcastic, embittered comment that YHWH always gets the court to decide things in YHWH's favor.[138]

The emotive distance between the opening of *this* prayer and the conclusion of Jeremiah's *last* prayer (11.20) becomes even clearer when Jeremiah announces his intention (almost against his better judgment)[139] to pronounce judgment upon YHWH! In every usage, דִּבֶּר pi'el + מִשְׁפָּטִים אֶת־ means 'to pronounce judgments on',[140] even containing the idea of 'passing sentence'.[141]

Lundbom seems a bit flummoxed by this, remarking with almost comic banality that this is 'uncommonly bold according to one line of thinking'.[142] What seems to be missing in Lundbom's analysis is an appreciation of the *emotive* dimension of Jeremiah's words to YHWH.

---

[137] The use of כִּי here has elicited several alternative translations. Berridge suggests: '*Whenever* I dispute with you'. Berridge, *Prophet, People, and Word of Yahweh*, p. 161, n. 253. Vriezen suggests: '*Even if now* I have to dispute with you'. Rudolph offers a third possibility: '*If I wished to* dispute with you'.
Commenting on these possibilities, Holladay remarks: 'One has the impression … they are offered in part because of the theological threat that a real quarrel [between YHWH and the prophet] would raise'. Holladay, *Jeremiah 1*, 376.

[138] In this context, 'the latter is a real possibility'. Craigie, Kelley, and Drinkard, Jr., *Jeremiah 1-25*, p. 179; however, it is not immediately apparent. 'On hearing the phrases of the second and third cola, then, one reconceives the first colon in a forensic context'. Holladay, *Jeremiah 1*, p. 375.

[139] Indicated by the use of the particle אַךְ, translated above as an adversative (i.e. 'Nevertheless').

[140] Though Volz and Rudolph try to suggest otherwise. Holladay, *Jeremiah* 1, p. 376.

[141] 'Translations have usually been softened because of sufficient ambiguity in the Hebrew' found in the pronominal object אוֹתָךְ. However, the prior colon uses the very clear אֵלֶיךָ ('to you'), which might also be the more proper rendering here. Lundbom, *Jeremiah 1-20*, p. 643.

[142] Lundbom almost stubbornly insists: 'At the outset Yahweh does not appear to be a defendant … Jeremiah is simply acknowledging Yahweh as the righteous Judge before whom his accusation is now being made.' It is not immediately obvious 'whether or not Yahweh himself is on trial'.
But Lundbom is forced to acknowledge that even 'if this does not constitute a direct censure of Yahweh, it is at least an oblique one, because to "make accusation" and "to speak judgments" is to confront the all-righteous Judge with a legal challenge and with judgments the prophet himself has made'. Lundbom, *Jeremiah 1-20*, p. 643.

This is not simply *legal* language;[143] most precisely, it is *legal* language used *affectively*. As Holladay says: 'To pronounce an acquittal of Yahweh is to be bitterly ironic'.[144] Taking the opening two lines together, then, show that Jeremiah's words at this moment are embittered,[145] belligerent,[146] frustrated,[147] despairing,[148] and perhaps even 'near-blasphemous'.[149]

The specific issue that has the prophet enraged with grief at YHWH is the issue of the 'prosperity of the wicked'. Though the question is presented in formal legal terms, the jaw-dropping opening of the prayer leaves the listener in no doubt that there is an 'intensely personal interest' at work here.[150] In the context of the prayer, the 'prosperity of the wicked' is Jeremiah's first 'judgment' on YHWH.

Once again, we have returned to speaking in generalities that marked the opening of the first confession. The 'wicked' are not explicitly identified.[151] And again, it only adds to the listener's

---

[143] See George W. Ramsey, 'Speech-Forms in Hebrew Law and Prophetic Oracles', *JBL* 96.1 (1977), pp. 45-58 (52).

[144] Holladay, *Jeremiah 1*, 375. In Jer. 2.29, Jeremiah uses the same kind of language to declare that Israel does not have a 'case' against YHWH. Here, Jeremiah certainly *does* feel that he has a legitimate 'charge' to make but is certain he has 'not the slightest chance of winning a verdict'. Craigie, Kelley, and Drinkard, Jr., *Jeremiah 1-25*, p. 179.

[145] This poem 'begins in a highly impassioned and embittered mood ... in bitter torment he stands up to his God and begins to remonstrate with him'. The expression מִשְׁפָּטִים אֲדַבֵּר אוֹתָךְ refers elsewhere to the activity of the judge (Jer. 1.16a; 2.12; 39.5; 52.9). But here, 'Jeremiah uses it of himself – against Yahweh! This alone should prove that it is rather more than a "calm, academic tone" that he uses.' Baumgartner, *Jeremiah's Poems of Lament*, p. 65.

[146] 'A belligerent note is evident from the outset in that the ironically polite admission of Yahweh's justice is followed by a determination to challenge it.' Allen, *Jeremiah*, p. 148.

[147] Jeremiah is frustrated 'that Yahweh will turn out to be innocent ... similar to the frustration Job expresses in Job 9.12-20'. Even there, though, Job is not half so bold as Jeremiah. Job is only speaking to his friends *about* YHWH whereas here, Jeremiah is saying this directly to YHWH's face! Holladay, *Jeremiah 1*, p. 368.

[148] 'Presumably he well knows that it is a hopeless enterprise to try to call Yahweh to account, that he will never get the better of him.' Baumgartner, *Jeremiah's Poems of Lament*, p. 65.

[149] Diamond, *Confessions in Context*, p. 45. McKane says the passage 'underlines the rebellious attitude of the prophet – he stands on the brink of contumacy. Over against the unthinkable thought that Yahweh's righteousness can be impugned, there is dissatisfaction with a faith which seems to be merely obscurantist, and there is an unwillingness to make lack of comprehension a theological virtue'. McKane, *Jeremiah*, p. 261.

[150] Allen, *Jeremiah*, p. 149.

[151] Lundbom, *Jeremiah 1-20*, p. 644.

confusion; after the astonishing opening, the hearer must ask: 'And who is Jeremiah talking about *now*?' Usually, the proximity to the mention of the 'men of Anathoth' is taken to provide the needed identification.[152] That, however, could be too easy an interpretive path.[153] We have already seen in the first confession how Jeremiah's conflict with the men of Anathoth is taken up as a microcosmic example of YHWH's conflict with the entire rebellious nation.

It is not at all surprising that the fear and anger generated by life-threatening local conflicts would stir up questions related to the existence and (apparently exalted) status of the wicked in YHWH's world. Thus, it follows with the emotive logic of these paired confessions that Jeremiah is speaking not now of specific individuals that he knows but of the wicked as a class of persons who are actively destroying justice by breaking YHWH's covenant and resisting the prophetic word.[154]

The language of 'the wicked' (רָשָׁע) in Scripture always includes within it the concepts of evil intent and injustice.[155] Perhaps the best way to understand the meaning of רָשָׁע is to note that its antonym is usually צָדֵק ('to act/do righteously').[156] Van Leeuwen suggests another key way to understand its basic meaning by suggesting רָשָׁע basically denotes 'to be impious'.[157] The term רָשָׁע is used first of all to refer to one who threatens the life of a fellow Israelite.[158] The idea is that wickedness is revealed by specific anti-social behaviors; by

---

[152] Brueggemann allows that we '*may* assume a carryover of the "men of Anathoth"' but clearly questions the wisdom of such an assumption. Brueggemann, *Commentary on Jeremiah*, p. 119, italics mine.

[153] Not to put too fine a point on it, but if Jeremiah had wished to question YHWH about why the conspirators were still prospering, he could have certainly mentioned the 'men of Anathoth' specifically.

[154] This classification would certainly have *included* the men of Anathoth who plotted Jeremiah's assassination, but is no longer *restricted* to that group. Lundbom, *Jeremiah 1-20*, p. 644; cf. Brueggemann, *Commentary on Jeremiah*, p. 119.

[155] In fact, רָשָׁע is 'used in parallel with almost every Hebrew word for sin, evil, and iniquity'. G. Herbert Livingston, 'רָשָׁע', *TWOT*, II, pp. 863-64.

[156] Eugene Carpenter and Michael Grisanti, 'רשע', *NIDOTTE*, III, pp. 1201-204. 'Eighty times (half of them in the book of Proverbs), רָשָׁע is placed in antithetic parallelism to 'צֶדֶק', often in focus on 'both the quality of lifestyle and the results of the two ways of living'. Livingston, *TWOT*, II, p. 864.

[157] C. Van Leeuwen, 'רשע', *TLOT*, III, pp. 1261-65. 'The measure of רָשָׁע is its contrast with the character and attitude of God" Livingston, *TWOT*, II, p. 863.

[158] Cf. Jer. 5.26; Prov. 12.6; cf. Pss. 119.95, 110; 140.5, 9.

behaving in those non-covenantal ways, a person *revealed* themselves as wicked.[159] The adjectival form used here occurs most often in the wisdom literature[160] but is rarely used in OT narrative.[161]

In Psalms, 'the wicked' is the short-hand designation for the one who 'stands diametrically opposed to the צַדִּיק',[162] the very term used to describe YHWH in Jer. 12.1! The רָשָׁע lives like an atheist[163] and can be described as YHWH's 'enemy'[164] and/or one who hates YHWH.[165] Because the רָשָׁע has no relationship with and no accountability to YHWH, the רָשָׁע also oppresses the poor and needy,[166] especially 'widows, orphans, and strangers',[167] though one day his own children will be fatherless and his wife a widow.[168] The רָשָׁע represent an imminent threat to all aspects of the community's well-being.[169]

---

[159] Thus, 'wickedness' in the OT is 'an objective fact [e.g. evidenced by specific actions] rather than a subjective phenomenon'. Livingston, *TWOT*, II, p. 863.

[160] Of the 263 occurrences in the OT, 214 are found in three books: Job (26x), Psalms (82x), and Proverbs (78x). The outlier is the book of Ezekiel, where the term is found another 28 times. Carpenter and Grisanti, *NIDOTTE*, III, p. 1202.

[161] Helmer Ringgren, 'רָשָׁע', *TDOT*, XIV, pp. 1-9.

[162] 'He is the archenemy of the godly individual.' Carpenter and Grisanti, *NIDOTTE*, III, p. 1202.

[163] Psalms 10.4; 36.2 [1]. In many ways, Ps. 10.3-11 is a summarizing 'profile' of the רָשָׁע:

They boast of their own desires and despise Yahweh in their arrogance ... and think that 'there is no God.' They prosper in their ways, pay no attention to God's judgments, and believe that they will never stagger. Their mouths are filled with deceit and oppression, they talk mischief and iniquity, saying that 'God has forgotten ... he will never see it.' One can accordingly call them the 'godless', since they do not take God into account, believing rather in their own strength; they withdraw from God's power and live by their own initiative' (Ringgren, *TDOT*, XIV, p. 5).

[164] Psalm 37.20.

[165] Psalm 68.2-3 [1-2].

[166] Psalms 10.2; 37.14; 82.4.

[167] In our discussion of the term 'vengeance' (נקם) above, special mention was made of Psalm 94 in relation to the 'emotive' dynamics of that term. It is interesting to note the presence of this triad (twice!) in vv. 3-6 as the object of the wicked person's hatred (see also Ps. 146.9). Carpenter and Grisanti, *NIDOTTE*, III, p. 1202.

This is relevant to our discussion of Jeremiah's confessions because *this same triad is found in Jeremiah 7.5-6* and represents a key link between the theology of the book of Jeremiah and the theology of the book of Deuteronomy, where the phrase is used repeatedly (see Deut. 10.18; 24.17, 19-21; 27.19, passim). William L. Holladay, *Jeremiah 2* (ed. Paul D. Hanson; Hermeneia; Minneapolis: Fortress Press, 1989), pp. 59.

[168] Psalm 109.9, 12. Carpenter and Grisanti, *NIDOTTE*, III, p. 1202.

[169] Cf. Exod. 2.13; Num. 35.31; 2 Sam. 4.11. Livingston, *TWOT*, II, p. 863.

Now, given their terroristic threat to the community, we might logically expect the wicked 'would always be kept under the restraints of law and order and suffer defeat every moment of life'.[170] However, Jeremiah claims that the wicked *prosper*! The term could not be more contradictive.

The root שָׁלָה essentially means 'to accomplish one's intention', that is, to be successful in all endeavors. The OT insists, over and over, that such 'prosperity' *only* results from the work of YHWH in a human life and is *only* available to those who seek YHWH with their whole heart.[171] By all that Jeremiah knows, the wicked *cannot* prosper. And yet Jeremiah's true word of YHWH is mocked and resisted at every turn. Powerful enemies in influential positions (eventually, even the kings of Judah themselves) attempt to silence his preaching. Even *his own friends* have joined a conspiracy to end his life! The wicked cannot prosper … and yet they do. There is no more absolute contradiction of terms than this, and it is tearing Jeremiah apart with anger, grief, and bewilderment.[172]

Perhaps here is the note of despair in Jeremiah's prayer: even if it proves out that YHWH is *not* responsible or complicit in the prosperity of the wicked, it remains part of Jeremiah's everyday reality. Even more frustrating than the apparent *guilt* of YHWH (for not judging the wicked as promised) is the wicked's apparently rampant *success*.

The question is put in, if possible, even *more* emotively powerful terms in the second half of the line: 'Why are the faithlessly faithless at ease?' The translation 'faithlessly faithless'[173] is an attempt to catch the poetic consonance of בֹּגְדֵי בָגֶד, which seems to imitate the earlier *multiclimatums* of 11.18 (הוֹדִיעַנִי וָאֵדָעָה)[174] and 11.19 (חָשְׁבוּ מַחֲשָׁבוֹת).[175] More importantly, however, is the fact that בָּגַד, which has at its core

---

[170] Unfortunately, this is 'not so'. Livingston, *TWOT*, II, p. 864.

[171] Cf. 2 Chron. 31.21; Josh. 1.8; Ps. 1.3. 'Joseph is called a prosperous man, for Yahweh turned all of his misfortune into benefit for Jacob's sons (Gen. 39.2-3, 23).' John E. Hartley, 'צָלַח', *TWOT*, II, p. 766.

[172] 'Normal expectations are overturned … such "rewards" are normally reserved for the righteous alone.' Diamond, *Confessions in Context*, p. 45.

[173] Following Lundbom's suggestion. See translation notes above.

[174] '[He] made me to know and I knew'.

[175] 'Schemed schemes'. As noted above, this is something of a Jeremianic 'signature'.

the idea of treachery, is clearly an important part of the theological vocabulary of the book of Jeremiah and has already appeared multiple times in key texts.[176] Klopfenstein finds three distinct legal spheres where the term is found: marriage, diplomatic relations, and sacral regulations.[177] Each of those categories is represented in Jeremiah's prior uses of the term: in Jeremiah 3, YHWH depicts Judah's sin as 'faithlessness' to the marriage vows;[178] in Jeremiah 5, Judah is condemned as a nation that has 'forsaken' (עָזַב) YHWH and has 'sworn' (שָׁבַע) fealty to foreign false gods; finally, in Jeremiah 9, Judah is condemned for not 'knowing' (יָדַע) and even 'refusing' (מֵאֵן) to know YHWH.[179] Judah has behaved treacherously in every possible way in every possible arena of life with YHWH and with the covenant people![180]

The verbal form of בגד expresses the unstable relationship between human action and external regulations; that is, as בָּגַד, humans cannot be relied upon to be obedient. In this sense, human בָּגַד is the ultimate contrast to YHWH's חֶסֶד.[181] This also indicates the explicitly religious usage of the term.[182] However, even though the term is

---

[176] Jeremiah 3.7-8, 10-11, 20; 5.11; 9.1 [2].

[177] See Exod. 21.8; Judg. 9.23; 1 Sam. 14.33, which Klopfenstein assumes are the three oldest usages of the term in the OT. M.A. Klopfenstein, 'בגד', *TLOT*, I, pp. 198-200.

[178] Judah's worship of false gods/betrayal of the covenant is 'likened to the betrayal of a wanton woman who is unfaithful to her partner'. Robin Wakely, 'בגד', *NIDOTTE*, I, pp. 582-95.

[179] Jeremiah 9.3-6 [4-7]. The context makes it clear that such 'knowing' is defined as obedience to the covenant.

[180] Perhaps the most significant 'shift' in the use of בגד in these earlier Jeremianic passages is its subtle 'broadening of reference'. In Jeremiah 3, the focus of the indictment is on the בגד of Judah, especially the ways in which it is worse that the בגד of Israel (cf. Jer. 3.11). However, in Jeremiah 5, the distinction between 'Israel' and 'Judah' disappears. Wakely, *NIDOTTE*, I, p. 587.

[181] Erlandsson, *TDOT*, I, p. 470. In fact, the unifying theme of several texts where the root בגד appears is 'the fate of the faithful and that of the faithless [cf. Ps. 59.6 (5); 73.15; 119.158]'. Wakely, *NIDOTTE*, I, p. 585.

[182] Such usage is not unique to Jeremiah but is also found in the earlier prophet Hosea (esp. Hos. 5.7; 6.7). In 5.7, 'the faithless acts of the people against Yahweh are compared with the birth of illegitimate children'; then, in 6.7, 'the expression בָּגְדוּ בִי, "they have dealt faithlessly with me", is used in connection with the people's transgression (עָבַר) of the covenant'. Erlandsson, *TDOT*, I, pp. 470, 472.

Also, 'most passages appear in the accusation of prophetic judgment speech', but also appear in 'the threat and in the lament'. It seems that the 'legal home of the root בגד required that the prophets use it for the accusatory indictment of apostasy'. Klopfenstein, *TLOT*, I, p. 200.

primarily used to depict Judah's treacherous faithlessness to YHWH – the incorrigible deceitfulness of their inner life – Jeremiah 9 very powerfully reveals the deleterious effects of *religious* treachery on *social* relationships. Faithlessness to God inevitably leads to acts of faithlessness against members of the community'.[183] Again, Jeremiah's complaint is here not rooted in threats to his *personal* safety but in the danger these 'faithless' ones pose to the entire community.

And it is these treacherous ones – these 'lying, deceiving, oppressing, stubbornly untrustworthy people who are all cheats'[184] – who are 'at ease' (שָׁלוּ)! The term means to be peaceful and quiet,[185] and typically designates what modern Westerners might call the 'easy life'.[186] So far, the term appears to be a synonym for צָלַח ('prosper') in the first cola.[187]

However, the term is also found in Ps. 30.7,[188] where the context seems to suggest that שָׁלוּ carries the connotation of 'the gross delusion that prosperity guarantees stability'.[189] In other words, the quiet of שלה might very well be negligent stupor rather than restful repose.[190] Thus, שלה is usually a 'blessing'[191] but can potentially be a 'curse'. Though it certainly does not work as a resolution of Jeremiah's distraught state, the usage of שלה here in the last line creates the tiniest of cracks in the wicked, faithless ones' armor of 'prosperity', providing a hint that all may not be well with them for very much longer. Of course, the prophet is still in such an enraged state that he seems to ignore this glimmer of hope, and rushes on in his address to YHWH, but the attentive listener should catch the hint.

---

[183] Wakely, *NIDOTTE*, I, p. 587.

[184] Wakely, *NIDOTTE*, I, p. 587.

[185] Lundbom, *Jeremiah 1-20*, p. 644.

[186] Philip J. Nel, 'שלה', *NIDOTTE*, IV, pp. 117-18.

[187] The usage in Jer. 12.1 is similar to Ps. 73.12. 'Such are the ways of the wicked. always *at ease*, they increase in riches'. K. Grünwaldt, 'שָׁלֵו', *TDOT*, XV, pp. 9-13.

[188] *BDB* mistakenly suggests this word is *only* found in Ps. 30.7. *BDB*, s.v. 'שָׁלָוה'. However, Holladay notes other appearances of the term. See *CHALOT*, s.v. 'שלה', which specifically notes שָׁלוּ as a form of the qal perfect and directly references Jer. 12.1 as an example.

[189] Victor P. Hamilton, 'שָׁלַה', *TWOT*, II, p. 927.

[190] Its use in Jer. 49.31 seems to carry this 'connotation of negligence'. Nebuchadnezzar calls the Arabian tribes גּוֹי שְׁלֵיו, a 'nation at ease', indicated by their lack of 'gates' (דְלָתַים) or 'bars' (בְּרִיחַ). 'A nation so unprotected is naturally easy prey.' Grünwaldt, *TDOT*, XV, p. 11.

[191] Job 20.20. Grünwaldt, *TDOT*, XV, p. 12.

Since we are exploring affective states, this is an important point to grasp because, at this point, the emotive reactions of the figure of the prophet and the attentive listener slightly diverge. This brief hint of hope pulls the listener back (just) a step from the precipice of emotional collapse on which Jeremiah stands. This does not mean that the listener loses any empathy with the prophet's emotional state – the listener was taken to the very brink of emotional chaos with Jeremiah's address to YHWH – however, the listener peeks into the potential for resolution *before the prophet does*. In a way, this actually serves to increase the listener's sympathy with the prophet: we actually feel his despair and grief and anger *more* acutely and hear even *more* clearly the inconsolability of Jeremiah's heart. This (slight) distancing of the listener and the prophet does not *lessen* but rather *increases* the emotive impact of Jeremiah's words.

Jeremiah's next statements make abundantly clear that this contradictory state of world affairs – the wicked prospering, the faithless at ease – is *YHWH's* fault. 'You have planted them; they are even rooted! They spread forth shoots; they are even fruitful!' It is impossible to miss here the inversion of Ps. 1.3.[192] That YHWH has 'planted' the wicked means their prosperity is not an accidental result of some oversight on YHWH's part; YHWH has *intentionally caused* the wicked's prosperity.[193] The use of the particle גַם in the second half of the lines serves to intensify the enormity of the claim by stressing the continued growth. The wicked are not only planted; they have also taken root![194] Not only have they grown; they have also produced

---

[192] Lundbom, *Jeremiah 1-20*, p. 645. Holladay takes careful note of how Jeremiah here plays on the imagery of Ps. 1.3, seeing the allusions that span the first two confessions as central to their interpretation. In fact, Holladay is convinced that the metaphor of Jeremiah as a 'tree' in Jer. 11.19 is where the allusions to Psalm 1 (esp. v. 3) begin, echoed again here in 12.2 and even later (and more explicitly) in 17.8, which offers the related noun יוּבַל 'stream' parallel with מָיִם 'water'. However, it is important to note that the parallel exists at the level of *imagery* not *vocabulary*. For example, Jer. 12.2 uses a different verb for 'plant' (נָטַע here; שָׁתַל there); also, Jer. 17.8 uses different terms for 'stream' (יוּבַל; פֶּלֶג in Psalm 1) and for the tree's flourishing (רַעֲנָן means 'luxuriant'; לֹא־יִבּוֹל in Psalm 1 means 'never wither'). The one term common to all three texts (Ps. 1.3; Jer. 12.2; 17.8) is פְּרִי, 'fruit'; that is, all three texts emphasize 'productiveness'. See Holladay, *Jeremiah 1*, pp. 372, 376-77.

[193] Holladay, *Jeremiah 1*, pp. 376-77. Jeremiah's charge is *not* that 'Yahweh has lost his grip and is no longer able to maintain his theodicy … Yahweh is said to cause the prosperity of the wicked'. McKane, *Jeremiah*, p. 262.

[194] This is a detail *not* included in Psalm 1's description of the wicked. Holladay, *Jeremiah 1*, pp. 376-77.

fruit! How ironic it is that it is *YHWH* who has 'planted' the very
ones who wish to 'cut down' (11.19) Jeremiah!

The apparent action of YHWH to prosper the wicked is an even
greater betrayal of the faithfulness of Jeremiah given the wicked's
clear *un*faithfulness to YHWH and YHWH's covenant. Jeremiah
feels the need to remind YHWH here: 'You are near in their mouth,
but far from their innermost being'.[195] In the first confession, Jeremiah had confessed YHWH as the one who tested the 'kidneys'
(כְּלָיוֹת). The accusation is plain: though there are pious motions, there
are no pious *e*motions. Though they may offer sacrifice and pray to
YHWH,[196] there is no inner affection that orients them to covenantal
love and obedience. Their *actions* are pious but their *affections* are godless![197] Some important points follow from this.

First of all, the audience, like the prophet, will find this state of
affairs absolutely confounding. While the idea of hypocrisy is quite
common in the NT, it was *not* a concept as familiar in the OT, which
assumed a rather direct connection between a person's inner self (e.g.
affections, thoughts, motives, desires) and external actions.[198] Therefore, observations such as this indicate 'a profound dislocation in the
expected order of things'.[199] One would as soon expect to rise in the
morning and find the dawn appearing in the *north* as expect that one
would profess fealty to YHWH and then live in utter disregard of
YHWH's commands, let alone that such outrageous treachery would
be so apparently blessed by YHWH with success and quietude!

Secondly, Jeremiah draws the line between righteousness and un-
righteousness, between existence in covenant and out of covenant, *at
the level of the affections*. It is important not to miss this. Jeremiah is
claiming that *he* is the truly 'righteous one' (Jer. 12.3)[200] because he is
the one who *feels* the right things. Jeremiah and the seemingly pious
wicked would perhaps have agreed at the level of *orthodoxy*; they
might have verbally affirmed at least some of the same claims about
YHWH and the role of YHWH's chosen nation of Israel. However,

---

[195] Literally, 'kidneys'. See discussion above in the interpretation of 11.18-23.

[196] Lundbom agrees that the 'wicked here are probably the outwardly religious'.
Lundbom, *Jeremiah 1-20*, p. 645.

[197] Thus, Jeremiah 'grounds the injustice of Yahweh's blessing to this group in
the hypocrisy of their relationship to him'. Diamond, *Confessions in Context*, p. 46.

[198] See above the discussion of the meaning of the Hebrew term רָשָׁע.

[199] Holladay, *Jeremiah 1*, p. 377.

[200] See comments below.

the ineluctable *distinction* between the righteous and the wicked is proposed here to exist at a level *deeper* than orthodoxy; it exists at the
level of *orthopathy*, rightly-ordered affections.[201]

Third, the connection of these 'hypocrisy' and 'planting' motifs
has another important effect that Diamond has noticed. The 'divine
planting' motif is used elsewhere in Jeremiah to reference the nation's
founding.[202] The present passage gains its rhetorical and affective
power by blending the imagery of the contrasted fates of the righteous and wicked with the imagery of the nation as the 'planting of
YHWH',[203] blended in such a way 'so as to place the latter[204] into the
former[205] just at the point occupied by the wicked'.[206] It is not just
that the nation has suddenly gone wicked; it is also that the nation is
wicked *from the root up*.[207]

5.3.2 Jeremiah's Innocence (12.3)

These three compelling incongruities intertwine as the source of the
emotive power of Jeremiah's plea, and lead us to the heart of

---

[201] Carroll, *Jeremiah*, p. 285, has noted a 'pious strand' in the Jeremiah tradition
that highlights

> the differentiation between outer appearances and inner realities; e.g. the people
> whose social lives are oppressive but who go to the temple and claim to be
> saved; the neighbours speaking *shalom* to each other but planning ambushes in
> their hearts [cf. Jer. 9.7 (8); the people whose penises are cut but whose minds
> are unreceptive.

[202] See Jer. 1.10; 2.21; 11.17; 18.9; 24.6; 31.28; 32.41; 42.10; 45.4.

[203] A common prophetic image; cf. Isa. 5.1-7.

[204] I.e. the nation of Israel.

[205] I.e. the contrasting fates of the righteous and the wicked.

[206] Diamond, *Confessions in Context*, p. 46.

[207] The introductory 'historical retrospective' of Israel's wilderness given in Jer.
2.2b, זָכַרְתִּי לָךְ חֶסֶד נְעוּרַיִךְ אַהֲבַת כְּלוּלֹתָיִךְ ('I remember you, your youthful devotion,
your love as a *new* bride'), will strike any listener familiar with the story of Israel's
wilderness wanderings in the Torah (especially the book of Numbers) as a very
romanticized retelling of that era of Israel's history. The wilderness period was
hardly a time of devotion and unquestioning obedience to YHWH's every command. Israel broke the first two of the Ten Commandments before Moses even
brought them to the people (cf. Exod. 32)! Rather, the Torah presents those wilderness days as a raucous time of rebellion and near-riot!
Clearly, the point in Jeremiah 2 is *not* that YHWH is somehow 'misremember-
ing' the early days but contrasting 'the idyllic origins of the community and its
recent experience [cf. Jer. 2.2, 5]'. Carroll, *Jeremiah*, p. 119. As Stulman says: 'The
fleeting memory of betrothal reveals what could have and should have been but
was not. It is a story of lost love. The marriage is over … Only in the distant past
does Israel love Yahweh. In the present, such devotion is altogether absent.' Stulman, *Jeremiah*, p. 48.

Jeremiah's prayer: 'But you, O YHWH, you know me, you see me'; more importantly, 'You test my heart toward you'. Perhaps what should fascinate us first of all is that where we would expect a *petition*, we find instead a *statement*;[208] instead of a plea to YHWH to set right this egregious wrong, Jeremiah instead reasserts his own intimate relationship with YHWH.[209]

The important verbs 'know' (יָדַע), 'see' (רָאָה), and 'test' (בָּחַן) link Jeremiah's claim to the call narrative (1.5)[210] and to Jeremiah's claim about YHWH's role as the scrutinizing Judge in the first confession (11.20). The claim here is *not* that *Jeremiah* knows YHWH, but that *YHWH* knows Jeremiah. As in multiple other contexts, the verb יָדַע here means *much* more than simply intellectual knowledge.[211] Rather, this is a knowing that implies a deeply intimate and totally transparent relationship.[212] Clearly, here, Jeremiah is somehow counting or calling on the intimacy of his relationship with YHWH as the catalyst that will bring about some change in the untenable national circumstances just described.

Though in statement form, it seems pretty evident that we have here a request for action, or, at the very least, a motivation to take action. That YHWH 'knows, sees, and tests' the prophet is tantamount to the prophet claiming that *his own* righteousness matches up to or equals YHWH's righteousness proclaimed in the opening line of 12.1.[213] This claim establishes Jeremiah's complaint as just; not

---

[208] 'It is striking that Jeremiah proclaims his innocence after questioning God's innocence.' Craigie, Kelley, and Drinkard, Jr., *Jeremiah 1-25*, p. 180.

[209] Perhaps as a partial justification for speaking to YHWH in such bold accusatory terms?

[210] Here, 'you have known me' (יְדַעְתָּנִי) answers 'I knew you' (יְדַעְתִּיךָ) in 1.5. 'Jeremiah is simply affirming the cornerstone of his life, his vocation'. Holladay, *Jeremiah 1*, p. 377.

[211] I.e. Jeremiah is *not* simply claiming that YHWH 'knows he exists'. Allen notes the 'polarization between vv. 2b and 3a'. Allen, *Jeremiah*, p. 149.

[212] J.A. Thompson, *The Book of Jeremiah* (NICOT; Grand Rapids. Eerdmans, 1980), p. 354, n. 32.

[213] Note that this claim for 'equal righteousness' is *only* made within the context of the prior claim of 'intimate relationship', presumably the source of the prophet's righteousness.

only is the complaint itself valid, but Jeremiah has the legal 'standing' (as a righteous man) to make this claim.[214]

This statement, then, is simultaneously a request and a statement of trust. Jeremiah *willingly* lays open his heart to the testing scrutiny of YHWH![215] Jeremiah is confident that YHWH will find no disjunctures between the content of Jeremiah's heart and his actions.[216] It is likewise an assertion that, though he is not prosperous or successful, he yet remains true to YHWH and YHWH's call.[217]

At one level, such a statement of profound trust and complete reliance on YHWH is inspiring to hear; however, careful listeners should be frankly shocked by the *dramatic* shift in tone. Just in the prior verse, Jeremiah had quite literally blamed YHWH for everything that was wrong with the world, accusing YHWH of collusion with the wicked to bring about their ill-gotten prosperity and ease. How or why would anyone then immediately express their trust in such a deity?

The solution lies within Jeremiah's claim that YHWH is a God who knows and sees all, including the innermost thoughts and feelings. We are to understand Jeremiah's angry, embittered, despairing, accusatory words in 12.1-2 as his exposure of the full contents of his heart. *Nothing* has been hidden from YHWH ... even the prophet's *negative* feelings. Jeremiah is claiming his prayer in vv. 1-2 as an act of audacious piety, but piety nonetheless; Jeremiah has *maintained* rather than *damaged* the intimacy of his relationship with YHWH by his outbursts.[218] What makes Jeremiah righteous is *not* that he has only

---

[214] Jeremiah and YHWH, 'the two of them, the poem claims, should agree about the accused wicked, who must surely be judged'. Brueggemann, *Commentary on Jeremiah*, p. 118.

[215] And, by extension, he lays his heart open to the scrutiny of the book's listeners' as well. Lundbom, *Jeremiah 1-20*, p. 645.

[216] 'Jeremiah's own life is all of a piece without any discrepancies between its surfaces and its depths.' McKane, *Jeremiah*, p. 262.

[217] Jeremiah is certain that YHWH knows 'his case is the precise opposite ... Outwardly, he is persecuted and poor but inwardly he is true to YHWH.' Baumgartner, *Jeremiah's Poems of Lament*, p. 285.

[218] Although there is no space to explore it here, this is of a piece with the massive ground shift in the theology of prayer presented in the OT, especially when compared to similar ANE theologies. Balentine correctly notes: 'Jeremiah uses prayer as a form for articulating his feelings of doubt and despair about God's presence in his life ... a way to cope with the circumstances, a way to reorient himself towards the presence of God in times of crisis'. Samuel F. Balentine, 'Jeremiah, Prophet of Prayer', *RevExp* 78.3 (1981), pp. 331-44 (341). See also Patrick

positive feelings for YHWH, but that he *does not hide any of his feelings* from YHWH.

Through its presentation of the prophet, the book is making an important affective claim upon the listener. It was noted above how the ambiguity in the term 'at ease' (שָׁלוּ) created a slight distance between the emotions of the listener and the figure of the prophet: we overheard a whisper of hope that the grieving prophet did not seem to discern immediately. However, with this petition for justice/expression of hope, the book, through the figure of the prophet, subtly re-invites the listener to give full expression to the emotive impact of the book. To do anything less than experience the full range of emotion is to be faithless to YHWH! Here, not only does the prophet authorize his own emotions as legitimate and faith-full expressions of a *true* relationship with YHWH[219] but also the book, *through* the figure of the prophet, authorizes the deep emotional reactions being stirred in listener's hearts as likewise legitimate and faith-full hearings of the book!

It is important to note this authorization at the apex of Jeremiah's prayer, for the very next line plunges the prophet and listener right back into an emotional melee of anger, grief, betrayal, and revenge. Once again, as at the middle of Jer. 11.20, we might yet expect a plea for salvation and protection; instead, we hear an even *more* vehement call for vengeance than in the first confession: 'Tear them out like sheep for the slaughter! Set them apart for the day of killing!'

The power of the request is effected by its reversal of the imagery of the first confession.[220] Jeremiah had described his innocence in the imagery of a helpless pet lamb being unwittingly taken to its

---

D. Miller, *They Cried to the Lord: The Form and Theology of Biblical Prayer* (Minneapolis: Fortress Press, 2000); Scott D. Ellington, *Risking Truth: Reshaping the World through Prayers of Lament* (PTMS; Eugene, OR: Pickwick Publications, 2008).

[219] This is just one among many ways 'the audience/listener/reader is led on the track of a structural identification between God and his prophet'. Else K. Holt, 'Word of Jeremiah-Word of God: Structures of Authority in the Book of Jeremiah', in John Goldingay (ed.), *Uprooting and Planting. Essays on Jeremiah for Leslie Allen* (LHB/OTS 459; New York: T and T Clark, 2007), pp. 172-89 (175); see also Margaret Zulick, 'The Agon of Jeremiah: On the Dialogic Invention of Prophetic Ethos', *The Quarterly Journal of Speech* 78.2 (1992), pp. 125-48.

[220] The verb here (נתק hiphil) means 'segregate, separate, single out', and clearly echoes 11.19, where Jeremiah is presented as a 'singled out' lamb. Holladay, *Jeremiah 1*, p. 378.

slaughter; now, that imagery of innocence becomes a rather-horrifying image of vengeance. It is important that we do not gloss the violence of the language here, or we miss its emotive impact. In sum, Jeremiah tells YHWH: 'Put them in the position of sheep which are dragged off to be slaughtered in circumstances where their wishes are a matter of no consequence'.[221]

Once again, the second line does not simply reiterate but exponentially intensifies the force of the request. The most obvious element of this intensification is Jeremiah's use of the language of 'setting apart' (קָדַשׁ).[222] The verb occurs only *one other time* in the entire book, in the hiphil stem, and that verb is found in Jeremiah's call (cf. Jer. 1.5).[223] Jeremiah, the one 'set apart' by YHWH to be YHWH's prophet, asks that the wicked be likewise 'set apart' for YHWH's judgment![224]

What makes this such a shocking term is that the root קָדַשׁ hardly ever occurs in a secular sense or setting; across the OT, it defines the realm of the 'holy'.[225] The idea of 'holy' objects/persons is quite difficult for modern listeners to comprehend.[226] To pronounce something 'holy' does not entail, it seems, some transfer of divine energies or qualities to the sanctified object.[227] Perhaps the best way to understand קָדַשׁ is having the sense of being dedicated or 'given over' to YHWH, from now on to be YHWH's possession.[228] Once this

---

[221] Jeremiah's imagery is *powerful* but not necessarily always *beautiful*. This verse describes a 'kind of absolute violence done to them and [they] are defenceless in the face of it'. McKane, *Jeremiah*, p. 262.

[222] Jack Naudé, 'קדשׁ', *NIDOTTE*, III, pp. 877-87.

[223] Given the paucity of occurrences, Holladay is right that the usage here 'must be heard in light of that occurrence in Jeremiah's call'. Holladay, *Jeremiah 1*, p. 378.

[224] Jeremiah 'appears to be saying, "You consecrated me to yourself when you called me, but you have treated me like a lamb consecrated for sacrifice; instead you should exercise your consecrating power upon my opponents-let them be dedicated to your purpose"'. Holladay, *Jeremiah 1*, p. 378.

[225] Thomas E. McComiskey, 'קָדַשׁ', *TWOT*, I, pp. 786-89.

[226] Müller argues that the idea of holiness as being 'set apart' is actually an *inferred* meaning because the entire idea of being 'made holy' as entailing an encounter with the 'wholly other … presupposes, for the most part, a point of departure in an understanding of the profane that has been suggested only by the absence of the numinous in modern concepts of normalcy'. H.P. Müller, 'קדשׁ', *TLOT*, III, pp. 1103-18.

[227] McComiskey, *TWOT*, I, p. 787.

[228] Naudé, *NIDOTTE*, III, p. 885. 'The causative concept "to dedicate, present" with God as the dative of the recipient dominates the hiphil'. Müller, *TLOT*, III, p. 1104.

transfer is complete, the person or object that exists within that sphere of 'the holy' and is subjected to 'cultic restrictions'; from then on, the person/object can only be used for a limited set of specific divine purposes.[229]

Perhaps Newman and Stine offer the best summary of the image: 'The meaning here is that they should be kept in a guarded palace until the time when they are put to death'.[230] In the prior confession, YHWH had assured Jeremiah of the coming destruction of the entire land (Jer. 11.22), but the wicked were still allowed, it seems, free rein until that judgment arrived; it seems Jeremiah is requesting that God reconsider or even reverse that decision and lock them up *now*. The sense of the text could be taken as highly ironic (and perhaps even a bit amusing) except that the listener is aware that Jeremiah is suggesting that the *only* divine purpose for the wicked is their destruction; there is no redemption or opportunity for repentance available to them. Their fate has been decided; let them away to it without delay![231]

Yet again, the paired terms are shocking in their contrast: while קֹדֶשׁ is a clearly sacral term, the terms טִבְחָה ('slaughter') and הֲרֵגָה ('killing') are both *domestic* terms without association to any cultic purpose.[232] The emotive power of the imagery comes from the clash of domestic and cultic terms. These who have refused to dedicate *themselves* to YHWH will be dedicated *by YHWH* to YHWH's ultimate purpose for them ... their death.

Again, the text has reached a moment of pause that draws the listener into reflection on what has just been heard. In our interpretation, we have worked quite extensively to show emotive movement *within* the selected texts, but this presents an ideal point to remind ourselves that emotive movement also occurs *across* Confession texts as well. In fact, Jeremiah's request here gains its emotive power from its juxtaposition to 11.18-23: without the prior image of Jeremiah

---

[229] See Neh. 12.47. McComiskey, *TWOT*, I, p. 787; Naudé, *NIDOTTE*, III, p. 886.

[230] Newman and Stine, *Handbook on Jeremiah*, p. 312. Even more ironic when we discover instances in the rest of the book of Jeremiah where the prophet is 'locked away'; cf. Jer. 36.5 (implied); 37.11; 38.6.

[231] Holladay suggests that Jeremiah is simply saying: 'God, get rid of them!' Holladay, *Jeremiah 1*, p. 378.

[232] See Jer. 11.19. Holladay, *Jeremiah 1*, p. 378.

being 'led like a lamb to the slaughter', his request that the wicked be pulled out 'like sheep for the slaughter' would appear morally outrageous. However, given the larger context, Jeremiah's request in 12.3 further clarifies what Jeremiah means in 11.20 when he asks to see YHWH's 'vengeance'. Considering both requests together affirms that the larger sense of divine vengeance at work here is more recompence than revenge.[233] Jeremiah is asking that YHWH do to his enemies (and all wicked) exactly as his enemies had planned to do him.

There is one other point for the listener to consider as we pause for a moment to think inter-textually rather than inner-textually. In the prior prayer, Jeremiah's cry for vengeance had *preceded* his statement of trust; in the present prayer, Jeremiah's cry for vengeance *follows* it. Holding the two confessions texts together (thus far) then yields the following emotive trajectory: fear/sense of impending doom (11.18-19); anger at conspirators (11.20c); affirmation of trust in YHWH (11.20d); angry accusation of YHWH (12.1-2a); anger at the prosperous wicked (12.2b); affirmation of relationship with YHWH (12.3a); cry for vengeance against the wicked (12.3b). Clearly, fear has faded into the emotional background and what is foregrounded so far is the prophet's wrestling with a sense of indignation *both* with the wicked of Judah *and* with YHWH. Underneath the outbursts of anger beats the solemn rhythms of heart-rending grief caused both by apparent betrayal by the people and YHWH and also by Jeremiah's clear sense of the doom that awaits his nation.

5.3.3 Jeremiah's Second 'Judgment' (12.4)[234]

Jeremiah had promised to pronounce his *judgments* (plural) upon YHWH; again, though the listener may have felt some sense of

---

[233] However, the conspirator's plots against Jeremiah had been quite drastic – i.e. his death and complete annihilation from social memory (Jer. 11.19) – so the requested 'payback' is *equally* shocking.

[234] Hitzig, Cornill, Volz, Rudolph, Hyatt, and Bright 'omit the verse except for the last clause on the grounds that it is out of place here'. Carroll, *Jeremiah*, p. 283; Giesebrecht omits all five cola. For Reventlow, the mention of the drought was the crucial indicator that this was a communal lament and, therefore, not an original part of this confession. Reventlow, *Liturgie*, pp. 244-51.

However, Craigie notes that if other laments of Jeremiah 'only concerned the fortunes of Jeremiah, then perhaps the deletion … would be justified'. However, the book makes an overwhelming argument for 'a link between the fortunes of Jeremiah and the people'. Furthermore, 'the people plotted against Jeremiah because they opposed God. Jeremiah mourns not only because of the plot against emotional resolution at the end of v. 3,[235] that sense of relief is quickly snatched away as Jeremiah embarks upon his second (but related) point of accusation. Above, our affective analysis revealed that a key concern about the existence of the 'wicked' (רְשָׁעִים) and the 'faithless' (בֹּגְדֵ) relates to their negative impact on the very fabric of reality. Their wickedness and rebelliousness are *never* condemned simply because of the *personal* harm it inflicts; rather, wickedness and faithlessness to YHWH *always* spill over into faithless acts that destroy order and bring about chaos.

For the prophet, the ultimate proof that the wicked *must* be dealt with forthwith is found in the languishing of the land. The drought-like conditions described here are presented as the after-effects of the curse the wicked have brought down upon themselves and their community.[236] The accusation is once more couched in lament language: 'How long will the land mourn and the grass of every field wither?'

The discussion of 'disaster in the land' is a quite common prophetic theme,[237] though very often, the actual depiction of the disaster is rather beside the point. The *real* issue is the prophetically-discerned connection between the people's covenant disobedience and the eventuation of the catastrophe.[238] However, here, Jeremiah takes a 'legal sentence'[239] and, by making it a rhetorical question, turns it into an accusation against YHWH.[240] The signs of drought become

---

him but also because of the sin of his people, revealed in the plot.' Craigie, Kelley, and Drinkard, Jr., *Jeremiah 1-25*, p. 180.

[235] Jeremiah has given full vent to his aggrieved anger at the prosperity of the wicked and has turned the matter over to YHWH for swift adjudication.

[236] Baumgartner, *Jeremiah's Poems of Lament*, p. 67.

[237] See Amos 1.2; 8.8; 9.5; Isa. 33.9; Joel 1; Jer. 4.27-28; 14; 23.10; Hos. 4.3. The last usage is particularly relevant. It is the last line of 'a prophetic judgment speech (4.1-3) which announces Yahweh's lawsuit against Israel'. The rest of the speech refers to Yahweh as the Judge 'who indicts the people for covenant infidelities (v 2) and then inflicts sentence … (v 3)'. The drought is presented there as 'the legal consequence of breach of covenant' and is described as bringing 'total devastation to the land'. O'Connor, *Confessions of Jeremiah*, p. 20.

[238] O'Connor, *Confessions of Jeremiah*, p. 20.

[239] Cf. Hos. 4.3; see above note.

[240] O'Connor, *Confessions of Jeremiah*, p. 20.

Jeremiah's evidence that YHWH is *not* acting to remove the wicked and restore order to the world.[241]

What is striking is Jeremiah's description of the *land* as 'mourning'. To be clear, אָבַל can mean *both* 'to mourn' *and* 'to be(come) dry'.[242] Lundbom asserts what we have here is another form of classical rhetoric called an *abusio*, a kind of implied metaphor where 'a word is taken from one usage and put to another'.[243] The term is most often used to describe the rituals for mourning the dead[244] though it can also be used figuratively as here.[245]

Even if Baumann is correct that the term is more focused on outward behaviors rather than inner feelings,[246] it is still the case that the *practice* of mourning in ancient Israel did involve the audible and visual expression of emotion.[247] Perhaps most intriguing is that the qal-stem of אָבַל is actually found *only* in the prophetic books, except for one instance in Job 14.22.[248] The term appears quite frequently in

---

[241] 'This is part of Jeremiah's whole argument: "Lord, even the land is suffering because of the wickedness of the people-and still you're not acting!"' Brown, *Expositor's Bible Commentary*, VIII, p. 213.

[242] Possibly either homonymous verbs or a single verb describing physical and psychological symptoms. Holladay, *Jeremiah 1*, p. 378. G.R. Driver popularized the idea that the root אבל meant 'wither'. 'A division of the root into אבל I "to mourn" and אבל II "to wither" is certainly unnecessary ... the same lack of distinction between physical and psychological conditions may also be observed with respect to אמל ["be weak"] and שׁמם ["be desolated, appalled"].' F. Stolz, 'אבל', *TLOT*, I, pp. 21-23.

Arnulf Baumann, 'אָבַל', *TDOT*, I, pp. 44-48, also notes that, if one follows Driver's assumption of

> two homonymous roots ... it is strange that in this division the hithpael participle and the substantive should only occur in I [e.g. 'to mourn'], while the qal and hiphil (in completely different ways) are assigned to both roots. It is more likely, then, that we are dealing with different meanings of the same root, although it is true that their inner connection is difficult to discern.

[243] Lundbom, *Jeremiah 1-20*, p. 129.

[244] E.g. Gen. 37.34; 1 Sam. 6.19; 2 Sam. 13.37; 14.2; 19.2; 1 Chron. 7.22; 2 Chron. 35.24. It is clearly 'a technical term for all these customs together that might be observed in case of a death'. The term 'often appears in connection with statements concerning periods of time [cf. Gen. 50.10; Deut. 34.8]'. Baumann, *TDOT*, I, p. 45.

[245] See Isa. 24.4: 'The land *mourns*'. J. Barton Payne, 'אָבַל', *TWOT*, I, pp. 6-7.

[246] Baumann, *TDOT*, I, p. 45.

[247] For audible expression, see Jer. 22.18; 48.36; for visible expression, see Gen. 37.54; Ps. 35.14; Mic. 1.8. It is also interesting to note that certain mourning rituals, such as tearing the hair or cutting the flesh were forbidden as pagan practices (cf. Lev. 19.28; 21.5). Payne, *TWOT*, I, p. 7.

[248] Anthony Oliver, 'אבל', *NIDOTTE*, I, pp. 243-48.

announcements of judgment,[249] emphasizing the after-effects of divine judgment upon the land and the people.[250]

Stolz thinks the term's *literal* meaning is 'to dry up, lay waste' and only *metaphorically* means 'to mourn'.[251] The connection, then, seems to be this: when the land is under divine judgment, it 'mourns' by stopping the expected rain cycle; the ensuing drought is taken as a symbol of nature's 'mourning'.[252] The imagery of the 'grass of the field' withering appears to be a variation on Gen 2.5, where the 'grass of the field' had not 'yet sprouted' (יִצְמָח) because YHWH had not yet 'sent rain' (הִמְטִיר) upon the earth. Thus, Jeremiah might be suggesting an analogy between the current state of the land and pre-creation chaos.[253] The drought conditions are *more* than just an unfortunate weather pattern; they are a *return to chaos* occasioned by the behavior of the wicked. There is a sense of incredulity or bafflement here on the prophet's part: is YHWH going to allow the wicked to continue to prosper until the entirety of creation is undone?

Jeremiah then lays the guilt for the natural chaos directly on the wicked: 'Because of the evil of those who dwell in the land, beast and bird are swept away'. The initial clause מֵרָעַה יֹשְׁבֵי־בָהּ (lit. 'because of the evil of those who dwell [there]in') could either conclude the prior sentence or begin the next. Holladay thinks the colon is better linked with what precedes than with what follows.[254] Though I translate the verse differently to balance the poetic lines, the best solution appears to be that the line is strategically and centrally placed as the explanation for *both* the drying up of the land as well as the disappearance of the animals.[255] Again, the focus on the passage is not simply

---

[249] Cf. Isa. 3.26; Hos. 4.3; Amos 8.8.

[250] Stolz, *TLOT,* I, p. 23.

[251] Stolz, *TLOT,* I, pp. 21-22; Oliver, *NIDOTTE,* I, p. 244.

[252] Probably due to it being the land's 'unnatural' (and usually calamitous) state. It is 'nature's symbiotic reaction to human wickedness [cf. Jer. 23.10]'. Allen, *Jeremiah,* p. 149. Describing the 'mourning' of the land expresses 'the totality or extensiveness of the judgment'. Even nature 'participates in the humiliation ... of the people struck with the calamity'. Baumann, *TDOT,* I, p. 47.

[253] Holladay, *Jeremiah 1*, p. 378. The disappearance of the birds is also a part of Jeremiah's vision of the return of chaos in Jer. 4.25. Lundbom, *Jeremiah 1-20*, p. 646.

[254] Holladay, *Jeremiah 1*, p. 378.

[255] 'In its meaning it relates to both statements.' Newman and Stine, *Handbook on Jeremiah*, p. 313.

complaining about difficult and/or unusual natural phenomena; the point is *explaining* these bizarre conditions by *blaming* the wicked for not keeping covenant and *demanding* that YHWH take action to remedy the situation.[256]

Oddly enough, this bridging phrase is also the most information the listener has been given so far as to the actual identity of 'the wicked'.[257] And, once again, the revelation is shocking: 'The wicked' are not some select few especially despicable persons – not some cabal hidden within the royal palace in Jerusalem, no! – rather, 'the wicked' who have brought this calamity down on both nation and nature are *all who dwell in the land*.[258] The magnitude of both the sin and its effects are truly horrifying!

Finally, Jeremiah offers the reason for both the disastrous situation of Judah and the coming destruction of the city and the temple. 'For they[259] thought to themselves, "He will not see our latter end".' Once again as in the first confession, the prophet appears to have been given access to the inner thoughts of the wicked. The listener should be astounded by both the stupidity and temerity of their claim.

The exact meaning of the phrase 'our latter end' (אַחֲרִית) bears a bit of discussion. Holladay and Lundbom both think the term means 'one's final situation',[260] that is, 'where we will end up' or 'our destiny'.[261] The people are rejecting YHWH's sovereign governance; in this they are *lying* to themselves, for, in Deut. 32.20, YHWH explicitly says, 'I will see their end'.[262]

The term אַחֲרִית, translated here 'latter end' is connected to the term אָחוֹר, which can mean 'back part' or 'rear',[263] but most typically

---

[256] What Jeremiah would *really* like to see is 'the punishment of the whole land to cease and the guilty to be punished instead'. Baumgartner, *Jeremiah's Poems of Lament*, p. 67.

[257] Diamond, *Confessions in Context*, p. 47.

[258] 'The whole nation is [now] in view.' Diamond, *Confessions in Context*, p. 47.

[259] I.e. the wicked 'dwellers in the land'.

[260] Holladay, *Jeremiah 1*, p. 379; Lundbom, *Jeremiah 1-20*, p. 646.

[261] 'It is a common biblical theme that the wicked mistakenly think Yahweh neither sees nor knows what they are about'. Lundbom, *Jeremiah 1-20*, p. 646. See Jer. 7.11; Ezek. 8.12; 9.9; Pss. 10.11; 73.11; 94.7; Job 22.13.

[262] Literally: אראה מה אחריתם. Holladay, *Jeremiah 1*, p. 379; Lundbom, *Jeremiah 1-20*, p. 646.

[263] Only in Exod. 33.23, when YHWH tells Moses that he will only see YHWH's 'back' and not YHWH's 'face', is the term used for 'the back of person's anatomy [anthropomorphically]'. R. Laird Harris, 'אָחַר', *TWOT*, I, pp. 33-35.

means 'backward' in the sense of direction.[264] In the most literal terms, then, the people are saying of YHWH, 'He will not see *behind* us'.[265] Thus, it seems this phrase may be open to *several* interpretive possibilities, especially given our earlier discussion of YHWH as the one who sees/knows/tests the kidneys as a description of the wicked person's vulnerability to YHWH's inspection and judgment because YHWH can see 'behind their back'. Thus, the claim 'He will not see behind us' could mean: (a) 'YHWH cannot see (i.e., control) our future'; (b) 'YHWH cannot see our innermost thoughts and feelings and therefore is too stupid to judge us'; or (c) 'YHWH will never see our 'backs' because we will never stop defying YHWH to YHWH's face'. Or, it could mean all three and be simultaneously a statement of mockery and defiance. It is precisely this contemptuous, defiant attitude of the wicked that guarantees their swift demise.

Something important but subtle has transpired in the prayer. We have moved from Jeremiah's almost-sarcastic, 'Innocent are you, YHWH!' to the wicked's defiant snicker: 'He will not see our end!' Though Jeremiah set out to pronounce 'judgments' on *YHWH*, Jeremiah's prayer ends exclusively focused on the wickedness of the land-dwellers – *and not YHWH* – as the source of the surrounding chaos. As we traced the emotive movement across 11.18-12.3, we noted the elision of fear into anger … but an anger that struggled to find its focal point, oscillating between being ultimately directed at YHWH or ultimately directed at the wicked. It is clearly too much to say that the ambiguity of Jeremiah's anger has fully resolved itself; however, it is important to notice that, by the end of the prayer, the prophet's anger is aimed at the wicked and *not* at YHWH. To put it more frankly, the attentive listener should be *much* more comfortable with how Jeremiah's prayer *ends* than with how it *began*. Jeremiah's tirade against the wicked and their obvious impact on the community and the land seems to imply that Jeremiah still believes YHWH is capable and willing to discipline those who break covenant.

---

[264] Jeremiah 7.24: 'They went backward (אחור) and not forward'. Harris, *TWOT*, I, p. 33.

[265] In the Hebrew conception of time, the past was 'behind the back' because it could not be seen. 'H.W. Wolff has likened the Hebrew conception of time to the view … [when] rowing a boat'. The person rowing 'backs into the future'. Harris, *TWOT*, I, p. 34.

5.3.4 YHWH's Reply, Part I (12.5-6)

Once again, the sense of emotive resolution is ephemeral, quickly overturned by the following verses. Clearly, the question-pair in v. 5 is meant to correspond to and balance Jeremiah's two questions in 12.1b-2, 4.[266] However, the divine answer here (like Jeremiah's prayer) is already astonishingly different than the equivalent material in the first confession. First, there is no formal introduction;[267] this already gives YHWH's reply a little more snap than the formality of 11.21-23.[268] Then, we find that YHWH's answer is not *nearly* the word of assurance found in 11.22-23. YHWH does not seem to 'overtly take Jeremiah's side' nor is there even 'an assurance of *postponed* punishment'. Instead, 'The divine judge refuses to take the case but issues an advisory brief'.[269]

Both YHWH's rhetorical questions follow the same basic format, offering a simile, and then applying it to Jeremiah's situation.[270] Each question moves from small to great; however, they have a cryptic coded feel.[271] The ambiguity here can lead to other affective constructions of YHWH's rhetoric. Holladay senses that the text is meant to present a *warning* to Jeremiah, echoing YHWH's words to Jeremiah about his enemies in Jer. 1.17.[272] Thompson finds it an exhortation for Jeremiah to remain faithful and courageous, even more so as greater troubles lay ahead.[273] Brown thinks that, though the answer is unsympathetic, it is a 'stark statement of reality' and a 'good example of the Lord's ruthless love'.[274] Lundbom thinks it is more reprimand than answer, and Rad says it is 'no answer at all'.[275]

---

[266] Allen, *Jeremiah*, p. 150.

[267] See Jer. 4.22; 5.7-9; 6.11b-12. This leads Carroll to argue that it is *not* a divine answer and 'should be read as a continuation of v. 4'. Carroll, *Jeremiah*, p. 286.

[268] Where YHWH's answer is formally introduced *twice*.

[269] Allen, *Jeremiah*, pp. 149-50.

[270] A similitude [*Gleichnis*] 'serves to ensure the effect of a sentence by juxtaposing a similar sentence from another field, whose effect is not in doubt'. It is a 'vivid and graphic manner of speech'. Baumgartner, *Poems of Lament*, p. 68.

[271] They are 'intentionally abstract ... almost proverbial'. This means then, that v. 6 is a 'more concrete explanation' of v. 5. Diamond, *Confessions in Context*, p. 48.

[272] He notes 'the verse presupposes diction suggestive of holy war ... adapted for the life of Jeremiah'. Holladay, *Jeremiah 1*, p. 380.

[273] As for the 'abruptness' of the reply, Thompson notes: 'This was nothing other than he might have expected from his initial call to fulfil the kind of ministry that was his'. Thompson, *Book of Jeremiah*, p. 356.

[274] Brown, *Expositor's Bible Commentary*, VII, p. 213.

[275] Lundbom, *Jeremiah 1-20*, p. 646.

YHWH asks the prophet: 'If you have raced with men and they have wearied you, how then will you challenge horses?' Apparently, the difficulties that Jeremiah is currently experiencing (e.g. resistance to the prophetic word, murder plots by home-town friends) is only a 'foot race' compared to the 'horse race' that is coming. The second question parallels the first: 'And if in a safe land you are collapsing, how will do in the jungle of the Jordan?'

The correspondence of the metaphors seems to be the threat of physical failure[276] or defeat. Ordinarily, a runner should have no problem competing with others on foot. The verb רוּץ may have special significance. In Jer. 23.21 it is used to describe the preaching of the false prophets; their 'running' (רוּץ) is contrasted with YHWH's 'sending' (שָׁלַח). The term is used again in Jer. 51.31 to refer to the running of a messenger. This suggests to Holladay that the terms of the first question may specifically refer to Jeremiah's prophetic career.[277] Also, it is difficult to imagine racing horses without having the imagery of *war* horses come quickly to mind.[278]

The other intriguing verbal issue is the word בּוֹטֵחַ, usually considered the qal participle of בָּטַח, 'to trust'. However, the existence of a homonymous verb that means 'to fall or collapse'[279] creates the possibility of hearing simultaneously two meanings: 'If in a land of peace you are trusting …' and, 'If in a safe land you are collapsing …'[280] It is important to note, along with Holladay, the verb is a participle not a perfect, speaking not of a 'specific action' but of a 'permanent attitude',[281] that is, an *affection*. Thus, what is at issue here is not only Jeremiah's *role* as YHWH's prophet – will he still 'run'[282] despite the increasing resistance from the people and the false prophets? – but

---

[276] Allen, *Jeremiah*, p. 144; McKane, *Jeremiah*, pp. 263-64; Smith, *Laments of Jeremiah*, p. 10.

[277] 'Running' then 'has a double reference, both to Jeremiah's function as a messenger of Yahweh, and to his effort to compete with others manifesting prophetic behavior'. He also wonders: 'Is there a hint here of Elijah's running in front of Ahab's chariot (1 Kgs. 18.46)?' Holladay, *Jeremiah 1*, p. 379.

[278] 'Likening the future troubles to a horse could be an oblique reference to the enemy from the north.' Craigie, Kelley, and Drinkard, Jr., *Jeremiah 1-25*, p. 180.

[279] See *CDCH*, s.v. בטח II'.

[280] There are simply no good 'middle terms' in English that can simultaneously represent both readings.

[281] Holladay, *Jeremiah 1*, p. 380.

[282] I.e. deliver YHWH's word.

also his *relationship* of trust with YHWH – will he keep trusting YHWH when there is no more שָׁלוֹם, or will his trust collapse?[283]

YHWH then moves to reveal that things have already gotten immeasurably worse for his own family has now turned against him: 'For even your brothers and the house of your father,[284] even they have dealt[285] faithlessly with you, even they cry out behind you, "Assemble!"'[286] This is the ultimate humiliation.[287] Even worse, by joining the growing resistance to the prophet, they have become part of the 'faithlessly faithless', the wicked ones who are responsible for the destruction coming upon the land and whom Jeremiah has just consigned to YHWH for judgment. Imagine for a moment Jeremiah's horror at realizing he has just condemned his own family to be slaughtered like defenceless sheep (Jer. 12.3).

This is then followed by YHWH's warning: 'Do not believe them when they speak to you good things'. Earlier, Jeremiah had warned Judah that no one was to 'trust their brother' because no one 'speaks the truth'.[288] This now even includes the prophet Jeremiah and his own brothers who are not to be believed even if they 'speak unto you good things' (רְדַבְּרוּ אֵלֶיךָ טוֹבוֹת). This term is drawn from the realm of international diplomacy; it is the language of 'treaty-making'.[289] It seems, then, that YHWH is forewarning the prophet that his family will approach him with an offer of help, a 'defence pact', as Diamond

---

[283] I.e. will he cease to open his heart to YHWH's close examination?

[284] The phrase 'house of your father' may be taken 'either as the equivalent to "your brothers" or else with the broader meaning of "all your relatives" ... as in "even your brothers along with all your relatives"'. Newman and Stine, *Handbook on Jeremiah*, p. 315.

[285] The verbs here are perfects but are *not* references to past actions but rather 'perfects of certainty'. Diamond, *Confessions in Context*, p. 218, n. 83. Thus, the phrase could also be translated: 'For even your brothers ... even they will certainly deal faithlessly with you'.

[286] The call to 'assemble' could 'refer to a banding together to destroy the poet' or to 'an invitation to the poet to gather with his family for defence/help'. In the latter case, 'the divine warning labels this as בגד and not to be trusted' and 'would parallel nicely the closing phrase "say nice things to you"'. Diamond, *Confessions in Context*, p. 49.

[287] The three-fold use of גַּם 'emphasizes the heightened indignity of family members turning against the prophet'. Lundbom, *Jeremiah 1-20*, p. 648.

[288] Jeremiah 9.3-4 [4-5]. Holladay, *Jeremiah 1*, p. 380.

[289] See 2 Sam. 7.28 for an explicit covenantal use. Cf. Michael Fox, 'Tob as Covenant Terminology', *BASOR* 209 (1973), pp. 41-42; W.L. Moran, 'A Note on the Treaty Terminology of the Sefire Stelas', *JNES* 22.3 (1963), pp. 173-76.

calls it.[290] They will offer Jeremiah peace 'to his face' (אֵלֶיךָ) while all the time conspiring 'behind his back' (אַחֲרֶיךָ).[291] Jeremiah is not to 'believe' (אָמַן) their words. Bracke here notes an important connection back to Jer. 11.3, 5. YHWH announced a curse on anyone who does not 'hear' (שָׁמַע) the covenant, to which Jeremiah replies: 'Amen (אָמֵן)!' While 'Jeremiah is not to say 'amen' to the good words of his relatives and friends, he [says] 'amen' to God's announcement of covenant curse'.[292]

As was noted briefly in the introduction to this textual section, YHWH's reply to Jeremiah has puzzled and provoked commentators; it is quite evident that no one is quite sure what to make of it. Perhaps Carroll is the most honest in his evaluation of YHWH's words: 'Silence would have been preferable to such an answer'.[293] Surely, silence would have been preferred to the unsympathetic reply of 'ruthless love' – an oxymoron if ever there was – that Brown has suggested. Baumgartner offers a valiant attempt to make sense of 12.5-6 as YHWH's reply to Jeremiah's impassioned prayer. For Jeremiah, with this final divine word, all illusion is stripped away and he recognizes he is quite alone.[294] YHWH ignores Jeremiah's accusatory questions in 12.1 because YHWH will not be held accountable by the prophet; YHWH expects-demands!-unquestioning service.[295] Thus, YHWH's answer is both 'terrible' and 'humiliating' for the prophet.[296]

Baumgartner is still convinced, though, that this lament ultimately does rise above the problem: 'Out of it speaks a resignation, a willingness to give up what has been dearest to him … [Jeremiah] accepts the burden … but no comforting thought weaves its way into his mind as we might have expected'.[297] However, this harsh answer is important for a reason far more crucial to Baumgartner's exegetical concerns; for him, this answer undoubtedly confirms the text's

---

[290] Diamond, *Confessions in Context*, p. 50.
[291] Holladay, *Jeremiah 1*, p. 382.
[292] John W. Bracke, *Jeremiah 1-29*, p. 113.
[293] Carroll, *Jeremiah*, p. 287.
[294] Baumgartner, *Jeremiah's Poems of Lament*, p. 69.
[295] Baumgartner, *Jeremiah's Poems of Lament*, p. 69.
[296] Baumgartner, *Jeremiah's Poems of Lament*, p. 69.
[297] Baumgartner thinks that this is a song 'in which both form and content rises far above the level of the Psalms'. Baumgartner, *Jeremiah's Poems of Lament*, pp. 69-70.

authenticity. Such a song can only come from a 'truly great man'[298] such as we know the prophet Jeremiah to be.

On the opposite end lies Diamond's evaluation, who finds 'confrontation and opposition … effected at every level of the passage'.[299] The central demand of Jeremiah's prayer is ignored, as are the prophet's nigh-blasphemous accusations. All in all, 'if the previous confession resolved its tensions … 12.1-6 leaves nothing resolved. There is only challenge and counter-challenge'.[300] To call this an 'answer to prayer' is to empty the term of all relevant meaning.

Once again, we find Brueggemann striving for a balance of perspectives. He grants that the answer is surprisingly 'hard-nosed', more reprimand and warning than reassurance.[301] YHWH's warning could be taken to mean 'Jeremiah is cast as an isolated voice', or it could be taken as YHWH's call to radical trust: 'Trust me, Yahweh, and only me. Trust me instead of them.'[302]

Taking the time to review the various options for hearing 12.5-6 as YHWH's reply has given the listener a reflective moment to reorient themselves to the text. As was noted at the end of the first confession, YHWH's answer which is so easily read as a complete resolution of the conflict is actually still invested with quite a bit of uncertainty.[303] So it seems only fair to ask of this second reply that seems to give no evidence whatsoever of resolution, if perhaps we might not be listening closely enough?

---

[298] 'The severity of the answer alone is sufficient to establish authenticity.' Baumgartner, *Jeremiah's Poems of Lament*, p. 69.

[299] 'Legal forms of speech are used in a surprising, unusual fashion. Motifs are joined in ways that produce contradictions in terms.' Diamond, *Confessions in Context*, pp. 50-51.

[300] The worst part of this lack of resolution is that 'Yahweh is depicted in collusion with the enemy and the primary threat to the prophet'. Diamond, *Confessions in Context*, p. 51.

[301] Brueggemann, *Commentary on Jeremiah*, p. 119.

[302] 'To serve such a God is not merely an act of dedicated loyalty and intentional decision-making. It is rather, an inescapable destiny once one has grasped a certain reading of reality.' Brueggemann, *Commentary on Jeremiah*, pp. 119-20.

[303] In fact, Melvin, whose argument I largely follow in my structuring of the second confession, says that in 11.21-23, 'Jeremiah's enemies are punished. So thorough will be their destruction that no remnant will remain.' Melvin, 'Why Does the Way of the Wicked Prosper?', p. 101. In point of fact, Jeremiah's enemies are *not* punished; YHWH only *promises* to punish them in the coming judgment on Judah and Jerusalem.

Only a few points need to be made. First, and most obviously, YHWH warns the prophet (again) of a looming danger, apparently some false offer of 'help' from family that is actually a cleverly-designed trap. Clearly, YHWH is still committed to protecting Jeremiah from harm.[304] Secondly, YHWH's cryptic questions imply that Jeremiah is somehow superior to the wicked who dwell in the land; this superiority means that YHWH 'has higher expectations for him than Jeremiah has [to this point] realized', but YHWH's prediction of greater resistance in coming days indicates YHWH already knows the future and is preparing the prophet for it.[305] In a sense, there is a lesser-to-greater logic at work here, too: if YHWH can foresee/reveal to Jeremiah an imminent event like his family's entrapment plot, then YHWH most certainly is in control of the ultimate fate of the wicked and the land. Thirdly, Jeremiah's anger and grief have not caused YHWH to give up on the prophet; YHWH does *not* refute Jeremiah's claim to be 'known' and 'seen' and 'tested'. Finally, and most importantly, *YHWH does not stop speaking.* At the end of v. 6, YHWH has *not* finished replying to Jeremiah's outburst of emotion. Therefore, though listening closely to this text has brought us to the point of emotional exhaustion, we need muster our courage to listen for just a little bit longer.

5.3.5 YHWH's Reply, Part II (12.7-11)

The most *immediate* connection between Jer. 12.7-11 and 12.5-6 is the catchword linkage of the terms for family in vv. 6 and 7.[306] However, the more *important* verbal link between the passages is surely the shared references to the 'mourning' of the land in 12.4 and 11.[307] Though most commentators agree that this passage is a divine lament, it should be noted that it lacks typical lament vocabulary.[308] The loss YHWH mourns here is a loss that *YHWH* alone causes; thus, this lament does double duty as a judgment-speech. That may

---

[304] Something that actually was *not* clear in 11.22-23.

[305] Holladay, *Jeremiah 1*, p. 32.

[306] The unit picks up from v. 6 'your family' (בֵּית־אָבִיךָ) with reference to Jeremiah and reuses it in a shorter version, 'my family' (בֵּיתִי) with reference to Judah. Allen, *Jeremiah*, p. 152.

[307] Craigie, Kelley, and Drinkard, Jr., *Jeremiah 1-25*, p. 184.

[308] Jeremiah 9.9-10, for example, contains terms like בְּכִי וָנֶהִי ('weeping and wailing') and קִינָה ('dirge'); all are absent here. Holladay, *Jeremiah 1*, p. 385.

provide some explanation for the love-hate relationship between YHWH and Judah expounded here.[309]

And yet it bears repeating; this is, first of all, a divine *lament*. The first expressions we hear are not expressions of anger or justifications of judgment but cries of pain born out of a deep and irrecoverable loss.[310] The YHWH of 12.5-6 appeared resolved, with all deep emotions safely in check; listeners are quite unprepared for this anguished outburst from the lips of YHWH![311]

The section breaks into near halves by topic: vv. 7-9 address the broken relationship; vv. 10-11 describe the broken land.[312] YHWH appears to make three key points: (1) the land has failed YHWH; (2) YHWH's judgment will come in the form of an invasion; and (3) the result of this invasion will be the desolation (e.g. desert-ification) of the land, returning it to the state of primordial wasteland.[313]

It is important, also, to recognize that this poetry is not *describing* what *has* happened but is *evoking* what *will* happen, expressing the inevitable result of Judah's waywardness. Here, 'the poetry is wondrously abrasive in presenting the disjunction between the peaceably ordered kingdom of Yahweh's vineyard and inheritance, and this community now gone berserk in its destructive, rapacious way'.[314] This poetry not only evokes the rebellious chaos of Judah's brokenness but evokes the emotional chaos within YHWH's own heart. Here is a divine speech where compassion, judgment, anger, remorse, grief, and despair all intertwine and interconnect,[315] in much the same

---

[309] Holladay, *Jeremiah 1*, p. 385.

[310] In Jeremiah 12.5-6, YHWH is 'momentarily described as aloof from Jeremiah ... uncaring about [Jeremiah's] fate'. If the passage ended there, 'Jeremiah could almost be perceived as morally superior to God'. However, 'the account does not end with Jeremiah's lament; it is answered by a lament from God. The divine lament portrays God as also suffering because of evil.' Craigie, Kelley, and Drinkard, Jr., *Jeremiah 1-25*, p. 185.

[311] Bracke, *Jeremiah 1-29*, p. 115. 'Yahweh's voice in the preceding poem (12.5-6) was harsh and uncompromising. That same voice now announces the devastation of the land of Judah.' Here, however, the words 'are exhausted grief by this One who so treasures the land and now finds it so abused that it must be abandoned'. Brueggemann, *Commentary on Jeremiah*, pp. 120-21.

[312] Allen, *Jeremiah*, p. 152.

[313] Brueggemann, *Commentary on Jeremiah*, p. 122.

[314] Brueggemann, *Commentary on Jeremiah*, p. 121.

[315] For Miller, the 'point of the text is, perhaps, best conveyed by v. 7b: "I have given the beloved of my heart into the hands of her enemies." The pathos of the whole section is caught up in that one sentence.' Miller, *NIB*, VI, p. 679.

way that numerous deep emotions intertwined in the opening of *Jeremiah's* prayer in 12.1.

YHWH's opening statements could not be more powerful: 'I have forsaken my house. I have abandoned my heritage. I have given the beloved of my soul into the hand of her enemies.' The emotive rhetoric here is so thick, it is almost impossible to parse. The opening use of the verb 'forsake' (עָזַב) is potent because of its use elsewhere in Jeremiah to describe Judah's action toward YHWH.[316]

Some have tried to differentiate the meanings of 'house' (בַּיִת), 'heritage' (נַחֲלָה), and 'beloved' (יְדִדוּת) as references to three specific things;[317] however, when the *affective* aspects of the terms are examined, such parsing becomes unnecessary and perhaps even a bit unhelpful.[318] These terms should be viewed as revealing multiple aspects of one reality, the relationship of Judah to YHWH; this is proven by the repeated use of the personal possessive pronoun 'my'.[319]

The opening imagery of YHWH abandoning YHWH's 'house' will certainly put the attentive hearer in mind of Jeremiah's Temple Sermon (Jer. 7.1-15), which is structured around the repeated phrase: בַּבַּיִת הַזֶּה אֲשֶׁר נִקְרָא־שְׁמִי ('the house which is called by my name').[320] There are three important points to be made. First of all, this description of the Temple effectively proclaims it to be YHWH's personal property.[321] Secondly, the rhetoric of the Temple Sermon is

---

[316] Jeremiah 1.16; 2.13, 17, 19; 5.7, 19; 9.12; 16.11 (2x); 17.13 (2x); 19.4; 22.9; 25.38. Brueggemann, *Commentary on Jeremiah*, p. 121.

[317] Especially Lundbom, citing Jer. 7.10-11, 14; 11.15; 23.11. 'House' is a reference to the temple; 'heritage' is a reference to the land; 'beloved' is a reference to the people; and the 'totality is achieved by accumulation, not by the first two terms having double or triple meaning'. Lundbom, *Jeremiah 1-20*, p. 654.

[318] Though Lundbom finds it essential to differentiate the meanings of 'house', 'heritage', and 'beloved', he does not give the same attention to determining the differences between 'abandoning' (עָזַב), 'forsaking' (נָטַשׁ), and 'giving (over)' (נָתַן), which would seem to be a logical and necessary exegetical move. Could not YHWH just as easily have 'forsaken' YHWH's house, 'given over' YHWH's heritage, and 'abandoned' YHWH's beloved to her enemies?

[319] YHWH is not simply speaking of 'house' and 'heritage' and 'beloved'; YHWH is speaking of '*my* house' and '*my* heritage' and '*my* beloved'. See above on structure.

[320] Cf. Jer. 7.10, 11, 14.

[321] See Bright, *Jeremiah*, p. 56. Moshe Weinfeld, noting the oft-recurrence of the phrase in Deuteronomy (Deut. 12.11; 14.23; 16.2, 6, 11; cf. also 1 Kgs. 9.3; 11.36; 14.21; 2 Kgs. 21.4,7), argues that this phrase is used to emphasize that the Temple is not *YHWH's* house but the house for YHWH's *name*. While Deuteronomy

structured around the term מָקוֹם ('place'), which is sometimes used as an explicit reference to YHWH's sanctuary (Jer. 7.7, 12), sometimes as an explicit reference to the land of Judah (Jer. 7.6, 14),[322] and sometimes as a reference to *both* (Jer. 7.1). Third, Judah's behavior in this 'place' (i.e., Temple *and* land) will lead to destruction (of the Temple) and exile (from the land) because YHWH will be forced to abandon both. In fact, the larger point of the Temple Sermon is to emphasize the interconnection of cultic observance and covenant obedience as necessary to maintaining YHWH's presence in the Temple and the people's presence in the land.

The term נַחֲלָה ('heritage') presents us with different imagery; if בַּיִת emphasizes that Israel is the place where YHWH 'lives', then נַחֲלָה emphasizes the way in which Israel 'belongs' to YHWH. A נַחֲלָה is that which is inherited; it therefore is the permanent belonging of the inheritor.[323] One's נַחֲלָה then, in OT law, is inalienable and enduring, though it does also include the idea of a specific allotment of something larger. Therefore, one receives a נַחֲלָה by virtue of membership within a specific group (e.g. family, clan, or nation), and it will remain a permanent possession for as long as the claims of the group on the *entire* נַחֲלָה remain valid.[324]

The term נַחֲלָה is used metaphorically, as here, to express Israel's relationship with YHWH. There is a kind of 'triangularity'[325] to the relationship of the land, the nation of Israel, and YHWH. Most

---

establishes the necessity of a centralized sanctuary, it simultaneously 'divests it of all sacral content and import'. Moshe Weinfeld, *Deuteronomy and the Deuteronomistic School* (Oxford: Clarendon Press, 1972), pp. 193, 197.

However, the function of the שֵׁם יהוה throughout the rest of Scripture challenges Weinfeld's distinction. The 'name of YHWH' is 'metonymical for the nature of the Lord … the name … does what the Lord does'; that is, 'the name of the Lord stands for God's essential nature revealed to people as an active force in their lives'. Allen P. Ross, 'שֵׁם', *NIDOTTE*, IV, pp. 147-51. Per Van der Woude, שֵׁם יהוה, like the expression פְּנֵי יהוה, 'means "Yahweh in person" or "Yahweh in … glory"'. A.S. Van der Woude, 'שֵׁם', *TLOT*, III, pp. 1348-1367.

[322] Unless, of course, we assume that in Jer. 7.6, YHWH is only banning murders within the Temple precincts. Lundbom, *Jeremiah 1-20*, p. 461.

[323] Leonard J. Coppes, 'נָחַל', *TWOT*, II, pp. 569-70.

[324] G. Wanke, 'נַחֲלָה', *TLOT*, II, pp. 731-34. Thus, any family or clan's claim to their inheritance within Israel is valid for as long as the nation itself remains within the stipulations of the grant; however, once the nation has violated those stipulations, *all* subordinate claims to a נַחֲלָה are immediately voided.

[325] 'The term נַחֲלָה the land as Israel's inheritance, the land as YHWH's inheritance, Israel as Yahweh's inheritance, and even Yahweh as Israel's … inheritance.' Christopher J.H. Wright, 'נחל', in *NIDOTTE*, III, pp. 77-81.

prominently in the OT, the *people of Israel* are YHWH's נַחֲלָה.[326] This carries the sense of Israel as YHWH's 'permanent possession', rather than Israel as something 'inherited by' YHWH.[327] This theme shows up in (again) Psalm 94.5 and 14; both times there is an explicit parallelism of נַחֲלָה with עַם:

> ⁵Your people (עַמְּךָ), O YHWH, they crush,
>> And your inheritance (נַחֲלָתְךָ) they humble ...
> ¹⁴YHWH will never forsake his people (עַמּוֹ);
>> His own inheritance (נַחֲלָתוֹ), he will never leave.

In fact, it is YHWH's possession of YHWH's own people – and *not* just YHWH's status as 'Creator of All' – that is a key distinction between YHWH and the 'false gods'.[328]

However, the claim here is that the people and the land *together* are YHWH's נַחֲלָה! As Creator, the *entire earth* is YHWH's נַחֲלָה (Ps. 47.4), and YHWH apportions it to the nations as YHWH sees fit.[329] YHWH's ownership and apportioning of the earth to the nations is precisely what obligates all nations to render service to the One True King.[330] While the logic of this understanding is clear, what is surprising is the scarcity of references to the *land* as YHWH's נַחֲלָה; it is a concept that occurs most often in the book of Jeremiah.[331] In particular, the land as YHWH's נַחֲלָה conveys YHWH's fond attentiveness to it,[332] as well as heightening the pain YHWH feels when YHWH's

---

[326] 'God's special created, chosen heritage is the people of Israel (Deut. 4.20; Ex. 34.9).' Coppes, *TWOT*, II, p. 569. 'According to OT tradition, Yahweh chose the people of Israel to make them his נַחֲלָה (1 Kgs. 8.53; Ps. 33.12), as Moses requested (Exod. 34.9)'; cf. Isa. 63.17; Jer. 10.16; 51.19; Ps. 74.2. E. Lipiński, 'נָחַל, נַחֲלָה', *TDOT*, IX, pp. 319-35.

[327] Lipiński, *TDOT*, IX, p. 331. As Wright wryly notes: 'From whom could YHWH have "inherited" the land of Canaan [or people of Israel]?' Wright, *NIDOTTE*, III, p. 79.

[328] Wright, *NIDOTTE*, III, p. 79.

[329] Since Israel is in a unique covenant relationship with YHWH, they are allotted the 'most prime real estate' of YHWH's נַחֲלָה, a land described as 'flowing with milk and honey' (cf. Deut. 31.20). Coppes, *TWOT*, II, p. 569.

[330] Coppes, *TWOT*, II, p. 569.

[331] 'In contrast to the richly attested concept that Yahweh is the grantor and guarantor of the נַחֲלָה of Israel and its tribes, the statement that Palestine is Yahweh's נַחֲלָה is remarkably rare.' G. Wanke, 'נַחֲלָה', *TLOT*, II, pp. 731-34. See Jer. 2.7; 12.7-9; 10.16=51.19; 16.18; 50.11; cf. 1 Sam. 26.19; 2 Sam. 14.16; Ps. 68.10 [9].

[332] The land of Israel is, to use modern imagery, YHWH's 'garden'.

land must be destroyed. The present passage is 'gives most poignant expression to this feeling'.[333]

And yet, Israel is not simply where YHWH *lives*, nor even just YHWH's prized possession; even more, Israel is the one whom YHWH *loves*. The phrase יְדִדוּת נַפְשִׁי ('beloved of *my* soul') is only found here in the *entire* OT.[334] This form, as well as the more common form יָדִיד, are used in reference to the person being loved, rather than the lover.[335]

The term is applied to Israel first in Deut. 33.12 but also in several psalms.[336] What is interesting about this term is its *lack* of covenant connections; when love is spoken of in covenantal terms, the verb אָהֵב is used.[337] The language of יָדִיד then applies the imagery of a 'beloved girl' to Israel.[338] To clarify, Zobel notes that the feminine name 'Jedidah' (2 Kgs. 22.1) comes from this same root and literally means 'darling' or 'favorite'.[339]

However, even the term 'darling' does not seem to come all that close to the emotive power of this phrase. Israel is not simply YHWH's יְדִדוּת, she is YHWH's יְדִדוּת נַפְשִׁי, the beloved '*of my soul*'. Quite literally, YHWH here calls Israel the 'love of my life'; YHWH's love for Israel comes from the very core of who YHWH is.[340] The irony here is that the term 'beloved' (in its more common form יְדִיד) occurs in the previous chapter Jer. 11.15; both here and there, the term 'beloved' appears in the context of an *accusation* made against Judah and a pronouncement of judgment![341]

---

[333] Cf. Jer. 50.11: 'From Yahweh's standpoint, the necessity of judgment was so painful precisely because of the precious relationship between himself and Israel as his inheritance'. Wright, *NIDOTTE*, III, p. 79.

[334] H.-J. Zobel, 'יָדִיד', *TDOT*, IV, pp. 444-48.

[335] The term דוֹד is used for 'lover', usually in an erotic sense absent from the primary meaning of יָדִיד and יְדִדוּת. P.J.J. Els, 'יָדִיד', *NIDOTTE*, II, pp. 408-409.

[336] Pss. 60.7 [5]; 108.7 [6]; 127.2.

[337] Els, *NIDOTTE*, II, p. 409.

[338] Els, *NIDOTTE*, II, p. 409.

[339] For Zobel, this is proof the term יָדִיד 'belonged by nature to the secular sphere, and expressed a relationship ... based on positive feelings of attraction'. Zobel, *TDOT*, IV, p. 445. This is 'lovers' language'; see Song. 1.7; 3.1, 2, 3, 4, which uses the similar phrase שֶׁאָהֲבָה נַפְשִׁי. Holladay, *Jeremiah 1*, p. 386.

[340] Zobel's claim that the Jeremianic term 'expresses Yahweh's favor toward his people ... and also the uniqueness of Israel' is something of a tragic understatement. Zobel, *TDOT*, IV, p. 447.

[341] Zobel, *TDOT*, IV, p. 447.

These usages, occurring so close together, create a moment of astounding emotive dissonance. First, the listener feels the heart-rending grief of YHWH. YHWH must judge, punish, destroy the one YHWH loves with every fiber of YHWH's being. YHWH must abandon, forsake, and hand her over to be ravaged by her enemies. The pathos of YHWH's opening words overmatches even the pathos of the opening of Jeremiah's prayer in 12.1. The listener feels the seething grief and rage of the betrayed lover. The shock of Israel's betrayal and lies is as great as the shock of the pronouncement of swift and total judgment.

YHWH then adds, almost as an aside: 'She has become to me like a lion in the forest. She has set her voice against me for which reason I hate her'. The imagery of the 'lion in the forest' is powerful because of its reversal of a common prophetic trope. Amos used the image of *YHWH* as a lion to depict swift judgment on the nations;[342] Jeremiah also uses similar imagery, especially in the central hinge of the book, ch. 25.[343] Here in Jer. 12, *Judah* is the lion who is *attacking* … not other nations, not the poor and oppressed, but attacking *YHWH*. The imagery expresses both her rebellion and her contempt.[344] 'Israel has taken on the prerogatives of Yahweh against Yahweh.'[345]

This 'reversal' in the YHWH-Israel relationship has turned 'love' into 'hate'. The statement is so abrupt that it stuns the heart and mind. YHWH had 'piled up' the affectionate descriptions of Israel in the first part – 'my house … my heritage … my beloved' – but, here, a single mention of YHWH's hatred is enough to reverse the rhetoric.

The use of the term 'hate' here does recall the use of divorce terminology in Jer. 3.1, 8.[346] Clearly, then, within Jeremiah, the term is used to designate the point of rupture in a relationship; once 'hate'

---

[342] Amos 1.2; 3.8.

[343] Jeremiah 25.30, 38; cf. Jer. 2.15; 4.7; 5.6, where the image refers to the human invaders.

[344] Lundbom, *Jeremiah 1-20*, p. 654. Lion imagery is 'often used in the OT to describe the ascendency of Judah (e.g. Gen. 49.8-10) … here the analogy is not flattering'. In fact, 'given the plot against Jeremiah described in the preceding verse, the roar could very well be the roar of the lion as it leaps on its prey'. Craigie, Kelley, and Drinkard, Jr., *Jeremiah 1-25*, p. 184. That is, the plot against the innocent lamb Jeremiah was a lion-like attack on YHWH because it was an attack on YHWH's spokesman.

[345] Holladay, *Jeremiah 1*, p. 387.

[346] Deuteronomy 24.3. Brown, *Expositor's Bible Commentary*, VII, p. 215.

has set in, the relationship has ended.[347] Though Lundbom wishes to equivocate, the OT term for 'hatred' used here (שָׂנֵא) includes an 'emotional attitude' of detestation and despising;[348] it is the determination of 'having nothing to do with' the object of one's hatred.[349] In precisely that way, hate is the opposite of love.[350]

Jenni notes that quite commonly in the OT, the term 'hater'[351] usually parallels אֹיֵב 'enemy',[352] which gives a good sense of the dimensions of 'hatred' in the OT. In fact, the nearest verbal parallel is תעב pi'el, 'to abhor', a term related to תּוֹעֵבָה ('abomination').[353] In the OT, hatred is manifested by distance. YHWH's 'hatred' of Israel in Jer. 12.8 is what had caused YHWH to 'abandon' (i.e. to get as far away from Israel as possible) in 12.7.[354]

After this barrage of emotional statements, YHWH returns to the rhetorical question format: 'Is my heritage a hyena's den? Are birds of prey circling around her?' The initial line, because of the oddity of the opening phrase, הַעַיִט צָבוּעַ, has generated wildly different translations. Reading הַעַיִט צָבוּעַ as a single phrase, Lundbom and Carroll render: 'Is my heritage to Me a speckled[355] bird of prey?'

---

[347] When the term is used of the relationship of a man and a woman, it signifies 'to love no longer, to develop dislike for'. E. Jenni, 'שָׂנֵא', *TLOT*, III, pp. 1277-79. See also Deut. 22.13, 16; Judg. 14.16; 15.2; 2 Sam. 13.15.

'One view holds that שׂנא originally referred to the mutual disappearance of feeling between spouses and to the cessation of sexual relations.' This understands the term as a 'stative verb designating an emotional condition'. E. Lipiński, 'שָׂנֵא', *TDOT*, XIV, pp. 164-74.

[348] Lundbom, however, notes here: 'Love and hate in the OT do not have the same bipolarity as in modern language (e.g. Mal. 1.2-3) or as in the language of the NT (Matt. 5.43-44)'. Lundbom, *Jeremiah 1-20*, p. 654.

[349] Gerard Van Groningen, 'שָׂנֵא', *TWOT*, II, pp. 879-80.

[350] Whereas love brings people together; hate drives people apart. Van Groningen, *TWOT*, II, p. 879.

[351] The substantive qal שׂונא and the piel participle משׂנא.

[352] Jenni, *TLOT*, III, p. 1279.

[353] For 'abhor', see Amos 5.10; Ps. 119.163; for 'abomination', see Deut. 12.31; Jer. 44.4; Prov. 6.16. Jenni, *TLOT*, III, p. 1278. Konkel says it is 'synonymous' with piel תָּעַב. Augustus H. Konkel, 'שׂנא', *NIDOTTE*, III, pp. 1257-60.

[354] In Amos 6.8, YHWH 'hates' the strongholds of Israel, which means that YHWH 'delivers up [the] cities to their enemies'. Lipiński, *TDOT*, XIV, p. 167.

[355] The description of Judah as a 'speckled' bird is 'referring not to beautiful plumage but to some sort of blemish'. Though the 'colored' plumage is often connected with Joseph's 'colored' coat (Gen. 37), Lundbom dismisses the association as only speculation. Rather, he chooses to connect the bird's 'speckled feathers' to the leopard's 'spots' in Jer. 13.23 which also are a negative attribute. Lundbom, *Jeremiah 1-20*, pp. 655-56.

Lundbom also feels Calvin is right that the 'speckling' of the plumage does not indicate a particularly *beautiful* bird[356] but rather the bird's 'strangeness' or 'wildness' that renders it unable to be domesticated.[357] Holladay, who seems to do the most textual emendation of any of the major commentators, reads: 'Does the hyena *look greedily* upon my possession?' Holladay replaces MT's הָעַיִט ('birds of prey') in the first line with הֲעֵיט[358] arguing that הָעַיִט was evidently miscopied into the first line.[359] Allen offers even a third alternative, closest to the rendering above: 'Did my home treat me as a denful of hyenas would?' He reads נַחֲלָה as a reference to 'social unit', yielding the translation 'den'.[360]

I would argue that the focus of the imagery here is not so much on the animal (e.g. bird of prey or hyena) but on the animal's *lair* (e.g. the hyena's *den* or the bird's *nest*) because the larger focus of the passage (since Jer. 12.4) has been the state of the *land*.[361] Hyenas are scavengers, known for feeding on dead corpses; their dens are filled with bones, filth, and rottenness.[362] Such an image also ties in nicely with the 'circling birds of prey'[363] in the following line to depict a land filled with death and waiting to die.

Before the stench conjured by the imagination has filled the nostrils, the listener hears YHWH's invitation: 'Let the wild beasts assemble! Bring them to consume her!' Most commentators get mired down identifying the 'vultures' and 'beasts' with particular historical players in the drama of Jerusalem's downfall.[364] McKane is right that too much focus on the *species* of animals named here has drawn many

---

[356] E.g. This is a bird 'with colors [that] excites all other birds against it'. Lundbom, *Jeremiah 1*-20, pp. 656.

[357] 'The bird representing Judah is acting aggressively toward Yahweh, just as the lion'. Verse 9 is then 'a simple shift in metaphor'. Lunbom, *Jeremiah 1*-20, p. 655.

[358] *BDB*, s.v. 'עיט', i.e. 'to dart greedily upon'.

[359] Holladay, *Jeremiah 1*, p. 383.

[360] Allen, *Jeremiah*, p. 152.

[361] As noted above, this is one of the rare instances where YHWH clearly speaks of the *land* of Israel as YHWH's נַחֲלָה.

[362] McKane, *Jeremiah*, p. 269.

[363] McKane follows T and sees a reference 'to the swift-moving armies which are encircling Judah'. He also notes there is a logic to the imagery. Judah 'has the disgusting habits of a hyena, and its cave, littered with partially devoured corpses, will attract vultures. The vultures … are the destructive agents, figures of the invaders who will execute Yahweh's judgment on Judah.' McKane, *Jeremiah*, pp. 270, 272.

[364] For example, Lundbom, following Kimchi, supposes the 'beasts' here 'are nations accompanying Nebuchadnezzar are his way to destroy Jerusalem [cf. Jer. 5.17]'. Lundbom, *Jeremiah 1*-20, p. 656.

away from the central point of the image: they are all *wild* beasts. This is the connection point with Judah's egregious behavior toward YHWH in v. 8. 'Snarling at Yahweh like a lion, [YHWH says]: You acted against me like a wild creature. Very well! You will be set upon by birds of prey and wild beasts.'[365] The second forgotten point is that they are all called to 'consume' (אָכְלָה).[366] Part of what we should note is the ordinariness of the term. אָכַל means 'to eat'; אֹכֶל means 'food'. As if YHWH stands at the door of the Temple and yells, 'Come eat! Dinner is ready!' The homeliness of the image increases its horror. The imagery is likewise filled with irony; Jeremiah's complaint in 12.4 indicated that the land is suffering a drought that has driven away all 'beasts and birds'. Without a doubt, many of the poorer Israelites are facing soon and certain starvation if the crisis-level conditions persist. And while the people of Israel cannot find any food to feed themselves, YHWH is preparing to make them a meal for the nations!

Verse 10 closely parallels the form of v. 7. The first half of the verse offers a 'double description' of Judah; the last half describes YHWH's 'surrender' of Judah to her enemies.[367] This creates an interesting frame around vv. 8-9, which were much more focused on the *sins* of Judah than on YHWH's *sufferings*, the focus of vv. 7 and 10. It is important to note how YHWH's suffering and mourning poetically surrounds these descriptions of Judah's sin and destruction. The focal point of YHWH's mourning is now the decimated state of the land; v. 7 mourned the 'trampled' relationship ... now v. 10 will grieve the 'trampled' land. In vv. 7-8, YHWH's 'love of my life' became 'the one that I hate'; here, YHWH's 'land that I cherish' will become 'land that is desolate'.[368] Clearly in agony, YHWH cries out: 'Many shepherds have destroyed my vineyard. They have trampled my portion; they have given over my pleasant portion to be a desolate wilderness'.

There is a doubled metaphorical shift: from wild beasts to shepherds as the agent of destruction and from YHWH's 'inheritance' to YHWH's 'field' as the object of destruction. This is signaled especially by the reoccurrence of the same verb[369] used in YHWH's statement in Jer. 12.7: 'I have *given* the beloved of my soul into the hand of her enemies'; here, is it the *shepherds* who 'have given' Judah over to destruction. One important point is the deliberate choice of the

---

[365] McKane, *Jeremiah*, p. 270.

[366] Literally 'the meal'; see translation.

[367] Craigie, Kelley, and Drinkard, Jr., *Jeremiah 1-25*, p. 184.

[368] Allen, *Jeremiah*, p. 153.

[369] Qal perfect נָתַן.

term shepherd, which is used in Jeremiah both as a reference to the kings of the enemy[370] or (more frequently) is a reference to *Judah's* kings who bear the brunt of responsibility for Judah's sure destruction.[371]

The most natural initial hearing would indicate that YHWH is speaking of foreign invaders.[372] However, the undertone of condemnation on the negligent 'shepherds' of Israel and Judah brings the listener to a moment of shocking (though delayed) revelation. the 'trampling' of Israel – even the 'devouring' of Israel – began long before foreign invaders threatened national sovereignty. Before foreign kings were oppressing the people and destroying the land, the arrogant kings of Judah were! Once again, we are subtly reminded that the horrific judgment that is coming is simply the reaping of the terrifying seed that has already been sown.

Again, the emphasis returns to the fact that this trampled land belongs to YHWH, who calls it 'my portion' (חֶלְקָה). The basic meaning of the term is simply 'field'.[373] As was noted in the translation, some commentators were troubled by the terminological shift and substituted the earlier נַחֲלָה for חֶלְקָה here. However, the root חָלַק, especially its nominative form חֵלֶק, shares many of the same theological connections as the term נַחֲלָה.[374] Though it is capable of a very generic construction,[375] in its most specialized use, it is the term used to describe the apportionment of the land in the book of Joshua.[376] The portion of land then, represented the individual Israel's connection to the covenant promise of YHWH and was not only their possession (Mic. 2.4) but signified their participation in the righteousness of God (Neh. 2.20).[377]

---

[370] Jeremiah 6.3; 25.34-36.
[371] Jeremiah 2.8; 10.21; cf. 23.1-2. Lundbom, *Jeremiah 1-20*, p. 656.
[372] Taking the shepherds as the enemy is, for Lundbom, the more precise meaning because it 'extends the imagery of punitive birds and wild beasts, both of which symbolize the enemy'. Lundbom, *Jeremiah 1-20*, p. 656.
[373] In the general sense of a 'piece of land (Hos. 5.7)'. Cornelis Van Dam, 'חלק', *NIDOTTE*, IV, pp. 161-63.
[374] Coppes mentions חֵלֶק as a 'near synonym'. Coppes, *TWOT*, II, p. 569.
[375] E.g. 'The portion coming to one by law and custom'. M. Tsevat, 'חָלַק II, חֵלֶק, מַחֲלֹקֶת, חֶלְקָה, חֲלֻקָּה', *TDOT*, IV, pp. 447-51.
[376] 'Since Yahweh is the original owner (and testator) of Palestine (e.g. Deut. 12.10), whoever receives a portion of the land ... has a portion in Yahweh's own property (inheritance) and whoever renounces his portion of the land has no portion in Yahweh (Josh. 22.25, 27; cf. 1 Sam. 26.19)'. Tsevat, *TDOT*, IV, pp. 449.
[377] Donald J. Wiseman, 'חָלַק', *TWOT*, I, pp. 292-93.
Though referring to a later usage of the term חֵלֶק, Fox's work on the meaning of חֵלֶק in Qohelet is helpful here. Qohelet 'does not use it to contrast a part

In *all* its usages, the main feature of the term is the sense of own-ership; a 'portion' always *belongs* to someone,[378] and someone 'be-longs' to that portion. Tsevat has noted that both the giver and the receiver have an equal, shared interest in the חֵלֶק.[379] Thus, each Isra-elite's 'portion' connected them to their family, clan, tribal, national, and theological identities. That 'portion' defines, as Schmid says, 'the place of the person in the world'.[380]

Clearly, the language of 'portion' was every bit as theologically freighted as the language of 'heritage/inheritance' in ancient Israel; but we must remember that here in Jer. 12.10, the imagery has been flipped. We are not speaking of the land as *Israel's* 'portion', but as *YHWH's*. And if loss of one's 'portion' left one without a 'place in the world', as Schmid suggested, is it possible that the text is coaxing us to imagine a homeless YHWH? Here, it is *not* YHWH who has turned the 'pleasant portion' into a 'desolate wilderness'; *the shepherds* have done that. YHWH is more victim/collateral damage than causal agent. *They* have destroyed YHWH's beautiful field; *they* have forced YHWH out of YHWH's own land![381]

The tones of mourning dominate YHWH's words in v. 11: 'They have turned her [into] a desolation! Desolate, it mourns to me. The whole land is laid desolate.' There is an extraordinary assonance in the original Hebrew, impossible to capture in English. Within the space of four lines, variations of the word שָׁמֵם ('to desolate') are re-peated four times. Furthermore, in the first three lines of v. 11, the word is found in nominal, adjectival, and verbal[382] forms; taken to-gether, those three forms could almost yield their own sentence: 'The desolate desolation lies desolate'. Meyer notes that such a

---

with the whole'; some have suggested that Qohelet sees a *contrast* between חֵלֶק ('por-tion') and יִתְרוֹן ('profit') along 'an axis of duration'. חֵלֶק is taken to mean 'temporary gain', while יִתְרוֹן indicates 'permanent gain'. Thus, for Qohelet, a חֵלֶק is only a 'piece … of the pie'.

Fox finds this distinction unhelpful for 'all possession is temporary, since it must end when life does … there is no point in complaining that there is no en-during profit in life when [humanity] does not endure'. Michael V. Fox, *A Time to Tear Down and A Time to Build Up: Rereading Ecclesiastes* (Grand Rapids: Eerdmans, 1999), p. 109.

[378] Fox, *A Time to Tear Down and A Time to Build Up*, p. 111.

[379] It is the portion 'that maintains the individual or small group [to whom it was given], and society is based upon the totality of all portions'. Tsevat, *TDOT*, IV, p. 448.

[380] H.H. Schmid, 'חלק', *TLOT*, I, p. 431-33.

[381] 'These verses … present an anguished God who is forced to abandon a precious heritage because Judah has turned against the Lord.' Bracke, *Jeremiah 1-29*, 116.

[382] Niphil stem.

concentration of variated usages of the same term makes for power-ful rhetoric but hampers precision in translation.[383] It is almost as if YHWH were sputtering or stuttering with grief.

Meyer asserts: 'There is no equivalent to שׁמם in any modern lan-guage'. The closest approximation in English is the word 'desolation' because it can imply inner feelings as well as outer geographical con-ditions.[384] The verbal form ('to desolate/be desolated') occurs most frequently,[385] usually with the sense of suffering destruction or, more precisely, the *aftermath* of destruction. It is used often to describe YHWH's judgment on Israel and its after-effects.[386]

The important feature of the verb is its differing objective and subjective aspects. Objectively (e.g. in describing a geographical re-gion), the term means 'to be lifeless'; however, the term subjectively refers to the psychological *reaction* to scenes of desolation, carrying the basic meaning of 'to be terrified/astonished'.[387] The term works to correlate perception and reaction.[388]

Within the book of Jeremiah, nearly all occurrences, as here, refer to the objective sense of the term, functioning more to describe scenes of desolation, though the visceral reaction of horror at such scenes is never far behind.[389] The one astounding exception to this

---

[383] I. Meyer, 'שָׁמַם, שָׁמֵם, שְׁמָמָה, שִׁמָּמוֹן, שַׁמָּה, מְשַׁמָּה, שִׁמְמָה, יְשִׁימוֹן, יְשִׁמֹן/יְשִׁימֹן, יְשִׁמוֹת', *TDOT,* XV, pp. 238-48.

[384] Meyer, *TDOT,* XV, p. 239.

[385] Around 55x. Tyler F. Williams, 'שׁמם', *NIDOTTE,* IV, pp. 167-71.

[386] See Ezek. 6.4; 25.3; 33.28; 35.12, 15; Amos 7.9; Mic. 6.13.

[387] F. Stolz, 'שׁמם', *TLOT,* III, pp. 1372-75. The basic distinction between שַׁמָּה and שְׁמָמָה 'seems to lie in the fact that שַׁמָּה in most passages stresses the horror caused by the desolation of judgment ... in שְׁמָמָה the stress is usually upon the desolation itself'. Hermann J. Austel, 'שָׁמֵם', *TWOT,* II, pp. 936-37.

'The verb ... occurs ca. 28x denoting the sense of revulsion or astonish-ment when confronted with the results of divine judgment and/or desolation'. Williams, *NIDOTTE,* IV, p. 170. Cf. Lev. 26.32; Job 17.8; Isa. 52.14; Ezek. 26.16; 27.35; 28.19; 32.10; Dan. 8.27.

[388] Austel, *TWOT,* II, p. 937.

[389] In Jeremiah, the synonymous term is used to describe the land of Israel (Jer. 2.15; 4.7; 18.16; 25.9,11); Judah and Jerusalem (Jer. 44.22), Jerusalem and its inhab-itants (Jer. 19.8; cf. 25.18); those left in Jerusalem after the 598 deportation (Jer. 29.18), those who fled to Egypt after Gedaliah's assassination (Jer. 42.18; 44.12); Noph/Memphis (Jer. 46.19); towns of Moab (Jer. 48.19); Bozrah (Jer. 49.13); Edom (Jer. 49.17); Babylon (50.23; 51.37, 41; cf. 50.3, 51.29, and 51.43); and, finally, the entire earth (Jer. 25.38).

is Jer. 8.21: 'Because of the breaking of the daughter of my people, I have been broken; I mourn,[390] seized by *desolation* (שַׁמָּה)'.[391] The prophet describes himself as a 'desolation' because of his grief over the plight of his people!

Though clearly dominating the verse, this extraordinarily powerful emotive term is not alone. Perhaps the most powerful link of all is the reappearance of the verb אָבַל ('mourn') from v. 4. There, Jeremiah's judgment had implied that YHWH was somehow deafened to the outcry of the land; however, here we learn that is not the case. The case is far, far worse: the land is 'mourning'[392] because YHWH has been forced to abandon it; the sin of Judah has forced YHWH to act in judgment.[393] Another powerful emotive affect is achieved by the use of the preposition עלי, which could mean either 'unto me' or 'before me'. The ambiguity here allows the land to be personified as *mourning to YHWH* and YHWH to be described as *mourning the land.*

Finally, the last line gives us the reason the land is such a sorry state: 'For no one turns their heart'. Employing the verb שׂים from the opening line of the verse to form an inclusio, the accusation is as obvious at it is painful: the land is ruined and no one really cares.[394] Only YHWH truly took the care of the land 'to heart' but has since been forced out, and no one has taken up YHWH's cause of caring for the land.[395] Here, *both* the neglected land, lying in desolation, *and* YHWH, gazing upon it, mourn together the land's uncared-for state.[396]

At this point, what is probably most prominent to the careful listener is the way that in which YHWH has gone from active to passive. Verse 7 is filled with divine actions: 'I have forsaken ... I have abandoned ... I have given'; vv. 10-11, in contrast, are filled with divine observations: 'They have trampled ... They have given over ... They have turned her into ...' In the opening, YHWH is clearly grieving

---

[390] קָדַר literally means 'to be darkened' and is 'used in contexts of judgment where the heavens and heavenly bodies are to be blackened (Jer. 4.28; cf. Joel 2.10)'. Leonard J. Coppes, 'קָדַר', *TWOT*, II, p. 786.

[391] The nominal form שַׁמָּה, though not used in Jer. 12.10-11, is 'largely synonymous with שְׁמָמָה', and is 'also used in similar constructions'. Most importantly, 'All its occurrences are in the context of judgment ... [and] of the word's 39 occurrences, 24 are in Jeremiah'. Meyer, *TDOT*, XV, p. 245.

[392] 'The meaning could be either that the land is personified as a mourner ("It laments before me in its desolate state") or that its desolation has a mournful effect on Yahweh ("Its desolation makes me mournful").' McKane, *Jeremiah*, p. 274.

[393] Bracke, *Jeremiah 1-29*, p. 116.

[394] Lundbom, *Jeremiah 1-20*, p. 657.

[395] 'Whereas once Yahweh had cared for the land (cf. Deut. 11.12), there would be nobody to care for the land anymore.' Allen, *Jeremiah*, p. 153.

[396] As a witness to the land's desolation (שׁמם), it is *YHWH* who is astonished!

but is still at work; at the conclusion, YHWH sounds, to be quite honest, exhausted by grief and a little helpless. It is not just the land that has been trampled; the people have also run rough-shod over YHWH to the point where YHWH cannot or will not intervene to save.

I suppose the only way to describe the listener's response to this movement in the divine *pathos* is consternation. And yet, by this point in our journey the listener should be prepared for emotive movements that surprise and defy expectations. If the listener is shocked at such divine passivity on the part of YHWH here in vv. 10-11, recall YHWH's reply to Jeremiah in vv. 5-6, which also seems to express a kind of divine apathy. No typical divine assurance there! Furthermore, we have already been shocked *several* times by the prophet's words (e.g. 11.19; 12.1-3).

5.3.6 YHWH's Reply, Part III (12.12-13)

The final part of YHWH's reply casts itself as a formal judgment speech, where YHWH is spoken *of* rather the one officially speaking; of course, there is no apparent change in speaker, so we must assume that YHWH is here giving YHWH's own formal pronouncement: 'Upon all the bare heights of the desert, spoilers have come. Indeed, a sword of YHWH consumes from one end of the land to the other – no peace for all flesh!'

Once again, the conclusion picks up key rhetoric from the prior section: 'desert' (מִדְבָּר) echoes the closing line of v. 10, evoking the desolated land; 'consumes' (אָכְלָה) echoes the close of v. 9, evoking the devouring enemies.[397] The prior unit had envisioned YHWH's withdrawal, a stepping-aside to allow consequences their full sway in the life of Judah; in this unit YHWH is again active.[398] Abandonment (v. 7) has suddenly become attack.

The 'bare heights of the desert' seems to depict militarily-advantageous ground, either high points from which best routes of attack could be plotted and/or broad flat spaces that afforded opportunities for swift movement and surprise attack.[399] Yet, the threat here is not invading armies with a keen grasp of desert warfare tactics. No, the direness of the threat comes from the חֶרֶב לַיהוָה, 'a sword of YHWH'. Earlier, the listener was aghast at the revolting image of every foul and wild beast consuming the rotting corpses in the land-turned-lair

---

[397] Allen, *Jeremiah*, p. 153.

[398] This unit 'speaks of a negative divine presence actively directing the destruction'. Allen, *Jeremiah*, p. 153.

[399] McKane, *Jeremiah*, p. 275; Lundbom, *Jeremiah 1-20*, p. 657.

of Judah (12.9). The listener learns here that the envisioned attack will be executed *by YHWH* ... it will be *YHWH's* sword that consumes. Reading the verses together creates an even more grim image. YHWH has invited all the wild beasts to feast on the remains of Judah; only now, we realize that *YHWH* is the Butcher who prepared the feast! YHWH's vengeance will be complete, covering the entire land[400] and 'all flesh'.

And yet, this utter destruction of grotesque proportions cannot be blamed on YHWH's vindictiveness. This is not the jealous rage of a jilted lover (though YHWH is that), nor is it retaliation against a rebellious people who refuse to be subject to their Sovereign's rule (though Judah is certainly that); rather it is something altogether more simple and horrifyingly tragic: 'They have sown wheat, and thorns they have reaped. They have wearied themselves to no avail'. The chiastic structure of the first line is visible even in English translation, sounding very much like an ancient proverb.[401]

The point, of course, is that Judah is only experiencing the unavoidable consequences of Judah's own rebellious actions. This utter destruction is the automatic result of rebellion against YHWH. Again, the second line intensifies the claim of the first. In all her labor (e.g. the 'sowing' of the first line), Judah has only succeeded in 'wearing herself out'. The root found here (חָלָה) can be used to describe any diminished state from tiredness/weakness[402] to generally ill health[403] to a terminal illness.[404] Furthermore, the term does not simply describe *physical* health; the verb can also be used of emotional suffering.[405] In that sense, חָלָה indicates *any* abnormal state of health; as such, to be in state of חָלָה essentially meant that one was *not* in a state of שָׁלוֹם, the language of good health, or, more accurately, 'wholeness'. However, most important for the term's usage here is the connection to the Jeremianic imagery of the נַחְלָה מַכָּתִי, the

---

[400] 'From one end of the land to the other' is clearly intended 'to describe the over-running of the entire land ... not even the remotest corners will be spared and no one will be immune from the blast of war.' McKane, *Jeremiah*, p. 276.

[401] Lundbom, *Jeremiah 1-20*, p. 658.

[402] Cf. Gen. 48.1.

[403] Cf. 1 Kgs. 14.1, 5.

[404] Cf. 1 Kgs. 15.23; 2 Kgs. 13.14. R.K. Harrison, 'חלה', NIDOTTE, II, pp. 140-43.

[405] Cf. Song 2.5; 5.8; Eccl. 5.12, 15. F. Stolz, 'חלה', TLOT, I, pp. 425-27. More evident in the Niphal stem. Amos speaks of those who are 'at ease in Zion' (Amos 6.1) but 'are not grieved (נֶחְלוּ) ... for the affliction of Joseph' (Amos 6.6).

Also, in Isa. 17.11 the prophet calls for a 'day of being sick (בְּיוֹם נַחְלָה)', usually translated as 'day of grief'. What is intriguing about that passage is the term occurs in another discussion of failed harvests. Carl Philip Weber, 'חָלָה', TWOT, I, pp. 286-87.

'incurable [e.g. infected] wound'.[406] All of Judah's labor (e.g. every-thing from her reliance upon Egypt to her abrogation of YHWH's covenant to her inveterate idolatrous worship) had led her to an un-wholesome state from which she could not recover. Stolz notes there are really only two possible experiences of illness: as a distressing state that leads one to cry to God for aid and mercy[407] or as an effect of divine curse.[408] Clearly, here Judah is feeling the effects of a divine curse.

The last two lines, though perhaps not technically so, at least have the emotive *effect* of a curse: 'Be ashamed of your harvests [of thorns and sickness] because of the burning anger of YHWH'. The idea of *commanding* shame[409] is quite startling, but it is mostly a result of the distance between ancient Eastern and modern Western worldviews; shame in ancient cultures had more to do with *social* position than with *psychological* disposition.[410] To put it another way, in ancient cultures, a person was *in* shame rather than *a*shamed.[411]

Shame entails dislocated relationships, both with the community and with YHWH. Again, as with other relational aspects of Israelite theology, here the one entails the other. Since Judah has rejected YHWH, turned her back on the covenant, she is now destined to be shamed before the whole world by her destruction at the hands of Babylon.

The reason for her shame is clearly not 'simply [no] crops in the field, but the life of an entire nation gone bad'.[412] The ultimate source of this shame is the 'burning anger' (מֵחֲרוֹן אַף) of YHWH.[413] This vivid term is important for two reasons. First of all, it participates in

---

[406] Cf. Jer. 8.20-23; 10.18-25; 14.17-20; 15.18; 30.12-17; 46.11; 51.8-10. See Chapter 3 above.

[407] Cf. Isa. 38.9; 8.37=2 Chron. 6.28; 2 Chron. 16.12.

[408] So here; cf. Deut. 28.59, 61; 29.11; Isa. 1.5; Jer. 10.19; 2 Chron. 21.15, 18-19. Stolz, *TLOT*, I, p. 427.

[409] בּוֹשׁוּ is a qal imperative plural, literally: 'You all be a/shamed'.

[410] 'The force of בּוֹשׁ is somewhat in contrast to the primary meaning of the English "to be ashamed", in that the English stresses the inner attitude, the state of mind, while the Hebrew means "to come to shame" and stresses the sense of public disgrace, a physical state.' John N. Oswalt, 'בּוֹשׁ', *TWOT*, I, pp. 97-98.

[411] 'Shame should be understood as a sanction of behavior within a society', particularly in 'those societies with a strong group orientation, in which the exposure to public opinion serves as a control over indecent forms of behavior.' Philip J. Nel, 'בּוֹשׁ', *NIDOTTE*, I, pp. 621-27. See Lyn M. Bechtel, 'Shame as a Sanction of Social Control in Biblical Israel: Judicial, Political, and Social Shaming', *JSOT* 16.49 (1991), pp. 47-76.

[412] Lundbom, *Jeremiah 1-20*, p. 658.

[413] NIV translates: 'Fierce anger'.

the book's recurrent theme of the anger of YHWH.[414] This is even more noticeable in that the prophetic and poetic books are 'relatively reticent' in their use of the term חרה ('to burn, kindle') of anger.[415] Of course, listeners are not surprised that, in a book about rejected prophets and broken covenants and the incomprehensible refusal to repent, anger surfaces as much as it does.

The second reason that the term is so important is that the word מֵחֲרוֹן picks up the verb תִּתְחֲרֶה[416] in YHWH's first rhetorical question to Jeremiah in v. 5. The verbal link is slight, a mere whisper. But the silken thread it weaves from the beginning of YHWH's reply to its end, the way it links the vivid imagery of Jeremiah hopelessly racing against galloping horses with the equally-inescapable approach of YHWH's 'burning anger',[417] is a thing of terrible beauty.

5.4 Summary

We have taken the time to listen to a significantly longer passage in our second foray into the confessions and have, it is hoped, been well repaid for the time spent. However, the careful listener might be forced to admit to some disappointment. The expectation was that listening to the *first* confession as it lurched from fear to anger to vengeance to trust would, in some measure at least, prepare us to hear the second.

But even our careful attention to those subtle markers did little to brace us for this next exchange between the prophet and his Master. From the outset, nothing was as it should be: a prophet – one

---

[414] Jeremiah speaks 'in oppressive frequency [24 mentions] of God's anger (אַף)'. To put that in perspective, Ezekiel, the book with the next most numerous mentions of God's אף has only *eleven* occurrences, *less than half* the number of occurrences in Jeremiah! G. Sauer, 'אַף', *TLOT*, I, pp. 167-69.

In fact, 'words for anger are connected with God three times as often as they are connected with man in the OT; אָנַף and חָרוֹן are 'used almost exclusively with God as subject. With few exceptions … combinations of several words for "anger" [as here in Jer. 12.13] have to do with the divine wrath exclusively.' E. Johnson, 'אָנַף, אַף', *TDOT*, I, pp. 348-60.

[415] Where the term does occur in the Prophets, it is consistent with the term's use in the Exodus and wilderness stories (cf. Exod. 4.14; 32.10-11, 19, 22; Num. 11.1, 10, 33; 12.9), referring primarily 'to Yahweh's anger that comes because of Israel's disobedience to divine commands'. Jerome F.D. Creach, 'חרה', *NIDOTTE*, II, p. 267. See Isa. 5.24-25; Hos. 8.5.

[416] תִּתְחֲרֶה is a tiphel form of חָרָה meaning 'to compete'. G. Sauer, 'חרה', *TLOT*, II, pp. 472-74; *CDCH*, s.v. 'חרה I'.

[417] Reinforcing that the 'galloping horses' of Jer. 12.5 are not-so-subtle a hint of the coming invasion.

designated to speak YHWH's Word *to* the wicked – was *accusing* YHWH of *aiding* them (12.1b-2). YHWH, whose words of reassurance had bolstered the prophet's (and the listener's) faith with the promise of coming (but not swift) judgment on those who resisted the prophetic word, suddenly seems to dismiss the prophet's anguished cry with little more than a brusque: 'You think it's tough now? Things are bound to get much worse!' (12.5). A prophet who *attacks* YHWH? A YHWH who *ignores* – even *rebuffs* – the prayers of the righteous? What is the careful listener supposed to feel but utter confusion, frustration, and despair? How does a listener faithfully hear a book they would rather not listen to it at all?

Yet, as we persisted in our listening, something changed in 12.7. YHWH began YHWH's *own* lament. And we heard something amazing. YHWH began to speak about the coming judgment of Judah, but in terms of endearment ... 'my house' ... 'my heritage' ... 'beloved of my soul'. It is the confounded language of the rejected lover; YHWH's shock at Judah's continued rebellion is palpable. Then, within the space of a phrase, that flame of love is snuffed out, replaced by cold rage: 'For which reason I hate her' (12.8).

Therefore, YHWH purposed to turn this 'heritage' – the clean, beautiful land that was YHWH's prized possession – into a fetid hyena's lair, a trampled vineyard, a desolated wilderness (12.9-10). Then, just as suddenly as it had departed, the keening returns. 'They have turned her into ... a desolation! Desolate, it mourns to me' (12. 11). YHWH's enduring love does not negate YHWH's righteous anger, does not cancel out the threatened judgment, does not deny or forget that Judah's judgment is but the just reward for the nation's own deeds ... but it does return.

Perhaps the easiest thing to miss here is that the prophet Jeremiah has not spoken one word since v. 4. Jeremiah 12.5-13 is *all* YHWH speech. In other words, the literary figure of the prophet has become, for the moment, one of *us*, the audience. It cannot be that Jeremiah cannot think of what to say – he said plenty in four short verses! – so the listener should assume the silence is intentional. A key part of that intention is reinforcing the identification of the book's audience with the figure of the prophet.

YHWH's words, in all the important ways, reflect every emotional dimension and dynamic of the prophet's cry. I would agree that

YHWH's reply, even when naturally extended to v. 13, does not offer Jeremiah or the listener a word of *comfort*. But what it *does* offer is *commiseration*, a sharing of grief, sorrow, anger, and frustration ... and there *is* some comfort in that. The resolution to this confession is to be found in the emotive mirroring of the divine and prophetic hearts evident at the end of the text.[418]

This affective reflection of the divine *pathos* in the heart of the prophetic figure is perhaps the Confessions' most significant contribution to the theology of the prophetic office. Recalling Jer. 12.3, Jeremiah's only basis on which to plead with YHWH for justice was simply: 'You know/see/test my heart, that it is with you'. That Jeremiah feels as YHWH does is then the needed proof that Jeremiah remains YHWH's true prophet, true to YHWH's heart.

Finally, our adoption of an interpretive strategy that attempts to take seriously the affective rhetoric and character development in the figure of the prophet has subtly moved the audience from prophetic sympathy (i.e. feeling sorry *for* the prophetic figure) to prophetic empathy (i.e. feeling *with* the prophetic figure). That is, the listening heart is slowly being shaped to mirror the prophetic heart, which prepares us to truly hear these powerful words of Jeremiah.

---

[418] Holladay, *Jeremiah 1*, p. 389, writes,

This poem offers to an extraordinary degree an expression of the love, sorrow, and anger of Yahweh over his people ... we are at the furthest remove here from the notion, insisted upon by the later church fathers influenced by Aristotle, of the impassibility of God ... all that Yahweh has held dear, all that has been considered inalienable to him, he is casting off, deserting.

6

CONCLUSIONS

6.1 Introduction

The goal all along has been to present a Pentecostal hearing of the Confessions in hopes that such attentiveness will elucidate new understandings of the function of those texts within the MT book of Jeremiah. That function seems to be two-fold: 1) to focus our attention on the literary presentation of the figure of the prophet;[1] and 2) by focusing on that figure, to provide an emotive guide to aid the audience's comprehension of the book's message.[2] This work understands the Confessions' function in the book of Jeremiah to be not simply an incidental recording of the *reactions* of the prophetic figure to the word of YHWH; rather, they also function as intentional *reception models* for the book's audience. This understanding of the Confessions uncovers new dimensions of these texts' integration into the structure of the book as well as highlights new aspects of their importance to its message. After our attentive hearing of Jer. 11.18-23 and 12.1-13, we have reached a critical point where the posited claims about the text must be evaluated in terms of our stated research question, aims, and interpretive method.

However, before any such an evaluation of actual achievements and relative success, there remains yet a final critical point of

---

[1] Especially important as an 'introduction' to the memoir material that comes to dominate the book in ch. 26.

[2] See Pamela J. Scalise, 'The Way of Weeping: Reading the Path of Grief in Jeremiah', *WW* 22.4 (2002), pp. 415-22.

discussion: the persistence of emotive patterning across the rest of the Confessions. To put the matter more precisely, do the affective patterns and terminology already identified in the first two Confessions show up in significant ways in *other* identified Confession texts? And are any such similarities enough to say that the first two Confessions are typical of the larger corpus and serve as a coherent and thematic, rather than accidental, introduction to the Confession texts?

6.2 The Confessions as a Listening Guide

It is clear from our close reading of the first two Confession texts in the prior chapter, that the emotive path the Confessions present is far from a linear movement from sadness to joy. Rather, we heard deep emotional tensions and unpredictable shifts of apparent mood within the prophetic figure: from fear to anger to vengeance to trust to even deeper anger and grief.

It was first argued that these wild emotions mirror the destructive and constructive nature of Jeremiah's prophetic calling within the narrative life of the figure of the prophet. Although the Word he proclaims tears his heart out, it simultaneously defines and defends his role as YHWH's true prophet. More surprising, though, our careful listening revealed the *same* emotional turmoil extant within YHWH's own heart, as YHWH wrestles with an unbearable position equal to that of the prophet, the impossible responsibility of being the One who both loves and judges Judah. Finally, these emotively overloaded texts have subtly but inexorably drawn the listener into that emotive space occupied by the prophetic figure and YHWH. The attentive listener now not only hears *what YHWH has said to Jeremiah* but hears YHWH's words *as Jeremiah heard them!* The same emotions – wariness, fear, frustration, shock, dismay, anger, grief – at war within the prophet's and YHWH's hearts now stir within the listener's own.

Is this a sustained pattern beyond Jer. 12.13? Has our chosen affective approach given the attentive listener new interpretive options for understanding these puzzling prayers of the prophet? Do these emotive patterns align the Confession texts with the primary deconstructive/constructive nature of the divine word presented in the book of Jeremiah?³ Does this make the Confessions *integral* to the overall message of the book rather than a kind-of chaotic *intrusion* upon an otherwise coherent text?⁴

The answer is, it would seem, a resounding, 'Yes!' Clearly, the destructive element becomes apparent in the first confession in the quoted words of Jeremiah's enemies (Jer. 11.19). They express a wish not simply to murder Jeremiah but to annihilate his memory.⁵ Their wish is for the prophet and his unwelcome words of censure and rebuke to disappear. The prophet does *not* flee or fade away, but doggedly persists in crying out to YHWH for justice against those wicked who overturn the moral order of the land (Jer. 12.1-4). Intimidation and fear of death (long the standard tactics of the powerful elite) are not enough to silence this prophet, who, though deeply grieved by the evil that confronts him, shows a courage worthy to be called heroic. Even while the prophet's reputation is being torn down by his Judean opponents, the Confession texts build up the prophet's renown with those who hear the book.

Jeremiah 15.10-21 seems to carry forward this pattern. First of all, the text is replete with the affective vocabulary of Jer. 11.18-12.13, using many of the same key emotive terms and phrases.⁶ We again

---

³ On other important texts related to Jeremiah's theology of the Word, see Wilhelm J. Wessels, "'My Word is Like Fire': The Consuming Power of YHWH's Word', *OTE* 24.2 (2011), pp. 492-510.

⁴ Is the book of Jeremiah a text *better* understood as a prophetic word *without* the Confessions than *with* them?

⁵ Fretheim, *Jeremiah*, p. 190.

⁶ רִיב, Jeremiah 15.10: 'Woe is me, my mother … a man of *strife*'; cf. Jer. 12.1: 'Innocent are you, YHWH, when I *contend* with you'. רָעָה, Jer. 15.11: 'Time of *trouble*'; cf. Jer. 11.23: 'For I shall bring *disaster* to the men of Anathoth', and 12.4: 'Because of the *evil* of those who dwell in the land'. נָתַן, Jer. 15.13: 'Your wealth and your treasures *I will give* as plunder'; cf. Jer. 12.7: '*I have given* the beloved of my soul into the hands of her enemies'. אַף, Jer. 15.13: 'In my *anger*, a fire is kindled that shall burn forever'; cf. Jer. 12.13: 'Because of the burning *anger* of YHWH'. יָדַע, Jer. 15.15: 'O LORD, you *know*'; cf. Jer. 11.18: 'YHWH *made me know* and I *knew*', and 12.3: 'But you, YHWH, *you know me*'. פָּקַד Jer. 15.15: 'Remember me and *visit* me'; cf. Jer. 11.22-23: 'Look, I will *reckon* with them … year of their *visitation*'. נָקַם, Jer. 15.15: '*Avenge* me on my persecutors'; cf. Jer. 11.20: 'Let me see your *vengeance* upon them'. אָכַל, Jer. 15.16: 'Your words were found, and I *ate* them'; cf. Jer. 12.12: 'The sword of YHWH *consumes* …' מָלֵא, Jer. 15.17: 'You had *filled* me with indignation'; cf. Jer. 12.6: 'Even they cry out behind you'/ 'Even they are in *full* cry behind you'. אָמַן Jer. 15.18: '[You are] like *untrustworthy* (e.g. לֹא אָמַן) waters'; cf. Jer. 12.6: 'Do not *believe* them when they speak to you good things'.

see the wish for the prophet's disappearance, but this time the wish is expressed by the figure of the prophet not the enemies! Certainly, Brueggemann is right that the 'complaint of Jeremiah is a reflection of the costliness of such a ministry of candor and discernment'.[7] However, Jeremiah's address to his mother and wish that he had never been born is also an indirect questioning of the legitimacy of his own prophetic calling, placed on him from his 'mother's womb' (Jer. 1.5). Here again, Jeremiah's crisis of calling is the result of the people's negative response to the Word the prophet speaks. His faithful obedience has rendered only 'strife', 'contention', and 'curse' (Jer. 15.10). Because of the word YHWH had given him to speak, the prophet complains of being ostracized by his mourning for the sin and imminent destruction of his people.

However, there is not only here a wish for self-destruction. First, YHWH gives Jeremiah a direct word of assurance phrased as a rhetorical question: 'Can iron break iron from the north and bronze?'[8] Of course, this is not a promise that the trouble will *end*; rather, it is the much more modest claim that the prophet will *endure* and will *not* crumble or succumb to the enemies' deadly desires. The constructive aspect of YHWH's word to Jeremiah, though, is seen most clearly when Jeremiah, out of his agony, reminds YHWH: 'Your words were found, and I *ate them*, and your words became to me a joy and the delight of my heart; for I am called by your name, O LORD, God of hosts' (Jer. 15.16). The prophet's ingestion of the divine word indicates that it has become a *part* of him. Hereby, Jeremiah is also

---

Also, though the precise words are different, there are phrases that are very similar to the phrasings of Jer. 11.18-12.13, especially in terms of emotive impact:

1) 'Your wealth ... I will give as plunder ... *throughout all your territory* (גְבוּלֶיךָ־ בְּכָל)' (Jer. 15.13); 'The sword of YHWH consumes *from one end of the land to the other* (מִקְצֵה־אֶרֶץ וְעַד־קְצֵה הָאָרֶץ)' (Jer. 12.12).

2) 'Your words became to me a joy and the *delight of my heart* (לְשִׂמְחַת לְבָבִי)' (Jer. 15.16); 'I have given the *beloved of my soul* (יְדִדוּת נַפְשִׁי)' (Jer. 12.7).

3) 'Why is my *wound incurable* (מַכָּתִי אֲנוּשָׁה)?' (Jer. 15.18); 'They have *wearied* (חָלָה) themselves' (Jer. 12.13), a term used in the more-common phrase נַחְלָה מַכָּתִי (also translated 'incurable wound') in Jer. 10.19; 14.17; 30.12.

[7] Brueggemann, *A Commentary on Jeremiah*, p. 144.

[8] Following Fretheim, who sees the 'iron' as a reference to 'the stubborn people Jeremiah face'; 'iron from the north' as a reference to the Babylonian army; and 'bronze' as a reference to the prophet Jeremiah, alluding to his call narrative (cf. Jer. 1.18). Fretheim, *Jeremiah*, p. 236.

acknowledging/claiming that his life experience is now inseparable from his prophetic calling and task![9]

In the final and perhaps most passionate Confession (Jer. 20.7-18), the verbal echoes take a different shape. לֵב reappears in 20.9 as the location of YHWH's irresistible, fiery Word.[10] In 20.10, Jeremiah's enemies gloat of their opportunity to enact their נִקְמָם upon the prophet;[11] however, in 20.11, Jeremiah is convinced of his enemies' soon-coming בּוֹשׁ.[12] They will not 'succeed'[13] and their dishonor will be 'never forgotten', cleverly inverting the enemies' intent in Jer. 11.19 that Jeremiah would never be remembered. However, the most important echo of the first confession is the near-verbatim quotation of 11.20 in 20.12, effectively forming a literary *inclusio* around the Confessions.[14]

In this last Confession text, we hear the destructive power of YHWH's Word in the life of the prophet reach a climax with the prophet's *cursing* the day of his own day of birth (v. 14)! The questioning of his calling seen in Jeremiah 15 here becomes an outright denial of that calling with his wish that he had never been born.[15] The prophet Jeremiah has come into agreement with the 'men of Anathoth' in 11.19. they had wished he would just disappear; now, so does he. The depth of Jeremiah's grief and despair is such that it overflows all proposed and imposed boundaries – even the textual boundaries marked by the *inclusio* – a grief that cannot be contained but must be poured out.[16]

---

[9] Here, the effect of this claim of 'identification' with YHWH is to remind YHWH and the book's audience that any injustice done to the prophet is, in reality, done to YHWH directly! However, within the broader scope of the book, this stakes out an amazing claim of identification between YHWH and the one who speaks YHWH's word.

[10] Verse 9, literally rendered: 'I will never speak again in the name of YHWH ... but in *my heart* a burning'.

[11] Verse 10: 'We can prevail and ... *take our vengeance* on him!'

[12] The full phrase is בֹּשׁוּ מְאֹד, literally 'much shamed'.

[13] In Jer. 12.1, Jeremiah had complained to YHWH that the wicked צָלֵהַ, which is also translated 'prosper' and carries with it the sense of 'constant success' as שׂכל does in Deut. 29.8. See Clines, *CDCH*, s.v. 'שׂכל I'.

[14] O'Connor, *Confessions of Jeremiah*, p. 88.

[15] Effectively, a wish 'that he had not become a prophet'. Fretheim, *Jeremiah*, p. 296.

[16] Here, I diverge from O'Connor's reading of the Confession texts as ending in Jer. 20.13. She is convinced the inclusion of Jer. 20.14-18 as part of the final

And yet again, we see a constructive dynamic also at work in the figure of the prophet. Here, the prophet's *ingestion* of the Word[17] has become outright *identification* with the Word! Even though wishing to resign his prophetic office, Jeremiah cries out instead, 'Your Word was *in* me!'[18] It is precisely in the final Confession that we see a total confluence of the destructive and constructive natures of the divine Word within the life of the prophet, expressed in a whirlpool of emotions, ranging from confident praise to near-suicidal despair. The prophetic Word at once sickens and strengthens the prophet. Though the prophet's *social* life has been effectively overthrown by his calling, though his inner life has been uprooted with emotional turmoil, yet the Word of God has been literally built into him![19] The figure of Jeremiah, who once faced the end of his life (Jer. 11.18b-

---

confession text has caused scholars to ignore this 'literary enclosure'. Jer. 20.14-18 can be excluded for the further reason that it does not conform to individual lament form like the other confessions but is a 'cursing poem' like Job 3. O'Connor, *Confessions of Jeremiah*, pp. 88-89.

Her conclusions on this point are clearly driven by another agenda – her wish to challenge the portrayal of the prophet as of weak character or an immature disposition. She goes so far as to claim that the Confessions instead present Jeremiah as a 'poet of Yahweh's praises. His confessions move from uncertainty and doubt to clarity of purpose in his vocation and confident trust in Yahweh'. O'Connor, *Confessions of Jeremiah*, p. 3. It seems that the preferred 'portrait of the prophet' has been selected ahead-of-time, and then the text is 'cut to fit' using the tools of form-criticism as the trimming shears.

Dubbink has questioned this decision: 'There is no reason to exclude vv. 14-18 *a priori* from the confessions. They have much in common with other texts, namely a report in the first person presented as a reflection of the prophet concerning his own situation.' Also, 'it is to be noted that the placement is surely related to 20.1-6. Not only is there a thematic connection between Jeremiah's lament and the repressive activity of Pashhur the priest; we also find in v. 10 the same term… "terror all around", which Jeremiah assigns to Pashhur as a nickname.' Joep Dubbink, 'Jeremiah: Hero of Faith or Defeatist? Concerning the Place and Function of Jeremiah 20.14-18', *JSOT* 86.4 (1999), pp. 67-84 (68-69).

Paying attention to the affective rhetoric also indicates that 20.14-18 should be included, since the very last line of 20.18 contains again a reference to the prophet's experience of בֹּשׁ, a key emotive term in Jer. 12.13. An affective approach does not 'ignore' the *inclusio* but instead addresses the way in which Jeremiah's overwhelming grief interacts with such a literary device.

[17] Jeremiah 15.16.

[18] Jeremiah 20.9.

[19] Psalm 102.3. 'Fire in one's bones signifies a fever in an individual lament Psalm', but here it signifies that, 'receipt of a divine oracle evidently brought with it a compulsion to declare it'. Allen, *Jeremiah*, p. 231.

19) has now become *living* Word! Jeremiah is conformed to the very word of God he embodies: *'as it is with God, so it is with Jeremiah'*.[20]

6.3 Summary and Conclusions

Having established the final point that our deduced affective themes and patterns remain consistent across the Confession texts, we can now effectively evaluate the presented findings in terms of the initial research question: what kind of figure does a Pentecostal hearing of the Confessions reveal the prophet Jeremiah to be and how is that presentation instructive for contemporary hearers of the book of Jeremiah?

Such a broad question contains within it several key aims: 1) to analyze how distinctively Pentecostal conceptions of Scripture and scriptural interpretation contribute to a distinctive hearing of the Confessions; 2) to articulate how a Pentecostal hearing of the Confessions causes the listener to conceptualize the theology of the Word presented in the book of Jeremiah; and 3) to articulate how this understanding of the Jeremianic theology of the Word may both challenge and enhance the Pentecostal conceptions of Scripture and the hermeneutic of hearing. The following section will address itself to each of these matters in turn.

To answer the research question in broad terms, the presented hearing of the Confessions has revealed the literary figure of the prophet Jeremiah as one consumed by and with the *pathos* of YHWH. In this claim, the present study breaks no new ground, following instead in the wake of the brilliant work of Abraham Heschel, who describes divine pathos as 'not an idea of goodness, but a living care; not an immutable example, but an ongoing challenge, a dynamic relation between God and man; not mere feeling or passive affection, but an act of attitude composed of various spiritual elements; no mere contemplative survey of the world, but a passionate summons'.[21]

---

[20] Jeremiah's claim of 'weariness' (לְאָה) in Jer. 20.9 matches the 'weariness' of YHWH in Jer. 15.16. God is 'weary of holding back the judgment on an unrepentant people'. Fretheim, *Jeremiah*, p. 292, italics mine.

[21] Abraham J. Heschel, *The Prophets* (Peabody, MA: Prince Press, 1999), II, p. 4.

To put it another way, the divine *pathos* is a particular orientation of YHWH to YHWH's created order; that is, divine *pathos* is the full expression of what we might otherwise term divine affections.[22] Perhaps, then, the *true* innovation of our claim is that, though Jeremiah the prophet cannot match YHWH in terms of sovereignty or power or wisdom or foresight, Jeremiah most certainly can and does match YHWH in terms of passionate longing and love for YHWH and YHWH's rebellious people. *Jeremiah loves Israel just as much as YHWH does, and this is so because Jeremiah loves YHWH just as much as YHWH loves Jeremiah.* Jeremiah's core orientation toward YHWH is revealed in and shaped by his sharing of YHWH's core orientation toward Israel. Each new emotive turn in the Confessions simultaneously reveals and deepens the shared *pathos* of YHWH and Jeremiah.

However, the claim of the present work pushes beyond even that stunning point to argue that a key purpose of the Confession texts is to re/orient the listener's heart to mirror the heart of the prophet as heard in the outcries of the Confessions. The emotive power of Jeremiah's poetry has long been recognized and even celebrated, but has, for all intents and purposes, never been well articulated.[23] The affective rhetoric and emotive imagery of the Confessions is offered with the precise intention of forming the affections of the attentive listener. The language *must* be powerful – the imagery *must* evoke the rawness of the tragic reality confronting Judah – in order to replicate the emotive impact that Word makes on the prophetic figure upon the *listeners*. Furthermore, if that is a key intention of the book, it is quite logical that such a book would include some examples of the prophet's *own* reactions to the divine Word to provide models for attentive listeners to emulate in their own hearings. Thus, the Confessions are neither incidentally included nor accidentally placed in the book of Jeremiah; rather, both their inclusion and their placement are intentional to the book's overall purpose.

Such attention to the impact of Scripture on affective formation is a distinctively Pentecostal exegetical concern. This should not be

---

In the earlier volume, Heschel claimed 'divine pathos' as the heart of the phenomenon of OT prophecy: 'The typical prophetic state of mind is one of being taken up into the heart of the divine pathos. Sympathy is the prophet's answer to inspiration, the correlative to revelation.' Abraham J. Heschel, *The Prophets*, I, p. 26.

[22] In the sense of YHWH's self-ordering 'loves'.

[23] It is *acknowledged* but never *explained*.

misunderstood as a claim that such an approach is *exclusively* Pentecostal; however, Pentecostal exegesis shows more careful attention to emotive aspects both of the text itself and of the listener's experience of the text than do other common current exegetical approaches.[24] Furthermore, such an approach is organic to the Pentecostal listener and their primitive-pragmatic approach to Scripture. For example, as Ellington has noted, many Pentecostal claims related to the authority of Scripture typically come down to very personal stories of God speaking to them or showing them something of immediate relevance within the text of Scripture.[25]

The *real* challenge, then, facing the formulation of a distinctive Pentecostal hermeneutic is not as much a matter of *developing its practice* as it is a matter of *articulating its fundamental structures* in terms recognizable within the broader field of biblical exegesis and hermeneutical theory. The affective strategy depicted here attempts to further such articulation by bringing together the tools and insights of rhetorical, narrative, and reader-response criticisms; clearly, what has been described is *a* Pentecostal affective listening strategy, by no means singular or definitive.

For Pentecostals, the Bible is a book that, more than anything else, makes an individual *feel* a certain way as we interact with it. Again, this does not equate to a *denial* that the Bible can be comprehended rationally; rather, a Pentecostal hermeneutic would humbly suggest that, if the Bible is *only* apprehended rationally, some very important pieces of its message may very well be missed ... sort of like reading a poem about a rose only concerned to determine if the poet's description was scientifically accurate.

---

[24] See ch. 2 for some examples.

[25] In his own discussions of biblical 'authority' with his students, Scott A. Ellington, 'Pentecostalism and the Authority of Scripture', *JPT* 4.9 (1996), pp. 16-38 (17), has observed that

> it was possible to question and even cast serious doubts on traditional understandings of and proofs for infallibility and inerrancy in Pentecostal groups without seriously challenging their understanding of the Bible as the authoritative 'Word of God'. This suggests to me that Pentecostals do not found their understanding of the authority of Scripture on a bedrock of doctrine, but that, in fact, their doctrine is itself resting on something more fundamental, dynamic and resilient; the experiences of encountering a living God, directly and personally.

The Pentecostal listener, then, is particularly primed for highly emotive texts such as the Confessions. Feeling what the Bible is saying is the entry point to scriptural exegesis.[26] That foregrounding of affective experience in the exegetical process creates a much more dynamic back-and-forth interaction between the emotive states depicted in the text and the emotive state/s of the listener/s, creating endless opportunities for texts to be heard afresh and anew, containing both stable, reiterated, reassuring themes as well as the always-present-potential for new insights and revolutionary reorientations. For the Pentecostal way of listening, the Bible can 'pull up and pull down, destroy and overthrow, build and plant' at any and every point.

Thus, the Pentecostal listener will discern in the Confessions a dialectical theology of the Word as both destructive and constructive. Those functions of the Word of YHWH in the book of Jeremiah can never be separated without doing great violence to book's overall message and theology. In a way, even to say that the book of Jeremiah is primarily a book about Judah's judgment and Jerusalem's downfall is something of a misnomer. True, those topics do occupy the most physical space within the book; however, just because the messages of hope and restoration do not receive equal space does not mean the book of Jeremiah is telling us that messages of hope are less important to the book than the messages of judgment.[27] The darker the room, the more noticeable and beautiful we find the merest glint of light; perhaps the very dominance of judgment serves to uplift the prophecies of hope in a way that an even balance would never have achieved.

Just as the Pentecostal approach to hearing Scripture informs the way we listen to the Confessions, so likewise does the theology of the Word presented in the Confessions speak to the Pentecostal understanding of Scripture. As the above analysis has revealed, the theology of the Word presented in the Confessions seems to affirm the

---

[26] Clearly, this relates more broadly to the role of 'affective knowledge' that also impacts Pentecostal theological construction as well as theories and practices of spiritual formation. See the discussion in James K.A. Smith, *Thinking in Tongues: Pentecostal Contributions to Christian Philosophy* (Pentecostal Manifestos; Grand Rapids: Eerdmans, 2010), pp. 48-80.

[27] The unique and prominent placings of surprising words of hope (cf. esp. Jer. 25.26; 30-33; 52.31-34) seems proof enough that the message of hope is 'strategic' to the book. The idea of 'equal time' for equally important ideas smacks again of the imposition of Western canons of balance and logic.

Pentecostal instinct that grants priority to the affective dimensions of the text. The affective hearing attempted above offered insight into form-critical and literary cruxes that have been perennial discussions and perhaps has helped move some of them in a positive direction. Such advances and contributions offered by a Pentecostal perspective should be recognized and celebrated.

Yet, the Confessions present a challenge to our foregrounding of the affective dimension. Perhaps of greatest concern is that our affective hearing of the first two confessions showed that YHWH *gives Jeremiah no real word of 'comfort' in either one.*[28] Furthermore, *there is no divine response given to the final confession.* The experiences that Ellington describes above as so foundational to the Pentecostal understanding of scriptural authority are *positive* experiences. That is, I, as a Pentecostal, believe in the authority of Scripture based upon my experiences of God *answering* my prayers, not based on my experiences of God's stony silence despite my most desperate pleas. It seems fair to ask if the Pentecostal affective approach to Scripture is fully prepared to grapple with the scriptural presentation of traumatic feelings and the absence of divine reassurances so clearly a part of the totality of scriptural witness. The present work has only peeked into that looming abyss.

6.4 Implications and Suggestions for Further Research

Clearly, this book has only begun to delve into the affective dimensions of the entirety of the book of Jeremiah. Three immediate possibilities for extending this research present themselves. First, an affective reading strategy could be used to look at other long-recognized textual units of the book of Jeremiah; for example, the Book of Comfort,[29] the 'Baruch Document',[30] and the collection of oracles against the nations.[31] One could also analyze textual segments that

---

[28] In fact, our affective method revealed that the supposed 'divine reassurance' in 11.22-23 was not all that reassuring, after all.

[29] Jeremiah 30-33.

[30] Brueggeman's designation for Jeremiah 37-45. Brueggemann, *Commentary on Jeremiah*, p. 338.

[31] Jeremiah 46-51.

share particularly stylistic features, such as the prose sermons[32] and the sign-acts.[33] Furthermore, as an affective hearing works both within and across texts, there is much comparative work to be done, from both chronological and canonical perspectives.

Another area with great potential for productive research is comparing the affective impact of MT Jeremiah (which has been the chosen text for this study) with the affective impact of LXX Jeremiah,[34] a text that is significantly shorter, radically rearranged,[35] and composed in an entirely different language. That last fact alone – the significant uptick in the precision of Greek affective terminology when compared to Hebraic terminology – could produce fascinatingly different hearings of apparently similar texts.[36]

A final area of particular personal interest is exploring further the concept of the Confessions as a listening guide for the entire book.

---

[32] Jeremiah 7.1-8.3; 11.1-17; 14.11-16; 18.7-12; 21.5-9; 22.1-5; 25.3-12; 26.3-6; 32.39-41; 34.8-22; 40.2-3; 44.2-10, 20-23. Allen, *Jeremiah*, p. 9. Stulman has pointed out the 'deconstructive' aspect of the prose sermons' function, which points to their affective power. See Louis J. Stulman, 'The Prose Sermons as Hermeneutical Guide to Jeremiah 1-25: The Deconstruction of Judah's Symbolic World', in A.R. Pete Diamond, Kathleen M. O'Connor, and Louis Stulman (eds.), *Troubling Jeremiah* (JSOTSup 260; Sheffield: Sheffield Academic Press, 1999), pp. 34-63.

[33] Perhaps the only agree-upon fact about prophetic sign-acts is that they were designed to add dramatic emotive 'impact' to the prophetic proclamation of YHWH's word. Jeremiah 13.1-11; 16.1-3; 18.1-11; 19.1-13; 27.1-11; 29.1-23; 32.1-15; 35.1-17; 36.1-10, 32; 44.8-13; 51.59-64. I have included Jeremiah's letter to the Babylonians, the scroll read and destroyed by King Jehoiakim, and the scroll of prophecies against Babylon sunk in the Euphrates River, following the suggestion of Martin Kessler that scroll writing should be considered a kind of symbolic action in Jeremiah. See Martin Kessler, 'The Significance of Jeremiah 36', *ZAW* 81.3 (1969), pp. 381-83 (382). Cf. Georg Fohrer, 'Die Gattung der Berichte über symbolische Handlungen der Propheten', *ZAW* 64.2 (1951), pp. 101-20.

[34] See A.R. Diamond, 'Jeremiah's Confessions in the LXX and MT: A Witness to a Developing Canonical Function?', *VT* 40.1 (1990), pp. 33-50.

[35] The different theological claims of the variant textual traditions is nicely summarized by Marvin Sweeney. For Sweeney, the LXX structure highlights 'an interest in presenting YHWH's plans for Israel/Judah and the nations, followed by a depiction of the consequences for Jerusalem for failing to abide by YHWH's will'. The book is a 'retrospective ... designed to explain the destruction of Jerusalem as a consequence of the people's failure to heed the prophet's warnings'.

The MT structure, on the other hand, 'indicates a prospective, hopeful interest in the book, insofar as it is designed to point to the rise of the Persian Empire as the agent of YHWH's restoration for Jerusalem and punishment against Babylon and the nations that oppress Judah'. Marvin Sweeney, *The Prophetic Literature* (Interpreting Biblical Texts; Nashville, TN: Abingdon Press, 2005), pp. 91-93.

[36] E.g. does the greater linguistic precision serve to *enhance* or *reduce* the overall emotive impact created by the in-built ambiguity of Hebraic terms?

Diamond, Smith, and O'Connor, for example, have presented fine contextual studies of the Confession texts. Diamond and Smith end their contextual studies of the Confessions at ch. 20; O'Connor extends her study to include chs. 21-25 as part of the Confessions' larger literary-theological context. However, none of the mentioned scholars consider the Confessions in relation to Jeremiah 26-52.[37]

In our brief discussion of the overall pattern of the Confessions that opened the current chapter, we noted that an affective reading would encourage the inclusion of Jer. 20.14-18 as part of the final Confession text, a move that O'Connor and others have been hesitant to make on form-critical grounds. However, making such a move creates an interesting ending to the corpus of Confessions text, juxtaposing the emotive high point of the entire corpus, the shout of praise in Jer. 20.13, with the prophet's lowest point of despair, the self-curse in 20.14-18. To put it another way, the ending of the Confessions refuses resolution[38] in favor of creating a sharp emotive juxtaposition. Such juxtapositions of emotive high and low points are demonstrably present in the latter half of the book.

For example, Jeremiah 25, which first declares Babylon the agent of Judah's judgment (v. 9), a *limit* to the length of Judah's punishment (v. 11), and the ultimate downfall of Babylon herself (v. 26) is juxtaposed to the story of the reception of Jeremiah's Temple Sermon in ch. 26, where the 'priests and the prophets and the people' forcibly seize him and condemn him to die (v. 8);[39] it is only by the unexpected, near-miraculous intervention of Ahikam ben Shaphan that

---

[37] What makes this even more puzzling is that it is in that section of the book where we begin to see the emotive reactions (both positive and negative) that Jeremiah's prophetic word generates in its various audiences: the people, the princes, the false prophets, the kings of Judah. Such responses are decidedly affective and are crucial to understanding the force and role of the prophetic word in Jeremiah. As Kessler says, 'Prophecy always presupposes the possibility of dialogue with the deity … it is not only concerned with the divine demand for the present, but also with the popular response which this demand draws'. Martin Kessler, 'Jeremiah 26-45 Reconsidered', *JNES* 27.2 (1968), pp. 81-88 (82).

[38] It is, to borrow another of Brueggemann's poignant phrases, an 'ending that does not end'. Walter Brueggemann, 'An Ending that Does Not End: The Book of Jeremiah', in A.K.M. Adam (ed.), *Postmodern Interpretations of the Bible–A Reader* (St. Louis: Chalice Press, 2000), pp. 117-28.

[39] *Before* he has even been officially tried. Brueggemann, *Commentary on Jeremiah*, p. 234.

the prophet escapes Jeremiah 26 alive.[40] In Jeremiah 25, the book appears to reach a rather poetic/emotive high with the proclamation of Babylon's eventual demise.[41] However, the book immediately plunges to a new low – Jeremiah is put on trial for high treason! – in Jeremiah 26. This pattern of emotive juxtaposition appears to repeat itself in Jer. 35/36,[42] 44/45,[43] and 50-51/52.[44] It is perhaps not entirely coincidental that these major emotive shifts appear to connect quite nicely with the suggested literary structure of the latter half of the book.[45]

I have chosen only to consider here the potential for further study within the realm of Jeremiah studies; however, that is simply for the sake of space and faithfulness to our primary subject. Most certainly

---

[40] See Kathleen M. O'Connor, '"Do Not Trim a Word": The Contributions of Chapter 26 to the Book of Jeremiah', *CBQ* 51.4 (1989), pp. 617-30.

[41] The opening of the chapter presents us with a 'summary' of Jeremiah's preaching (vv. 3-7) and concludes with Jeremiah fulfilling his role as 'prophet to the nations' (Jer. 1.5). See Robert P. Carroll, 'Halfway Through a Dark Wood: Reflections on Jeremiah 25', in A.R. Pete Diamond, Kathleen M. O'Connor, and Louis Stulman, *Troubling Jeremiah* (JSOTSup 260; Sheffield: Sheffield Academic Press, 1999), pp. 73-82; see also in the same volume, Martin Kessler, 'Function of Chapters 25 and 50-51', pp. 64-72.

[42] E.g. the contrast between the faithfulness of the Rechabites to their covenant with their ancestor Jonadab and Jehoiakim's unfaithfulness to YHWH demonstrated by his burning of Jeremiah's scroll.

[43] The unfaithfulness of the Judean refugees in Egypt openly refusing to halt their worship of the Queen of Heaven in contrast with YHWH's word of promise to Jeremiah's scribe and faithful supporter Baruch. Notably, this is the only example where the emotive low point is *followed by* the high point. See Marion Ann Taylor, 'Jeremiah 45: The Problem of Placement', *JSOT* 12.37 (1987), pp. 79-98.

[44] The elaborated oracle against Babylon which contains several promises related to Judah's restoration to the land is followed by what looks to be an almost-unnecessary repetition of the story of Jerusalem's fall (already related in Jeremiah 39). See Kenneth T. Aitken, 'The Oracles Against Babylon in Jeremiah 50-51: Structures and Perspectives', *TynBul* 35 (1984), pp. 25-63; Moon Kwon Chae, 'Redactional Intentions of MT Jeremiah Concerning the Oracles Against the Nations', *JBL* 134.3 (2015), pp. 577-93; Else K. Holt, 'The Meaning of an *Inclusio*: A Theological Interpretation of the Book of Jeremiah MT', *SJOT* 17.2 (2003), pp. 183-205; H.G.L. Peels, '"You Shall Certainly Drink!": The Place and Significance of the Oracles Against the Nations in the Book of Jeremiah', *EuroJTh* 16.2 (2007), pp. 81-91; Pierre J. P. Van Hecke, 'Metaphorical Shifts in the Oracle Against Babylon (Jeremiah 50-51)', *SJOT* 17.1 (2003): pp. 68-88.

[45] Gary E. Yates, 'Narrative Parallelism and the "Jehoiakim Frame": A Reading Strategy for Jeremiah 26-45', *JETS* 48.2 (2005), pp. 263-81. See also T.R. Hobbs, 'Some Remarks on the Composition and Structure of the Book of Jeremiah', *CBQ* 34.3 (1972), pp. 257-75; Richard Duane Patterson, 'Of Bookends, Hinges, and Hooks: Literary Clues to the Arrangement of Jeremiah's Prophecy', *WTJ* 51.1 (1989), pp 109-31; Christopher R. Seitz, 'Prophet Moses and the Canonical Shape of Jeremiah', *ZAW* 101.1 (1989), pp. 3-27.

Jeremiah's close interactions with other biblical books such as Deuteronomy and Psalms point toward opportunities for affective analysis of those books, perhaps especially so at their points of contact with the book of Jeremiah.[46]

6.5 Confessions of a Pentecostal Hearer – A Concluding Postscript

At the end of a book such as this, it seems only appropriate to return to where I began, those many years ago in a Bible college classroom. I must admit my disappointment when I discovered, to my shock, that the 'fire' shut up in Jeremiah's bones in Jer. 20.9 was not zeal but pain and heartache. I recall that questions quickly filled my mind. What else about the book of Jeremiah did I fundamentally misunderstand? What other sermons that had been anchor points of my maturing Pentecostal faith had been based on apparently poor exegesis and inattention to proper contextualization?

It truly was a moment where preconceptions were deconstructed, leaving my faith much more like a reed shaking in the wind than a heavily fortified bronze wall. However, looking back, it was *that* moment that I determined I would get to know this mysterious prophet named Jeremiah who sickened at YHWH's awful words. I had no clue then where such a determination would lead, nor how I would return again and again to the book of Jeremiah as my scholarly pursuits and inquiries began to shape themselves into a true passion for this weeping prophet.

This book is the end of a very long journey to discover the *real* reason why I have been so enthralled with the figure and book of Jeremiah. There was something so bold … so honest … so authentic … so *raw* … about a prophet who could stand eye-to-eye with YHWH and say: 'Your Word makes me want to be sick'. It was frightening, thrilling, and inescapable.

And what I have discovered at the end of this path is that all those preachers whose fiery voices echo in my youthful memories with calls

---

[46] Walter Brueggemann offers a helpful summary of Jeremiah's connections to the rest of the OT corpus. Walter Brueggemann, *The Theology of the Book of Jeremiah* (Old Testament Theology; New York: Cambridge University Press, 2007), pp. 134-83.

to feel the fire of God's Holy Word kindling in my very bones were not so very wrong in their hearing of Jeremiah after all. For Jer. 20.9 *is* a claim about Jeremiah's passion for YHWH's Word – it *is* perhaps the most vivid image given in the book of YHWH's possession of the prophet. My faith has now returned, built up by greater understanding and more deeply rooted in my life experience.

I have come to understand that passionate zeal for YHWH's Word came at a high price for the figure of the prophet; the passion that drove Jeremiah was burned into his soul by the bright flame of YHWH's burning anger against Judah's unstoppable sin. Jeremiah's zeal was never just his own; it was first and always *YHWH*'s. The reason why the book is still considered some of the most powerful rhetoric in all of the OT is simply this: the book is, at the end of the day, not primarily a portrait of a prophet; rather, it is a beautifully conceived artful portrayal of YHWH *through* the portraiture of Jeremiah. In the book of Jeremiah, YHWH's grief takes on a human face in the weeping of Jeremiah, while Jeremiah's plaintive cries are lifted up to the plane of divine beauty and grace. Though I did not know it at the time, I now understand that what I had heard as a boy in the voice of Jeremiah was the echo of the voice of YHWH. It has shaped within me a longing that has given my life a measure of meaning I never would have thought possible.

BIBLIOGRAPHY

Adam, A.K.M., *et al.*, *Reading Scripture with the Church: Toward a Hermeneutic for Theological Interpretation* (Grand Rapids: Baker Academic, 2006).

Ahuis, Ferdinand, *Der klagende Gerichtsprophet: Studien zur Klage in der Überlieferung von den alttestamentlichen Gerichtspropheten* (CTM 12; Stuttgart: Calwer Verlag, 1982).

Aitken, Kenneth T., 'The Oracles Against Babylon in Jeremiah 50-51: Structures and Perspectives', *Tyndale Bulletin* 35 (1984), pp. 25-63.

Allen, Leslie W., *Jeremiah* (OTL; Louisville, KY: Westminster/John Knox Press, 2008).

—'Jeremiah. Book of', in Mark J. Boda and J. Gordon McConville (eds.), *Dictionary of the Old Testament Prophets* (Downers Grove, IL: InterVarsity Press, 2012), pp. 423-40.

Allen, Ronald, 'Feeling and Form in Biblical Interpretation', *Encounter* 43.1 (1982), pp. 99-107.

Alter, Robert, *The Art of Biblical Narrative* (New York, NY: Basic Books, 1981).

Archer, Kenneth J., *A Pentecostal Hermeneutic: Spirit, Scripture, and Community* (Cleveland, TN: CPT Press, 2009).

Autry, Arden C., 'Dimensions of Hermeneutics in Pentecostal Focus', *Journal of Pentecostal Theology* 1.1 (1993), pp. 29-50.

Avioz, Michael, *'I Sat Alone': Jeremiah Among the Prophets* (Piscataway, NJ: Gorgias Press, 2009).

—'The Call for Revenge in Jeremiah's Complaints (Jer. 11-20)', *Vetus Testamentum* 55.4 (2005), pp. 429-38.

Bak, Dong Hyun, *Klagender Gott-Klagende Menschen: Studien zur Klage in Jeremiabuch* (BZAW 192; Berlin: Walter de Gruyter, 1990).

Baker, Robert O., 'Pentecostal Bible Reading: Toward a Model of Reading for the Formation of Christian Affections', *Journal of Pentecostal Theology* 3.7 (1995), pp. 34-48.

Balentine, Samuel E., 'Jeremiah, Prophet of Prayer', *Review & Expositor* 78.3 (1981), pp. 331-44.

Barr, James, *Comparative Philology and the Text of the Old Testament* (Oxford: Clarendon, 1968).

Baumgartner, Walther, *Jeremiah's Poems of Lament,* (trans. D.E. Orton; Sheffield: Almond Press, 1988).

Bechtel, Lyn M., 'Shame as a Sanction of Social Control in Biblical Israel: Judicial, Political, and Social Shaming', *Journal for the Study of the Old Testament* 16.49 (1991), pp. 47-76.

—'The Perception of Shame within the Divine-Human Relationship', in Lewis M. Hopfe (ed.), *Uncovering Ancient Stones: Essays in Memory of H. Neil Richardson* (Winona Lake, IN: Eisenbrauns, 1994), pp. 79-92.

Berridge, John Maclennan, *Prophet, People and the Word of Yahweh: An Examination of Form and Content in the Proclamation of the Prophet Jeremiah* (BST 4; Zürich: EVZ-Verlag, 1970).

Berrigan, Daniel, *Jeremiah: The World, the Wound of God* (Minneapolis: Fortress Press, 1999).

Bezzel, Hannes, *Die Konfessionen Jeremias: Eine redaktiongeschichtliche Studie* (BZAW 379; Berlin: Walter de Gruyter, 2007).

Biddle, Mark E., *Polyphony and Symphony in Prophetic Literature: Rereading Jeremiah 7-20* (SOTI 2; Macon, GA: Mercer University Press, 1996).

Black, C. Clifton, 'Rhetorical Criticism and Biblical Interpretation', *Expository Times* 100.7 (1989), pp. 252-58.

Blank, Sheldon H., 'The Confessions of Jeremiah and the Meaning of Prayer', *Hebrew Union College Annual 19* 21 (1948), pp. 331-54.

—*Jeremiah, Man and Prophet* (Cincinnati, OH: Hebrew Union College Press, 1961).

—'The Prophet as Paradigm', in James L. Crenshaw and John T. Willis (eds.), *Essays in Old Testament Ethics* (New York, NY: KTAV, 1974), pp. 111-30.

Bockmuehl, Markus, 'Reason, Wisdom and the Implied Disciple of Scripture', in David F. Ford and Graham Stanton (eds.), *Reading Texts, Seeking Wisdom: Scripture and Theology* (Grand Rapids: Eerdmans, 2003), pp. 53-68.

Botterweck, G. Johannes, Helmer Ringgren, & Heinz-Josef Fabry (eds.), *Theological Dictionary of the Old Testament* (Grand Rapids: Eerdmans, 1974-2006).

Bracke, John M., *Jeremiah 1-29* (Westminster Bible Companion; Louisville, KY: Westminster/John Knox Press, 2000).

Briggs, Richard S., *The Virtuous Reader: Old Testament Narrative and Interpretive Virtue* (STI; Grand Rapids. Baker Academic, 2010).

Bright, John, *Jeremiah* (AB 21; New York, NY: Doubleday, 1965).

—'The Apodictic Prohibition: Some Observations', *JBL* 92.2 (1973), pp. 185-204.

—'Jeremiah's Complaints: Liturgy or Expressions of Personal Distress?' in J.I. Durham and J.R. Porter (eds.), *Proclamation and Presence: Old Testament Essays in Honour of G.H. Davies* (London: SCM Press, 1970), pp. 189-214.

Brown, Francis, S. Driver, & C. Briggs, *The Brown-Driver-Briggs Hebrew and English Lexicon* (Peabody, MA: Hendrickson, 1996).

Brown, Michael L., 'Jeremiah', in Tremper Longman and David E. Garland (eds.), *Expositor's Bible Commentary* (Grand Rapids: Zondervan, 2006), VII, pp. 21-572.

Brown, William P., *Seeing the Psalms: A Theology of Metaphor* (Louisville, KY: Westminster/John Knox Press, 2002).

Broyles, Craig C., *The Conflict of Faith and Experience in the Psalms: A Form-Critical and Theological Study* (JSOTSup 52; Sheffield: JSOT Press, 1988).

Brueggemann, Walter, 'An Ending that Does Not End: The Book of Jeremiah', in A.K.M. Adam (ed.), *Postmodern Interpretations of the Bible-A Reader* (St. Louis: Chalice Press, 2000), pp. 117-28.

—*Exile and Homecoming: A Commentary on Jeremiah* (Grand Rapids, MI: Eerdmans, 1998).

—'Jeremiah: Portrait of the Prophet', in Patrick D. Miller (ed.), *Like Fire in the Bones: Listening for the Prophetic Word in Jeremiah* (Minneapolis, MN: Fortress Press, 2006), pp. 3-17.

—*The Theology of the Book of Jeremiah* (Old Testament Theology; Cambridge: Cambridge University Press, 2007).

—*Theology of the Old Testament: Testimony, Dispute, Advocacy* (Minneapolis: Fortress Press, 1997).

Burkitt, Francis C., 'Justin Martyr and Jeremiah xi 19', *Journal of Theological Studies* 33.132 (1931-32), pp. 371-73.

Cargal, Timothy B., 'Beyond the Fundamentalist-Modernist Controversy: Pentecostals and Hermeneutics in a Postmodern Age', *Pneuma* 15.2 (1993), pp. 163-87.

Carroll, Noël, *The Philosophy of Horror* (New York: Routledge, 1990).

Carroll, Robert P., *From Chaos to Covenant: Uses of Prophecy in the Book of Jeremiah* (London: SCM Press, 1981).

—*Jeremiah: A Commentary* (OTL; Philadelphia: Westminster Press, 1986).

—'Halfway Through a Dark Wood: Reflections on Jeremiah 25', in A.R. Pete Diamond, Kathleen M. O'Connor, and Louis Stulman (eds.), *Troubling Jeremiah* (JSOTSup 260; Sheffield: Sheffield Academic Press, 1999), pp. 73-86.

Caruth, Cathy, 'Introduction II, Recapturing the Past', in C. Caruth (ed.), *Trauma: Explorations of Memory* (Baltimore: Johns Hopkins University, 1995), pp. 151-57.

—*Unclaimed Experience: Trauma, Narrative, and History* (Baltimore: Johns Hopkins University, 1996).

Castelo, Daniel, 'Tarrying on the Lord: Affections, Virtues, and Theological Ethics in Pentecostal Perspective', *Journal of Pentecostal Theology* 13.1 (2004), pp. 31-56.

Chae, Moon Kwon, 'Redactional Intentions of MT Jeremiah Concerning the Oracles Against the Nations', *Journal of Biblical Literature* 134.3 (2015), pp. 577-93.

Chatman, Seymour, *Story and Discourse: Narrative Structure in Fiction and Film* (Ithaca, NY: Cornell University Press, 1978).

Childs, Brevard S., *Introduction to the Old Testament as Scripture* (Philadelphia: Fortress Press, 1979).

Clements, R.E., *Jeremiah* (IBC; Atlanta: John Knox, 1988).

Clines, David J.A., 'Story and Poem: The Old Testament as Literature and Scripture', *Interpretion* 34.2 (1980), pp. 115-27.

—(ed.), *The Concise Dictionary of Classical Hebrew* (Sheffield: Sheffield Phoenix Press, 2009).

Condamin, Albert, *Le Livre de Jérémie* (Etudes Bibliques; Paris: J. Gabalda, 3rd edn, 1936).

Cornill, Carl Heinrich, *Das Buch Jeremiah* (Leipzig: Chr. Herm. Tauchnitz, 1905).

Craigie, Peter C., Page H. Kelley, and Joel F. Drinkard, Jr., *Jeremiah 1-25* (WBC 26; Dallas: Word Books, 1991).

Davies, Andrew, 'What Does It Mean to Read the Bible as a Pentecostal?' *Journal Pentecostal Theology* 18.2 (2009), pp. 216-29.

Davies, Eryl, *Biblical Criticism* (Guides for the Perplexed; London: T & T Clark, 2013).

Dearman, J. Andrew, 'Jeremiah: History of Interpretation', in Mark J. Boda and J. Gordon McConville (eds.), *Dictionary of the Old Testament Prophets* (Downers Grove, IL: InterVarsity Press, 2012), pp. 441-49.

Diamond, A.R., *The Confessions of Jeremiah in Context: Scenes of Prophetic Drama* (JSOTSup 45; Sheffield: JSOT Press, 1987).

—'Jeremiah's Confessions in the LXX and MT: A Witness to a Developing Canonical Function?' *Vetus Testamentum* 40.1 (1990), pp. 33-50.

Driver, G.R., 'Birds of the Old Testament', *Palestinian Exploration Quarterly* 87.1 (1955), pp. 5-20, 129-40.

Dubbink, Joep, 'Getting Closer to Jeremiah: The Word of YHWH and the Literary-Theological Person of a Prophet', in Martin Kessler (ed.), *Reading the Book of Jeremiah: A Search for Coherence* (Winona Lake, IN: Eisenbrauns, 2004), pp. 25-39.

—'Jeremiah: Hero of Faith or Defeatist? Concerning the Place and Function of Jeremiah 20.14-18', *Journal for the Study of the Old Testament* 86.4 (1999), pp. 67-84.

Duhm, Bernard, *Das Buch Jeremia* (Tübingen. J.C.B. Mohr, 1901).

Dunn, James D.G., 'Criteria for a Wise Reading of a Biblical Text', in David F. Ford and Graham Stanton (eds.), *Reading Texts, Seeking Wisdom: Scripture and Theology* (Grand Rapids: Eerdmans, 2003), pp. 38-52.

Ellington, Scott A., 'Pentecostalism and the Authority of Scripture', *Journal of Pentecostal Theology* 4.9 (1996), pp. 16-38.

—*Risking Truth: Reshaping the World through Prayers of Lament* (PTMS; Eugene, OR: Pickwick Publications, 2008).

Fish, Stanley, 'Literature in the Reader: Affective Stylistics', *New Literary History* 2.1 (1970), pp. 123-62.

Fohrer, Georg, 'Die Gattung der Berichte über symbolische Handlungen der Propheten', *ZAW* 64.2 (1951), pp. 101-20.

Fowl, Stephen E. & L. Gregory Jones, *Reading in Communion: Scripture and Ethics in Christian Life* (BFT; Eugene, OR: Wipf & Stock, 1998).

Fox, Michael V., *A Time to Tear Down & A Time to Build Up: Rereading Ecclesiastes* (Grand Rapids: Eerdmans, 1999).

—'Tob as Covenant Terminology', *Bulletion of the American Schools of Oriental Research* 209 (1973), pp. 41-42.

Fretheim, Terence E., *Jeremiah* (SHBC; Macon, GA; Smyth & Helwys, 2002).

Giesebrecht, Friedrich, *Das Buch Jeremia, übersetzt und erklärt* (Göttinger Handkommentar zum Alten Testament; Göttingen: Vandenhoeck & Ruprecht, 1894).

Gerstenberger, Erhard, 'Jeremiah's Complaints: Observations on Jeremiah 15.10-21', *Journal of Biblical Literature* 82.4 (1963), pp. 393-408.

Green, Chris E.W., *Sanctifying Interpretation: Vocation, Holiness, and Scripture* (Cleveland, TN: CPT Press, 2015).

Greenwood, David, 'Rhetorical Criticism and Formgeschichte: Some Methodological Considerations', *Journal of Biblical Literature* 89.4 (1970), pp. 418-26.

Grey, Jacqueline, *Three's a Crowd: Pentecostalism, Hermeneutics, and the Old Testament* (Eugene, OR: Pickwick Publications, 2011).

Habel, Norman, 'The Form and Significance of the Call Narrative', *Zeitschrift für die alttestamentliche Wissenschaft* 77.3 (1965), pp. 297-323.

Har-El, Menashe, 'The Pride of the Jordan: The Jungle of the Jordan', *Bibilcal Archaeology* 41.2 (1978), pp. 65-75.

Harris, R. Laird. 'Kidneys', in Geoffrey W. Bromiley (ed.), *International Standard Bible Encyclopedia* (Grand Rapids: Eerdmans, 1986), III, p. 13.

Harris, R. Laird, Gleason L. Archer, Jr., and Bruce K. Waltke (eds.), *Theological Wordbook of the Old Testament* (2 volumes; Chicago, IL: Moody Press, 1980).

Hayes, Katherine M., *The Earth Mourns: Prophetic Metaphor and Oral Aesthetic* (AcBib 8; Atlanta: Society of Biblical Literature, 2002).

Henderson, Joe, 'Duhm and Skinner's Invention of Jeremiah', in Else K. Holt and Carolyn J. Sharp (eds.), *Jeremiah Invented: Constructions and Deconstructions of Jeremiah* (LHB/OTS 575; New York: Bloomsbury, 2015), pp. 1-15.

—'Jeremiah 2-10 as a Unified Literary Composition: Evidence of Dramatic Portrayal and Narrative Progression', in John Goldingay (ed.), *Uprooting and Planting: Essays on Jeremiah for Leslie Allen* (LHB/OTS 459; New York: T & T Clark, 2007), pp. 116-52.

Heschel, Abraham J., *The Prophets*, (Peabody, MA: Prince Press, 2001).

Hitzig, Ferdinand, *Der Prophet Jeremia* (KEH 3; Leipzig: Verlag von S. Hirzel, 2nd edn, 1846).

Hobbs, T.R., 'Some Remarks on the Composition and Structure of the Book of Jeremiah', *Catholic Biblical Quarterly* 34.3 (1972), pp. 257-75.

Holladay, William L., *The Architecture of Jeremiah 1-20* (Lewisburg, NY: Bucknell University Press, 1976).

—(ed.), *A Concise Hebrew and Aramaic Lexicon of the Old Testament* (Grand Rapids: Eerdmans, 1971).

—*Jeremiah 1* (ed. Paul D. Hanson; Hermeneia; Minneapolis: Fortress Press, 1986).

—*Jeremiah 2* (ed. Paul D. Hanson; Hermeneia; Minneapolis: Fortress Press, 1989).

—'Jeremiah and Moses: Further Observations', *JBL* 85.1 (1966), pp. 17-27.

Hölscher, Gustav, *Die Profeten: Untersuchungen zur Religionsgeschichte Israels* (Leipzig: J.C. Heinrichs'sche Buchhandlung, 1914).

Holt, Else K., 'The Meaning of an Inclusio: A Theological Interpretation of the Book of Jeremiah MT', *Scandinavian Journal of the Old Testament* 17.2 (2003), pp. 183-205.

—'Word of Jeremiah-Word of God: Structures of Authority in the Book of Jeremiah', in John Goldingay (ed.), *Uprooting and Planting: Essays on Jeremiah for Leslie Allen* (LHB/OTS 459; New York: T & T Clark, 2007), pp. 172-89.

Houberg, R., 'Note sur Jérémié xi 19', *Vetus Testamentum* 25.3 (1975), pp. 676-77.

Hubmann, Franz D., *Untersuchungen zu den Konfessionen Jer. 11, 18-12, 2, und Jer. 15, 10-21* (Forschung zur Bible 30; Zürich: Echter Verlag, 1978).

Hyatt, J. Philip & Stanley R. Hopper, 'The Book of Jeremiah', in G.A. Buttrick (ed.), *The Interpreter's Bible* (New York: Abingdon Press, 1956), V, pp. 777-1142.

Iser, Wolfgang, *The Act of Reading: A Theory of Aesthetic Response* (trans. D.H. Wilson; Baltimore: Johns Hopkins University Press, 1978).

Ittmann, Norbert, *Die Konfession Jeremias Ihre Bedeutung für die Verkundigung des Propheten* (WMANT 54; Neukirchen-Vluyn: Newkirchener, 1981).

Jenni, Ernst and Claus Westermann (eds.), *Theological Lexicon of the Old Testament* (3 vols; trans. Mark E. Biddle; Peabody, MA: Hendrickson Publishers, 1997).

Jenson, Robert W., 'The Religious Power of Scripture', *Scottish Journal of Theology* 52.1 (1999), pp. 89-105.

Jobling, David K., 'The Quest of the Historical Jeremiah: Hermeneutical Implications of Recent Literature', *Union Seminary Quarterly Review* 34.1 (1978), pp. 3-12.

Jones, L. Gregory, 'Formed and Transformed by Scripture: Character, Community, and Authority in Biblical Interpretation', in William P. Brown (ed.), *Character and Scripture: Moral Formation, Community, and Biblical Interpretation* (Grand Rapids, MI: Eerdmans, 2002), pp. 18-32.

Kalmanofsky, Amy, 'Israel's Open Sore in the Book of Jeremiah', *Journal of Biblical Literature* 135.2 (2016), pp. 247-63.

—*Terror All Around: The Rhetoric of Horror in the Book of Jeremiah* (LHB/OTS 390; New York: T & T Clark, 2008).

Kessler, Martin, 'The Function of Chapters 25 and 50-51 in the Book of Jeremiah', in A.R. Pete Diamond, Kathleen M. O'Connor, and Louis Stulman (eds.), *Troubling Jeremiah* (JSOTSup 260; Sheffield: Sheffield Academic Press, 1999), pp. 64-72.

—'A Methodological Setting for Rhetorical Criticism', in David J.A. Clines, David M. Gunn, and Alan J. Hauser (eds.), *Art and Meaning: Rhetoric in Biblical Literature* (JSOTSup 19; Sheffield: Sheffield Academic Press, 1982), pp. 1-19.

Kort, Wesley A., *Story, Text, and Scripture: Literary Interests in Biblical Narrative* (University Park, PA: The Pennsylvania State University Press, 1998).

Kuhn, Karl Allen, *The Heart of Biblical Narrative: Rediscovering Biblical Appeal to the Emotions* (Minneapolis: Fortress Press, 2009).

Kumaki, F. Kenro, 'A New Look at Jer 4, 19-22 and 10, 19-21', *Annual of the Japanese Bible Institute* 8 (1982), pp. 113-22.

Lalleman, Hetty, *Jeremiah and Lamentations* (TOTC 21; Downers Grove, IL: InterVarsity Press, 2013).

Land, Steven Jack, *Pentecostal Spirituality: A Passion for the Kingdom* (Cleveland, TN: CPT Press, 2010).

Lewin, Ellen Davis, 'Arguing for Authority: A Rhetorical Study of Jeremiah 1.4-19 and 20.7-18', *JSOT* 10.32 (1985), pp. 105-19.

Lundbom, Jack R., 'Jeremiah', in David Noel Freedman (ed.), *Anchor Bible Dictionary* (New York: Doubleday, 1992), III, pp. 684-98.

—*Jeremiah: A Study in Ancient Hebrew Rhetoric* (Winona Lake, IN: Eisenbrauns, 2nd edn, 1997).

—*Jeremiah Closer Up: The Prophet and the Book* (Hebrew Bible Monographs; Sheffield: Sheffield Phoenix Press, 2010).

—*Jeremiah 1-20* (AB 21a: New York. Doubleday, 1999).

Magonet, Jonathan, 'Character/Author/Reader: The Problem of Perspective in Biblical Narrative', in L.J. de Regt, J. de Waard, and J.P. Fokkelman (eds.), *Literary Structure and Rhetorical Strategies in the Hebrew Bible* (Winona Lake, IN: Eisenbrauns, 1996), pp. 3-13.

Martin, Lee Roy, *The Unheard Voice of God: A Pentecostal Hearing of the Book of Judges* (JPTSup 32; Blandford Forum, UK; Deo Publishing, 2008).

—'Delighting in Torah: The Affective Dimension of Psalm 1', *Old Testament Essays* 23.3 (2010), pp. 708-27.

—'Longing for God: Psalm 63 and Pentecostal Spirituality', *Journal of Pentecostal Theology* 22.1 (2013), pp. 54-76.

—(ed.), *Pentecostal Hermeneutics: A Reader* (Leiden: Brill, 2013).

—'Rhetorical Criticism and the Affective Dimension of the Biblical Text,' *Journal for Semitics* 23.2 (2014), pp. 339-53.

—'Fire in the Bones: Pentecostal Prophetic Preaching', in Lee Roy Martin (ed.), *Toward a Pentecostal Theology of Preaching* (Cleveland, TN: CPT Press, 2014), pp. 34-63.

Mauser, Ulrich, *Gottesbild und Menschwerdung: eine Untersuchung zur Einheit des Alten und Neuen Testaments* (BHT 43; Tübingen. Mohr, 1971).

McConville, J. Gordon, *Judgment and Promise: An Interpretation of the Book of Jeremiah* (Winona Lake, IN: Eisenbrauns, 1992).

McCracken, David, 'Character in the Boundary: Bakhtin's Interdividuality in Biblical Narratives', *Semeia* 63 (1993), pp. 29-42.

McKane, William A., *A Critical and Exegetical Commentary on Jeremiah: Jeremiah I-XXV* (ICC; Edinburgh: T & T Clark, 1986).

—'SPY(Y)M with Special Reference to the Book of Jeremiah', in A. Caquot and M. Delcor (eds.), *Mélanges bibliques et orientaux en l'honner de M. Henri Cazelles* (AOAT 212; Neukirchner-Vluyn: Neukirchener Verlag, 1981), pp. 319-35.

McQueen, Larry R., *Joel and the Spirit: The Cry of a Prophetic Hermeneutic* (Cleveland, TN: CPT Press, 2009).

Meeks, Wayne, 'A Hermeneutics of Social Embodiment', *Harvard Theological Review* 79.1-3 (1986), pp. 176-86.

Melugin, Roy F., 'Muilenburg, Form Criticism and Theological Exegesis', in Martin J. Buss (ed.), *Encounter With the Text: Form and History in the Hebrew Bible* (SemeiaSup; Philadelphia: Fortress Press, 1979), pp. 91-100.

Melvin, David P., 'Why Does the Way of the Wicked Prosper? Human and Divine Suffering in Jeremiah 11.18-12.13 and the Problem of Evil', *Evangelical Quarterly* 83.2 (2011), pp. 99-106.

Mendenhall, George E., *The Tenth Generation: The Origins of the Biblical Tradition* (Baltimore, MD: Johns Hopkins University Press, 1973).

Mihelic, Joseph L., 'Dialogue with God: A Study of Some of Jeremiah's Confessions', *Interpretation* 14.1 (1960), pp. 43-50.

Miller, Patrick D., 'Jeremiah: Introduction, Commentary, and Reflections', in Leander E. Keck (ed.), *New Interpreter's Bible* (Nashville: Abingdon, 2001), VI, pp. 553-926.

—*They Cried to the Lord: The Form and Theology of Biblical Prayer* (Minneapolis, MN: Fortress Press, 2000).

Moore, Rickie D., 'Canon and Charisma in the Book of Deuteronomy', in *The Spirit of the Old Testament* (JPTSup 35; Blandford Forum, UK: Deo Publishing, 2011), pp. 19-34.

—'Deuteronomy and the Fire of God', in *The Spirit of the Old Testament* (JPTSup 35; Blandford Forum, UK: Deo Publishing, 2011), pp. 35-55.

Moran, W.L., 'A Note on the Treaty Terminology of the Sefire Stelas', *Journal of Near Eastern Studies* 22.3 (1963), pp. 173-76.

Mowinckel, Sigmund, *Zur Komposition des Buches Jeremia* (Oslo: Kristiania, in Kommission bei J. Dybwald, 1914).

Muilenburg, James, 'Form Criticism and Beyond', *Journal of Biblical Literature* 88.1 (1969), pp. 1-18.

Newman, Barclay M. and Philip C. Stine, *A Handbook on Jeremiah* (UBS Handbook Series; New York: United Bible Societies, 2003).

Nicholson, Ernest W., *The Book of the Prophet Jeremiah: Chapters 1-25* (CBC; Cambridge: Cambridge University Press, 1973).

Noel, Bradley Truman, *Pentecostalism and Postmodern Hermeneutics: Comparisons and Contemporary Impact* (Eugene, OR: Wipf & Stock, 2010).

O'Connor, Kathleen M., 'The Book of Jeremiah: Reconstructing Community after Disaster', in M. Daniel Carroll R. and Jacqueline E. Lapsley (eds.), *Character Ethics and the Old Testament. Moral Dimensions of Scripture* (Louisville: Westminster/John Knox Press, 2007), pp. 81-92.

—*The Confessions of Jeremiah: Their Interpretation and Role in Chapters 1-25* (SBLDS 94; Atlanta, GA: Scholars Press, 1988).

"Do Not Trim A Word': The Contributions of Chapter 26 to the Book of Jeremiah', *Catholic Biblical Quarterly* 51.4 (1989), pp. 617-30.

—*Jeremiah: Pain and Promise* (Minneapolis, MN: Fortress Press, 2011).

Olbricht, Thomas H., '*Pathos* as Proof in Greco-Roman Rhetoric', in Thomas H. Olbricht and Jerry L. Sumney (eds.), *Paul and Pathos* (SBL Symposium Series 16; Atlanta: Society of Biblical Literature, 2001), pp. 7-22.

Olson, Dennis T., *Deuteronomy and the Death of Moses: A Theological Reading* (OBT; Minneapolis: Fortress Press, 1994).

Overholt, Thomas W., *The Threat of Falsehood: A Study in the Theology of the Book of Jeremiah* (SBT 2.16; London: SCM Press Ltd, 1970).

Patterson, Richard Duane, 'Of Bookends, Hinges, and Hooks: Literary Clues to the Arrangement of Jeremiah's Prophecy', *Westminster Theological Journal* 51.1 (1989), pp. 109-31.

Peels, H.G.L., '"You Shall Certainly Drink!': The Place and Significance of the Oracles Against the Nations in the Book of Jeremiah', *European Journal of Theology* 16.2 (2007), pp. 81-91.

—*The Vengeance of God: The Meaning of the Root NQM and the Function of the NQM-Texts in the Context of Divine Revelation in the Old Testament* (OtSt 31; Leiden: Brill, 1995).

Pinnock, Clark H., 'The Work of the Holy Spirit in Hermeneutics', *Journal of Pentecostal Theology* Issue 2 (1993), pp. 3-23.

—'The Work of the Spirit in the Interpretation of Holy Scripture from the Perspective of a Charismatic Biblical Theologian', *Journal of Pentecostal Theology* 18.2 (2009), pp. 157-71.

Pohlmann, Karl-Friedrich. *Die Ferne Gottes-Studien zum Jeremiabuch. Beiträge zu den 'Konfessionen' im Jeremiabuch und ein Versuch zur Frage nach den Anfängen der Jeremiatradition* (BZAW 179; Berlin: Walter de Gruyter, 1989).

Polk, Timothy, *The Prophetic Persona: Jeremiah and the Language of Self* (JSOTSup 32; Sheffield: JSOT Press, 1984).

Rad, Gerhard von, 'The Confessions of Jeremiah', in Leo G. Perdue and Brian W. Kovacs (eds.), *A Prophet To the Nations: Essays in Jeremiah Studies* (trans. Anne Winston and Gary Lance Johnson; Winona Lake, IN: Eisenbrauns, 1984), pp. 339-47.

Ramsey, George W., 'Speech-Forms in Hebrew Law and Prophetic Oracles', *Journal of Biblical Literature* 96.1 (1977), pp. 45-58.

Rashkow, Ilona N., 'In Our Image We Created Him, Male and Female We Create Them: The E/Affect of Biblical Characterization', *Semeia* 63 (1993), pp. 105-13.

Reventlow, Henning Graf, *Liturgie und prophetisches Ich bei Jeremia* (Gütersloh: Gütersloher Verlagshaus G. Mohn, 1963).

Rudolph, Wilhelm, *Jeremia* (Tübingen: J.C.B. Mohr, 3rd edn, 1968).

Scalise, Pamela J., 'The Way of Weeping: Reading the Path of Grief in Jeremiah', *Word & World* 22.4 (2002), pp. 415-22.

Seitz, Christopher R., 'The Place of the Reader in Jeremiah', in Martin Kessler (ed.), *Reading the Book of Jeremiah: A Search for Coherence* (Winona Lake, IN: Eisenbrauns, 2004), pp. 67-75.

—'Prophet Moses and the Canonical Shape of Jeremiah', *Zeitschrift für Alttestamentliche Wissenschaft* 101.1 (1989), pp. 3-27.

Sherwood, Yvonne K., 'Prophetic Scatology: Prophecy and the Art of Sensation', *Semeia* 92 (1998), pp. 183-224.

Siebert, Johanna, *The Construction of Shame in the Hebrew Bible: The Prophetic Contribution* (JSOTSup 346: London: Sheffield Academic Press, 2002).

Skinner, John, *Prophecy and Religion: Studies in the Life of Jeremiah* (Cambridge: The University Press, 1948).

Skoss, Solomon L., 'The Root בטח in Jeremiah 12.5, Psalms 22.10, Proverbs 14.16, and Job 40.23', in Salo W. Baron and Alexander Marx (eds.), *Jewish Studies in Memory of George A. Kohut, 1874-1933* (New York: Alexander Kohut Memorial Foundation, 1935), pp. 549-53.

Smith, James K.A., *Thinking in Tongues: Pentecostal Contributions to Christian Philosophy* (Pentecostal Manifestos; Grand Rapids: Eerdmans, 2010).

Smith, Mark S., *The Laments of Jeremiah and Their Contexts: A Literary and Redactional Study of Jeremiah 11-20* (SBLMS 42; Atlanta: Scholars Press, 1990).

Stulman, Louis, *Jeremiah* (AOTC; Nashville: Abingdon, 2005).

—'Jeremiah the Prophet: Astride Two Worlds', in Martin Kessler (ed.), *Reading the Book of Jeremiah: A Search for Coherence* (Winona Lake, IN: Eisenbrauns, 2004), pp. 41-66.

—*Order Amid Chaos: Jeremiah as Symbolic Tapestry* (BibSem 57; Sheffield: Sheffield Academic Press, 1998).

Taylor, Marion Ann, 'Jeremiah 45: The Problem of Placement', *Journal for the Study of the Old Testament* 12.37 (1987), pp. 79-98.

Thiel, Winfried, *Die deuteronomistische Redaktion von Jeremia 1-25* (Neukirchen-Vluyn: Neukirchener Verlag, 1973).

Thomas, D. Winton, 'מלאי in Jeremiah iv.5: A Military Term', *Journal of Jewish Studies* 3.2 (1952), pp. 47-52.

Thomas, John Christopher, 'Women, Pentecostals, and the Bible: An Experiment in Pentecostal Hermeneutics', *Journal of Pentecostal Theology* Issue 5 (1994), pp. 41-56.

Thompson, J.A., *The Book of Jeremiah* (NICOT; Grand Rapids: Eerdmans, 1980).

Trible, Phyllis, *Rhetorical Criticism: Context, Method, and the Book of Jonah* (GBS; Minneapolis: Fortress Press, 1994).

Tull, Patricia K., 'Rhetorical Criticism and Intertextuality', in Steven L McKenize and Stephen R. Haynes (eds.), *To Each Its Own Meaning: An Introduction to Biblical Criticisms and Their Application* (Louisville, KY: Westminster/John Knox Press, 2nd edn, 1999), pp. 156-80.

Van Gemeren, Willem A. (ed.), *New International Dictionary of Old Testament Theology and Exegesis* (5 vols; Grand Rapids: Zondervan, 1997).

Van Hecke, Pierre J.P., 'Metaphorical Shifts in the Oracle Against Babylon (Jeremiah 50-51)', *Scandinavian Journal of the Old Testament* 17.1 (2003), pp. 68-88.

Vischer, Wilhelm., 'The Vocation of the Prophet to the Nations: An Exegesis of Jer. 1.4-10', *Interpretation* 9.3 (1955), pp. 310-17.

Volz, Paul, *Der Prophet Jeremia* (KAT 10; Leipzig: A Deichertsche Vergasbuchhandlung, 1922).

Waard, Jan de, *A Handbook on Jeremiah* (TCT 2; Winona Lake, IN: Eisenbrauns, 2003).

Wacker, Grant, *Heaven Below: Early Pentecostals and American Culture* (Cambridge, MA: Harvard University Press, 2001).

Weinfeld, Moshe, *Deuteronomy and the Deuteronomistic School* (Oxford: Clarendon Press, 1972).

Wessels, Wilhelm J., '"My Word is Like Fire": The Consuming Power of YHWH's Word', *Old Testament Essays* 24.2 (2011), pp. 492-510.

Wimmer, Donald H., 'The Sociology of Knowledge and the Confessions of Jeremiah', in Paul J. Achtemeier (ed.), *SBL Seminar Papers, 1978* (SBLSP 15; Missoula, MT: Scholars Press, 1978), I, 393-406.

Yates, Gary E., 'Narrative Parallelism and the "Jehoiakim Frame": A Reading Strategy for Jeremiah 26-45', *Journal of the Evangelical Theological Society* 48.2 (2005), pp. 263-81.

Zulick, Margaret, 'The Agon of Jeremiah: On the Dialogic Invention of Prophetic Ethos', *The Quarterly Journal of Speech* 78.2 (1992), pp. 125-48.

INDEX OF BIBLICAL REFERENCES

INDEX OF AUTHORS

www.ingramcontent.com/pod-product-compliance
Lightning Source LLC
Chambersburg PA
CBHW070014100426
42739CB00023B/3201